First Gyro

Dedication

To my long-suffering yet continually supportive family, close friends and fellow RNLI crew-members – my sincere apologies that my journey took so long to complete!

Special thanks to the fantastic NHS staff, specialist nurses, surgery and oncology teams at Royal Victoria Hospital Belfast, Belfast City Hospital, The Northern Ireland Cancer Centre and the Mater Hospital Belfast, whose combined and collective life-preserving efforts over many years, allowed me to attempt this journey...

With special thanks to cover illustrator Daniel di Paolo, and my editor Matt Phillips and my sister Norah Crammond for jointly knocking my early first drafts into shape.

And extra special thanks to my lifelong record setting inspiration – Aunt Isabel Woods (né Clements), whose stoic sense of single-minded determination and tenacity in achieving long-distance cycling records, has endured down through generations of our extended family.

First Printing, 2022

First Gyro

THE LAST AIRCRAFT TYPE TO CONQUER THE WORLD

Norman Surplus

Publishing

Contents

Introduction

Late in 2003, I was diagnosed with advanced stage bowel cancer. I was 40 years old, married (to Celia) with two young children (Felix and Petra), aged five and two respectively, and still had so much life ahead of me to live. Yet my bleak prognosis gave me only a 40% chance of living for the next 18 months.

I was not ready to give up without a fight.

I underwent immediate surgery, followed in early 2004 by six months of gruelling chemotherapy. Being relatively young, I was prescribed as much chemo as my body could physically take by my oncologists, in the hope of hitting the cancer as hard as possible. It was extremely rough going, but gradually, month after month, year after year, I managed to pull through until I eventually emerged out the other side. I then began to live life to the full again. A life beyond cancer.

While lying in my hospital bed, recovering from the bowel surgery, a daytime TV show caught my attention. It was a restoration programme, repairing old, broken machinery back to working order, and this particular episode just happened to be restoring an aged, single-seat, gyroplane aircraft (aka autogyro or gyrocopter). I had heard of them before. I even knew of *Little Nellie* in the James Bond film *You Only Live Twice*, but the programme immediately reminded me of their existence.

So, I thought to myself...

"If I ever manage to get myself out of this mess, someday I might like to have a go at flying one of those things."

Over the next few years (and with the *mess* thankfully much diminished...) I went on and learned how to fly, under the expert guidance of my instructor Chris Jones, of Chris Jones Gyroplanes flight school, Kirkbride Airfield, Cumbria. During my early training, I became aware of a British Army helicopter pilot named Barry Jones (no relation) who was attempting to fly the first gyroplane around the world. His attempt sadly was cut short when his aircraft was submerged under six feet of flood water in north-east India during an unusually heavy monsoon season, but his pioneering first circumnavigation attempt had proved that such a thing might just be possible. After about a year of training, I gained my CAA PPL(G) – Private Pilot's Licence (Gyroplanes). I purchased a bright yellow RotorSport UK MT-03 Autogyro aircraft and registered it G-YROX. For several years I consolidated my training with regular flying and short multi-day touring adventures to new destinations, including flying to the south of France. During these numerous cross-country jaunts, I often thought back to Barry Jones' expedition and slowly, slowly, bit by bit, a crazy idea formed in my head that perhaps I too, could also try to circumnavigate the world in a gyroplane.

I began to research the history of flying around the world and made a terrific discovery. Of all the fundamental types of flying machine that have ever taken to the skies, only one type remained that had never made a circumnavigation… and that was the gyroplane.

There are only seven fundamental ways that you can get airborne:

The Magnificent Seven

Fixed-wing aeroplane: conventional three axis-controlled aircraft (includes motor-gliders, bi-planes, fast jets, airliners, ekranoplans); first circumnavigation – US Army Air Service World Flight aircraft *Chicago* and *New Orleans* **1924**

Airship: gas filled for lift, propelled by engines (includes rigid and semi-rigid dirigibles and blimps); first circumnavigation – the *Graf Zeppelin* **1929**

Rocket: using propellant thrust rather than aerodynamic wings for lift (includes all rockets and aircraft reliant on rocket/

jet/ion propelled thrust to remain airborne); first circumnavigation – Uri Gagarin first orbit of Earth in *Vostok 1* **1961**

Helicopter: using a powered rotating wing/propeller/ducted fan for lift, mounted on either vertical or horizontal axes of rotation (includes multi-rotor drones, cyclocopters, hovercraft, ducted fan jets, tiltrotors); first circumnavigation – *Spirit of Texas* **1982**

Flex-wing aeroplane: weight-shift/wing warping controlled aircraft with flexible wing structure (includes microlights, ultralights, ornithopters, powered parachutes); first circumnavigation – *Global Flyer* **1998**

Free balloon: heated air/gas for lift, non-propelled aerostat (includes all forms of balloon and non-powered lighter-than-air aircraft); first circumnavigation – *Breitling Orbiter 3* **1999**

Gyroplane: using an unpowered rotor for lift, propelled by engine (includes gyrodynes, rotodyne convertiplanes, gyrogliders and kites); first circumnavigation – ...

Footnote: some aircraft may encompass two or more categories. (For example, the Space Shuttle could be viewed as part rocket (on take-off) and part fixed wing (on landing), or the tilt-rotor Osprey is part helicopter and part fixed wing). But *all* flying machines use at least one of the seven fundamental types listed here to achieve flight.

It was a terrific realisation, at least one example of every other type of flying machine had already circumnavigated the globe other than the humble gyroplane. I felt that it had been forgotten about, even though the first gyro had flown in 1923, only 20 short years after the Wright brothers had first taken to the skies.

The gyroplane represented the last global challenge still left to conquer. Until humanity comes up with a completely new way to fly, there would be no more maiden circumnavigation flights after this one. Realising this fact, gave me even more encouragement to seriously consider making an attempt.

During my cancer treatment I had benefited greatly from the on-going research and charity support given to patients and I wondered if this flight idea could be a good way for me to give something back. I could raise both awareness of the condition and help to raise much needed funds by supporting the most appropriate charity for me, Bowel Cancer UK. I also wanted to send out a strong message of hope and encouragement to all recently diagnosed cancer patients – I had been in exactly the same dark place as them only a few years previously, and yet look now, beyond treatment, I was thinking of flying an aircraft right around the world!

I kicked the circumnavigation idea around for a while until, almost as a hypothetical exercise, I started to study a map of the world to research how exactly it could be done. I sketched out a rough route: Northern Ireland, England, France, Italy, Greece, Egypt to Oman, Indian Sub-continent, Myanmar, Thailand, Malaysia, Philippines, Japan, Russia, Alaska, western Canada, the lower US States, eastern Canada, Greenland, Iceland, Faroe Islands, Scotland, Northern Ireland. I understood early on that the most difficult part would be gaining permission to fly across Russia to reach the Bering Strait, so one day in late 2009 I decided to shoot an email off to the British Embassy in Moscow. It was a simple enquiry as to what the likelihood would be of getting the go ahead for such a flight from the Russian authorities.

I heard nothing back from the embassy for about six weeks, until, quite out of the blue, my mobile phone rang with a curiously short number popping up on the screen. It was the British Embassy calling to say that they had turned my initial enquiry into a formal request to the Russian Ministry of Foreign Affairs, and the good news was that they hadn't said "no".

The mood in the follow-up communications with the Russian authorities was upbeat and even encouraging. It all seemed to be quite possible if I could comply with a few easy-to-meet pre-conditions, such as carrying a satellite phone and organising for a Russian navigator to sit in the back seat (to act both as navigator and translator on the radio).

I was amazed at the news and immediately discussed its full implications with Celia. We had always shared a common spirit of adventure, since we met while both studying for outdoor recreation degrees at Ilkley College in Yorkshire. She understood why I was keen to pursue the idea and was supportive for me to attempt the flight (though, admittedly at that time, we both assumed it would only take about four months to complete). Celia grasped both the personal challenge and the wider goals associated with taking on such a major expedition, and in fact she has since undertaken a similar solo, long-distance journey of her own. Riding on horseback and leading a pack-pony, she navigated the length of the Pennines (a ridge of mountains and fells that form the great backbone of Britain) with her two Fell ponies, *Foxy* and *Juno.*

So, with the go ahead from the family (and the Russians) in place, it meant my gyro world circumnavigation attempt was on.

Prologue

"I'm upside down!"

My aircraft was lying on top of me. I was submerged underwater. And I was in darkness.

Still in my seat straps, I could reach to feel the bottom of the lake above my head. It had an oozy muddy texture, the sort that I might normally feel squeezing through my toes when paddling in bare feet.

Only this did not feel normal, not normal at all.

My immediate thoughts: "What have I done to end up in this situation? Why am I not flying?"

Moments before, I had been saying my farewells to my new-found friends at the airfield and then, so suddenly, I found myself to be an uninvited guest in their lake.

Thankfully, there was no panic.

The violence of the impact was quite surprising. After a slow, inevitable descent towards the lake shoreline, I was instantaneously pitch-poled forward as the gyroplane tripped over its nose in the shallow water. Upside down, though not fully inverted, my aircraft was leaning slightly onto its right side, and this simple fact, as I shall explain later, would directly help to save me, the aircraft and ultimately the whole expedition.

But wait, I should correct myself; there was no panic, *initially*...

At first, I sensed an inner calmness in my head, and I attribute this to having already experienced many very violent crashes into water. Not from flying admittedly, but rather from windsurfing in high winds on rough seas. The effect of being thrown from my board, slammed into the water at 20 knots and being momentarily disorientated, felt very similar to my current tricky situation. When tangled up and held submerged under a large sail, made heavy with overlying water, the best course of action was always: to mentally control any immediate sense of panic; to take stock of my situation; to work out my orientation and escape route; and, finally, to simply float my way out from under the obstruction as calmly as possible to regain the surface.

Thankfully then, when it came to attempt my escape from a suddenly inverted, ditched and damaged aircraft, my body and brain thought instinctively that this was a fairly normal experience.

1

Preparations for Departure

For a hectic six months after the British Embassy call had come through from Moscow, I worked feverishly on pre-flight route planning from my hometown of Larne, Northern Ireland. A great variety of things had to be arranged and coordinated in quick succession, not least the fact that my aircraft required some special upgrades and servicing. I was also advised to arrange a press launch event "somewhere close to London". It was clear that I was going to need to fly a pre-circumnavigation mini tour of Britain as the best way to fit it all in. Aircraft maintenance in Shropshire would be followed by a press launch in Duxford, Cambridgeshire and then back up north to Larne again, via Kirkbride in Cumbria, where I had originally learnt to fly. Only then, after all these preliminary preparations were completed, could I look towards starting the circumnavigation in earnest.

10 March 2010: Press launch day

A bright and frosty early spring morning greeted me on arrival at the Midland Gliding Club on top of Long Mynd hill in Shropshire. Unlike the resident cable-launched gliders, which use this lofty locale to get an immediate leg up at take-off, I was here to prepare to fly over to Duxford for the media launch event of my attempt to become the first-ever gyroplane aircraft to circumnavigate the world. In the process, I also hoped to set an official FAI (Fédération Aéronautique Internationale/World Air Sports Federation) speed around the world (eastbound) record.

My gyroplane 'G-YROX' (she was yet to be christened *Roxy* by my Facebook followers), had spent the previous week ensconced in the cosy workshop hangar of Gerry Speich's Rotorsport UK Headquarters in the valley directly below *The Mynd.* Here, during major under-carriage surgery, she had her maximum take-off weight (MTOW) upgraded from 450kg to 500kg. This would provide me with valuable extra fuel weight-carrying capacity, notably to extend my flight range for the long open water sea crossings that lay ahead.

To get an early start, the aircraft had then endured the night sitting out atop the misty heights of Long Mynd's 1000ft plateau. A thick crust of hoar frost adorned every surface of the open cockpit, as temperatures had dropped well below zero during the night. As I drew a line with my finger on the frozen white surface of the seat fabric, I reflected on why I had not thought to bring my aircraft cover on this particular flight. Having been kept previously in the workshop, I had just assumed that she would not have been sitting outdoors all night at this time of the year. At least I took some (cold!) comfort from the fact that the seat covers were waterproof, so no harm had been done. As I continued to draw patterns on the frosted windscreen, I pondered on what would be the events of the day ahead.

Shortly after my daily pre-flight checks were complete my mobile rang to link me through to BBC Radio Cambridgeshire. I was greeted with a cheery, live interviewer for the early Breakfast show who was playing 'The Dam Busters March' in the background. They were clearly trying to create some ambiance and to set the scene for a derring-do story. The interview came off as a mixture of James Bond doing a Phileas Fogg, and had me dancing from foot to foot to ward off frost-bite while talking to everyone who was at home eating their cornflakes in warm dressing gowns.

So began the first of many bizarre media interviews conducted in various obscure locations right across the globe.

Radio interview over, it was time to saddle up and depart. I had arranged to rendezvous en route with John Butler, a fellow pioneering 'gyronaut' and good friend. Our intention was to fly in formation across from his home airstrip south of Birmingham to Duxford in Cambridgeshire for the press launch. In a two-ship formation flight, we could share navigation and communication duties around the busy south-east of England airspace, and ensure that we arrived as planned over the threshold of Duxford's parallel grass and tarmac runways at 10.30am prompt.

I called John on the mobile as I left Long Mynd and he was already at his strip getting his gyroplane (registration G-PPLG) ready for my arrival. His weather on scene was fair, but the forecast further east was for low cloud, rain showers and murky visibility; just normal conditions for a couple of UK-registered gyros!

Landing on John's pleasantly manicured grass strip, I made for the nearest hedge as in-flight toilet facilities in a gyro are, well, *challenging* to say the least. After a quick call through to Duxford to reconfirm our arrival time, we were off again. Rain periodically spattered the windscreen as we proceeded eastwards north of London, maintaining 800ft above ground level (AGL) and flying low under the steadily thickening blanket of cumulus cloud. On the plus side, the deteriorating visibility and generally murky conditions ahead would help to keep the normally busy skies predominantly free of other low level General Aviation (GA) traffic. Gyroplanes, as with many other light aircraft types, are only equipped with a basic level of cockpit instrumentation and therefore have to be flown according to Visual Flight Rules (VFR). This means their pilots are required to be able to see the Earth's surface below them at all times and need to avoid flying above unbroken cloud, as the flight instruments carried on board are not advanced enough to guide the aircraft safely down through the cloud layer below. In marginal weather conditions, the result is often a low VFR transit across country, scooting along just below the cloud base.

'The Dam Busters March' from the radio was still running through my head as we made a low-level final approach over the threshold of Duxford Aerodrome. It was a wholly appropriate and fitting soundtrack for arriving at one of the UK's best-known war-time airfields and where the on-site Imperial War Museum exhibits many original aircraft from the Battle of Britain era.

We appeared from under the low gloomy cloud at Duxford, exactly on time. The air traffic controller (ATC) had given me radio clearance for a flypast as long as I stayed clear of the surrounding villages and didn't fly directly over the museum buildings. Flying a gyro, I was able to assure ATC that I would be able to easily remain within the boundary of the airfield. In actuality, I completed all the manoeuvres (consisting of a series of low passes and tight turns) over the grass runway in a box probably no larger than 200 metres square, such was the highly agile flight characteristics of my wonderful machine.

The assembled flock of press photographers, who were tightly perched together like hi-vis-vested starlings on the upper balcony of the control tower, snapped away with their long-range lenses. Landing immediately below them on the grass apron, I was reminded of all the historic British-built aircraft that would have put down here over the years, including many of the great 1940s' war-time examples. These classic old aircraft designs demonstrated some of Britain's finest aviation ingenuity and pedigree at the time and represented a rich history of past struggles and conflicts that were intent on taking command of all of Europe's skies. Ironic then, that now in 2010 I should be making my dramatic low-level approach and flypast sitting in a fabulous 21st Century aircraft that actually started its flying career from an ultra-modern factory based in... Germany.

John landed some minutes after me and as we slowly taxied across to the parking area beside the tower, he once again took up position as my trusty right-hand wingman.

The relatively high workload I had upon approach, landing and taxiing was briefly followed by an oasis of calm and quiet as I shut down the roaring engine behind me and signed off on the radio. As soon as I turned off the GPS units and took off my sunglasses, the yellow-vested starlings jostled down the stairs of the tower, hi-vis plumage all ruffled and left a-flapping in the rush. They then proceeded to fan out and formed a half circle in front of me. Some of them were kneeling, whilst others crouched, but all were gesturing and waving to attract a smile in their direction. From an initially unorganised scrum, a glorious natural pecking order then ensued, and one that Charles Darwin himself would have been proud of.

The press agency photographers outnumbered everyone else by about five to one, and so they took first preference, snapping away merrily in all sorts of permutations of poses. The video cameras took longer to set up for their respective interviews, and therefore they commanded second place. Following them were the radio interviewers, before, finally, seemingly at the bottom of the journalistic food chain, the newspaper and magazine journalists. The latter – jotting down their hand-written comments – were the slowest of media creatures, but perhaps therefore the most deep thinking and considered.

With the interviews in the can, memory stick and notepad, John and I were suddenly released from further scrutiny, and the fluorescent flock drifted away back to their respective paparazzi roosts.

* * *

"Is it nearly time for lunch?" was the call from friends and family who had assembled, by special invitation no less, to witness the event. I had decided to call the expedition GyroxGoesGlobal, and good friend and worldwide media organiser Tom Burns from World Reach Comms was there to help coordinate all of the assembled 'birdlife', as was my sister Norah, brother-in-law Geoff and father-in-law Wally who all happened to live close at hand. En route to the excellent tearoom at the museum, we stopped off to pay homage (and to photograph) the World War II vintage gyroplane (an Avro 671 Rota Mk 1 (C.30A) registered G-ACUU) that is on permanent display in the Battle of Britain exhibit hall.

Standing next to this 70-year-old warbird, I was initially taken by its sheer size (a much larger gyro than my modern version, though both carry just two people) and then by its simplicity (extremely few instruments and simple mechanical controls). While similar to G-YROX in its in-flight capabilities, it clearly lacked the advanced materials, construction techniques and sophisticated electronic technology that we now take for granted in the modern era. Photos were taken while I was still wearing the (now somewhat iconic) bright red flying suit, which made for a stark (but intentional) contrast to the drab camouflage colours of the old gyro. It was of course painted to be unseen as much as possible during the war, whereas my red suit and bright yellow aircraft were coloured for exactly the opposite effect – for safety, I wanted to always be as visible as possible. Photos over, it was time to finally head off for that jolly nice cup of tea (and a spot of lunch old boy!), as I often found myself starting to think like a waxed moustachioed wing commander in such places. As such, after lunch, it was all "Tally Ho!", "Chocks away!" and "Back home in time for tea and medals." Only, at that precise moment, I didn't have a particular home to go to for the night.

Much of the effort of the previous few days had been geared towards making that precise 10.30am arrival at Duxford on the appointed day, and little detailed planning had been made beyond that point. So as to how, exactly, I was going to get home again was still up in the air (excuse the pun!). In gyro flying, a certain amount of *making it up as you go along* is usually factored into most multi-day journeys, as the cumulative effects of weather, fuel availability, visibility (especially fog) and daylight hours can all play their part to suddenly change even the best-laid plans. However, I was not totally unprepared. I had various strategies up my sleeve to call on, depending on the weather conditions. I could either go up the east side of the Pennines, via York, or up the west side towards Preston. On both sides, I had contacts and people to call with if I needed somewhere 'gyro friendly' to stop off.

After studying the weather forecast and consulting on the phone with another fellow gyronaut, Phil Harwood in Rufforth, York, it was decided the east side would work fine. A quick splash of avgas (aviation-rated fuel) from the resident fuel bowser truck and we were swiftly bidding fond farewell to friends and family. John pre-flighted, saddled up and departed for the shortish return flight north-west back to his home strip. Meanwhile I also made my pre-flight checks and preparations, which notably on this occasion included securely strapping a stout cardboard-boxed consignment of homemade pickled onions onto the rear seat. These dozen big jars were courtesy of my father-in-law, who keeps us readily supplied throughout the year (though more typically, they have previously arrived via an EasyJet flight from Stansted!).

Departing Duxford was a much more subdued affair than our colourful arrival some four hours earlier. The flight north took me along the course of the River Trent, which was easy to trace for miles ahead by the regularly spaced power station cooling towers. Their steaming plumes of artificial clouds spilled up into the chilly, dishwater grey sky, and were brightly lit by the late afternoon sun. Arriving at Rufforth, I was met by aforementioned chief instructor Phil, his current crop of gyro students and an exceptionally courageous chap called Dave Sykes who was planning a microlight flight from London to Sydney.

Over a very convivial meal at Phil's favourite curry house that evening, amid much reminiscing of previous adventures, we talked through both my own and Dave's upcoming routes and schedules (as it happened, Dave was planning to take a remarkably similar path to me all the way down to the south of Malaysia). It was soon realised that as Dave was due to depart in the autumn, a few months behind my starting date, any feedback coming out of my experiences en route (good or bad!) could then also act as useful advanced information for his own subsequent flight planning. His trip was going to be made all the more remarkable by the fact that he was planning a solo attempt despite being confined to a wheelchair when on the ground. Following a motorbike accident (that was not of his making) some years ago, he was subsequently able to adapt a flex-wing microlight with full hand controls.

After this meeting, and throughout my own flight down as far as

Malaysia, I would frequently recall the thought that Dave would be passing through many of these same airports. He would have similar trials and tribulations, but his would be made much more complex, no doubt, by his more restricted mobility. I was constantly humbled (and encouraged) by the fact that no matter how tough it got for me, there would always be a much harder prospect facing Dave if he found himself in the same sorts of tricky situations.

(Footnote: Dave's departure from the UK was delayed until 28 April 2011, but he successfully completed his intrepid journey on 30 August 2011).

11 March 2010: back to base

The following morning, after more chatting with Phil and organising his kind sponsorship of the SPOT global satellite tracking system for G-YROX, it was back to the airfield to continue north and home. The weather was flyable, though low cloud was barring my way across my normal high Pennine routing through the more remote parts of the North Yorkshire moors and Cumbrian fells. Over the years this route had become a poignant one for me because it gave me glimpses of what it could be like out in the real wilderness on my circumnavigation. It was here, above these harsh windswept uplands, with their desolate nooks and crannies, that I first had any tangible sense of being truly alone within a hostile landscape. Inevitably these were only fleeting sensations, because almost as soon as I had entered these mini-wildernesses, I was quickly spat out again and delivered back into civilisation once more. Indeed, I would have to wait until the world flight was well under way before I would experience the real meaning of remote solitude over any significant length of time.

On this occasion, however, to successfully cross the Pennines I elected to become an aerial HGV driver and followed the main truck route of the A1 road north to Scotch Corner and then the A66 westward across the bleak open moorlands. This great arterial link road between the North East and North West of England follows a natural low pass through the uplands, and in a similar fashion I could safely traverse the hills while remaining below the blanketing cloud level.

Over the high ground on either side of me, the cloud was threatening to touch down to surface level, which would have made flying across it impossible.

Safely navigating through the pass was like flying through the open slot in a letter box, but the added advantage to this route was to keep in visual contact with the road, useful in case I ever needed to use it as an emergency runway. It also gave me a much better chance of waving down say, a lone truck driver, to hopefully give me assistance (as long as he hadn't already run me over!).

Later, while I was flying in the more remote parts of the world, I would continue this strategy of flying close to roads, railways and other infrastructure. The reassurance of spotting a human-made feature down below, was always especially welcome after I had been flying for any length of time across inhospitable terrain. And the idea that someone could be close at hand to offer assistance was also particularly reassuring. Little did I know then, over the A66 that I would have to perform such unscheduled emergency landings not once, but three times before I would even reach Thailand.

These thoughts were all in the future however, as I tootled across the Pennines with chilly fingers and toes. There was still a good deal of late winter snow on the ground and sitting in the open cockpit was probably best described as *bracing* to say the least. I pondered that this could well be the sort of conditions I would encounter even at the height of summer in the higher sub-arctic latitudes of Russia, Alaska, Canada and Greenland. For good reason, the A66 has long snow poles planted all year round on each side of the road to show the snow ploughs where the road lies buried beneath.

Reaching the western edge of the highest ground, I was extremely relieved to drop down to a lower and slightly warmer altitude again and fly on over the much flatter terrain of the Eden Valley. Passing overhead Appleby, famed for its annual horse fair, I could easily spot the great loop of the River Eden that coils itself along the edges of the village like a long lazy snake. I continued towards the Solway Firth on the west coast of Cumbria, intent on calling in for a late-lunch visit to

Kirkbride Airfield. With my body and soul gradually warming, I was now entering into my old flight training grounds.

Kirkbride was where I had first learnt how to fly a gyroplane under the watchful guidance of instructor Chris Jones. The familiar waypoints of Penrith, Skelton aerials, Great Orton Wind Farm and Wigton all came sequentially into view. Place names which, during my training, became not only crucial local navigation landmarks, but also challenging milestones on my first solo cross-country flights away from the comforting circuit pattern of this quiet training airfield. As a trainee solo pilot, the early challenge of successfully navigating from say, Kirkbride to Carlisle Lake District Airport about 15 miles away, via waypoints at Skelton and Penrith, felt just as daunting then as any present flight I was contemplating now. One thing I was sure of though, was that irrespective of what stage of flight training or numbers of hours flying experience I had, whilst flying solo I always had little option but to just grit my teeth and cope with whatever situation unfolded before me, good or bad. It was unavoidable, as there was simply no one else up there to land the aircraft for me.

These feelings of self-reliance and self-resilience, mixed with heavy doses of apprehension and nervousness, were similar to those that I faced when embarking on my last life-changing personal journey. That adventure did not take me to the air or across continents, but instead it saw me fighting cancer with surgery and chemotherapy in 2003 and 2004.

Now, I should point out here, right at the outset of this description, that I use the words 'adventure' and 'cancer' together in this context not in any casual or flippant way. Cancer treatment cannot and should not, of course, ever be trivialised and belittled in this way, as if it is some mild amusement carried out for sport or enjoyment like many recreational adventures are described. It was (and still is) a very real experience for me, with very real consequences, many of which, sadly, often cannot have an altogether positive outcome. Rather, I use the word 'adventure' as part of my own mental defence mechanism, and as an internal method of dealing with the diagnosis that, at the time, had come quite suddenly out of the blue. I resolved that as I embarked on this unexpected trip through the treatment process, that I would have to meet this dreadful thing head on and come to terms with it by regarding it as a sort of unique challenge to face. I would almost treat it like an expedition or voyage of discovery, scrutinising it with the same sort of mixture of curiosity and cautiousness that I would regard any upcoming adventurous, uncertain journey.

Therefore, in squaring up to the unknown challenge ahead, I projected a positive thought process, a mindset where I knew that this could be fought and (hopefully) tamed successfully. I perhaps even went so far as to (almost) foster a sense of enthusiasm for getting to 'know my enemy' as they say. At the time of my diagnosis, tremendous advances were under way into new methods and medicines to further combat many forms of cancer. This in turn gave me further encouragement that perhaps soon there might be incredible new ways that this age-old enemy could be fought and even with luck, if not fully conquered, at least controlled and put in its place. I was fully fired up and motivated to give this advanced bowel cancer a really good run for its money. In the end, it wanted a good fight, and I certainly gave it one.

And that dear reader, is why, some sixteen years later, I was fortunately still around to start writing about my global flying adventure!

Approaching Kirkbride Airfield, the big white hangar doors (remnants of the prolific 1940s' war-time infrastructure) were a friendly landmark looming into sight through the murky conditions. I made the customary call to Kirkbride radio to announce my imminent arrival, and then positioned for a straight-in long final approach path. With no other traffic reported, I throttled back as I arrived over the threshold and, as is quite normal for a gyro, I dropped in steeply and plummeted towards the tarmac. Levelling off at about 6ft, I then continued to hover-taxi my way along the runway to eventually land next to the taxiway at the far end. Resident chief instructor Chris Jones was on hand to meet me, along with a group of his current trainee gyro pilots. We all soon retired for warming cups of tea into the classic brick built

WWII control tower, which had been skilfully adapted in recent years for the gyro school's use.

Many a happy morning and afternoon had been spent in this remote outpost while I was flight training. Despite being a rookie student armed with a shiny new pilot's logbook to fill, all manner of things would often come along to hinder me from gaining precious hours in the air. Low-lying mist, high winds, driving rain, ice and snow could all contribute to keeping me firmly on the ground. Inclement conditions that would act only as an encouragement to reach again for the kettle in order to make yet another cup of that reconciling tea.

As a trainee, the anticipation of preparing to go flying was almost as enjoyable as the actual flight itself. The idea that in a few minutes or even several hours' time I (along with my fellow student tea-drinkers) may be up there, magically off the ground, gave me a powerful surge of nervous adrenaline. On safe return to the ground after surviving these early flights, feelings of accomplishment and satisfaction would then wash over me in a euphoric sense of wellbeing. Like after a ride on a fun fair roller-coaster, I'd regain the earth with slightly wobbly legs and relief at being once more back on *terra firma.* But, of course, at the same time I was always itching to turn around and go do it all again!

Even on those days where the weather conditions at the airfield were well beyond a trainee's abilities, the adrenaline was still evident, as was camaraderie between fellow students. The excitement I felt was purely because there was *still a chance* that if the weather suddenly improved I might, just might, get to go flying later on in the day. Such hope and optimism would see us all happily turn up to the airfield day after day at 9am, only to be sometimes still sitting drinking tea by late afternoon. In such conditions, keenly watching for subtle changes to the angle of the windsock became an activity in itself. If it was flying horizontally, stretched out at a full 90 degrees to the mast, it indicated 20 knots of wind, which was far too breezy for a low-hours student to handle. But when the windsock angle dropped below the horizontal, the chances of flying increased accordingly. So by constantly checking the windsock, perhaps every five minutes or so, a comforting (almost institutionalised) ritual would develop to while away the hours of waiting.

"Has it dropped?"

"No."

"More tea anyone...?"

Shortly followed by...

"Has it dropped?"

"Nooooo. Big gusts coming through now."

"More tea?"

The only risk with this cosy arrangement was of becoming *too* cosy and sluggishly slow to leap into action if the windspeed did eventually drop off, particularly in the late winter afternoons when there was perhaps only an hour of daylight left in which to squeeze in a quick flight session. The real effort in those circumstances was then to extricate myself from my comfy armchair, don my chilly flight suit, grab my helmet and gloves, and step out into the cold, grey, afternoon air. This feeling of lethargy however would then promptly vanish, replaced by the familiar warm glow of adrenaline as I approached my aircraft, a fantastic machine that could literally transport me as if on a flying carpet, into that magical third dimension, up and away from the flat, flat earth.

Tea and Carpets! I am afraid we have wandered well off course dear reader, let us return to the story in hand. The talk in the Kirkbride Control Tower that wintery afternoon was predominantly about the adventurous and ambitious target I had set myself. What was the driving force behind my somewhat out-of-the-blue decision to fly off around the world? Being only the second serious attempt to circumnavigate the globe by gyroplane (the first being UK military pilot Barry Jones in 2004), I knew I wanted to attempt the rounding for a wide variety of reasons, some of which I wouldn't fully get to grips with or even fully understand until well into the flight itself.

One of the notable threads in the conversation with Chris was on my strategy of attempting the flight solo and completely unassisted by a travelling ground crew. Many first attempts by various other (often larger) aircraft types had been conducted with at least two flight crew members on board, to share pilot and navigation duties en route. During my attempt, as with Barry Jones' before me, our light two-seat gyro machines didn't really have a viable option of dual crew. This was predominantly because I needed to use the back seat passenger space (and weight allowance) for extra fuel, which was required to increase the overall range of the aircraft and enable me to achieve the longest sea crossings. Without this ability to make extended flights it would have been logistically impossible to stitch the whole route together, from country to country and continent to continent.

In the build-up preparations to the flight, I did briefly consider and discuss the possibilities of flying in formation with another gyro in company, a technique that fellow gyronauts and I had used many times previously on extended trips through the UK and France. Having a wingman certainly had its advantages: in the air it allowed the sharing of navigation and communications duties, as well as the ability to keep a watch on each other's aircraft from outside the cockpit for potential defects; and on the ground it helped with logistics and onward flight planning. It also could have given a morale boost and psychological strength through a feeling of 'safety in numbers' and a social camaraderie element that could have helped greatly when encountering the numerous unforeseen challenges ahead.

That said, there were also drawbacks, the main one being that flying in company could effectively double the technical risks. There would be two aircraft collectively to take care of, with perhaps twice as much equipment to go wrong. We would also have had a slower group pace, and perhaps even the odd disagreement during tricky or complicated circumstances. Faced with uncertain and stressful situations in the air, differing views on what actions or strategy to take may have not only caused friction, but perhaps also dangerous outcomes.

When travelling solo many of these aspects became non-issues. In the air I had no one else to convince but myself that my actions were appropriate for the ever-changing situation. Mentally, I only needed to focus on the welfare of myself and no one else, which meant I had a better understanding and control of my complete picture as I flew along. And on the ground, there were no potential arguments (with myself!) about planning and logistics either.

Solo flight was not all upside though. For starters, it was quite difficult to keep an eye on the exterior of my own aircraft, unless I were to perhaps employ a mirror on a stick (don't try this at home). Also, the mental repercussions from embarking on long-distance solo flights of this nature could not be overlooked – as they could easily create feelings of tremendous loneliness, isolation and vulnerability.

***

At least there were no such feelings of loneliness in the busy Kirkbride Control Tower – its functional white painted concrete-and-brick construction gave a practical, no-nonsense feel to this gyro training school. There were also none of the plush black leather seats, chrome fittings and other fancy trappings often found at some high-end GA flying clubs. Kirkbride has always had a much more inclusive and friendly feel for anyone who may be just dropping in for a chat about learning to fly, accompanying a would-be flying partner or simply hoping to watch some incredible flying machines being put through their paces close at hand.

Above all it has been the strong active community of like-minded gyro pilots at Kirkbride, led by Chris Jones, who have developed and shaped the flight school in the intervening years since I first made my own pilgrimage there to learn how to fly. I was one of Chris's first *ab initio* trainee pilots since he himself had qualified as an instructor, such was the small community of U.K. gyro pilots and instructors that existed at that time. It felt like new ground for both of us.

But how exactly did Chris manage to teach me, as a complete beginner, to be able to eventually jump in an aircraft and fly it unaided? The answer of course, was to do it in small but logical steps.

It was about building my confidence slowly, gathering a familiar pattern of sensations into my brain. These things then became common and formed just another ordinary sequence of events, just like riding a bicycle. Many hours were spent in getting the basics correct and in becoming comfortable with the sensations of flight and feedback from the aircraft. First lessons and repeated exercises were usually handling in the air: flying straight and level, holding a steady course, and gentle turns. All these training sorties were focussed on helping me know how to handle the aircraft, and to understand how it would react to my (nervous) first inputs on the flight controls: the stick (right hand); throttle (left hand); and rudder pedals (both feet). Flying correct approaches and landings were next up with, rather surprisingly, the take-off being one of the last basic skills to be taught. This was primarily because the take-off called for some of the most advanced manoeuvring skills – it was the culmination of all the knowledge and newly acquired skills that I had learned combined into producing the glorious act of committing both body and machine into the air. For this, I needed to be ready. I couldn't just hope to *sort of* take-off in some loose approximate way. I either fully committed to doing it or I didn't. And if I did do it, then I was fully focussed on flying the thing and getting it safely back down again sometime soon. And as you would expect, having now flown myself into this aerial predicament, the *getting down again* immediately became my next number one priority.

All too soon, time was up on my Kirkbride pitstop. With 100 nautical miles still to fly, heading due west and out over the Irish Sea, I needed to get going and continue my homeward journey.

Farewells, good lucks and best wishes were exchanged with everyone, and I taxied out towards runway 28 on Kirkbride's enormous (by gyro standards) tarmac runway. I had to pay particular attention to an occasionally used farm access road that dissected the runway halfway along its length. Heavy trucks, tractors and even the odd rally car training near the perimeter fence were all regular traffic here, though thankfully aircraft were (usually) given the right of way.

Lined up for take-off, my first task was to push the control stick fully forward and pre-rotate the main rotor above my head. This meant taking power from the engine and temporarily feeding it through a system of drive shafts to spin the rotor blades up to around 250-260 rpm. With the aircraft held stationary on the ground by use of the main wheel brakes, I throttled up the fixed-pitch propeller behind me until the engine was running at about 4000 rpm. At this point, such was the thrust generated by the prop, the brakes had difficulty holding back the aircraft, and I disengaged the pre-rotator mechanism. Pulling the stick fully back towards my seat then caused the rotor head (and therefore the whole rotor) to tilt back to allow as much air as possible to flow into the underside of the rotor disc (the circular area beneath rotating blades). Finally, I then released the brakes to allow the gyro to begin its extremely short take-off roll. As the aircraft moved forward more air flowed into the underside of the spinning rotor, and just as in a free-spinning windmill, the blades were encouraged to spin faster and faster. With this new source of energy, the lightweight rotor blades rapidly built up momentum to exceed 300+ rpm and reached the trigger point at which the aircraft really wanted to fly. Such is the magic of gyroplane rotary flight that this very healthy and flight-worthy rotor speed was attained with minimal actual forward ground speed. Gyros can therefore typically achieve flight with a ground speed of only 20-25 mph.

As the take-off roll continued for the few short metres needed to attain flight, initially the nose wheel became light and then pulled itself off the ground due to the increased lift being generated by the windmilling blades. I then brought the stick forward again slightly, which allowed the aircraft to literally balance on its two main wheels. Now, a fixed-wing aeroplane at this point typically would hold this wheel balancing profile until, at a certain critical airspeed, the pilot would pull back on the stick and allow the aircraft to climb away into the air. I however did not need to do this in a gyro, I simply held both the stick and the wheel balance profile steady, until the rotor built up enough upward thrust to overcome the gravitational pull of the aircraft's own weight. This resulted in the main wheels becoming light, bouncy and skittery on the ground until the aircraft magically and rather majestically pulled itself up into the air. Sitting in the cockpit, it felt as if the ground just dropped away from below the aircraft (rather than experiencing any pulling up and climbing away sensation) and suddenly, I was airborne.

Climbing out from Kirkbride on the way home always had mixed emotions for me. I was keen to arrive safely home after my various adventures, but at the same time slightly saddened by the fact that I was leaving the great camaraderie of fellow flying enthusiasts behind. Normally, I would take comfort in the fact that I would soon be back to bother them all again on the next trip across the pond, but on this occasion, things felt significantly different. I knew on take-off that my route south in a few short weeks' time, marking the start of the world circumnavigation flight, would bypass this part of Cumbria. The more direct routing would see me depart Northern Ireland and take a slightly longer sea crossing to make landfall on the Cumbrian coastline over Saint Bees Head to the west of Workington. So the logic followed that the next time G-YROX would see her old stomping ground of the Solway Firth would be after she had actually flown completely around the world.

Quite a sobering thought at the outset, and flying home, there was much soul searching and reasoning as to the sanity of this whole seemingly crazy idea. But I had gone and done it now. I had *lit the blue touch paper* and set off the fireworks with the Duxford press launch event.

The flight along the northern shore of the Solway estuary was a lovely trip, especially viewed from the unique perspective of the open cockpit of a gyroplane. Generally flying much lower than a fixed wing, typically around 800-1000ft, gyro pilots always have a real bird's eye view of the scenery, in all directions. At this height I was often low enough to see people walking around below me, busily going about their normal business. Sometimes I could even smell the fields of crops, pine forests and wood smoke, and also take in the sea air while watching sets of wave patterns on the beach. Occasionally, I might see a farmer walking out of perhaps a milking shed to cross the farmyard carrying a bucket or some such thing, and on hearing a light aircraft passing overhead they would invariably stop in their tracks to instinctively glance up at me. The really nice thing was that in an open cockpit I could then lean slightly outboard and give them a big wave to say hello! And in response most felt compelled to wave back at me. Kids, on the other hand, often went berserk!

Once, I remember a group of children charging around like mad things at the fun of it all, only for two of them to run off completely in a different direction to the others. Playing and waving up from their farmyard, they ran away off into the front garden of their farmhouse. This intrigued me greatly, and I wondered what they were up to. The answer soon became apparent when they leaped onto a large circular trampoline and started to bounce and wave at me like members of the Whirling Dervish Society's bungee jump display team. It seemed that their sole mission had been to attempt to bounce just that tiny bit closer to my height! I was so impressed that I made a point of flying a tight circle around the farmhouse so we could all fit in some extra waving at each other. Long after I'd turned back onto my original course, I was still smiling to myself.

The straight-line crossing from Kirkbride to Larne is 100 nautical miles and, depending on the wind strength and direction, it would usually take me anywhere between 55 minutes (strong tailwind) to two hours and 30 minutes (strong headwind). An added advantage was that my route direction was always pretty much due west, flying into the setting sun and thus gained me an extra few minutes of precious daylight.

Crossing the Solway Firth was the first real overwater flying I had undertaken when flying the aircraft home from Kirkbride back in 2006. And whereas back then I had tentatively skirted around the edge of the estuary, clinging to the security of the shoreline as much as possible, I soon gained enough over water confidence to take a more direct routing. The course out over the sea was not only shorter, but it also avoided the air turbulence that was often created over the numerous nearby mountains and forests. Typically, at this point I would make a quick call to Scottish Information (or after first radio contact, simply 'Scottish' for brevity) on the VHF Radio, and then, with air traffic communications established I would be off and running, homeward bound.

Scottish was always a great comfort on this route, as by periodically relaying my position to them, either by a direct call over the radio or by them interrogating my radar transponder, I could rest assured that at least someone always knew of my whereabouts on this relatively empty and isolated coastline. Through a bit of trial and error over numerous trips, I also found that flying at a low altitude and surrounded by hills, there was always a 10-minute radio blackout area just to the east of Scotland's National Book Town, Wigtown.

Entering this blackout area, I often felt like an Apollo astronaut who had just gone behind the Moon. After an enforced radio silence, it was always a relief to hear the cheery voice of someone receiving my calls once more. Except it was not a Texan accent ringing in my headphones, but a Scottish one as I continued out west and considered my next obstacles, a series of restricted airspace zones and active military firing ranges.

Often at weekends and sometimes during the weekdays these various gunnery ranges were declared cold or inactive. On these occasions, I always looked forward to the possibility of transiting across these normally out-of-bound areas, as it gave me a fascinating glimpse of the artillery shooting ranges set up within their boundaries. Heavily bunkered huts were strategically placed, virtually buried into the hillsides save for a small observation window staring out towards the sea (and at the target zones by the shore). From here, I could easily imagine the firing range observer radioing back the accuracy score that a heavy piece of artillery had just shot into one of the targets, much like an oversized game of darts. I often wondered if the observer was ever tempted to shout out on the radio, "One hundred and eightyyyyy!" when a perfect hit was made.

Travelling on westwards, I approached yet more firing ranges at Luce Bay, only a few miles from my crossing point for the Irish Sea. When the Luce Bay range area was 'cold' I was permitted a marvellous low-level flight right along the length of the often-restricted beach. On one such crossing, I was in communication with Scottish about allowing me a direct flight path right across the middle of Luce Bay, effectively straight through the firing line. The danger zone area was active at the time, and a message came back to me after some minutes: "Golf Yankee Romeo Oscar X-Ray (G-YROX), you may transit directly across the bay as soon as the Harrier jet (that was five minutes ahead of me) has completed its (bombing) run and has safely cleared the zone."

In other words, I was given permission to cross the active zone while there was a short gap in the Harrier training traffic and (most probably) when all the RAF staff on the ground would be pausing for a quick cup of tea and a biscuit. This was all very well and good, but as I subsequently made my 10-minute dash at 95 mph across the bay, I couldn't help having this uneasy feeling that I was surely being watched through the telescopic crosshairs of a dozen control tower observers nearby. Momentarily distracted from properly dunking biscuits in their tea, this quirky little radar blip must have resulted in a lot of soggy and broken custard creams having to be hastily fished out of government-issued mugs that day. It was all I could do to stop imagining those little red laser dots used for weapons guidance appearing on the sides of my fuselage, as they do in all the top action movies.

On approaching the quaint Scottish fishing village of Portpatrick, it was customary to change radio frequencies from Scottish Information to Belfast Approach. This handover meant replacing the Scottish accent talking to me in my headset with a familiar Northern Ireland voice, and if I had been away on a lengthy trip this was always my first sign of home. 'Belfast' would then track my progress across the Irish Sea on the short hop over to my hometown of Larne. This stretch of water was familiar to me as I had sailed it many times in both cruising yachts from East Antrim Boat Club and RNLI lifeboats, but a crossing that took perhaps four plus hours by sailing boat was quickly reduced to only around 25 minutes by gyro! During my sea crossing, depending on the altitude I was flying at and the visibility on the day, I could often see 100 miles or more in all directions. Glancing southwards, I could sometimes see as far as the Isle of Man, famous the world over for its motorbike TT (Tourist Trophy) time trial road races, and northwards, occasionally I could see up beyond the Mull of Kintyre towards the Scotch Whisky producing western isles of Islay and Jura.

It was here in mid-channel that I once saw one of my most memorable sights on what was otherwise an uneventful trip home. The visibility on that particular summer's day had not been so clear, a hazy murk had established itself and although still within the legal minima for VFR flight, it meant that as I coasted out from Portpatrick, I couldn't readily see the coastline of Northern Ireland stretching out ahead of me. Flying along in this murk, my eyes were kept busy watching out for the confirmation of the far coastline, which I felt would surely appear suddenly out of the gloom. It was then that I saw a strange object on the water, which at first resembled a large dark grey box. As I flew closer it grew even larger, though I was still at a loss to know what it actually was. It certainly wasn't the shape of a ship or even the rear end of a very boxy-looking ship. What could it be? It was only when the box slowly rotated in the water that it suddenly dawned on me what I was peering at through the haze.

I was staring down at the conning tower of a Royal Navy submarine!

What a treat to see one of these most elusive and secretive of creatures out in its natural habitat. Drawing closer, I could now see its somewhat minimal markings, only visible whilst on the surface. A bright White Ensign flag fluttered in the stiff breeze and three hi-vis clad crew stood huddled in their cramped quarters up in the flying bridge.

Now I had a real dilemma on my hands. What to do? Three options sprung to my mind:

Option 1 - Make a polite 'excuse me' manoeuvre designed to allow both parties to remain unflustered and unidentified (and therefore not blow the submarine's cover). Basically, I would hastily leave the area, as soon as possible, in a semi-dignified manner.

Result - This erratic behaviour might have made me appear to be more suspicious than ever and perhaps would even have attracted the unwanted presence of those pesky red laser dots again (or worse).

Option 2 - Swoop down out of the hazy sun at full throttle to *really* give them something to worry about! Buzz around three laps of the deck at only 50ft off their bows, all the while humming (again) that theme tune from *The Dam Busters* movie.

Result – Err, perhaps not a good plan...

Option 3 - Maintain present course, altitude and speed, and perhaps give them a cheery wave while flying past (and get one back in return?).

Result – yes, as you might have guessed, I went with this option, though I could not be quite sure whether those were really waving hands or shaking clenched fists from atop the flying bridge. I like to think it was the nicer of the two gestures.

Once I had safely passed a respectful distance beyond the sub, I paused to snap a quick picture, just to prove back home later that, yes, I really did see it. It was such a rarity that I happened to be coinciding my crossing of the Irish Sea with their surface manoeuvres that day. As it was so murky, if I had been flying perhaps 10 miles north or south of my current track, I might have easily flown right past and not seen them at all.

I also did spare a thought for the three poor unsuspecting lookout crew on board the sub. I imagined them receiving a message from their tactical warfare officer below decks to watch out for an unidentified incoming target. Being tracked on radar, I would have appeared to be heading straight at them at a little over 90 knots. With one hand on the CRASH DIVE alarm button (there must surely be one, and it would be painted bright red of course), they would have been scouring the horizon, only to report back down to the ops room the following urgent communiqué: "Bridge deck to tactical warfare officer. Affirm, target sighted. Appears to be a... small yellow bumblebee... Stand by... One person on board. They are waving, and in a cheery fashion." At precisely which point, the entire bottom half of the tactical warfare officer's custard cream would have plopped off into his mug of tea.

***

Approaching Larne on the County Antrim coast, I was struck, as often was the case, by the natural beauty of my own backyard. On a good weather day, the shoreline of East Antrim and the world-famous Antrim Coast Road, which heads north from Larne, winding its way along the coastal fringes and around the many valleys and headlands that make up the nine Glens of Antrim, is truly a sight to behold. Over the course of the circumnavigation route, I would of course see many thousands of miles of coastline in all sorts of countries, but all in all, I would definitely say that the scenery of the Antrim coast could easily hold its own against the best that the rest of the world has to offer.

As a driving route, it even gives California's Big Sur a good run for its money. The fantastic contrasting geologic strata of stark black basalt, earthy red sandstone and brilliant white limestone, combine to give a unique, underlying ruggedness to the landscape. A wild terrain that is then smoothed and tamed by a blanketing patchwork quilt of lush green grass fields and intersected by peaty-brown fast moving-rivers. It is simply stunning to see on a sunny day.

Almost home, I signed off with Belfast Approach as I descended to touch down on the undulating fields of my private farm strip, which is on the home farm of long-time family friends, the Wilsons, just a couple of miles outside Larne. Using a 'private strip' sounds very grand but in my case, it was not so much an example of enjoying VIP treatment, more like avoiding getting splashed by sheep-dip treatment! A grass-roots status that I much preferred and greatly appreciated... However, landing here certainly had its own peculiarities. Late on final approach, I needed to line up in a certain way to avoid the large trees growing in the hedgerows. I then had to slot down into a relatively short landing strip, of roughly 100m hedge to hedge, that was frequently shared with an assortment of sheep, cattle and silage (winter fodder of cut grass, the length of which depends on the various intervals of the farming calendar). This was true 'farm strip' flying, which in my case at least, was only made accessible by arriving in a gyro. For what other aircraft could possibly land in a few metres, stop its rotor and then taxi along a tree-lined farmer's lane, before driving into the farmyard and straight into an old barn (sorry, that should read 'hangar'). The only concession to aviation that has ever been needed on the farm, is a homemade windsock planted in a hedgerow – I made it from an old plastic bucket with the bottom cut out, which was then sewn up with some ripstop nylon.

I put the dust covers back on G-YROX in the hangar and reflected back on the journey just completed. The quick round-trip tour of Britain, which saw me fly down the west side, do some ongoing maintenance, and then hop over to Duxford for the world circumnavigation launch event before running back up the east side, was all done and dusted in less than a week. The quick round-trip tour of the globe however would prove to take considerably longer as we shall soon find out.

12–21 March 2010: the final build up to launch day

Although the build-up phase started long before this period, the last few days of preparations were now full of continuous, relentless pressure. Like rushing around frantically packing for your holidays whilst constantly worrying that you had forgotten to pack that one vital item that would come in handy somewhere half a world away. But whereas on normal holidays you might have a rough idea of the conditions you are likely to expect at your destination and could therefore pack your bags accordingly, I now had none of this reassurance. I had to expect and prepare for *every* type of condition such was the extreme climatic variation of my routing around the world. That mesh mosquito hood may have been very handy during a forced out-landing in the endless forests of the Far East of Russia, but it was not going to be much use to me passing through the customs arrivals hall at Doha's Hamad International Airport. The issue of what to bring and what to leave out, with a finite weight allowance governing everything, was therefore a major concern for weeks before the departure.

With no handy '*How to fly around the world guidebook*' to refer to, everything for me just seemed to be a case of 'make it up as you go along'. But I did have plenty of extremely helpful support too. Tom Burns (Ireland) was helping with media interviews and press releases, and also organising my website along with Eddie Gould (Egypt) who additionally managed my GyroxGoesGlobal Facebook page. Also on-line, my sister Norah (UK) administered our Just Giving page for charity donations. Phil Harewood (UK) of The Gyrocopter Experience aided me with the SPOT tracker system, while Geoffrey Boot (UK) helped with route planning and liaising with the FAI to coordinate the multiple world speed and distance records that I hoped to set throughout the circumnavigation. Mendelssohn Pilot Supplies (UK) sorted my air navigation charts and arranged GPS equipment with coverage for the whole world. International flight permissions were initially organised by Mike Gray at White Rose Aviation (UK) and latterly by Eddie Gould of General Aviation Support Egypt. Devising the design of my soon-to-be-famous bright red immersion/survival suit was Sauli Jankari of professional drysuit specialists Ursuit (Finland), and last but definitely not least, was the creation of my long-range fuel delivery system, a combined effort by Laszlo Torok of Turtle Pac (Australia) and aircraft manufacturer RotorSport UK.

2

UK: the Circumnavigation Begins

22 March 2010: Larne, Northern Ireland – Brook Farm, Lancashire, England – Long Mynd, Shropshire, England

Circumnavigation launch day had arrived at last! With a lot of the hectic preparation work now already completed, I had time to slow things down a bit and take stock. Before I set off up to the farm to fly the aircraft down to the official FAI starting point in Sandy Bay Playing fields at Larne Harbour, Celia and I were able to sit down and have a last, peaceful cup of coffee. The kids were both at school, and so we were able to soak up a few moments of relative calm and normality before the big day started in earnest.

The logistics of the launch were fairly easily worked out from what was physically possible. The take-off field at the farm was too short to take off fully loaded with all my expedition kit and the spare fuel needed for the first leg of the journey, so an alternative plan was devised. Celia and I loaded all the bags and fuel into the car, and while all the other people were heading for Sandy Bay, we were heading in the opposite direction up to the Wilsons' farm. Celia dropped me off at the barn with my gleaming red flight suit and then took the car and equipment a further two miles down to the local Larne Rugby Club pitches. Meanwhile, I made my final checks of the aircraft, warmed up the engine and flew all of two minutes across country to also arrive at the rugby club.

Once all the bags were unloaded by the side of the pitches, Celia then drove the car back into Larne to meet up with everyone else at the Sandy Bay playing fields. Meanwhile I busied myself packing all my expedition baggage and fuel into the aircraft and was soon ready to go. Taking off this time from a much longer and smoother grass surface, I was able to hop across to Sandy Bay in another two-minute flight. The only person to witness my departure from the rugby club was a local man called Ronnie Lough, who just happened to be down to cut the grass that morning.

It was all a little surreal. I had told everyone I knew, and it had also been reported in the local paper, *The Larne Times*, that I would fly in at 11am. And so it was that I flew across Larne Lough and performed a sweeping turn onto a short final approach to land down on the council's manicured grass playing surface. I made a short taxi to a holding pen that the ever-helpful council groundsmen had earlier constructed from crowd control barriers. This meant that when I stopped the engine and climbed out, I was surrounded on three sides by the assembled crowds. The local Olderfleet Primary School students, including both Felix and Petra in their ranks, were cheering like mad and had constructed some fabulous 'Good Luck' banners. There was even a remote Sky TV broadcasting unit there, beaming me live into their studios in London.

Bidding everyone a fond and emotional farewell, I lined up on the grass playing fields and took off over the harbour.

This was it. I was on my way! As if on autopilot mode, my standard procedure for crossing the Irish Sea kicked in, I contacted Belfast Approach for a basic (radio) service to see me to the mid-channel and then changed to Scottish Information to watch out for me after that. As I coasted out over Muck Island, a little self-doubt crept in when thinking of the enormity of what I was taking on.

I reflected to myself, "Well, you've gone and done it now!"

After all the many months of preparations, I had just committed myself to undertaking the flight (and adventure) of a lifetime.

"You'll be fine. Just take it one flight at a time."

My initial tactics were to ease myself into the flight by retaining as much familiarity as possible. So my first stop was Brook Farm airstrip in Lancashire, home base for Pete Davis who is a well-known gyroplane international display pilot. Calling in for a quick cup of tea and a catch up with Pete was a good way to settle in and focus on my most immediate tasks ahead, particularly after the emotionally charged atmosphere of my departure from Larne earlier in the day.

There was also a practical reason for the stop. I had spare fuel in the Turtle Pac fuel bladder, which was strapped into the back seat. This auxiliary fuel capacity was eventually going to be used as part of my inflight refuelling system, but the bladder had not yet been plumbed into the aircraft. So while on the ground, I had to manually decant the spare fuel directly into my main fuel tanks. When fully operational this additional Turtle Pac fuel system would allow me to extend my flight endurance range from around three hours to over seven hours, which was essential for making long open water crossings at various points around the world. I planned to have it factory fitted over the next few days by RotorSport UK in its Shropshire-based workshop at Long Mynd.

23–24 March 2010: Long Mynd, Shropshire, England (non-flying days)

Roxy was treated to two days of last-minute pampering and preparations in the RotorSport UK's workshops, in the capable hands of Gerry Speich and his team of design engineers and mechanics. Her long-distance Turtle Pac fuel system was fitted, including a safety restraint that would anchor the fuel bladder to the main rotor mast so that, in the event of a crash landing, the Turtle Pac would be prevented from lunging forward on impact and potentially smashing its way through the back of my seat. It was seen as a mandatory UK Civil Aviation Authority (UK CAA) safety measure but one that would most likely never be needed.

Little did I know then that I might end up testing it out for real in the coming weeks.

25 March 2010: Long Mynd, Shropshire,England – Stoke, Kent, England

Final rotor-balancing flight checks slightly delayed my departure from the Midland Gliding Club, but once underway I made up good time. The original plan had been to swing by John Butler's farm strip on the way south, but because of the earlier delay, I rearranged that John and his MT-03 Autogyro (registration G-PPLG) would join me in the air as I flew past overhead. It worked a treat, and together we continued south towards Kent in loose formation, electing to avoid all of London's busy airspace by skirting eastwards around the capital.

En route however, just north of London, I had one extra special task to do. Watching out for a local water tower landmark, I broke off from our formation to overfly a very particular house, that of my sister Norah and brother-in-law Geoff (both of whom attended the Duxford launch). Sure enough as I passed overhead, they were in the back garden with their family, all waving madly alongside a huge good luck sign that had been laid out on the lawn. It was my last direct contact with family members before leaving the UK.

We arrived overhead Stoke airfield, a small grass strip squeezed in along the shoreline of the River Medway estuary, in good spirits. Unusually, the runway has a slight kink in it, being flanked on one side by the curved estuary shoreline and on the other by an equally curved line of rather intimidating high-voltage transmission lines, which certainly helped to sharpen the attention. As we were landing in gyros however, there was nothing much to worry about, and soon enough we were warmly welcomed in the clubhouse by Kai Maurer. He was the resident gyroplane flight instructor and also a good buddy to John and me, since our shared early student days up in Kirkbride Airfield. More recently, we had all spent a pleasurable week of flying together in France in 2009.

Kai put John and me up at his house nearby, and we spent an enjoyable night reminiscing of our past adventures. The next day I was leaving the UK behind, and the idea of setting off to fly around the world was all now becoming much more real.

3

Europe: France to Greece

26 March 2010: Stoke, Kent, England – Le Touquet, France – Chartres, France

Flying down through England had so far been comfortable. I had been passing through pre-flown territory and was welcomed at every stop by familiar friendly faces, all keen to provide me with fuel, food and friendship. Today however, was going to be different.

Although I had flown across the English Channel the year before, with John and Kai on our mini-tour of France flight, I had not yet ventured such a distance completely unsupported and on my own. So with no group strength to call on and nobody else to blame but myself should things go wrong, I psyched myself up to cross the Channel in what was very much a rites of passage solo flight.

From Kai's house, we made our way back to the airfield exceedingly early, to be met by a Kent journalist who then had to wait, very patiently I might add, to get the story and pictures of my departure. This would become a recurring theme of many departures. I would be busying myself with the essential task of making sure everything was tied down and in its proper place, as well as going about my other routine daily checks of the aircraft and equipment, when I'd spot out of the corner of my eye someone (or even a sizable group in busier places) hovering nearby. Usually with camera(s) in hand, they would be standing around, seemingly expecting some action.

"Hurry up and get going so I can get some dramatic, all-action pictures."

This was never actually said out loud of course, but I got to know their impatient body language as they shifted from one foot to the other, getting bored with the apparently endless tasks that that 'gyro guy' was doing. I'd imagine the other thoughts running through their heads: "What's he fiddling about with now, surely he has checked those straps three times already? And look, he is not even in his famous red suit yet. What sort of supposed debonair dashing pilot runs around in ripped shorts and a manky old T-shirt anyway?"

After take-off from Stoke, we had a four-ship flight down to the south coast. *Roxy* and I were accompanied by Kai (and his trainee student pilot), John Butler in G-PPLG and flying duo Mike King and his wife Trish. Such is the close-knit gyroplane community in the UK, that I had first met all these flying escorts at various stages during my training at Kirkbride or shortly afterwards. Each of them had kindly turned up to wish me well with the expedition and to give me a proper send off. On subsequent flights, thoughts of these simple actions would help keep my spirits up in many lonely parts of the world. Often, when I was several hundred miles away from any civilisation, I would think back and take great heart from the companionable flying I had experienced today.

Flying down over the Kent countryside, we chatted away whilst in loose flight formation and took air-to-air photos for posterity. When Dover Castle and the Port of Dover came into view however, I knew that all too soon I would have to leave this cosy 'guard of honour'. I was about to be launched out on my own, "To infinity and beyond!" as Buzz Lightyear would say. One by one the other aircraft bade me a heartfelt *bon-voyage* and peeled off the formation to commence their homeward journeys. My final radio messages to each of them were all of a similar vein: "You had better make sure you are able to come and meet me up in Scotland!" The last aircraft to turn was John – as he wanted to snap a photo of me leaving the shoreline with the White Cliffs of Dover in the background. All that remained was for me to have a quick chat with Dover Coastguard, whose premises I was now flying over. I then changed frequencies to contact London Information, who were to handle my flight out across the Channel.

London Info's friendly and busy radio chatter with a myriad of local aircraft served as a fitting audio backdrop as I coasted out above numerous container ships and vehicle ferries that were plying up, down and across this busiest stretch of the Channel. This was far more congested than my local patch of water across the North Channel of the Irish Sea and the fact that I could already see the French coast made the sea crossing appear even shorter.

My final reporting point for London Info was to be at the mid-Channel flight boundary between UK and French controlled airspace, and it arrived quickly. The last words from 'home' were telling me to free-call my onward destination frequency, which allowed me to sign off with London and contact the French controllers when I was ready. Suddenly I was done with the UK air traffic system and I was off and running on my own, attempting to fly solo around the globe. I was now out in the big world!

* * *

The early strategy for the world flight was to cut my teeth on the run down through France. This was certainly abroad, yet for now, it still remained very familiar *pre-flown* territory. So while I was still finding my wings with the heavily loaded aircraft and the newly installed (and as yet not fully field tested) Turtle Pac re-fuelling system, my plan was to minimise my workload and revisit some of the airfields John, Kai and I had used the previous year. In this way Le Touquet, Chartres and the lovely little airstrip of Sarlat-Domme would all serve as friendly, pre-rehearsed destinations. Approaching Le Touquet would be familiar as I already knew the landmarks to watch for, the radio reporting points and the general layout of the runway, taxiways and apron. And on arrival I would know where to park and where to pay my landing fees and clear customs (I would even know where the toilets were!). All these things were a great psychological help, which would at least give me the appearance of knowing what I was doing. My plan was then to be well into the swing of things by the time I reached more unfamiliar airports on the south coast of France.

I made landfall with France at Cap Griz-Nez and followed the coastal route south towards Le Touquet – Côte d'Opale Airport. The fabulous beaches that had been teeming with life last May now seemed empty, lonely and windswept. There were no wild bunches of kids staring up from their sandcastles and ice creams to wave and shout crazily at me. This time around there was just the odd lone dog walker wrapped up well against the cold to witness my little yellow craft buzzing by. A stiff sea breeze had picked up by the time I arrived on final approach to the airfield. The controller had warned me of this fact on the radio and had added that the wind was not only strong and gusting, but its direction was a full-on crosswind blowing at 90 degrees across the single runway. This meant that my landing needed to be a little more unusual compared to the standard, straight in approach used by conventional fixed-wing aircraft as outlined below.

Crosswind landings in a strong breeze are usually regarded with some deserved trepidation by pilots of light aircraft, as it requires them to keep their wits and reflexes sharp. It calls for the pilot to make their final approach in a crab-like fashion (a little bit sideways to the direction of travel) to compensate for the strong side wind, in order that their glide path can remain aligned over the runway centre line right through to touchdown. Crucially however, the wheels cannot be left pointing at this slight sideways angle on first contact with the ground as this could easily trip the aircraft over onto its side. Therefore, a kick of rudder is often required in the last seconds of the landing, to align the aircraft up with the runway and the direction of travel. Furthermore, once the wheels are on the deck, great care then has to be taken to ensure that the aircraft wings don't catch the wind (blowing in from the side). This could unbalance the aircraft and either push it off course, or worse still, flip the aircraft over completely.

So little wonder that the ATC sitting in the control tower at Le Touquet sounded a little nervous and apprehensive as he resigned himself to the fact that he would now be obliged to give *Roxy* and me permission to land on his precious pristine runway. As if that wasn't enough for the unfortunate controller's nerves, as I made my final approach it appeared that I wasn't going to land on the runway at all, as by now I was plummeting towards the ground about 50m to the left side of the tarmac, out over the scrubby grass outfield.

However, this unusual manoeuvre was all in my game plan. A gyro in a reasonable headwind can perform a zero-roll landing, in other words it can settle down onto its main wheels without any forward rollout at all. I could achieve this by flaring the aircraft moments before touchdown, which would then scrub off all the forward airspeed. I always liked to compare this action to a seagull coming in to land on a beach – gracefully swooping down and manoeuvring at high speed until the very last seconds, when it casually sticks its undercarriage legs out and plops down the last few inches, to land exactly on its chosen spot on the sand. A bit of a shake and a shrug of its feathers as it stows its wings away and the coolest of seabirds is all sorted to strut off and find its lunch, hiding under a rock.

So by deliberately flying to the far left side of the runway, I was allowing myself space to turn in, hard right, on a very late final approach and land directly *across* the runway. Yes, this was at a full 90 degrees to a 'normal' approach, but more importantly it meant I was landing directly *into* the strong wind. I was able to make a spot landing on the centre line of the runway, right at a T-junction with a taxiway. I then simply taxied straight ahead off the active runway and headed for the ATC's control tower and the airport's terminal buildings.

Appreciating the ease and control with which I had landed in the testing conditions, the much-relieved ATC greeted me over the radio with a lovely expression, "*Ahh! C'est une formidable machine!*" and I thanked him for his warm welcome. It made me smile that he could readily recognise a fantastic flying machine when he saw one. Taxiing ahead towards the apron, I paused to apply the rotor brake onto the rotor hub, an action that stopped the blades from freely rotating and allowed me to align the two rotor blades fore and aft along the length of the aircraft. On the ground at least, *Roxy* was now only as wide as her main wheel span (less than 2m). I then searched for the familiar yellow square with a big black letter **C** on it. This sign denoted the reporting point in the terminal building for any visiting pilots. After spotting it, I went to park on the adjacent apron parking area, which on this occasion was quite full of light fixed-wing aircraft of various breeds and pedigrees. The way all the aircraft had been parked reminded me of a supermarket carpark near to closing time, where vehicles are dispersed randomly with gaps here and there in between. Akin to manoeuvring a supermarket trolly, I was then able to weave *Roxy*, (my now slender aircraft), in and out through these spaces until I finally arrived, triumphant in pole position, right in the front row just outside the terminal building. No other aircraft type, including helicopters, could have executed such a flexible manoeuvre when taxiing around in these confined spaces.

The stop here on the ground was quite short, only a quick visit to pay landing fees and review the weather for the next leg to Chartres. It was long enough, however, to pause for photographs with some of my growing band of online supporters. This was my first inkling that the trip was being followed online by people en route and it was reassuring to know that such local well-wishers were able to offer me their encouraging support from time to time, as my journey progressed.

Taxiing back out to the runway, I spoke again to the *formidable* ATC duty controller. After our previous friendly exchanges, I requested to take off much in the same fashion as I had landed, as the wind strength and direction had changed little during my short stay. By warning the ATC of my intentions, he was not then unduly alarmed to see me line up on the extreme left side of the tarmac, pointing at about 70 degrees away from the conventional runway take-off direction. I knew with a runway width of about 50m, in the given wind strength, I would most likely be off the ground before even reaching the centre line, never mind the far edge of the runway. Once airborne and climbing out, I was then able to bank to my left and follow the regular climb-out path along the main runway as any other conventional aircraft would do.

I was off and running again for the second flight of the day. I had successfully coped with my first port of call in a foreign land and as I headed inland towards the second, Chartres, I wondered how the hundred or so landings at other foreign airports would work out. As we will soon discover dear reader, not all were as smooth or as well-planned as this first day abroad.

We had flown into Chartres from Le Touquet the year before as part of our mini-Tour de France trip, so the landmarks and terrain en route were all fairly recognisable. However, the previous year we had arrived quite late in the evening, so much so that we found the whole place had shut up shop (and hangars). Everyone had gone home. All we could do was break out our aircraft covers in the setting sun, park the three gyros close in beside the hangars (and out of sight from the road) and hail a taxi to take us into town. We then had a tremendous (albeit unscripted and impromptu) sightseeing tour of the town as we careered around, hunting for accommodation and food. This time I had arrived much earlier in the day and had the added luxury of being able to stow *Roxy* safely in the maintenance hangar overnight. And rather than repeating the previous year's magic roundabout joyride around town, I now easily found an out of tourist season low-cost room, at the Hotel Campanile within walking distance of the airfield.

27 March 2010: Chartres, France – Sarlat-Domme, France – Carcassonne, France

Returning to the airport, I busied myself with the regular pre-flight checks and had a visit from Jane Colous, a local contact who had already been following the progress of my flight online. She had brought her son along to meet me and kindly offered up some food for my journey. So once my pre-flights were complete, I gratefully squeezed the baguette sandwich she gave me in amongst my luggage as I re-packed *Roxy*. It would prove to be most appreciated later in the day.

The flight from Chartres to Béziers via Sarlat-Domme was to be the first real test of the Turtle Pac and the refuelling system I had devised in order to significantly extend the mileage range of *Roxy*. This meant that the weight allowance normally allocated to carrying a passenger was used for carrying extra fuel instead. The tricky part however, had been finding a convenient method of stowing the additional fuel within the aircraft. In other similarly sized aircraft, this was normally achieved by fitting a rigid fuel tank on the back seat. This approach however was far too inflexible (excuse the pun), as I needed to retain the ability of potentially carrying a passenger (ie. a Russian Navigator) on the back seat at the same time as carrying additional fuel. So I was very fortunate when I found that Laszlo Torok and his Turtle Pac company in Australia could provide me with an ideal flexible solution. All I then needed was an approved method of installing it into *Roxy's* back seat.

Laszlo and I had exchanged emails and design sketches until we ended up with a workable solution. We would use an 80-litre flexible Turtle Pac that was approved to hold either regular motor unleaded petrol (mogas) or aviation fuel (avgas). Similarly, discussions with Gerry Speich's team at RotorSport UK brought us also to a workable fuel line delivery system. The idea was that the Turtle Pac would be strapped in place in the back seat just like a human passenger, only this one would not talk much and would get considerably thinner during each flight. Then to operate my *in-flight refuelling*, I could activate a shut-off valve by my seat in the cockpit to allow the additional fuel to flow by gravity (no pump required) down into the main tanks sitting below the passenger seat. The hidden beauty of the system however, would not really come into play until the aircraft was back down on the ground.

The *pièce de résistance* was that the Turtle Pac was easily removed, via a quick-release fuel line system more commonly used with fuel tanks for marine outboard motors. This system enabled me to disconnect the empty Turtle Pac, roll it up, put it under my arm and then take it to the nearest petrol station. This proved invaluable time and time again, especially as transferring unleaded petrol from a normal auto garage forecourt out onto an airport apron was usually a challenge. During my travels, all manner of imaginative transport – taxis, taxicles (don't ask!), service trucks, local contacts' vehicles, baggage trolleys and even loaves of bread (definitely don't ask!) – would then be employed to ferry the refilled Turtle Pac back to the aircraft.

My plan was to use the whole of France as a testbed for this new fuelling system. Should things go awry, I was safely flying over land and could hopefully resolve and fix any teething problems before I had to take on the serious business of crossing the Mediterranean Sea. By filling the Turtle Pac at Chartres, I could stop and check it was decanting through properly at Sarlat–Domme, and then fly directly onto Béziers without the need for any additional refuelling stops. This would also save me a lot of time, as during a typical re-fuelling stop, I would have to approach, land, ground manoeuvre, find willing staff and transport, locate fuel at a local garage (a mini adventure in itself), return to the airport, perhaps smuggle the fuel past security(!), pay landing fees, refuel, taxi out in the queue of departing traffic, line up and depart again. Even the briefest of fuel stops would usually take me at least an hour.

* * *

The flight southwards to Sarlat-Domme was pleasant and relaxed, as the scenery was still familiar to me from having flown the same route the previous year. The main aerial hazards that I needed to navigate through in this part of France were the fast-jet military air routes that crisscrossed the country. These were corridors in the sky that effectively funnelled the jets from their training bases in the interior of the country, out to their high-speed playground for war games over the Atlantic Ocean. For me to cross these no-fly corridors, I could either fly above them at a few thousand feet or below them at a few hundred feet. As *Roxy* was a highly manoeuvrable, ultra-low-level capable gyroplane, I opted to limbo dance my way under the restricted airspace every time.

As the miles quickly ticked by on my GPS screen and with numerous limbo dances completed, I flew on through lovely rolling countryside dotted with classic French châteaux. These large imposing country retreats, with sweeping drives and manicured gardens, were a sight to behold and I was privileged to be able to take a visual tour of them from above. Going by the drawn shutters and complete absence of any *l'autos* sitting on the gravel outside the big French doors, a surprising number appeared to be devoid of residents. I surmised that perhaps these were all grand summer palaces for well-to-do Parisians, and that no doubt the gravel courtyards would be chock-full of limousines come the summertime.

Little sleepy villages also glided by beneath me, again equally bereft of people. Where was everyone? Was the whole of France shut? Apparently so. It was late afternoon before any evidence of life re-emerged from behind shuttered windows and doors, as the odd clapped out Citroën van bounced along a rough farm track and people once more took to the streets to reopen their village shops and businesses. Peering down from my elevated viewpoint, rural France certainly looked to have a very relaxed and idyllic pace of life.

Standing prominently for miles around, Sarlat-Domme is in a terrific location for an airfield. Much like the Long Mynd back in Shropshire, it sits atop an elongated hill so that on my approach I felt as if I was coming into land on a giant tabletop. The airfield was deserted apart from one club member who was incredibly surprised to see me. I knew that as long as the Turtle Pac was working as planned, I had plenty of fuel onboard and so I hadn't needed to make any local fuel arrangements in advance. In reality, this stop was more like pulling into a layby to check that the luggage on the roof rack was still tied down and I was soon able to confirm that the fuel bag was indeed functioning properly and that the two straps used to keep it tensioned were working correctly. These straps had been a further necessary invention, installed only a few days before my UK departure.

Before setting off, I had been concerned that when the Turtle Pac got thinner, it would start to flap about in the seat belt that had originally been nicely tightened around it, when it had been a more XXXL-sized passenger. The two additional straps provided the bag with further restraints that could be operated remotely from the front seat. After all, there was no way I was going to be able to activate an autopilot (as if I had one), get up out of my seat and walk back down the cabin to have a quiet word with this troublesome passenger, telling them that although I appreciated their *crash diet,* it was still no excuse for them to suddenly start thrashing about rather violently in their seat. The solution had been simple – I worked out a system where I tied the two adjustable straps to the bottom corners of the bag (in effect the passenger's legs) and securely attached the tails of these straps under my front seat, so that I could reach them as I flew along. As the fuel drained out of the bag, I was able to reach down and tighten the straps by a few centimetres every 30 minutes or so and stretch out the passenger, as if they were on some medieval torture rack.

With 'the rack' performing as expected, and all other parts of the aircraft in good order, I gratefully stuffed Jane's delicious (though now slightly squished) baguette down my own refuelling hatch and once more took to the air. I was feeling extremely pleased and buoyed up by the refuelling system – it was working exactly as planned and was going to allow me to fly a tremendous distance in a single flight. Another uncertain part of the circumnavigation jigsaw had been slotted into place and I was beginning to settle in and enjoy this fantastic journey. My enjoyment was short lived however, as a growing amount of thick and menacing cloud started to loom over the high ground ahead.

Routing towards Béziers, I initially kept myself well clear to the west of the Massif Central, a 5000ft-high plateau that dominates a good deal of eastern France. By flying this less direct dogleg, I was then able to remain at a relatively low altitude and stay as warm as possible in my open cockpit. It was still March after all, and the ambient air temperature proved to be quite nippy once I climbed even to just a few thousand feet. Eventually however, I still needed to head south-east in order to reach the much-anticipated coastline of the Mediterranean and so I hoped to cut the corner and climb over the southernmost foothills of the plateau. Alas, as I approached this point, I could see that there was a very low-level cloud base lurking over the hill tops. At least when dealing with poor visibility out over the sea, I always had the comfort of knowing the surface was flat and that I wouldn't suddenly fly into anything. High ground being hidden by low clouds, such as I was facing now however, was a much more dangerous mix.

I didn't want to climb into these much riskier mountain conditions, so I began to skirt around the lower reaches of the hillsides. In doing so I kept my escape route open to my right-hand side, out over the flatter lower ground towards the south and west. But staying safe by flying around the edges was also gradually lengthening my overall routing, in both time and distance; it was clear I was going to need a contingency plan. The thought of running extremely low on fuel became a constant worry, as did the turbulence. The winds had been favourable all the way down through France, and at times I had been covering the ground at over 125mph for a given airspeed of only 95 mph. While this extra tailwind had been welcomed over the flatter terrain, it was now generating severe turbulence in the undulating foothills. The gusting winds were deflected by the ridges and resulted in a very confused and unsettled airflow. Ideally, I needed to find a suitable alternative airfield or landing spot, from where I could take stock of the weather and perhaps source further fuel.

Continuing my skirting manoeuvre, I called two smaller airfields that happened to be en route. Unfortunately, neither appeared particularly active, and the thought of making an unannounced precautionary landing into a deserted airfield did not appeal. I may have ended up on the ground feeling even more isolated, behind locked fences and with little immediate prospect of reaching any assistance whatsoever. Luckily however, another alternative plan had also been forming in my mind. If I carried on contouring around the foothills, I would eventually clear the high ground close to Carcassonne. This would still be perhaps 50 minutes' flight-time short of Béziers, my intended destination, but I knew that Carcassonne would have all the facilities I would need. And importantly, for maintaining my morale in this increasingly uncertain flight, I also had the psychological boost of having flown into Carcassonne before. Admittedly, this had only been as a normal tourist in a commercial passenger jet, but even this was enough to make the place seem more familiar. As I was passing over a last ridge of the foothills, the ancient walled city of Carcassonne appeared in the distance, dominating the wide-open plain that lay ahead and I was soon able to make contact with the airport control tower. I passed on my hastily created diversion details, citing the cause as bad visibility and weather to the north-east. Familiar with the poor flying conditions in the mountains, the reassuring and friendly French controller's voice put me at ease immediately as she recognised that I must have already experienced quite a difficult last two hours of flying. With the worst of the uncertainties behind me, I was then able to relax and enjoy making my final approach to land.

It was a very weary and relieved gyro pilot that eventually touched down on the Carcassonne runway. I had virtually flown down the length of France in a single day and was now in much need of some rest and recuperation. After some discussion, I was allowed to squeeze *Roxy* into the flying club hangar, and local club member Yves Pueyo, was a big help in organising the necessary fuel run and local accommodation.

Another budget motel, which are very popular in France, was handily close to the airfield and again proved ideal for my needs, though I had to remind myself that this could be viewed as luxury accommodation, when compared to what I might expect later on in the journey.

By this time, I was also gradually discovering the best way to pack *Roxy*. When I left the UK, I knew that I had all the kit I needed on the aircraft, *somewhere*, though exactly *where* it was stored was not always obvious or convenient. And so it had taken until now, the South of France, for me to reorganise and repack the luggage into some sort of logical order. There isn't much in the way of luggage space in a two-seat tandem gyroplane – I basically had the area of the passenger's footwell, the space under my front seat, two small storage pockets on either side of my seatback, lightweight storage in the nose, and whatever space I could spare directly under my legs. The passenger seat was predominantly taken up by the Turtle Pac and perhaps a light rucksack strapped on top of it. This then, along with some big pockets in my red flying suit was all that I had to play with.

I quickly devised a system where, overnight, I needed to only remove a small rucksack (holding my computer, journal, flight logs and camera equipment) and two small fuselage-shaped pannier bags. One contained my spare clothes and wash kit, while the other held my tracker, phone, electrical chargers and my two removable GPS devices. These three bags, along with the empty rolled-up Turtle Pac under my arm, would then regularly pitch up at the check-in counter of the nearest local hotel, motel or guest house. They would usually be accompanied by their dishevelled, wind-burnt owner, who would grace the lobby sporting that certain *Eau de Gasoline* cologne that is often associated with racing car mechanics and diesel fitters the world over.

Rarely used items such as spare parts, spare flying helmet, emergency sleeping bag, extra warm clothes for the colder climates, first aid kit, air charts etc. were all kept in one large holdall bag that remained in the rear seat footwell. The aircraft dust cover, which could also cope well with light rain, was conveniently stuffed into one of the front seat pockets. Whenever it emerged, it always looked like a huge yellow scarf being pulled from a magician's top hat.

28 March 2010: Carcassonne, France – Cuers, France

Although the motel was only 600m from the airport, the Sunday morning trek back to the hangars felt a long way in the hot spring sunshine. Thankfully I had been helped to source fuel the previous evening, and so now all I had to carry were my three bags. Arriving at the small flying club entrance door at the rear of the hangars, I was amazed to find that the interior, which had the night before been stuffed full of light aircraft of all shapes and sizes (including *Roxy*), was now completely empty.

My G-reg (UK) aircraft (G-YROX) was sitting in pride of place, outside on the apron alongside all the resident F-reg (French) aircraft. The club members were gathered around, setting out trestle tables and busily preparing for – wait for it – a Sunday lunchtime paella party! And even better, I was invited!! What luck to have diverted to Carcassonne, only to then find this club event in full swing. It was a great way to meet and chat with all the flyers, and a pleasant couple of hours were spent by all.

Initially, my onward plan had been to travel in the direction of Corsica along the French Riviera coastline, but because of the weather the previous day, I was now starting from farther back in my routing than expected. I therefore needed to re-jig the next flights slightly. I consulted with the local flyers and initially enquired about arranging to land at Toulon, but a quick call to their tower confirmed that I was too light as they had a minimum aircraft weight limit of five tonnes. After checking out a few other possibilities, my next best option was to fly to Cuers.

I called the authorities at Cuers civil airport but was immediately told that they couldn't permit me to land as their runway was only open to their own resident aircraft. A few confused phone calls later however, I was put through to the Cuers military authorities who then said there would be no problem in using their airfield. At this point I was under the impression that there were perhaps two separate airfields, a short distance apart, and that I had presumably been given permission to land by officials at the military base. It was only when I arrived overhead later in the day that it dawned on me that in fact it was two separate airfield zones, military on one side, civil on the other, but who then jointly shared the same runway in the middle. On landing, I was subsequently directed to park up on the civil side, but when I finally met with the airport staff the following morning to pay my landing fees, the manager was most indignant that I had ignored his strict advice not to land.

"I told you on the phone yesterday you were not to land here, but I now see that you flew here and landed anyway!" was my warm greeting on entering his office.

He was fuming and banging the desk at my impudence, but I remained calm and waited for my chance to reply. To my great relief, earlier in the day, I had found out that the *whole airfield* was actually owned by the military. The civil side was only tolerated under a licence agreement, though to be fair this was probably the reason why they had been nervous about me being there in the first place. Presumably they didn't want to upset their military landlords. So at the right moment in his ranting lecture on my disobedience, I was quite happy to smile back and calmly divulge that I was actually there by *kind invitation* from the military. A few moments of stunned silence followed, until the penny dropped with the manager and he realised that I had just been able to pull rank on him! It was no surprise that he then became much more friendly for the rest of the conversation.

***

The flight along the Mediterranean coastline to reach Cuers had been an extremely pleasant jaunt, especially when compared to the drama of the diversion in the mountains the day before. The short climb out over Carcassonne from the airport gave me a terrific low-level view of the ancient high city walls and the tightly packed buildings squeezed inside. An hour spent heading for the coast saw me skirting alongside the ATC area for Béziers, but rather than calling in, I stayed to the edge of their zone and met up with the coastline, just to the west of the seaside town of Cap d' Agde.

Situated along the shoreline of 'Le Cap' is a world-renowned naturist village resort, which in the height of summer can accommodate up to 40,000 people who love nothing more than to strip completely naked on the beach. This wasn't the case in chilly March however, as the beach was now virtually deserted, and my only greeting was the odd wave back from a few hardy beachcombers and lone dog walkers; all of whom remained well buttoned up in their overcoats against the cold.

Navigation was comparatively easy along this stretch, as I basically meandered along the coastline at about 600-800ft for a couple of hours soaking up the scenery. Numerous sea defences were evident, as were lagoons, inland lakes and wildlife. At one point I spotted a large flock of pink wading birds, and as I flew closer I was amazed to find that it was a huge *flamboyance* of flamingos (such an appropriate collective noun for these birds!), numbering in their thousands and feeding off the bright pink algae that lives in the salty marshes. I was really surprised, as I certainly hadn't expected to see such exotic birds overwintering in the South of France!

On landing and taxiing to the civil side of Cuers airfield, I was delighted to find that I was not in fact the only gyroplane in town. There was a small gyro club, complete with their own sign on the door. And tucked up in a far-away hangar were not one but two single-seat models. The French have long since held these aircraft in fond regard and one of Europe's biggest gyro fly-in events is held every year at Bois de la Pierre near Toulouse. This was the event that I attended in the summer of 2009 with John and Kai, when we saw a fantastic static display of ingeniously created gyroplane aircraft – of all shapes, sizes and imaginations – that were put on show along the flight line. One sharply angular homemade two-seater even had the appearance of a flying lean-to greenhouse, while others had been designed to replicate more natural flowing lines and curves. The welcoming camaraderie of the pilots and spectators had been warm and heartfelt, as if we were being greeted as old friends. We three gyronauts, who had flown the farthest distance to attend the event, were given VIP treatment, and in the evening fêted at dinner as only the French know how. On returning north from the fly-in, we detoured a little and flew past the world-famous Millau Viaduct, a road bridge designed by Lord Norman Foster. As John and I flew alongside each other, he took a terrific photo of *Roxy* and me crossing over the mist-filled Tarn river gorge with the bridge in the background and I subsequently used the dramatic image as the headline banner for my GyroxGoesGlobal blog page. In one single image, I think John managed to capture something of the extraordinarily uplifting spirit of adventure that I was to experience throughout the circumnavigation.

I left *Roxy* hangared in good company with the other two gyros, and I was whisked away by a club member to track down a local motel and a takeaway pizza. We then made plans for my morning pick-up, however the usual arrangements ended up being slightly different than I had expected.

29 March 2010: Cuers, France – Bastia, Corsica, France

As a nod to local diplomacy, the flying club thought that an early morning visit to meet the mayor in his palatial civic offices would be most appropriate. We travelled into Cuers and to the town hall, where on being presented to the mayor, I took the opportunity to go out onto his 1st floor balcony and wave down majestically to the assembled 'crowd' of one (who was taking photos with my camera). Although tempted, I then resisted the urge to launch into a lengthy rabble-rousing *"Liberté, Égalité, Fraternité"* speech from the parapet, as suddenly time was running short and I had a flight to catch!

Returning to the airport I was pleasantly surprised and amazed to be met by an Irish family, who had been holidaying nearby. They had been following my exploits online over the past few days and as the satellite tracker was showing me in Cuers, they had decided to come along to say hello. We had a nice chat as I introduced them to *Roxy* and a little later the mayor also appeared on the apron, to inspect my flying steed for himself. However, between all this social activity and excited chatter around the aircraft, I was ever conscious that I still had a significant flight to make that day.

It was going to be my longest sea crossing to date, a jaunt of about 180 nautical miles (210 miles) or so across the Med to the island of Corsica. My longest previous over-water flight had been about 70 nautical miles across the Irish Sea, from Larne direct to Saint Bees Head in Cumbria. However, if I had ever suffered any sort of emergency over the Irish Sea, I always had the reassuring option of heading immediately for the nearest point of dry land, as I was never that far away from the surrounding coastlines. By contrast, coasting out from the French mainland over to Corsica, gave me no such psychological security blanket. Once totally committed to being out over the Mediterranean, any proximity to dry land vanished, literally over the horizon. Clearly, I was going to be much more isolated and alone for the majority of this upcoming flight. I had one alternative fallback option early on, to make haste for the coastline of the Côte d'Azur off to the north-east if needs be, but as the flight progressed that option soon diminished as landfall became farther and farther away.

We pushed *Roxy* over to the avgas fuel pump on the airfield and topped up the tanks. As previously noted, it was such a bonus that my Rotax 914 engine could run on either avgas (aviation fuel) or mogas (ordinary unleaded gasoline). There would be many times during the world flight that I could only get one or the other fuel (rarely would both be seen for sale at the same place). On this occasion I had the added luxury of not having to remove and manhandle the Turtle Pac, which was best lifted with two or three people when it was full of 80 litres of fuel. At the pumps here, it was a simple task of topping up the main tanks under the passenger seat and then filling the fuel bag in situ.

Next up was a quick visit to the briefing office to submit my flight plan. Originally, I had hoped to fly to the island of Elbe, which would have meant entering the Italian domain, but a NOTAM (notice to airmen) recently issued from Nice stated that Marina di Campo Airport on the island, was shut for winter maintenance. Undeterred, such was the necessary flexibility of my en route planning, I simply elected to go to Bastia-Poretta Airport instead, situated in the far north of Corsica and still part of *la France*.

Take-off from Cuers was once again (as in Le Touquet) angled across the runway and into the stiff crosswind that had developed. Thankfully however, this also gave me a favourable tailwind for the sea crossing. I had a short corridor of controlled airspace to negotiate on the way out toward the coast, and then within a few minutes I was off out over the wide expanse of sea. Stretching out before me, the Med offered no visible sign of any landfall ahead. Unlike my short channel hopping flights back home, this was now real expeditionary stuff!

I had made plenty of long sea passages prior to this flight, though admittedly, these had been mostly *on* the water rather than *above* it.

During family sailing holidays we had cruised around Scottish waters and I had also spent the previous 15 years serving as second coxswain of the Larne RNLI lifeboat. Therefore navigationally at least, I now hoped that the upcoming flight would still feel quite routine and familiar. All I had to do was follow a straight-line course to steer across a flat, featureless seascape and to arrive unscathed at an unfamiliar destination, where I hoped the locals would be friendly.

The greenish-blue sea state was moderate, with the tailwind just blowing up the odd white horse on the surface below. It was also surprisingly empty of surface vessels, and I only passed one solitary yacht in almost 200 miles. Quite a stark contrast to the busy traffic these parts would have during the summer months, no doubt. The only other sign of life that I happened upon was a large pod of dolphins. From my relatively low vantage point I could clearly make out their body shapes in the water. Although when I gave them my usual cheery wave as I passed by overhead, not a single one bothered to wave back!

It was a relaxed, turbulent-free crossing and the smooth air enabled me to trim the aircraft for steady, level flight. By pressing one steadying knee against the stick, I was then able to free up both hands to search out some apples and bananas from the pannier bag stored just under my right leg. Munching away merrily, I thought, what a great place for an aerial picnic. The cloud base was low, only 800ft (dropping to 600ft at times), but more significantly for me it was *consistently* low. I viewed this as a good thing as I could happily scrape along just below this blanket of cloud all day long and easily for the next 200 miles if necessary. What I didn't want was any surprises, such as constantly shifting cloud formations that didn't quite know what to do with themselves (though I would experience plenty of these more extreme scenarios in the weeks to come). My only real difficulty with the current cloud conditions came right at the end of the flight.

The northern tip of Corsica has a long mountain ridge jutting out and rising quite dramatically out of the sea. Unfortunately, the day I arrived I found those same mountains were now also rising dramatically straight up into the low cloud base. Not such a welcome sight. I viewed this wall of rock topped with cloud from about 10 miles out and pondered on my options. My intended route had been to basically hop over this coastal ridge and drop back down to the airport on the flat coastal plain beyond. But now this direct route was completely blocked. My only option was to fly a long dog leg to the northern tip of the island at Cap Corse to get around the mountain range, and then fly back down on the other side. Fortunately, I had plenty of fuel on board and I contacted Bastia Tower to advise them of my intended diversion due to weather. This was duly accepted by the airport, and everyone was now happy with my impromptu revised plan of action.

Everyone that is, apart from one unfortunate group of online adventurers. A growing number of GyroxGoesGlobal followers were watching my progress live, every day, online via the SPOT satellite tracking system I was carrying on the aircraft. The SPOT tracker was beaming real-time position reports to our tracker page linked to the website. This small lightweight transceiver, fixed just above the instrument panel (or on my lifejacket over water), was a fantastic tool for keeping people advised of my progress as it sent out a positioning GPS signal every 10 minutes during my flights. Up to the point of diverting, my online GyroxGoesGlobal spotters had seen that I'd been flying steadily for 200 miles in a straight line. They knew nothing about the low cloud problem and so had been left guessing as to why my SPOT trace had suddenly become a squiggly line and then appeared to be heading back out to sea! Had a rogue wasp or bee managed to get inside the Red Suit perhaps? Happily, the confusion was short lived and there was relief all around when I finally arrived at the airport unscathed.

The 'squiggle' had recorded me traversing along the coast, parallel to the ridgeline as I searched for a suitable gap in the mountains that would allow me safe passage through to the other side. I had been prepared to fly right around the northern tip if necessary, but after a few miles north, one such gap appeared between a lower section of the mountain ridge tops and the overhead cloud base. Timing my run to coincide with some slightly thinner cloud, I then posted myself through the letter-box slot, just as I had done crossing the Pennines and over the Cumbrian moors. Once safely on the other side of the ridgeline, I reduced power and dropped back down into clear coastal air once again.

Approaching Bastia, the tower gave me an immediate "Number one" to land and allowed me to fly a straight-in approach. Helpfully they also permitted me to land directly on the wide taxiway alongside the runway, as it allowed me a much shorter ground taxi run to the stand. Soon enough I was placed in the very capable care of Jean, who proved to be a highly resourceful resident maintenance mechanic. On refuelling my 'passenger', Jean and I were concerned to find that I had somehow inadvertently damaged an O-ring seal on the fuel filler cap. This meant the system was now leaking a small amount of fuel, which was never a good situation. What to do now? As luck would have it, with one glance at the damaged seal, Jean was able to calmly reach into a workshop drawer and produce a new O-ring of the exact same dimensions. I was extremely relieved that we had found a solution so quickly. He also gave me two extra seals as spares for good measure, proving he was as generous as he was resourceful. *Roxy* spent the night in the maintenance hangar while Jean dropped me off at a small tourist hotel nearby. Though still being March, and well before the busy summer season, yours truly appeared to be the only guest and my dinner was quite a solitary affair in a large tourist restaurant close by. On such occasions, it was useful to have either one of the GPS units for flight planning or a diary for note taking with me, in order to occupy the long 20 or so minutes between ordering and receiving my food. Taking in my surroundings, it struck me that these types of holiday restaurants always appeared so forlorn outside the tourist season, a mere shadow of what they'd be like at the height of summer. Beachcomber trappings of coastal paraphernalia festooned the walls – old fishing nets, coloured glass floats, fake lobsters and seashells – all conjuring up images of holiday families playing in warm seas and on sandy beaches during endless sunny days. In the early spring, however, these things all took on a slightly fraudulent quality. Particularly on this occasion when I was viewing them in the close company of an old battered bottled gas heater that was trying desperately (but failing miserably) to compete against the cavernous volume of cold air around me.

Alas, there was no Wi-Fi connection in either the restaurant or back at the hotel. But I did nevertheless receive an important message via my phone regarding the way I should tackle the heavily restricted Italian skies ahead. It was timely information, as in an instant it transformed what could have been one of the more difficult technical legs of the journey so far, into one of the most sublime.

30 March 2010: Bastia, Corsica Island, France – La Porta delle Aquile, Pescara, Italy

This was another significant day because it marked my first flight into wholly new territory. France had been 'abroad', but John, Kai and I had already flown around it the year before, so it didn't feel as foreign as this upcoming flight into Italy was going to be. In the planning phase, I had been studying aeronautical charts for Italian airspace and was somewhat disheartened by how much of it was restricted. Huge swathes of airspace were sanctioned for military use, often down to the ground or to such low levels that they even negated my limbo tactic. Worse still, in some areas the restricted airspace zones then conspired to join together; they overlapped and formed an unbroken barrier stretching right across the country from coast to coast. Trying to find a path of least resistance, it quickly became clear to me that with so many areas effectively closed off, I was going to find it almost impossible to fly down the 'boot' of Italy.

Fortunately, the timely assistance that had arrived via my phone in Corsica, was from a contact called Jean Marco. He was an Italian flying enthusiast who had been following my progress online and was keen to offer any help I needed on the flight through Italy. To my great relief he was able to provide me with a neat solution, as explained below.

The Italians themselves recognised that their lower airspace had historically been smothered by a plethora of military airspace zones, many of which now appeared to be rarely (if ever) used. Even basic mathematics would indicate that a country that is over 600 miles long could not possibly be regularly over flown *everywhere* by a modern air force whose aircraft numbers were now a small fraction of those from decades ago, when the military zones where conceived. Recognising that fact, the local light aviation fraternity had worked out a tremendous system that, in a practical sense at least, seemed to deliver a workable solution. Rather than becoming bogged down in a myriad of permission processes to gain access to transit across restricted blanket military zones, the microlight community adopted a much simpler unwritten rule of thumb. That was to fly anywhere they liked, outside normal air traffic restricted zones – around airports, build up areas, hazardous/danger areas – as long as they only flew at a maximum height of 500ft AGL during the week (rising to 1000ft at the weekends). This revelation solved everything.

By simply *turning off* my aircraft transponder, which is the electronic device on board that reacts to incoming radar signals and responds by giving out my aircraft position, altitude and call sign, I was able to become just another slow-moving, low-level, Italian microlight bumbling across the terrain seemingly without a care in the world. No transponder meant that my visibility on radar systems at nearby airports would be much reduced, and which then meant equally that the controllers would not be unduly alarmed by seeing a rogue target on their screens that was not accounted for in their system. For me, this change meant a couple of days flying along as a nobody, an aerial 'gentleman of the road' (sorry of course that should read 'air'). I'd be keeping my head down and answering effectively to no one, as long as I kept out of the way and did not trespass into the approach path of any landing Alitalia jets.

The downside however of this tactic, was that I would be also on my own if anything was to go amiss during the flight. There was not much use calling ATC in an emergency and making polite introductions as to where I was and the nature of my predicament, all from 500ft. I would rapidly already be down on the ground before I could make a hurried mayday call to the nearest control tower. With this in mind, I had to now revert to flying more defensively, just as I would normally do when cross-country flying back home. All low-level flying in a gyro is best carried out with the somewhat pessimistic, but in this case very healthy, mindset of constantly needing to land – immediately. Therefore, flying defensively now meant favouring as much as possible landscapes that were friendly for sudden emergency landings, such as open fields, flat terrain, long sandy beaches, forest tracks, riverbanks, race tracks, golf courses etc. Throughout the world flight, these open spaces became my best friends as I flew along admiring the view, and likewise dense forests, heavily urbanised areas, very steep terrain and areas crisscrossed with electricity pylons became my worst enemies and were to be warily avoided wherever possible.

And so I could now expect some lovely low-level flying across the fantastic undulating Italian countryside, navigating around rather than through the various civilian airport ATC zones en route. At times it felt, whilst sneaking past an airport perhaps five miles distant, like I was flying past some villain's secret base in a James Bond movie. By seeking out low ridge lines in the rolling countryside and flying along below them in the valleys, I was effectively hidden to the eyes and ears of the nearby ATC. I pictured them, no doubt, sitting behind a big bank of computer monitors, and perhaps stroking a white cat... "Ah! Come in *Commander Surplus*, we've been expecting you."

Departing Corsica and landing in Italy also involved filing an international flight plan, which was especially relevant for the overwater section across the Tyrrhenian Sea to get me across to the Italian mainland.

My tactics now became clear-cut, I would use the flight plan primarily for the sea crossing and to conform to the same requirements as any aircraft travelling between jurisdictions. Then, once safely across to the mainland, I would attempt to become just another local microlight aircraft. How best to achieve this however, proved to be not quite so simple.

As I crossed the Italian coastline, at the requisite 500ft, I attempted to raise Pisa ATC in order to close out my international flight plan. Unfortunately, they were unable to close it for me as I wasn't intending to land in Pisa. Instead, I was referred to contact Rome control, but I had no luck making contact with them at all, due to my poor radio signal range at such a low altitude. This meant yet again, I now had a real problem. What to do? If I didn't officially close the flight plan, I may have been later classed as missing, which could have easily then triggered a countrywide search for my whereabouts. I dodged about in the sky for about 10 minutes deciding what to do. Thankfully, a sudden brain wave hit me and I pulled out my mobile phone. In this case, flying at such a low level was an advantage to acquiring a phone signal, and I made a quick call to Jean Marco. Once he was aware that I had safely crossed the water he said he would be able to phone Rome to explain the situation and to also close the flight plan for me. Bingo! Job done! I was now free to turn off my transponder, turn inland towards the Apennine Mountains and simply *disappear* for the next two days. Ciao baby!

***

The Apennines are a ridge of high mountains that run right down the middle of the entire country to form the backbone of Italy. I knew whilst route planning that to transit across Italy, I would have two options: to run down the west coast (past Rome) all the way around the distant 'toe' of the 'boot' or continue directly across the high central mountains and then fly down the eastern coastal plains. Taking the first option I could certainly have avoided the mountains, but instead it would have caused a massive diversion from the most direct route to the bottom end of the 'heel', which was where I was planning to jump across to the next stop at Corfu in Greece. There was therefore no real tactical advantage to opt for the west side, particularly as I'd also have to do battle with the extremely busy air traffic system around the greater Rome area. So that left me with the second option, to find a flyable route across the Apennines and reach the flat Adriatic coastline on the eastern side, as soon as possible. From there, it would then be an easy low-level run down the coastline to my launch point over the Adriatic Sea to Greece.

My strategy for approaching this first major mountain range crossing was simple:

1. Aim for an area where the overall mountain flying was going to be the shortest distance possible.
2. Find a suitable coll, or gap, between the high peaks, where the ridgeline dipped down significantly lower than the cloud base above, to give me a 'letter box' of clear visibility.
3. Approach with caution, but be ever ready to retreat back using an 'escape route' if the conditions became unflyable at any point. If everything remained stable and I could clearly see my unobstructed exit route down through to the other side of the coll, then I'd fully commit to crossing the ridgeline and post myself through the opening.

I made good progress inland from the Italian west coast with a brisk tailwind pushing me onwards towards the looming barrier of the Appennine ridgeline ahead, a formidable wall of rock that just got bigger and bigger as I apprehensively approached. I knew I would need to be incredibly careful in this situation; these were not the gently rolling hills and glens of the Antrim Plateau that I was used to back home. Even the higher and more rugged mountain landscape of the Lake District in Cumbria, which I had flown through many times previously, now suddenly seemed like mere molehills compared to some of the jagged monsters that were currently towering up ahead of me. At least and in my favour, I was quite used to flying in rough turbulence and strong gusty winds over hills; Northern Ireland is after all located right on the doorstep of the raging North Atlantic. I was just now setting out to face these similar conditions on a much grander scale. All I could hope for was that the basic laws of physics concerning the complex movement of air currents in mountainous terrain would still apply, even if they would now be somewhat amplified.

My plan was initially to make for a small GA airfield, Castiglion Fiorentino, that Jean Marco had briefed me about, which was situated just to the west of the mountains. I didn't need to land necessarily, but from overhead of this field, I would then be able to observe the immediate prevailing conditions up on the ridge ahead and give myself a go or no-go decision on continuing my ascent towards the high ground. If necessary, this airstrip could also act as my alternate airfield, a place of retreat if, after pressing on, I had then to abort for any reason and backtrack to sit out on the ground and wait for a better weather window to develop.

I had two main factors to consider: the restless thick blanketing cloud that sat heavily atop the ridgeline, brought about by the moist sea air being forced to rapidly rise up the mountain slopes until it condensed to form the clouds; and also the resultant turbulence that this rising air would then cause to my aircraft as I flew close to the ridgeline, both on the upwind side and potentially much more dangerously on the downwind side of the ridge.

In any light aircraft the combination of these adverse factors, especially the unpredictable, gusty turbulence, could easily cause a pilot to quickly backtrack to safer territory and reconsider waiting for calmer conditions. However, I was not in *any* light aircraft. I was in a gyroplane, and this often underrated, almost forgotten type of aircraft has a few hidden tricks in its highly manoeuvrable repertoire that can assist greatly in such circumstances. In the rising air of the upslope that is upwind of a ridgeline, a gyro is buoyed up by the updraught, often allowing it to soar and hover, much like a seabird can soar seemingly effortlessly, for hours above the sea cliffs. Turning to fly slowly into a strong headwind allows the gyroplane to hover, stationary in the air, which has proved very useful when I've ever needed to 'pause' for a few minutes to assess my situation. Now approaching the Apennines, I was able to use this technique while watching to ensure that the cloud formation was giving me a stable gap through which I could see my clear exit route to fly beyond the ridge. Further, being a rotary-wing aircraft, I also had the advantage of the fast-spinning blades being able to cut through gusty turbulence much more effectively than a slow-flying, fixed-wing aircraft. In gusty conditions, whereas a light fixed-wing aircraft would be in risk of being tossed all over the sky, a gyro (or helicopter) merely shrugs off any offending gusts with a much dampened and less violent movement. This allowed me to ride out the gusts almost as you would steadily ride over the waves of a moderate sea in a sailing boat.

However, the truly remarkable and unique manoeuvrability of the gyro would be saved for use on the much more turbulent, down-draught-prone back slope of the ridgeline, which was lying in wait for me downwind of the mountains. In this zone, I decided that I would use a 'descending hover' tactic.

This is a slow controlled descent that both a helicopter and a gyroplane can perform, but not to an equal ability. A gyro, with suitable height to play with, can approach this manoeuvre with relative impunity, as the air passing upwards through its auto-rotating blades during descent is free to become turbulent above the rotor, well out of harm's way to the aircraft. However, when a helicopter performs a similar type of descent, such as to drop vertically into a tight landing location, it has an inherent risk of creating a potentially dangerous 'vortex ring' state. To remain airborne, a helicopter is constantly grabbing at the air above its rotor and thrusting it down through its blades and below the aircraft, much like a frantically swimming man trying to constantly tread water to keep his head above the waves. This downward airflow creates the downwash effect below any helicopter, and this is often observed (and felt) easily when it is close to the ground. It is this downwash that creates the great enveloping whoosh of sand and gravel that accompanies any helicopter landing on loose ground. When a helicopter establishes itself in a hover, the downwash is pushed downwards and outwards to form an expanding ring of air below and around the helicopter, and in certain flight conditions this can create a ring-doughnut shaped vortex of circulating air immediately below the aircraft. The centre of this vortex can have a considerably lower air pressure than the surrounding air, and herein lies the real danger. If the helicopter wants to descend vertically then the risk is that the aircraft is effectively being asked to descend into its own turbulent airflow, and if vortex ring conditions are present then the big risk is that the aircraft can, in effect, fall through its own turbulence, through the low-pressure hole in the middle of the doughnut. This is a situation that may become irrecoverable if the aircraft happens to be too low to the ground. Therefore, the speed of any helicopter's vertical descent must be closely monitored to avoid this situation arising. And while this may be OK in clear, stable air conditions, in gusty turbulent conditions the air may be much more volatile and present a much greater concern to the helicopter pilot. By contrast, a gyroplane given the same conditions can continue to descend without the same concern as no vortex ring state condition can ever exist below the aircraft. The gyro, with its free-spinning blades, drops vertically down exactly like a sycamore seed, at its own self-governing speed of descent. Importantly however, the gyro cannot continue this hover all the way down to the ground. For a safe landing it must once more build up forward momentum and airspeed from about 400 ft above ground level so that it can then continue with making a normal landing approach.

Maintaining the hover of a helicopter is always a fine balancing act of playing available engine power against blade pitch angle against pedal yaw control. Mentally, the pilot is performing a three-dimensional ballet, constantly, with both hands and both feet highly active in order to keep the aircraft in its desired position and attitude. This can present the pilot with an extreme workload even in calm conditions, never mind while operating in high turbulence and gusting winds. The gyro pilot in a descending hover on the other hand is simply *parked up*, making a somewhat leisurely descent, with not a lot to do in particular, just sitting in the cockpit admiring the view and waiting for the aircraft to bring them down to where they want to be. In these circumstances, the throttle is fully closed, the rudder is just fixed in one position and the stick is simply held back to maintain zero forward airspeed – it's left largely to the autorotating, self-governing rotor to do the rest.

And so dear reader, now armed with a bit more theory of fluid dynamics under our belts, we should get back to the story. You will remember that we were poised upwind, holding in a hover and assisted by the rising updraught from a sharp, jaggy ridgeline, high up in the Italian Apennines. So how exactly are we going to get down from here?

Well, there is one more thing we need to examine before we can tackle the descent, and that is a little skiing lesson. When skiing in very icy conditions there is a trick you can use to navigate your way down a steep, icy slope in relative safety. The technique is known as side-slipping, and it involves standing side-on to the direction of slope. By relaxing the grip that the edges of your skis have on the hard compacted snow and allowing them to slide sideways in a controlled way down the hillside, you can finely regulate your descent. Digging in your edges allows you to slow down or stop, while relaxing your edges has the opposite effect. Further, you can also traverse across the slope either by moving slightly forwards or backwards and angling the skis to avoid obstacles in your path such as rocks, grass (if the snow is thinning) and other skiers. Tips down will move you forwards, while heels down will slide you backwards. We'll now see how I used this technique to help me up on the Apennine ridge.

Eyeing up my crossing point while hovering close by, I could see that beyond the ridge the ground fell away again just as steeply as it had risen up on the upwind side. This left only a very sharp knife edge arête of rock to cross over, taking only a few seconds. Once safely across to the downwind side, my first manoeuvre was to turn sideways to the now almost sheer face of the cliffs dropping away below me. This was a defence strategy, to know my enemy so to speak. The villain in this instance was the jagged rockface that I was now attempting to sidle down beside, hopefully without being noticed too much by the gusting winds. I knew there would be heavy rotor turbulence for a considerable distance out from the cliff face on the downwind side, where the airflow that had been forced upwards over the mountains would now tumble and spill over itself downwards over the back face of the cliffs, not unlike running water spilling over a fixed rock obstruction in a stream bed.

I quickly realised that by staying closer in to the mountainside there was a considerable lee effect, a sheltered eddy with much less turbulent airflow, as most of the disturbed wind was passing by harmlessly much higher overhead. Such are the flight characteristics of a gyro, using the slow, near vertical, descending hover technique to quickly lose over 1000ft in height was now easily achievable. I adopted a right-hand, side-on attitude to the mountain so that I could keep a close eye on the topography of the rockface as I descended alongside. I didn't want any pinnacles of rock suddenly jutting out and surprising me, and just as in skiing I induced a degree of sideslip into the descent by biasing the stick slightly left of centre. By adjusting the stick forward and aft I could also effectively traverse along the cliff forwards and backwards to allow for ravines and buttresses in the main face. The steepness of the slope meant that at any moment I could still safely break away from the close proximity of the rockface by simply allowing myself to roll out and dive away to my left side and go from say 200ft of clearance from the ground to 2000ft in just a few seconds.

Indeed there had been many times on previous flights, especially in the Lake District, where I rapidly transitioned from flying close to the terrain, such as over a rounded peak, to suddenly then flying out over the edge of a cliff with perhaps an abrupt 1500ft drop to the valley below. This action could sometimes give me a mild sense of vertigo. I imagine it must be because my brain was somehow momentarily fooled into thinking I had just jumped off the cliff edge and out into this vast open space. The effect was only fleeting however, and easy to guard against mentally once I was aware it could happen. I simply visualised the action taking place before I reached the edge, so that my brain was fully up to speed with what was going to actually happen a few moments later.

Slowly descending from the ridge at about the same speed as a parachutist, I was able to drop vertically down to well below the lowest cloud base and continued in this way until the ground below me began to shallow out. As it opened up into a wide valley floor, I regained normal forward cruise speed but remained ever mindful that rogue downdraughts could still strike, even a considerable distance downwind of the peaks. With all the high drama behind me, I was able to relax once more and enjoyed a pleasant flight now safe in the knowledge that I would soon reach the flat coastal plains once more. From there, I planned to fly down the east coast towards my afternoon's destination near Pescara. I was feeling extremely pleased that the mountain crossing had all worked out as planned, as mentally at least, it had previously been an ongoing nagging concern for several days, with so many uncontrollable and unknown variables to consider. Now I had the added delight of skimming along at 500ft admiring the Italian landscape and following the contours of the gently undulating countryside.

Next, I had to locate the small grass airstrip of Alanno la Porta delle Aquile, where I was going to be accommodated for the night. The area surrounding the airstrip was made up of many small hummocky hills that even encroached onto the runway, giving one end of the grass strip the appearance of a mini ski jump. On touchdown, I landed on the downhill part of the ski jump and rolled out onto the flat runway surface beyond.

I had done it! I'd touched down in Italy, the first of many 'new' countries on my global itinerary. As I taxied across the grass, I wondered what sort of reception now awaited me.

I did not have to wonder for long. Three very jolly Italians came out to meet me on the edge of the strip and stood applauding while I taxied to a standstill and shut down the engine. The buzz of excitement at my sudden arrival was lovely to share with these guys in the late afternoon sunshine, and soon a fourth fellow appeared riding on an electric scooter, after he'd spotted me coming in to land. The euphoria was contagious, and I got the feeling that welcoming an international arrival like this didn't happen very often. Yet this local grass airstrip was exactly the sort of place I was aiming to use wherever possible on the trip. They were typically populated by small, but very enthusiastic grassroot aviation communities, who would happily go about their own local flying activities with little need or desire to grow their airfield much bigger in size or complexity. So to suddenly have a globetrotting gyroplane drop in on the doorstep, as you can imagine, certainly caused quite a stir.

A somewhat disjointed English conversation followed where I explained that I was on my way around the world and this naturally added to the overall sense of occasion. *Roxy* was soon bedded down in a nearby hangar, and we all retreated to the small clubhouse for beer and cake, the latter being a swirly sort of vanilla and chocolate sponge. During the celebrations, my FAI world record paperwork was ceremoniously filled in and signed off.

As the afternoon was progressing into early evening, the clubhouse was locked up and I was taken by car to find a local hotel that could accommodate me out of season. We stopped briefly at the family house of my driver, and I had a brief glimpse of rural Italian home life in these parts. I was invited to sit in the big busy kitchen while both family and close neighbours gathered around to greet such an unusual traveller. Within a few hours of me landing in Italy, I became aware of an immediate curiosity and kindness from complete strangers, something that I would experience time and again around the world.

Much discussion in Italian followed, and I could only guess that they were debating which hotel would suit me best. Soon enough, we were back in the car, and I was delivered to a local tourist chalet complex with a restaurant attached. As it happened, I was the only diner in the restaurant and I got the distinct impression (as in Corsica), that I was, once again, the only guest.

31 March 2010: Pescara, Italy – Torre Sant'Andrea, Italy – Corfu, Greece

Breakfast was also a solitary affair, but after a real Italian cappuccino, some yoghurt and four(!) slices of cake, I was ready for anything the Mediterranean was going to throw at me on my onward journey to the Greek island of Corfu. I was collected by car and we made a quick stop at the local Agip garage to fill the Turtle Pac up with petrol, much to the curiosity of the locals at the pumps.

I suspected that my take-off was going to be unusual, given the steep slope at the end of the runway. Initially, I had to taxi up the hill feeling the heavy weight of the additional fuel onboard and I then turned to point downhill ready for take-off. It gave me such an odd viewpoint, as I was now sitting some 20m above the surface of the main runway stretching out ahead of me. I had to now work out how best to use the slope to my advantage. If I took off too early, before the slope flattened out, I risked being airborne but holding a 'downhill' nose-down attitude and I would then risk flying back into the ground. So instead, I elected to use the slope to only build groundspeed and then, once I reached the flat portion of the runway, I applied full throttle and took off in the normal way.

Today's flight, leaving Italian airspace and entering Greece, was going to be in two legs: first a flight down to the small grass strip of Torre Sant'Andrea on the 'heel' of the Italian boot and then, the second leg would see me coast out over the sea on a direct flightpath towards Corfu.

The flight down the south-eastern coastal plains of Italy was fantastic. Like the previous day, I was still flying in *microlight stealth mode* without transponder at 500ft above ground level, which afforded me tremendous views of the surrounding countryside. I was not so much flying *over* the landscape but *through* it. Cruising through gentle rolling valleys with hills on either side, I enjoyed covertly flying *under the radar* coverage of the neighbouring regional airports and for my own amusement, I continued to stay as undetected as possible. All the while, I had a welcome tailwind on my starboard quarter, pushing me along at about 90 mph ground speed for an airspeed of only 75 mph. To make things even better, the sun was out, and the air was beginning to feel quite warm and pleasant. All my previous worries of how I was going to navigate through overbearing Italian military airspace were now behind me, and I was able to relax a little and enjoy the journey.

I continued to soak up the scenery. Acres of olive groves covered the rolling countryside as far as the eye could see in every direction. As I proceeded south, funny little beehive-shaped stone huts began to appear in the groves, first the odd one and then they were littered all over the landscape. I later discovered that these dry-stone huts with a distinctive conical roof were called *trulli.* They have been around for centuries in this part of Italy and in rural areas, they were built as field shelters and storehouses. Sleepy little picturesque Italian villages slid past and yet strangely, as I had found in rural France, the landscape was devoid of people. One of the real perks of flying at only 500ft was the ability to see lots of detail on the ground, and that included people to wave at and interact with. But I could only interact with people if I happened to spot them and as yet, I hadn't seen anyone.

Surely they couldn't all be stuck indoors on such a lovely spring morning? I then made a discovery as I was skimming over yet more olive groves. I caught the odd glimpse of bright colour through the tightly packed branches of the trees, and I also noticed the odd battered Fiat hidden under the dense canopy. Next to catch my eye were tall ladders, poking up through the branches, and sure enough on the ladders I then spotted the farmers themselves. These olive farmers were actually present in great numbers, but were hidden in the branches of their trees, busy pruning and shaping them for the upcoming growing season.

Excellent! Now I had the prospect of another 150 miles of elusive farmer-spotting to look forward to. I began to make shallow zigzags across the landscape to visit each patch of olive grove in my path ahead. Olive trees? Check. Beat up vehicle? Check. Ladder? Check. Farmer? Check. Waving farmer? Check! A score! And of course, I never forgot to wave back.

This game was going great until one farmer, who had spotted me coming from some distance away, was so enthusiastic about vigorously waving some sort of cloth over his head, that he overbalanced himself on the ladder. Wobbling precariously for a few seconds, thankfully I saw he had regained his footing before he finally passed out of my view. It just goes to show, waving to excited Italians could prove to be quite dangerous.

The small grass strip I planned to use for my brief final stop in Italy was exactly what I needed. There were no local airspace restrictions, no officialdom from overzealous airport staff and no lengthy taxi and flight handling procedures that could double (or triple) my time spent on the ground. What I needed was a quick, no-nonsense landing, followed by some uninterrupted peace and quiet to thoroughly pre-flight the aircraft (and my sea survival safety kit) for the upcoming over-water crossing. I then planned to make a brief call through to Milan, for my international flight clearance, and then I would be all set for an immediate departure onwards to Greece. It all seemed a good workable plan, but in reality, it turned out a little differently...

I made a blind call approach to the airfield, but the place seemed deserted. So on landing, I taxied across to a small row of light aircraft hangars to see if anyone was around. Almost immediately, the only resident of the airfield came happily strolling across to meet me, only it wasn't quite what I expected – it was a stray dog that had somehow managed to squeeze itself inside the perimeter fence. It was friendly enough, but its sudden appearance forced me to immediately shut down the engine; after all a wagging tail in close vicinity of the prop was definitely not what I needed at this point. I then had to get out and push *Roxy* the last few yards to reach the hangars.

Although no one was around, I was encouraged by the fact the side door to the end hangar was open. Someone would turn up soon, they often did once word had travelled around that an odd-looking mini helicopter had just been spotted coming into land. My first task was to re-check the aircraft ready for the upcoming over-water flight to Corfu. I then rang Milan on my mobile to pass on my flight plan, only to hit another snag.

Milan were most insistent that I provided them with details of an emergency alternative airfield for my flight to Greece. But as the straight-line flight over to Corfu was 99% over water, there were simply no alternate airfields for me to use en route. If a problem arose while I was flying, I would have to either push on to my destination, or if the distance was shorter, turn back and land again at the nearest airfield back on the Italian side, which of course happened to be the very same airfield I was now departing from. I tried to convey this information to Milan, that my designated alternate airfield would also have to be the same as my departure airfield. However, in an Italian version of the classic *Little Britain* TV sketch show, I was then informed by the Milan flight controller:

"Sorry, *the computer says no*! It's not possible to have the same airport designated as your alternate *and* departure airport. So what *is* your alternate airport?"

"But there isn't one. There is only sea!" I replied.

"No sir, the computer must have an alternate, otherwise clearance cannot be given," was their retort.

Eventually, after some further back-and-forth discussion, I elected to give the name of the next nearest available airport, which was 20 miles north of my current position. With much relief all round, that seemed to please the fussy computer, and my clearance came through instantly. I was good to go, safe in the knowledge that if I did have any sort of emergency out over the sea and had to turn back, I would at least now have a *computer approved* option of extending my emergency condition out for an extra 20 miles back up the Italian coastline. On the way past I could then overfly my perfectly good departure airport and even perhaps give my stray doggy friend a little wave.

Just prior to take-off, a solitary walker did eventually turn up and became the only person to witness my final departure from Italian soil.

Thankfully the flight over to Corfu was fairly uneventful. I had already flown reasonable distances over water on the legs to and from Corsica and I reasoned to myself that I had to become as comfortable as possible with these first few Mediterranean flights, as they were only relatively short hops compared to the major ocean crossings I would have to undertake later in my journey.

Soon enough, I made contact with the Greek ATC unit at Corfu. Being a major holiday destination, the airport was quite large for the size of the Island and, although not yet in peak tourist season, it was still surprisingly busy with the traffic movements of many different types of aircraft. It was certainly the biggest airport I had approached to date and on first contact, ATC did a great job of understanding what my capabilities and limitations were in my unusual aircraft. To simplify things, I suggested that they might prefer to vector my approach directly in over the main runway threshold. This avoided sending me out on a long eight-mile final approach, which would have slowed all the other incoming traffic down considerably. All was going well on final approach until ATC requested that, because of holding traffic, could I expedite my landing as quickly as possible. I had to inform them I was already fully *expediting,* with my air speed indicator showing 100 mph during my descent. In response, ATC passed on the instruction, "Continue to hold" to a twin-engine private jet waiting to depart.

"Imagine," I thought, "a luxury private jet having to hold back, just for little ol' me!"

Roxy and I had certainly hit the big time now and this theme continued when an aircraft handler driving a 'Follow Me' truck came out to meet me on the apron and led me past the main passenger terminal towards an area normally reserved for helicopters. My handler jumped out at a stand next to a Swiss-registered helicopter and proceeded to give me the full treatment with his marshalling wands (ie. table tennis bats). With a big grin on his face and in a somewhat tongue in cheek manner, his arm signals directed me right onto the stand just as if I were a jumbo jet. He proceeded to give me the thumbs up, as I shut down the engine. Welcome to Greece!

The pilot of the Swiss helicopter strolled over for a chat while I was unpacking my gear. His conversation was laden with a mixture of professional curiosity, genuine concern and a certain incredulity at what I was proposing to do.

"You're hoping to fly right around the world in... *that*?"

This slightly condescending, professional pilot's response was echoed in many of the larger airports around the world, but I did notice that the incredulous tone of their voices gradually dropped away as my circumnavigation flight progressed, especially after I'd achieved a few of the more major over-water challenges en route. Indeed, some of the most encouraging responses I could hope for actually came from search and rescue helicopter pilots. These guys were the real professionals in my view, quietly confident, calm and unassuming, but flying their missions day in and day out, in some of the most testing and brutal conditions imaginable.

***

It appears a very odd practice, if you are not used to it, but often the very first question that aircraft handlers all over the world asked me on arrival was:

"When are you leaving Captain?"

In the busier places there was simply no operational need for a nice chit chat to ask, "How was your flight?" or even a courteous, "Pleased to meet you".

By immediately asking when I was leaving, it sounded as if their sole aim was to get rid of me again as quickly as possible, that somehow my very presence was a gross inconvenience to the smooth running of *their* airport operations. The real reason that they asked, of course, was that they needed to rapidly work out what my onward requirements were likely to be. Did I need refuelling immediately because I planned a quick turnaround within the hour or was I planning to stay for a week and therefore needed long-term hangarage or an outlying (and cheaper) parking stand.

Usually for me, I was just staying overnight, which meant finding my 'Big Four' items: fuel, transport, accommodation and food. In Corfu, fuel was sorted out first as soon as I had landed. Unleaded petrol wasn't available, so the mobile avgas refuelling truck was summoned. The refueller was very cautious on which fuel I was able to use in my flying motorbike, so much so that he actually repeated the following line about six times before pouring it into my fuel tanks: "Now, it *is* definitely *avgas* that you want, Captain?"

The other three items were then gratefully achieved in a matter of minutes afterwards. Kate, one of the operations' staff, gave me a lift over to the terminal, organised a local hotel for me near the harbour and, as luck would have it, was also then able to drop me off in town as it was on her way home. Sorted.

Greece was the first country en route that I had not visited before, even as a tourist. Indeed, from now on and until I reached Malaysia, I would be on my own and in completely unfamiliar territories every few days, which was quite a sobering thought. I wondered how the local people in these places would react to the quirky double-act of a man in a bright red onesie appearing over the horizon in his little yellow whirligig aircraft.

1 April 2010: Corfu, Greece – Kythera, Greece

The flight from Corfu to Kythera was a very pleasant one. As an overall strategy, I always preferred to follow coastlines wherever possible, this was for a number of reasons: it helped with ease of navigation; there was less gusty turbulent airflow (compared to flying over mountains); and it also avoided excessive flying over potentially harsh and unforgiving rugged terrain. So on this flight, I elected to skirt around the edges of the Greek mainland and relished the discovery of picturesque small outlying islands with pristine hidden coves and beaches. Meanwhile on the radio, I was being passed, relay fashion, from the ATC of one military airbase to the next and then to the next. The sun was warm, the sea was blue, and the remote fishing villages were brilliant white, petite and picture perfect. There was certainly plenty to enjoy on this somewhat unique sightseeing journey.

I approached a long thin island that had a mountainous ridge running down its entire central spine. Due to its orientation, I needed to work out how best to cross the island over its middle section, as to fly around the southernmost tip would have added a considerable diversion to my direct routing. I thought it best to fly up and over the ridge in a diagonal line, then drop off the other side back down towards sea level at a similar angle. By flying a path at 45 degrees to the ridgeline I was also giving myself some extra leeway to veer away from the mountainside should the air suddenly become too turbulent.

The early afternoon sun was warming the air nicely and I had a very welcome updraught to help me gain altitude up towards the ridge. The rising air was so smooth that it felt as if an invisible hand was helping to lift *Roxy* and me skywards. But as I approached the point where I would cross the ridgeline, I was on full alert. "After all, what goes up must come down," I thought. I was watching out for heavy rotor turbulence causing sudden and severe downdraughts on the other side of the ridge. All my senses were heightened, feeling for any twitch in the aircraft that might indicate an imminent downward gust of air that could, if left unchecked, easily force *Roxy* down into the rocky scree slopes below. Instead, what I felt came as a fantastic surprise – no downdraught, nor rotor turbulence effect at all, just more lovely updraught! But oddly this time, on the other side of the mountain.

It took me a few minutes to be sure that this was not just a fluke. But no, the updraught definitely continued, as smoothly and steadily on this side of the ridge as it had been on the other side. This was truly a win-win situation.

I tried to figure out how this could be happening and came to the conclusion that the warm air on the Island was rising on *all* sides of the mountain. The resulting rising thermals were strong enough to override any notion of a prevailing wind acting from any one particular direction. So rather than having to do battle with turbulent downdraughts, I could now throttle back and coast down the back side of the ridgeline as leisurely as I pleased. I spent the 10 minutes or so that it took to descend back down to my usual 1000ft altitude by having a snack and enjoying the view. It was easily as good as parking up at any motorway rest area.

I made first contact with Kythira airport ATC with about 30 minutes to run, however the controller sounded a little disappointed. He had obviously already received word from the neighbouring airfields farther north that I was on my way, but he hadn't appreciated my relatively slow ground speed. He would just have to remain patient and wait a little while longer.

Soon afterwards, the Kythira ATC controller made contact again.

I sensed that I was probably one of very few, if not the only, aircraft that was arriving during his shift. Such was his enthusiasm, he called again to update my arrival when I was still 18 miles out and then again when I was 12 miles away. All was going well, until at six miles out, a small business jet suddenly appeared on frequency and called 'finals' to land. Suddenly our man in the tower went from being an underutilised Greek plane spotter to being the *Air Boss* of his very own Kythira-Class aircraft carrier.

He immediately swung into action to deal with the other landing traffic, and the jet soon aced its landing onto his carrier flight deck. Traffic conflict averted, there was however still one more snag. Whilst real aircraft carriers can align themselves directly into wind to present a smooth and constant airflow across their flight decks, this *solidly constructed* Kythira-Class carrier was of course, by its very design, stuck to the seabed and therefore had very limited manoeuvrability (aside from earthquakes and other plate tectonic movement of the Earth's crust). All this meant that I was obliged to land yet again into a very gusty 25-knot crosswind. Gyroplanes of course love such conditions, and although it was bumpy on final approach, the spot landing was gentle, controlled and angled at about 45 degrees across the runway centreline.

I quickly applied the hub brake to my rotor blades and taxied behind the main terminal building to escape the worst of the gusting winds. After some discussion concerning the lack of hangarage, I was allowed to tie *Roxy* down in the staff car park, which, at least, was partially in the lee of the buildings. My lightweight yellow aircraft cover, which although waterproof was mainly used more as a dust sheet, began to flutter worryingly in the stiff breeze. With all alternative shelter close into the buildings frustratingly deemed out of bounds, all I could hope for was that the strong afternoon wind was a diurnal effect and that it would die down once the heat of the day had subsided. Thankfully, I was pleased to find that this did indeed happen later in the evening.

With *Roxy* sorted for the night, I headed off once again in search of my 'Big Four' requirements. The airport was in a fairly remote spot on the island, so the first arrangement was for transport and here, a spot of luck came along. The man working at the small car-hire desk in the terminal building had already seen me being interviewed the night before on Greek national TV, when I had first landed in Corfu. So when I now suddenly appeared in front of him at the counter, he was beside himself with joy. He just couldn't believe that 'Mr. Norman' was actually here, in person, on his island, and was actually going to hire a car from him. Unfortunately, his gushing enthusiasm didn't quite extend to allowing me to use one of his cars overnight for free. But nonetheless, he did give me a good discount and then also rang around his contacts to find me a cheap rental room in the village of Kapsáli on the south coast.

I was sorting things out nicely. Next I took my hand luggage, along with the empty Turtle Pac under my arm, out to find my waiting *celebrity limousine* in the rental carpark, which in reality turned out to be a thoroughly clapped out 4x4 jeep with a very uncertain pedigree. The phrase, "Yes I can give you a very 'special price' Mr. Norman" was constantly ringing in my ears for some time. "Yes, it was a very special price for a very *special* car indeed," I thought as I bumped, clanked and rattled my way along the dusty roads towards Kapsáli.

Still, I was in Greece. On a lovely little Greek island, with all the charm, challenging logistics and limited capabilities that small island communities seem to thrive on. Driving along the single-track roads I saw a Greek Orthodox priest, dressed entirely in black robes, complete with his very distinctive black hat and a long white beard. He was being chauffeur driven, with I might add, some considerable majesty and sense of occasion, in a motorised vehicle that was evidently just as clapped out as mine. I took some small comfort in the fact that whatever was good enough for the island's top religious dignitaries, would certainly also be good enough for me.

I spent the evening in the charming Lemon Café, within earshot of the Mediterranean lapping around the small fishing quay. Being early April, the air temperature was pleasantly warm in the daytime, but considerably cooler at night. Just before dusk I took a stroll around the bay, which was virtually empty of life, apart from a solitary angler sat on the end of the pier. He was hunched intently over his small fishing rod, and when viewed from behind, rather bizarrely, his upper body appeared to be as wide as it was tall. I imagined how this peaceful little bay must erupt in the height of summer, no doubt packed out with tourists, souvenir stalls and the angry roar of passing jet skis.

2 April 2010: Kythira, Greece – Sitia, Crete, Greece

A leisurely breakfast and coffee at the Lemon Café was followed by a quick visit to the bank and a pause on the road, somewhat randomly, to take pictures of some wild goats. The last item of my essential four requirements was easily found on the way back to the airport. Half-way through filling up the Turtle Pac, I glanced at the price; a litre of fuel was about 30% more expensive here than on mainland Europe. I thought this was a bit pricey, even for super unleaded. To my chagrin, I then realised it was not so *super* after all, but just regular unleaded. Still fine for my Rotax 914 engine to run on, but by comparison just even more expensive. The garage attendant was mightily pleased as I had bought a whopping 80 litres of his very pricey product. On such a small Island with a very limited road infrastructure, local vehicles might only have used that amount in a whole month of driving. I quickly learnt that all I could do in such unforeseen and expensive circumstances, was to smile and appear happy. And perhaps watch closely for the cartoon dollar signs to flash up in the eyes of the smiling pump attendant stood before me.

Returning to the airport, I was met by the hire-car man, the airport refueler and a fireman who all helped me manhandle the now-full Turtle Pac in through the terminal and past the security checks. A big crowd of bystanders, camera phones in hand, began to gather as I uncovered the aircraft, made my daily pre-flight checks and stowed away my bags under the seats. A visit up to the control tower allowed me to check the weather, file my flight plan and unfortunately learn that ATC at Sitia Airport, my next destination on the island of Crete, would be shutting early today, at 13:30UTC (4.30pm local) due to the upcoming Easter weekend. This was unexpected, otherwise I would have planned my day differently and perhaps spent less time eating breakfast and talking to goats. Luckily however, the Kythira controller was actually from Crete, here on secondment, and was able to contact the Sitia controller on duty, who was also his friend. Between them they were able to keep the airport open for my arrival if I ended up being late. As it happened I was, though only by about 15 minutes.

An expeditious departure followed, as I was now up against the clock. Final stowage, hook up of the fuel line, donning the red suit, answering many curious questions from spectators and visiting the airport manager for the almost ceremonial signing and stamping of the FAI landing and take-off certificates, all followed with as much urgency as I could muster. This hasty procedure was not helped by the fact it was all carried out under a sweltering early afternoon sun. However, while the heat was the main disadvantage of setting off so late in the day, there was one overriding advantage – the Mediterranean's afternoon breeze was now up to a healthy 20-25 knots, which would serve as a very useful tailwind all the way to Crete.

With this heavy crosswind once again blowing over Kythira's *carrier flight-deck*, I was able to angle the gyro directly into it, a full 60 degrees across the runway. It appeared to the observers in the tower that I was aiming to fly back towards them along the taxiway, but I was up and airborne after a take-off roll of only about 20m, not bad for a fully loaded aircraft. I flew up past the tower to wave at everyone gathered there. It was a lovely send off from a lovely island, even the fire engine had sounded its horn for me as I had taxied out.

The flight across to Crete was a direct route down from the northwest. The air was warm, the visibility was good with only occasional, wispy clouds high above, and I had the healthy tailwind to boost my morale. Occasionally I was reaching 125 mph over the ground for an indicated airspeed of 95 mph, just what I needed as I was in a hurry. Numerous white horses danced across the Sea of Crete below, indicating that the Force 4-5 (on the Beaufort scale) breeze was almost directly behind me. As I closed with Crete's northern coastline, I became increasingly concerned about encountering thermals of air rising off the hot, rugged landscape stretching out before me. This, combined with the stiff onshore sea breeze, could have easily brought me all sorts of unwanted turbulence. I decided therefore to hold off crossing onto the land mass and continued to fly in the relatively comfortable, smooth and fast airstream out at sea. I made contact 17 miles out from Sitia, keen to hear of any potentially conflicting air traffic in the area. I needn't have worried though, as it turned out that there had only been two flights throughout the whole day; and one of these was my own.

Like Kythira, Sitia also had a strong crosswind blowing over the runway. With no other traffic expected and the airport now effectively closed for the day, I requested to land directly onto the taxiway, which again like Kythira, was aligned directly into wind. I love landing into a strong wind as the approach is always so slow and controlled, and in a gyro that allows me to settle down onto the ground for a pinpoint landing with zero roll out. The controller's voice over the radio sounded both pleased and relieved that I had landed in such challenging conditions without any fuss. (Maybe afterwards I should have introduced him to the ATC at Le Touquet, to set up the 'Gyro crosswind landing appreciation society'!) I quickly applied the hub brake to my main rotor and taxied the short distance to the control tower building where I was yet again able to find *Roxy* some welcome shelter from the wind.

I was greeted on arrival by George, a young Greek handler, who spoke his English with a strong Australian accent. He turned out to be of great help over the Easter weekend, which I spent waiting for permission to make my onward flight into Alexandria in Egypt. With international permissions, I could perhaps arrive into a new country a little later than planned but never earlier. So there was no choice but to sit tight in Crete until the following Monday.

3–4 April 2010: Sitia, Crete, Greece (non-flying days)

Having a couple of days off was very relaxing. I explored the town even though the commercial centre was quite empty due to it being Easter. However, at one point I did come across a 'Gyro' for sale on a restaurant menu. Intrigued, I ordered one… It turned out to be what I would know as a Turkish Döner Kebap (kebab) in the UK. The meat was carved from a rotating spit (hence 'gyro') and then wrapped in pitta bread. Later on, I enjoyed an ice cream whilst sitting by the harbour and fell into conversation with a family on holiday from the UK. As we got chatting, they were amazed that I had managed to fly myself all the way to Crete in such a small aircraft. As they had a car, my new-found holiday friends Alex, Annabelle and Kate, then offered to take me for a sightseeing tour of the island, which was really kind of them. It was nice to be able to spend the day doing touristy things in the pleasant company of people from back home.

On Easter Sunday, I was picked up by flight handler George and taken for a traditional Greek meal in his family home. We played a fun Easter custom called *tsougrisma,* where each person takes a boiled egg (dyed red for the occasion) and taps the end of it against their neighbour's egg until one of the eggshells cracks. The winner, who is bestowed much luck, is the one whose egg remains intact for the longest tapping time. Later, we all attended a fascinating Greek Orthodox Church service and were deafened by hundreds of firecrackers exploding in the streets.

Although I had been pleasantly distracted for a couple of days, in the back of my mind was a constant state of nervousness. My very next flight was going to attempt a 320 nautical mile open water crossing of the Mediterranean Sea.

4

Middle East: Egypt to Oman

5 April 2010: Sitia, Crete, Greece – Alexandria, Egypt

Leaving Crete would prove to be an extremely significant flight. I was challenged with the prospect of the first major open water crossing of the circumnavigation, and it was something that had to be conquered, both physically and mentally. I was also leaving behind the relative comfort of the European Union. Next up were the more uncertain and unknown mysteries of North Africa and the Middle East.

I had organised a local taxi to take me the short distance from my accommodation, the small harbourside tourist hotel Flisvos, up the hill to the airport first thing in the morning. My plan was to persuade the driver to stop en route at a fuel station to allow me to fill up the Turtle Pac. But as I hurriedly loaded my assorted luggage into the rear of the taxi, I tripped over a loose kerbstone and badly sprained my left ankle. The day was not starting well. With no time to waste, I just consoled myself with the thought that at least my ankle would get a nice sit-down rest on the four-hour plus flight across to Alexandria. The fuel stop to fill the Turtle Pac went without a hitch, much to the amazement of the taxi driver, and happily he was even allowed to drive through airport security and right up alongside *Roxy*. Things were now looking up. Alex, Annabelle and Kate even turned up to wish me bon voyage. They also helpfully offered to backload a lot of excess baggage, such as now-redundant flight charts for France and Italy, back to the UK for me.

Bidding a fond farewell, I taxied out the short distance to the main runway and faced into the stiff, but now familiar crosswind. Taking off at a 45-degree angle to the main runway, I was eye level with the ATC as I passed close by the tower a few seconds into the flight. Not many international departure travellers can wave cheerio directly into the controllers' window on take-off and see them waving back!

Clearing Crete airspace, I lost radio contact with Sitia after about an hour, so for the rest of the open water crossing until I closed into the Egyptian coastline, I reverted to listening out on the internationally recognised Distress and Diversion radio frequency, 121.5 MHz. This frequency acts as a safety net for any pilot that may find themselves in difficulty, as all commercial aircraft flightcrew monitor it whilst airborne. In this way, one aircraft's 'all-stations' broadcast for assistance will lead to other local aircraft responding to their distress message directly, and/or alert and relay the message onward to the relevant authorities on the ground.

As it happened, the crossing turned out (physically at least) to be fairly uneventful. The weather was calm, the sunshine was bright, and the air was warm. Mentally, I simply tried to project the confident thoughts that I had built up from previous, much shorter, open sea crossings onto this one. The main difference was that it was a much longer flight duration, and there was a complete lack of alternate landing possibilities en route. I was also expecting a long VHF radio silence, but as it turned out, other aircraft were regularly using the 121.5 frequency. Though nobody was speaking to me directly, simply knowing that there were people out here listening, gave me a warm feeling inside, for the time being at least.

The aircraft and all its systems had no issues and were humming along nicely, I was off on a big adventure into the unknown, and I was even flying between continents.

* * *

The fact that it was a quiet, non-dramatic flight, provided me with time to reflect on how life could take on a completely different context during a lengthy open sea crossing. Everyday objectivity and rationality that were maintained on the ground now became almost suspended or frozen as I flew through this empty space, as if hanging in limbo. Things that seem to matter greatly on the ground somehow now found no relevance. Here, there seemed to be no point in dwelling or mulling over earthly concerns, as they simply didn't help me in this realm. Often this state of mind dominated my thoughts until I once more approached civilisation and prepared to return to all the hassles and conformity of the modern aviation world.

But for a brief few hours, whilst completely isolated and on my own, I could afford myself a gloriously different existence, almost a purer state of consciousness, one where the only things that truly mattered could be distilled down to a simple list: the ongoing performance of the aircraft; my navigational skills; my (sometimes sporadic) communications with passing traffic; the immediate and imminent weather conditions; and my own mental and physical wellbeing. It was a glorious existence because it was so simple. At that precise moment in time nothing else mattered, *nothing*. In the same way that a climber might be wholly committed to scaling a technically difficult rock face or a canoeist wholly committed to shooting white-water rapids, my focus of attention and commitment was placed solely on the immediate task in hand. For me, that was safely piloting the aircraft, to the exclusion of many other mundane thoughts that seemed now to become completely irrelevant and redundant. How any of these challenging tasks were handled successfully was purely down to the adventurer's skill and management of both their mind and body while constantly interpreting and instantly reacting to their ever-changing physical environment. To avoid potential mistakes, at no point could they afford to lose their positive grip on mental awareness and stability.

Long-distance, isolated flying however was often a vastly different experience to other forms of adventure. The physical conditions, both in and surrounding the aircraft, for 99% of the time, were (hopefully) very stable. When in such an uncertain environment, *boring* and *uneventful* could be regarded as good news. There was often truly little to do physically in the cockpit apart from minor course adjustments, monitoring the radio and generally maintaining a good overall lookout. Often in this vacuum of physical stimulus, it was left to the mind to do all the real work.

Central to keeping my brain gainfully employed in this way was to maintain a positive, cheery disposition. I found that this was of great benefit to me mentally, even if this cheeriness was entirely for myself. After all, there was no one else up there to appreciate my jolly mood or even to laugh or complain about my bad singing. Keeping up such an internal positive morale in an uncertain environment, as demonstrated by people who whistle when they are nervously walking alone down a dark alley, is a natural defence mechanism that we all share. The idea that we try to convince ourselves that everything is OK, even when perhaps it is not, allows us to keep our mind active in a positive way and not to dwell on what future upsets may (or may not) befall us. This was a tactic that I also employed when faced with dealing with my cancer treatment.

I searched for the positive in every aspect of the treatment process. Potentially unappealing and lengthy sessions sitting in a treatment chair, whilst receiving my unique concoction of 'chemo soup' through an intravenous drip could, mentally at least, be turned into different thoughts in my head.

"Well at least I'll get a nice sit down and maybe find something interesting on the TV."

Time spent watching daytime TV was not a usual activity for me, so it was a marvellous mental distraction to find myself avidly engaged in house hunting, selling antiques, celebrity cooking or any of the other activities the daytime schedules happened to be showing. Rather bizarrely at times, I would even be concerned that my treatment session might actually finish *before* the programme I was watching.

"I wonder is there a way of slowing down my chemo drip? Perhaps I could kink that tubing a bit, slow the flow rate a little and make the delivery stretch out for another 10 minutes. I really need to see if that carefully selected Royal Doulton figurine is going to fetch the auction price needed to win the day."

Usually during my regular weekly visit to the treatment rooms in the Northern Ireland Cancer Centre in Belfast, which stretched over a 24-week period, I would be assigned a reclining chair to sit in while receiving my intravenous chemotherapy. On the very odd occasion however, and only when all the chairs were already taken, I was directed instead to lie on a normal hospital bed for the treatment. On these rare occasions, in my mind at least, I was able to luxuriate in the knowledge that I had received a *free upgrade*, a first-class flatbed passenger seat instead of the usual economy-class recliner if you will.

In my mind, I would be cruising at 44,000ft with *NHS Airlines*, halfway across the Atlantic Ocean en route to my private Caribbean Island (which had been easily purchased by auctioning off just a tiny fraction of my vast Royal Doulton figurine collection). I would be waiting for the first-class tea trolley to come around by my flat bed. The deluxe range of international beverages on offer, extending to *both* tea or coffee, would then be served in the finest Royal Doulton bone china mugs, accompanied by a complimentary offering of milk and sugar. To round off my first-class culinary experience, I would finally be offered a selection of *petit four biscuits*, including *les custard crèmes du posh, les digestifs de chocolat* or *les dodgeres de jammie* (polite notice – maximum two biscuits per patron – thank you very much).

By playing these internal mental games with the TV, the furniture or the tea trolley, I was able to deflect (as much as possible) the impact of the painfully real, oppressive, and often relentless aspects of coping with the highly invasive chemotherapy treatment.

Similar mental games could be employed in the air.

During remote sea crossings, cloud formations could take on a whole personality or structure of their own. Enormous caverns the size of cathedrals, and deep gorges of crystal-clear air between lightly scattered fluffy clouds, would present themselves as a constantly restless maze of landscapes in which to fly under, around, over or through. Likewise, brilliantly white three dimensional 'icebergs' would appear, just ready and waiting for me to pilot my 'aerial submarine' around, providing a fantastically fanciful underwater maritime adventure, all played out at perhaps 4000ft above the sea!

Arriving at the destination airport, thoughts would swiftly return to the real terra firma world, where airfield personnel would invariably be asking me how the flight went. My stock answers were often to say: "Fine, nothing much to report"; "All went well"; or "Very uneventful transit". The dreamlike solo experience that I had *actually* encountered somehow always felt too complicated to convey to my new hosts. What seemed therefore to bystanders as a fairly standard, uneventful trip was actually often, mentally at least for me, quite something else.

But imagine if I had tried to convey that just two hours ago, beyond the horizon and away out over the sea, I had been commander-in-chief of my very own stealth submarine, cruising along at 85 knots and playing dodgems with icebergs in the sky. The chances are that I would have been gently led away by the hand from my aircraft, presented with an extremely fashionable white jacket with lots of smart buckles on the sleeves, and sent off to stay indefinitely in a very exclusive hotel room complete with the latest trend in padded wallpaper.

* * *

Just as I was mentally trying on my straitjacket for size, I was abruptly brought back into the here and now, when I heard Cairo ATC on the radio. At about 3.5 hours into the flight, I was still too far out of range to call their designated frequencies, but close enough to at least monitor them and build up a mental picture of what aircraft traffic was entering and leaving Egyptian-controlled airspace. As I drew closer to the shoreline, I could hear more of the routine traffic, only every time an aircraft called "Cairo" it often sounded like they were calling "gyro" and my ears would unnecessarily prick up. ATC on the other hand sounded like they were sitting in a tin bath, which was not ideal when you are contemplating your first-ever approach and landing at a mid-sized international airport.

Once established with Alexandria approach, I was vectored in directly over the very beige and dusty looking city at 3000ft. My initial nervousness of approaching and landing correctly on the huge complex of available runways eased as I discovered that this airport was being fully decommissioned in a few months' time, meaning that most of the commercial airliner traffic had already shifted to the new airport close by. It meant I was arriving at a virtually empty international airport. As I taxied onto the deserted apron to take up my allotted stand, I thought, "Happy days. This is not going to be as difficult as I had imagined."

This early euphoria was short lived.

I should have guessed something was up when, as soon as I was parked up on the stand, the ground staff rushed forward to chock, front and back, all three wheels. I got the impression *Roxy* was being handled exactly the same as a Boeing 747, but I thought they were just being super cautious and following procedures, so I said nothing. Unfortunately, worse was yet to come. The stand I was put on was only about 100m from the terminal entry door. But as I picked up my luggage to stroll over to the open doorway, the ground handler immediately sprang into action.

"No Captain. That is not possible. You must wait here."

I then thought, well, if I couldn't walk on the apron, I would just hitch a ride in the front seat of the pickup truck the ground handler had arrived in.

"No Captain. That is also not possible. You must wait here."

After four hours and 30 minutes in the air, I just wanted to finish up with the airport as quickly as possible and get some rest. I didn't need any of this seemingly unnecessary delay.

"How long are you going to keep me here for?" I enquired. The sun was beating down and I was overheating nicely.

"Just a few more moments, Captain. Ah! Here is your official transport coming now," said the ground handler.

And then it all became crystal clear, as a decrepit old passenger bus hove into view and steadily worked its way across to where I was standing. Indeed, I could have easily walked into the terminal building twice as fast as the bus took to wend its way across the tarmac to meet me.

I had worked it out. My international flight was being met by the passenger bus not to help offload my 350 imaginary jumbo jet passengers, but simply so that as I climbed aboard, as the sole occupant save the driver, it would allow the airport authorities to add a considerably hefty *bus transfer fee* to my other handling charges. How very innovative. Welcome to Egyptian bureaucracy, working hand in glove with Egyptian ingenuity.

To add further insult to injury, thereafter during my whole stay I was subsequently allowed to simply walk in and out of the terminal building unhindered back and forth to the aircraft. Suddenly there was now no need for the official bus. After all, why would there be? The pilot had been fully charged for the bus already, so there was no further operational need to actually provide the service.

That said, the local handling agents did a slick job of getting me quickly through customs, quarantine and Immigration. But, of course as with many things, speed costs money. Airport Security also ended up being very interested in my GPS units and cameras, with serial numbers taken and recorded to make sure all the same equipment would return to the aircraft the next day.

Once clear of the airport, I was taken directly to an executive hotel that the local handler had already arranged. This was a problem, as it really wasn't necessary for me to stay in one of the most expensive hotels in town. I hadn't arrived in a fancy VIP corporate jet and I certainly didn't need the same sort of costly, lavish attention to detail that more discerning clientele might automatically expect and pay for. Here for the first time, I felt I was not a customer, a client, or a respected guest, but rather I was simply a commodity, a source of cash, to be squeezed, billed and charged at every creative opportunity. Later on in my journey, along with a change in handling agent, I became much more aware of the pitfalls, ruses and rackets that could easily catch out the unwary traveller, but even still it would not be the last time I was put upon in this way.

I was met in the evening by three local guys who had become aware of my flight through a growing band of online supporters. Ahmed El Heity from Cycle Egypt and his two pals came along to meet me and take me out to sample some local foods, notably *kushari*, a flavourful dish of macaroni, rice, chickpeas, lentils, caramelised onions, fried liver and a rich chilli sauce. We also visited the Alexandria Aero Club. After all the officialdom and bureaucratic nonsense in the airport, I was grateful to be once more in the company of genuine, friendly local people.

6 April 2010: Alexandria, Egypt – Cairo, Egypt

"What practical use is being booked into a luxury hotel room if I have to then leave it so early in the morning," was my thought as I left for the airport at 7.15am. I made my way as quickly as possible to *Roxy* to repack my overnight bags and to refuel from a rickety old avgas truck. I then made my way, on foot across the previously un-walkable apron, to meet with ATC up in the tower.

The terminal administration building felt huge, and yet was also strangely quiet and empty, much like a school building devoid of pupils over the summer holidays. With this airport scheduled to close down in a few months, I guess that most of the support staff had begun to transfer operations over to the new airport. I was brought into a flight-briefing office just behind the main control room where I could discuss filing my first-ever flight plan outside Europe. Filing such a plan was usually a fairly simple procedure. Most of the basic information could be copied from one plan to the next, but a trick that I learnt quite early on was to let the local ATC take a handholding role when planning the actual routing. The reasoning was simple; these people were local, they knew their patch better than anyone and they could therefore give sage advice on any possible hazards en route, such as military or civil exclusion zones, radar/radio black spots, weather, reporting points etc.

All things that I could have needlessly stayed up until 3am worrying about.

It is important to remember that I was, of course, always aiming to fly these routes only once, unless weather or a mechanical issue would force me to turn back for any reason. I would therefore only have to know the joining/leaving procedures and reporting points for any one particular airport on the single day that I was using it. Subsequently, I developed a mastery of short-term memory for instructions from ATC. I flew each day as it came, temporarily structured and guided by local ATC rules, or on occasions where this was lacking, sometimes just by the seat of my pants.

And so it was with Alexandria ATC. The briefing room was dusty, worn out and very antiquated. A high counter stretched across the whole room as you would perhaps see in a bank or hotel lobby. Only this counter was up at chest height. It was definitely designed to project the authority and power of those officials behind it over those mere pilots and lowly navigators who stood, as if accused in the dock, before it. It was slightly intimidating at first glance until, on commencing my by-now-well-tested "Could you please help me with some of the finer details of my routing today?" patter, I spied that there was a bed rigged up on the other side of the counter. It was an old wrought-iron bedstead affair, complete with sagging mattress and threadbare bed linen to match. Any grandiose visions of Egyptian ATC wielding 100% power over their mighty territory were, in this office at least, gone in an instant. No doubt the bed was there for good reason, probably used for a solo officer working overnight on the graveyard shift. But in my mind, it just conjured up what could be a fantastic plot twist in an airplane disaster movie...

"Mayday! Mayday! Alexandria, can you read me!" calls the captain.

"It's no use Captain. We can't raise the airport. The ATC must already be in their pyjamas and tucked up in their office bed by now," replies the first officer dejectedly.

* * *

With my flight plan submitted, the clock was now ticking. It was standard practice on the flight plan to state my intended departure time, and once that time was set in the system, the aircraft was then obliged to take off within a few minutes of the plan becoming active. In some countries, to allow for any minor unforeseen delays, there was often an extension window of up to one hour to get airborne, however in other countries this window was sometimes reduced to only 30 minutes. Timing out and going over the extension period without departing, risked the immediate cancellation of the active flight plan and this then required the tedious task of resubmitting a whole new flight plan. Not wanting to overshoot my departure time, it was easy to understand why the countdown clock was always ticking away in my head, very loudly.

I was making reasonable progress. I was already fully loaded, suited and booted, and was about to climb into *Roxy* when I remembered that I had forgotten one very important task: to get my FAI world-record attempt forms officially signed and stamped by the airport staff. As these forms gave the necessary official proof to the FAI that I had indeed landed and taken off from this location in G-YROX, on this date and time, then it was imperative that I got someone in authority locally to sign the forms as a witness.

"No problem," I thought, "I'll just grab the forms from my bag and nip up to the ATC duty officer in the Tower". I made the top of the tower in double quick time, still in my full immersion suit as this wasn't going to take more than a couple of minutes, or so I thought. After a quick explanation to the duty controller about him putting his signature on the forms to basically confirm I was indeed standing right there in front of him, he slowly considered his reply.

"I think we will need to ask my supervisor if it is OK for me to sign your forms," he replied.

"No problem," I said.

We then went back to the rear of the tower to the supervisor's desk, where I had to explain the whole signing procedure again. The supervisor, in turn, carefully considered my request. In front of him were my two forms for signing, along with my own pen in readiness for a quick getaway down the stairs. The remaining minutes of my active flight plan were steadily ticking away.

"I'm not sure I can sign these forms Captain, as they are not ours. I think it is better if we check first with the airport operations manager. His office is downstairs."

"OK..."

With growing frustration and gritted teeth, I followed the tower supervisor down the stairs, clutching my precious but as yet unsigned forms in my fist. Approximately 50m down a long, dimly lit internal corridor was the airport operations manager's office.

Knock... Wait...

Inwardly fume...

The door eventually opened and in we went. Once more the full explanation of the FAI forms was needed.

"They are not official travel documents," I add for clarity. "I just need someone to witness that I did indeed pass through this airport, at this time and date with my aircraft. Anyone in the airport can probably sign it" I said. My desperation was growing, so I continued. "In Italy, a guy who just happened to be walking his dog on the edge of a small grass runway was able to witness that I had indeed landed there. Honestly, it's no big deal for one of you guys to sign it."

The operations manager then looked at the supervisor for unspoken support.

"Yes!" I thought, the ops man is going to sign it and I will be out of here, pronto. He picked up the papers and the pen. Yes! Here we go, get signing.

"We will have to ask the airport's general manager. Come! We all go to his office now!" he said with gusto.

My precious papers were now firmly in the fat fingered grip of the ops man. I immediately felt like just grabbing them back and making a run for *Roxy*. But I was trapped. Held firm in an idiotic bureaucratic process that I had rather foolishly brought upon myself. There was no way out apart from letting the course of events slowly work through to their natural conclusion. Once more we headed out into the myriad of drab, shabby staff corridors and staircases; I was looking into places where the travelling passengers just never see.

This time there were three of us knocking and waiting when we arrived at the GM's door. More silent fuming. Beads of sweat were now running off my face. I was dressed for doing battle with the elements at 6000ft, not for an airlessly hot corridor surrounded by crumpled white shirts and body odour.

"Come!" came a booming voice from inside, and we were duly summoned into the high commander-in-chief's inner sanctum. We had indeed gone right to the top to see the airport's *Mr. Big*.

"Welcome! Welcome! Sit down! Sit down! Would you like to have some tea?" he bellowed.

Once again, I was duty bound to now take Mr. Big through the whole same laborious explanation of signing the FAI forms. More minutes wasted. Tea was served and then yet again the whole signing matter was duly considered afresh. The pen was picked up by Mr. Big, and the papers were carefully set out, just so, in front of him...

"Just sign the bloody forms and let me go!" I seethed under my breath.

Pen was almost put to paper, but then a hesitant pause. A new consideration had flickered in Mr. Big's mind.

"This form is not one of ours. It is a highly unusual request. I'll just ring Cairo to check that it is OK to sign it."

"Be calm. Breathe. Sip tea. Look relaxed," I was doing everything to stop myself exploding. "He **is** helping you, even if it's a really, really, slow type of help."

Thankfully, Cairo was fine with letting Mr. Big make such a big decision about his own airport. And so he did sign the forms, eventually. However, he appeared like he was signing his own death warrant while doing it. What should have taken three minutes at the most had now taken 30, but at least it was signed. I was home and dry, until I made one last error of judgement.

On receiving the forms back again I made a casual remark that they may also like to use the airport stamp, just if it was handy, as there is a nice place on the forms for them to be stamped.

"Oh yes! The official stamp is very necessary. We must use it!" Mr. Big decreed to his attendants. "Where is it?"

Kicking myself, I responded: "Ahh... It's not totally necessary, you understand. It's just nice to have on the forms if you have it handy." Alas my backpedalling was to no avail. Again, I had stupidly opened the way for yet more totally unnecessary delay.

It took a further 10 minutes to locate the airport stamp in another part of the building. A full 10 minutes that I just couldn't afford. I told them to go and find the stamp on their own and bring me the completed papers down to G-YROX. I had the engine running and was ready to taxi out when the signed and freshly stamped papers were finally stuffed back into my hands.

Lesson learnt. Let's go. The whole of Egypt awaits!

* * *

My flight plan was for an initial hop of just one hour and 40 minutes towards Cairo, and then I would proceed onwards up the Nile valley towards Luxor. I wanted to avoid the undoubted congestion of the main Cairo International Airport, and therefore opted for the much smaller and quieter 6th October Airport situated out to the west of the city.

My departure from Alexandria after such a hectic pre-flight period was largely uneventful. I taxied out to runway 04, and after take-off, I was vectored out of their immediate controlled airspace. I then changed radio frequency from the tower to be controlled by radar. I had been cleared to fly at 2500ft, which was quite high compared with my flights so far through Europe. Little did I know what awaited in the next few days. It was a comfortable altitude to fly at however, not too hot and not too cold, sitting in the open cockpit whilst admiring the view. I felt that I was now really on my way. I was flying across a different continent, with a very different landscape rolling out ahead of me.

Initially I was flying over orderly agricultural fields, not surprising given the Nile Delta provides the vast majority of Egypt's domestic food production. This all still felt quite familiar, not so far removed from Southern Europe. That was until I sensed a looming presence of something quite unfamiliar, something I had yet to come to terms with. Slowly the rich agricultural land was being invaded by sand. It was encroaching into the fertile soils, making the fields gradually more and more barren until, as I flew on, agriculture gave way completely to a huge proper desert on a scale that I had never before witnessed.

A very odd sensation then came over me. My routing according to my GPS waypoints simply took me the most direct route, out over a huge swathe of the desert en route for 6th October Airport. But even though this was the most direct route, I found myself skirting around the edge of the desert for a short time, just as if I was contemplating setting out over a vast ocean and was reluctant to leave the relative safety of the shoreline. It was an odd, irrational nervousness of an unknown type of terrain. I soon rationalised that I had already been quite happy to set out over significant stretches of open water, so why not a desert? Indeed, there was the added advantage that if I had to 'ditch' in the desert for any reason, at least the aircraft would not sink in the sand (I hoped) like it would do in the water. With irrational fears allayed, I was then much happier to take a deep breath and push on out over the hot desert sands.

I approached 6th October Airport at 2000ft but then had to wait for other traffic and training aircraft to complete their circuits before I could land. To slow my approach, I 'paused' in the air and made a vertical descending hover from 2000ft until the circuit traffic cleared ahead of me. Then, while on 'short finals' to land, I was further advised that I could hover-taxi directly to the apron. Although this manoeuvre was normally used by helicopters, it allowed me to hop across the infield taxiways and land conveniently on the apron to take up my stand ahead of the other fixed wing traffic still taxiing in from the main runway. So far so good.

It was here that I first made contact with Eddie Gould (or *Eddie Gold* as he would be nicknamed on social media) and his good friend Ahmed Hassan M. Aly. Eddie and his wife Anthea were British expats living in Cairo. Being long-time aviation enthusiasts Eddie and Ahmed took great interest in any General Aviation flights that happened to be flying past their doorstep and I was no exception. The great thing was that now with the power of online social media, we were able to communicate beforehand, and then arrange to meet up in person when I arrived. Psychologically, the idea that I would be able to meet a friendly face from home in such a remote far-flung place meant a great deal. We struck up a good friendship immediately and after the usual heavyweight Egyptian bureaucracy, I was eventually allowed to leave the airfield in the company of Eddie and Ahmed to go off into town to find some unleaded petrol. On the way we stopped in a fast-food restaurant so that I could be interviewed for a local English-language magazine. We then went onwards to claim our main prize of the day, a very welcome petrol station that supplied 95 octane unleaded gasoline.

Most of the local garages could only supply up to 92 octane fuel, but it was preferable for my Rotax engine to use the 95-rated fuel wherever possible. The higher-octane rating gave the fuel slightly more bang for my buck, which helped boost performance. Eddie and Ahmed were treated to the spectacle of filling up the Turtle Pac on the garage forecourt, and both were suitably impressed with its simplicity and versatility. Fuelled up, we headed back out to the airfield with the intention that I would then proceed with my second flight of the day onwards towards Luxor.

With some fast talking by Ahmed and Eddie we were able to carry the Turtle Pac in by a side gate at the airport and plumb it once more into the fuel system on the back seat of *Roxy*. I was well within my schedule of getting back into the air before over-officious Egyptian bureaucracy sadly caught up with me once again. Initially from Alexandria, I had planned to make it as far as Luxor in one day, and my flight called for two short stops en route at Cairo (6th October airport) and at a place farther up the Nile called Asyut. But now departure delays leaving 6th October Airport threatened to throw that whole plan out of the window.

As I had managed to find 95 octane fuel here, I reasoned that I could probably now skip out landing at Asyut altogether and instead simply fly a longer distance direct to Luxor. Missing out the Asyut stop would save me the considerable time that would have been wasted on the ground there – it felt like a good compromise, and I would still end up in Luxor that evening. However, spirit-sapping bureaucracy soon kicked in yet again, as I had already stated in my original flight plan that I would land at Asyut. When I later suggested that I should bypass it, to save me time overall, it was dismissed straight away.

"No Captain. You must land at Asyut first and then land at Luxor. It is simply not possible for you to fly directly to Luxor," was the official word.

I suspect the "not possible" was probably much more to do with Asyut International Airport missing out on being able to charge me a handsome landing and commercial handling fee rather than for any credible aviation safety issue. I argued the point, citing that I now wanted to file a new flight plan instead, one that would simply take me overhead Asyut (still using it as a radio reporting point) and directly on to Luxor. This threw the officials slightly as they had no technical counter argument as to why they could still insist that I land at Asyut. They reluctantly agreed that this would be an option open to me.

I may have won that particular bureaucratic battle, but I did not win the war this day. My revised flight plan still had to be approved by Cairo. To save time I got suited up and warmed the engine while waiting for approval of my new submission. I would be ready to taxi out to the runway as soon as the tower indicated that approval had arrived from Cairo. I sat in the mid-afternoon heat watching the time tick away, waiting and waiting.

It had been a tight schedule in order for my new plan to work, and I needed the clearance to take off soon or else I was going to run out of daylight during the flight. Alas, as the time ticked on, it eventually became clear that there was no way that I could now reach Luxor before dark. I had no option but to scrub the flight, and somewhat dejectedly, I contacted the tower to advise them that I would now be returning to the stand. As if to add insult to injury, as I was taxiing back to the apron, the tower came through to tell me that approval had arrived and that I was OK to now depart for Luxor. Thanks, but no thanks.

On the positive side, every cloud has a silver lining and on this occasion, it meant that I was able to meet up with Eddie and Ahmed again. They had waited patiently to watch me take off but had soon realised something was amiss when I returned to the stand. Eddie was very generous and offered to put me up for what would now have to be a two-night stay in Cairo due to the airport being completely shut the next day, a Wednesday. I was very relieved to climb back into Eddie's arranged transport and temporarily forget all about the frustrations of the local airport bureaucracy. I slumped down into the car seat and suddenly felt dog tired; it had certainly been a long day.

As we headed into the city to stay at Eddie and Anthea's place, the traffic in Cairo was just wild. It took a full hour and 30 minutes to drive across town. Everywhere car horns were blaring, and drivers were constantly jostling for position, inching forwards on the hopelessly congested roads. It was mayhem. A short time later Eddie took me to his local British expats club for a few beers and a falafel. Compared to the bedlam witnessed out on the streets, the small backroom-style club was an oasis of calm and normality. After the high tension of making my first long open water crossing from Crete and then navigating in the novel airspace challenges of Egypt, not to be flying the next day came as a big relief. It allowed the several beers to taste even better.

7 April 2010: Cairo, Egypt (non-flying day)

A relaxing morning was followed by Eddie's grand tour of Cairo. I had lamented to Eddie earlier that but for the delay in flying on to Luxor, I would have departed 6th October Airport and flown up the Nile Valley without even seeing the Great Pyramid of Giza. In retrospect, it would have been shameful to fly right past Cairo without even glimpsing the last-remaining wonder of the ancient world. Now at least, with an enforced free day in hand, Eddie planned that we could fix that injustice with a visit to the pyramids on foot.

The most unexpected aspect of visiting the pyramids and the Great

Sphinx of Giza is how close they are to the edge of the city's suburbs. In all the classic photos, the pyramids are set against a backdrop of uninterrupted desert. So I imagined they might be a 100 miles from any civilisation. Yet this is just an illusion. Eying the scene from one strategic direction, the desert does indeed stretch away to the horizon, but swinging your gaze through 180 degrees, you are immediately greeted with the grimy, noisy and dusty bustle of Cairo, right there in your face.

Jostling tour buses manoeuvred incredibly around the narrow streets before spilling out their tightly scheduled gaggles of River Nile cruising day-trippers, who in turn, immediately became easy prey for the street hawkers and stall vendors. On our arrival into this melee, Eddie, Anthea and I were able to pick our own way up towards the pyramids. With all the confidence that visiting with an experienced local can bring, I avoided the worst of the hassling. Although at one point, just for fun, Eddie still couldn't resist asking if I would like to have my picture taken with a camel.

The pyramids were quite simply spectacular. It was only when I got right up close that I could appreciate the finest detail, measurements and craftsmanship that created this feat of civil engineering on such a mindboggling scale.

After a late lunch on the terrace balcony of a local café overlooking Giza, we once more braved the traffic to visit an old market area of the city. We wandered through the vibrant Khan el-Khalili bazaar for a few hours, complete with its 200-year-old café. I thought this was impressive enough, until I was further advised that the café had actually been open non-stop, 24 hours a day, for those past 200 years! A regular all-night café or 24-hour diner will never again be seen in quite the same league by comparison. It seemed all manner of everything exotic was on sale at Khan el-Khalili: spices, carpets, shiny bowls, pots, kettles of all shapes and sizes, and more. I happily soaked up the historical significance of the place, set in the heart of Old Cairo.

Later in the evening Ahmed and I ventured out from Eddie's place on a special mission. Our quest was to find suitable top-up oil for my

Rotax engine. After trying half a dozen local petrol stations, we finally found what we were searching for at a Shell garage, some six miles away. This find was significant, as I was well aware that from Cairo onwards, I would be heading out into much less-resourced country. I therefore took the opportunity to stock up on essential spare parts and consumables. Oil was fine for now at least, but the same could not be said with confidence for always finding the right fuel…

8 April 2010: Cairo, Egypt – Aswan, Egypt

On first arrival into Egypt, I had imagined rather fancifully that I might fly past the pyramids at 500ft and get to wave at everyone on my way up the Nile. I quickly learned however from Alexandria's ATC office, that my presence anywhere in Egyptian airspace was going to be very tightly controlled. My aircraft was, by international necessity, equipped with a mode A, C and S transponder. This device is activated by detecting an incoming radar signal from a nearest airport or ground station, to which it then pings back my aircraft's position to the radar controller's screen. Information on my position (mode A), current altitude or flight level (mode C) and my call sign G-YROX (mode S) could all be shown on the screen, and this helped ATC to coordinate my target blip with all the other on-screen traffic being displayed. This was always assuming that the ground station had equipment capable of receiving and processing all the information; and indeed, not all airports could.

The upshot of all of this in Egypt, was that the local ATC radar operators used this all-seeing power to its maximum effect. They gave me strict orders to fly my aircraft on a precise course, as if it was simply a radio-controlled aircraft on a grand scale. Even deviating by just a mile off course, perhaps to skirt around a low cloud base, would result in me receiving a rapid interrogation over the radio by the controller to get me back on my *exact* track immediately. I think the trouble all stemmed from the fact that there was so little non-commercial traffic flying in Egypt. Local General Aviation aircraft just seemed to be non-existent. Therefore, this meant there were no small light aircraft jaunting about on quick Sunday afternoon flights to the next airstrip for a cup of tea and a bun, or bumbling around their local countryside airspace for an hour on their way to fly over their Great Aunt Matilda's house. And with that, it followed that the controllers were used to handling only commercial or military traffic. In their eyes I was just another commercial jet, albeit a rather slow and low one, on their radar screens. It had advantages in that I was not going to be allowed to get myself lost over the desert, but the disadvantage was the total lack of sensitivity on how a small, slow-flying, open cockpit private aircraft operates compared to a commercial jet. This rigidity of strictly applying commercially orientated rules would very nearly lead to an incident a few days later over the Red Sea, and also gave my departure from 6th October Airport a bizarre twist.

* * *

The day had started normally enough by Egyptian standards. We had battled the early morning Cairo traffic to reach the airport in good time for my planned 10.00am departure slot. However, overly enthusiastic yet extremely sluggish guards at the airport entrance gate then created the first of my delays. Next, close scrutiny of my newly revised, direct flight plan to Aswan, which now missed out Luxor altogether, accounted for yet more delay and this all resulted in my eventual departure being at midday, a full two hours later than expected.

After fond farewells to Eddie, Anthea and Ahmed, I finally taxied out to take off. Then came the most bizarre request from the tower on the radio.

"Golf, Yankee, Romeo, Oscar, X-Ray. On departure, please rise vertically to 8500ft over the airfield."

I sought some clarification.

"October Tower. You want me to climb to 8500ft while remaining above the airfield. Is that correct?"

"Affirm. Please climb to 8500ft within the area of the airport perimeter fence," came the reply from the tower.

"What were they thinking?" I thought. Fully fuelled and taking off heavy in the midday heat, *Roxy* would climb like a fully laden Canadian Goose. It might take me 20 minutes to reach that altitude, and in that time I should have been 20 minutes closer to my final destination. No matter, I had no option but to cooperate with my remote controllers and dutifully, albeit fuming under my breath, I made a painfully slow set of climbing orbits above the runway to finally reach 8500ft. I'd not only wasted 20 minutes of my time, but also 20 minutes' worth of valuable fuel. I was raging inside.

Unceremoniously, I was then passed to Cairo Control and they vectored me into the air route southwards towards Asyut, Luxor and Aswan. So much for hopes of sightseeing the Nile at 500ft. Compared to me sitting at 8500ft in their route corridor, I would have had a much better view of the Nile valley observing it on Google Earth. It was spectacular all the same, with the Nile's ancient river course being a predominantly green ribbon of agriculture sandwiched on both sides by the ever-present desert backdrop. The varied landscape featured some fantastic desert scenery, sometimes rugged, sometimes serenely sandy, and there were strange markings, the origins of which were hard to decipher. Desert roads would come and go, some with seemingly quite random short strips of tarmac laid down within them.

Even though I was over the desert, the altitude meant that it certainly wasn't warm cruising along at 8000ft for five hours. After a while the cold seeped into my bones, which was such an odd feeling when staring down at the baking hot sand below. I lost Cairo on the radio fairly early on into the flight and flew on listening to 121.5 for about 150 miles until I was picked up by Asyut radio. I got the impression that the controller there had not had much traffic to deal with during his shift, I may even have been the main event of his day. He was however most insistent that I should cross directly overhead of his runway and not just bypass him by a few miles, in order to shorten my direct routing toward Luxor. Sensing his obvious enthusiasm, I complied to his instruction and his voice seemed most happy to see me fly over, wishing me a safe onward flight. Likewise, Luxor were also keen to make contact with me as soon as possible. Initially, I was too far out to make direct two-way contact with them, but they managed to relay a call via a passing Air Berlin flight to gain an update on my position. Perhaps due to busier airspace, Luxor was the opposite to Asyut and requested me to NOT overfly them, but to stay well out to the west of their local ATC zone.

Eventually, after a bum-numbing five hours and 20 minutes, I made my final approach for Aswan. The visibility had turned very murky, with a light brown dust hanging in the air, but fortunately I could still see distant objects through the haze, albeit with some difficulty. After some minutes of anxious peering through the gloom, there was welcome relief when I finally recognised the distinct markings of runway 35 looming into view. I briskly taxied to the stand only to be delivered once again into the overly eager hands of the Egyptian ground staff.

"Yes Captain, you *must* have our ground handling. Chocks, ground marshal and our bus to the terminal."

And immediately followed by...

"Your bill is US$215 sir. Pay now please."

I began to argue with the guy. After five extremely cold hours in the air, I was not ready to exchange any pleasantries. It felt that I was being 'officially' robbed as I didn't either need nor want any of these services. At the same time, the rest of the ground staff were gathering around excitedly taking pictures of my aircraft as seeing a gyroplane was such an unusual event. In a frustrated moment I lost my cool and shouted.

"Well, if I am being charged US$215 to park here overnight, then all you guys can pay me US$10 for each photo you are taking of my aircraft! And no, I am not joking!"

The gaggle of airport staff I was speaking to all suddenly went noticeably quiet. My little outburst didn't help, of course. I still had to pay up... eventually, but at least it made me feel a bit better to prove a point of how inflexible (and expensive) their system was to small GA aircraft.

* * *

Aswan was a significant milestone in the journey. Mentally, up to this point, I had fashioned an adequate coping strategy with the aim to ease myself as gently as possible into the enormity of the global challenge I had set. Passing through the UK, my mantra had been, "I haven't really got going yet, so it's all OK." In the rest of Europe this became, "It's still very similar to flying in the UK, therefore it's still all OK." When crossing the expansive Mediterranean, I stretched this sense of wellness, but at least I was already familiar with over-water flying and this was just more (albeit a lot more) of the same; so it was "still all OK". It was landfall in North Africa however, that started to chip away at my defences. Lots of things, even small things normally taken for granted, now felt immediately different. But then meeting up and staying with Eddie had provided a welcome and safe respite, that despite being surrounded by a very unfamiliar landscape, I managed to temporarily still say "all was OK" in Egypt. And so that had helped me to cope at least until I reached Aswan.

But I now felt well and truly out on my own. On the positive side, at least *Roxy* was safe and securely (if expensively) parked at the airport, and so once I had found a taxi and a reasonable local hotel for the night, I was able to try to relax a little and reassure myself that all would be well. I also took some comfort from the very real progress I had made to get even this far in my journey.

As luck would have it, it was *buffet night* at the hotel. Served on the restaurant veranda, it enabled me to sit outside in the pleasant warm evening air, write up my flight diary and plan for the upcoming flights in finer detail. The next stop would be in Jeddah, Saudi Arabia, with a flight across the Red Sea thrown in for good measure. How unbelievably crazy was this flying adventure already shaping up to be, I mused. Internally, I flitted from nervousness and apprehension of the unknown (and of the unknowable) to a strangely calm confidence and an overall excitement for the whole adventure, all in equal measure. It felt almost that the whole journey up to this point was only the preamble, the warm-up, for the *real* flight that was yet to begin. Very similar feelings to those which I had experienced on departure day from Larne, only now, they felt much more magnified, much more significant and much more serious. It was a set of feelings that would return to me at several crucially significant points during the journey, and at each time I would help myself mentally prepare for whatever was yet to come, by focusing and building on the experiences that had gone before.

9 April 2010: Aswan, Egypt – Jeddah, Saudi Arabia

This turned out to be a big day.

I had slept well enough, assisted by my physical fatigue from the previous day's flight, but I was awakened at dawn by the first calls to prayer. They were sounding out all over the city of Aswan from loudspeakers. Slowly, thoughts of the day ahead of me started to creep into my consciousness. I would attempt to fly across the Red Sea and land in Saudi Arabia. This realisation triggered a rush of adrenaline, and there was no drifting back to sleep after that.

I had arranged with my previous day's taxi driver to come back and pick me up from the hotel. Very full of life and eager to help, he hailed from Namibia. He'd agreed to find me two 20-litre containers that we would fill up with fuel en route to the airport. Along with refilling the Turtle Pac, I would then be able to load up with an extra 120 litres for the expected long flight across the Red Sea to Jeddah. My taxi driver duly arrived with containers in hand, and we set out to find the best fuel we could. However, after searching several local fuel stations, the best grade we could muster was only 92 octane.

Like sourcing a well-poured fresh pint of Guinness back home, I could only hope and pray that a busy fuel station, that seemed like it had plenty of daily customers, would also turn out to have the freshest fuel in town. So, I simply picked the one that appeared the most popular. It was not the best way to allay any worries of fuel quality for my crossing of the Red Sea in a single engine aircraft, but I figured at least I had an hour of flight time over land first, in order to test the fuel before I ventured out to sea. And besides, it was all I could source locally anyway. Fuel bought, we then headed back out to the airport where another bizarre event took place.

I'm not sure what I was expecting the airport security team on duty at the main doors would make of my five pieces of luggage: one small carry-on rucksack, one overnight bag and three containers holding a total of 120 litres of highly flammable unleaded petrol. Just your typical everyday tourist essentials! I tried to pre-empt a potentially tricky situation and asked the staff if we could go and drop the three fuel containers off at a side entrance gate to the apron. From there we could then organise to get them transferred directly out to where the aircraft was parked. However, the security staff of course had their own ideas, and in their esteemed wisdom decreed instead that *all* five pieces of my luggage, petrol included and now stacked high on a regular airport luggage trolley, should be ushered directly ahead into the main airport terminal lobby where they would then be loaded onto the conveyor belt and passed through the standard airport baggage X-ray machine. I held my breath as the sloshing containers jiggled their merry way over the conveyor belt rollers...

With 120 litres of highly flammable petrol duly scanned, cleared and delivered, I could never again pass through an airport security line without having a wry smile each time they said that I couldn't take through any liquid containers holding more than 100ml.

With refuelling sorted, I re-packed *Roxy* with my normal luggage and I was about ready to go. The last thing to complete was to settle my airport fees and charges. I had already complained about the highly extortionate charges on first arrival, and now I was prepared to take this up with the airport manager in his office. We argued the finer points, but the bulk of the US$215 charges remained stubbornly fixed. As I didn't have unlimited time to fight my corner, I reluctantly relented and set about settling the newly revised US$206 bill in cash using US dollars. Without having any bills smaller than US$20, I handed over US$220.

"Oh, I am sorry sir, but we don't have any change for US dollars," he replied in an oily voice.

It was so well-rehearsed that I just knew he had used this excuse before. Already feeling aggrieved at the extortionate fees, the sense of injustice at now also being squeezed for every last dollar, just added fuel to the fire and I erupted.

"NO CHANGE! NO CHANGE! WHAT DO YOU MEAN YOU HAVE GOT **NO CHANGE**? YOU ARE SUPPOSED TO BE RUNNING AN INTERNATIONAL AIRPORT HERE, NOT SOME MONEY-GRABBING STREET STALL!"

The manager was visibly shaken, not surprising perhaps as I was deliberately shouting as loud as I could, sure in the knowledge that all of his staff in every office down the long corridor would also be able to hear every word of our conversation echoing around the building. Indeed, numerous heads then popped out into the corridor to see what all the commotion was about.

Knowing that I had claimed the moral victory, he quickly moved to calm the situation. Within two minutes one of his staff came running in with a petty cash box, full of – surprise surprise – low denomination US dollar bills.

Well, suffice it to say, I got my exact change (all fourteen dollars of it), and was very satisfied to do so.

Delayed yet again by these exchanges, by the time I made it out to the aircraft I was really fired up to get into the air. I had now just about had my fill of flying in Egypt and this last incident had just brought it all home. Although the general population were incredibly nice, Egyptian airport authorities appeared to be truly inflexible, petty and tedious. The bureaucracy had steadily worn away at my usual upbeat, easy-going, optimistic self. I now just wanted to fly out of the country as soon as possible.

This however, proved not to be that easy…

I'd flown to Aswan, well south of Luxor, so that I would have the shortest distance over the Red Sea to reach the city of Jeddah in Saudi Arabia. But on reviewing my upcoming flight plan with the tower in Aswan, it quickly transpired that I had made an error. The air corridor that exists between Aswan and Jeddah only operated in one direction, from Jeddah to Aswan and not the other way around. I had missed this small but very significant detail. Talking through what to do about it, ATC advised that I would have to fly initially from Aswan back up towards Luxor and then fly down a different, two-way, air corridor to Jeddah from there. In theory this sounded OK, until I flagged up to the ATC that for me to fly back up north to Luxor would add another hour of flight time and a significant unnecessary dogleg onto my already lengthy flight schedule. Furthermore, flying towards Luxor was also flying back against the prevailing wind and overall fuel endurance would also then become an issue. After more discussion, a compromise of sorts was finally reached. A plan emerged where I would fly back up towards Luxor until I cleared the immediate airspace around the Aswan airfield, from there I would then be allowed to turn and cut the corner across to the adjacent two-way flight corridor that led from Luxor directly to Jeddah.

I set off to enact the plan. Imagine a clock face for a moment, the centre point being Aswan, 12 o'clock being Luxor and 4 o'clock being Jeddah. As I headed up towards 12 o'clock from the centre, I wanted desperately to be allowed to turn 120 degrees to the right and fly directly towards 4 o'clock. The closer I flew towards 12 o'clock the farther away I was actually getting from my eventual destination at 4 o'clock.

Shortly after take-off, I began repeatedly asking permission from Aswan ATC to change course to a new bearing that would see me heading directly for Jeddah. But ATC's response was stubbornly the same each time, to continue on my current course towards Luxor. Something was not right. I then realised that the ATC officer that I had spoken to personally in the tower at Aswan, who had given me the verbal assurance that I would be able to cut the corner off once underway, was not now the same person controlling me in the air. The tower could see every move I was making via my transponder and its radar screens.

I tried to slowly veer off course to the right, but each time I did so the controller would rigidly correct me and insist that I maintain a proper course directly for Luxor. Once more I felt like I was simply his remote-controlled aircraft, and yet I was the one who would be ending up getting very wet if, by his actions, he ran me out of fuel over the Red Sea. All the while I was watching my elapsed flight time, calculating my speed over the ground, and estimating my distance to run and fuel endurance. My safety margin of fuel reserve was constantly being eroded. I could not fly even for another 15 minutes in this wrong direction without having serious concerns about running out of fuel. It was time for more desperate measures.

At one point I tried turning off my transponder, as I thought that if he couldn't see me then he couldn't control me in quite such a draconian way. All went quiet for a few moments, then ATC asked if I was still OK.

"Yes," I replied, pretending not to notice that my transponder was not functioning.

He became agitated, and asked me to recycle my transponder, which was a way of resetting or rebooting the signal. I pretended to do so, hoping that he might then just assume the transponder was malfunctioning and let me be. I would then simply fly off out of Egypt unseen and unhindered. So what if the Egyptian ATC were unhappy, or even wanted to deport me, I was after all, already in the process of deporting myself.

I underestimated this controller, however. He became increasingly disturbed, warning me that if I did not return immediately to Aswan then he would activate a military search and rescue aircraft to come and find me. This was getting out of hand. All I wanted was to be allowed, as agreed earlier, to turn towards Jeddah and then get out of Egyptian-controlled airspace as quickly as possible. There was no way I wanted to return to Aswan. But as the threats of military involvement escalated, I reluctantly turned the transponder back on, citing a connecting wire must have come loose.

But the last few calls from ATC were also telling me another story – in the background, I could hear a heated argument taking place in the tower. I guessed (and hoped) that my original flight planner must now have finally got involved, and I was probably right because after much more shouting in the background, the duty controller came back onto the radio to give me a curt instruction:

"G-YROX, right turn 120 degrees. Proceed direct route for final destination."

"Thank you, *very much*" was my equally curt and barbed reply.

There was definitely no love lost between us at this point. I sharply banked the aircraft, rolling to my right and I was off and running as fast as I could out of Egypt.

I may have been out of that particular difficulty but the whole time-wasting and distance-increasing episode was to have serious repercussions later in the flight. As I tried to settle myself into the journey, I was able to focus more positively on my progress. I had managed to get turned onto the new course in time and now had a good tailwind, good ground speed and my fuel endurance was still within an acceptable safety limit. Perhaps I wouldn't be getting wet on this day after all. One vital element of the equation was missing though, and after several recalculations, I came to the stark realisation that my situation was no longer looking so bright, literally.

Daylight. I was going to run out of it. By my calculations the sun would set 20 minutes before I reached Jeddah. However, there was not a lot I could do about this. Turning back was no longer an option as I was now well out over the Red Sea, and the current tailwind would become a stiff headwind in that reversed direction. All I could hope for was that the dusk after sunset would linger long enough for me to get a visual sight of the runway and get me down safely. It was a big hope.

Dusk fell after six long hours of flying, five of which had been spent out over the Red Sea. Unfortunately, I still had about 30 minutes before I was due to land. As I have explained earlier, my aircraft was designed to fly visual flight rules and in daylight only. It was simply not equipped for night or instrument flying. I reviewed what instruments I did have available. The two Garmin GPS units were very useful of course, and I was able to pre-set the required radio frequencies. I could be (willingly this time) vectored by ATC using my transponder and

Roxy was at least visible, with flashing white strobes and standard red/green navigation lights so I was as set as I could be. Initial contact with Jeddah was encouraging; they were happy to vector me in directly over the city at 5000ft and I suggested that if required, I could make a hovering descent immediately over the runway threshold. This turned out to be particularly useful for them, if only for the fact that Jeddah was a very busy international hub airport with *three* active runways. It was a glimmer of good news set within the growing darkness.

Flying over the city was spectacular, even though I was a bit preoccupied to appreciate it fully. Under the streetlights the whole of Jeddah was glowing a light brown colour, and beyond it I could see from my lofty viewpoint, a big dark patch of nothingness. Referring to my Garmin, I worked out that I was in the vicinity of the airport, but the runways were not yet recognisable. This was because I was looking down from a direct overhead view. Airfield approach lights are exactly that; they are lights that are designed to be visible when you are on a shallow angled final approach and staring straight into them. Tilted at a slight upward angle, they don't actually illuminate the ground in front of them, which then made them hard for me to see from directly above.

Initially I was not worried on this point. As long as the approach ATC could vector me in directly over the correct runway threshold, then I would be sure to land on the tarmac in some shape or fashion. Soon enough, I was 'over the numbers' and was given the go ahead to make a descending hover directly down from 5000ft(!) to land on runway 34R. This was the relatively easy part. With the throttle on idle, stick held slightly back, the aircraft showed zero forward airspeed and began its slow descent. On the way down I began to gain some visual references below, but without landing lights I was worried about being able to see enough ground definition to accurately judge the height needed to land in a controlled way.

If I landed in complete darkness, I might easily misjudge where the ground was and either try to touch down while still 10ft up in the air, or impact into the ground whilst thinking I was still 10ft above the runway. Both scenarios were bad news. Luckily on the way down I found a solution, and it was my only option. The only visible light-source when viewed directly from above, was at the runway intersections, where a few surface lights sunk into the tarmac helped to give out a glimmer of all round visibility. By carefully timing my rate of descent and moving forward on the correct glide path, I could hopefully aim to land directly at the main intersection in the middle of the runway. Once I realised this plan could work, a huge sense of relief came over me.

The landing was not my best ever, I will freely admit that I probably dropped in from about 2ft. But it was controlled and safe and had the added advantage that being in complete darkness, no one else had been able to witness it anyway. With no time to lose, I quickly taxied off the main active runway onto the first taxiway I could find.

My next problem was that I didn't actually know where I was on the airport. I contacted ground radio and they were obliging enough to send a 'Follow Me' car out to find me and bring me in. It proved to be a wise move and I could relax as they safely navigated our little convoy in between the three active runways and myriad of taxiways. The last hour of darkness had all been quite an ordeal and I was so pleased to finally see a friendly hangar and welcoming (if slightly amazed) staff gathering around to greet me.

Wow! I was now in Saudi Arabia! It was amazing to think I had flown myself here all the way from Northern Ireland. Only one slight problem remained however, I had been denied a visa to enter the country. Normally this could have been a big issue, but I aimed to use a plan that had worked well for many other globetrotting private aircraft pilots before me. If I was able to remain 'airside' through all the airports I visited in Saudi Arabia, then I would never have to pass through immigration and passport control. Technically, I would not then be classed as entering the country, even though I was flying through it. I hoped therefore to use this strategy at every overnight stop.

Being an international hub, Jeddah was well used to serving many foreign national aircraft crews transiting through the airport, so helpfully they already had a system in place to work around the visa problem. On arrival, they simply took my passport and issued me with a 24-hour pass that allowed me to be taken to a local airport hotel. They drove me there in a secure minivan, along with some other international air crew and told us all not to leave the confines of the hotel until they returned to pick us up again in the morning. No worries on that score, I thought. After the day I had just had, all I wanted to do was get some food and some serious sleep.

10 April 2010: Jeddah, Saudi Arabia – Al Ta'if, Saudi Arabia

Sitting at breakfast, I could see across towards the open-plan hotel lobby. It was a busy time of the morning, and numerous people were coming and going, but it was only when two women briefly appeared from a side corridor, quickly crossed the lobby and clambered hurriedly into a waiting vehicle with blackened out windows, that I suddenly realised something incredible. I had not as yet seen any other women in the country. All the reception staff, waiters, airport staff and drivers, everyone I had seen anywhere, were all men. These two ladies, completely covered head to toe in black flowing robes and niqābs, were the first (and only, as it turned out) women that I would see throughout my time in Saudi Arabia.

Later, during the minibus drive back to the airport, I kept an eye out but there were simply no women to be seen outside at all. Then on the freeway, I saw the most unusual sight of all: a huge roadside advertising billboard depicted a mother with her pre-teen daughter in a modern living room. Both were dressed in contemporary, Western-style clothing and were pictured demonstrating the use of some sort of domestic appliance. It seemed like a million other regular billboards around the world, only on closer inspection, this one was anything but regular. While the young girl was shown quite normally in the picture, happy and smiling, I was startled and amazed to find that the head of the mother had been deliberately blurred and pixilated, so that any onlooker would not be able to actually see her face. This country was clearly going to have a very unfamiliar culture and society to experience.

Back at the airport I was able to pick up some avgas, which I thought would help to boost the performance of the remaining 92-octane mogas from Aswan. I also managed to get the rotor head greased in a lean-to shed used to maintain all the airport airside vehicles.

As my options for overnight stops while crossing the desert interior of Saudi Arabia were limited, I planned initially on making a short flight of just one hour and 35 minutes in the early afternoon. This would get me as far as Al Ta'if, and from there I would then be able to fly over the bulk of the Saudi desert in one long flight to reach the capital, Riyadh, the following day.

I was actually very glad of making such a short flight. The previous flight into Jeddah had really pushed the operational envelope of both body and machine. Although I had flown to the best of my ability, at maximum efficiency and cautiously within my own sense of safety margins, in hindsight I could also admit to myself that I had been flying well beyond my comfort zone. I knew that I never again wanted to be forced into such a compromised position, brought about by the actions of an overzealous airport official. To be honest, I was still quite shaken from imagining all the 'what if' scenarios that could have made things really unravel and go very wrong in a big way. So now a short, no-nonsense flight was really what I needed to reset my confidence and get back onto a normal footing once more.

The day was hot, 37°C in the shade, but a lot of the airport staff still came out to wave me off. It had cost me over US$500 for *Roxy* to stay here for one overnight, a fact that no one apart from me seemed to mind in the slightest. I made again my point of wanting to charge everyone US$10 per photograph. And once again, this comment was laughed off as everyone clicked away with their phones. I was the only one not laughing.

***

Climbing away from Jeddah was much less traumatic than my late arrival. I had briefed the tower and they now knew the full capabilities and limitations of my aircraft. They allowed me a departure route that avoided all commercial traffic and so I very quickly found myself out at the edge of their zone and bidding them a good-natured farewell. As I headed inland from the coast, I thought this was the real desert at last. Egypt had been real enough, but there I was also following the more densely populated Nile valley. Here, I was heading out for the first time into a much greater wilderness. I was excited and very curious as to what lay ahead, but also a little apprehensive about the remoteness and what I would have to do to survive in the case of having to make a forced landing out in the desert.

Not all my thoughts were quite so serious, however.

"Right then, I wonder if I will see a wild camel?"

I was not disappointed. Within 15 minutes I spied a small black dot up ahead. As I got closer, I realised that it was indeed a dark brown camel and diverted my track slightly to fly overhead to try to get a photo. I was only at about 1000ft above ground level, low enough that I got a good view of it, but not so low as to disturb it. I was very pleased with myself for being able to spot some actual wildlife from the air, even though a camel was quite a big target. My initial euphoria at spotting an elusive creature was short lived however, as over the following 15 minutes I had spotted a further 50 of them. Indeed, so many that the last couple of dozen hardly even got a sideways glance.

I landed at Al Ta'if with little fuss as it was much quieter than Jeddah, which suited me just fine. I was ushered into a VIP waiting area and confined there for the next three hours while there was a concerted effort by the local security staff to try to get me a visa clearance. Even though all the while, I said that it didn't matter as I had my sleeping bag with me in the aircraft, so I could simply bed down on the airside of the airport and then be off on my merry way, early the next day. Eventually this was accepted as the best plan, and I gave one of the staff US$50 to get the Turtle Pac filled at a local gas station. Airport fees might have been eye-wateringly steep at Jeddah but at least petrol prices in such an oil-rich country, were now going to be much cheaper.

Fuel and accommodation were both sorted, and transport was unnecessary, so all I needed now was food. It was decided that I should share a takeaway with the two overnight security guards. Once airport operations were finished for the night, I was shown into the crew rest area, which was a plain carpeted room with bed rolls stacked in the corner. I was intrigued to find that the takeaway food arrangements were quite different to what I was used to back home, both inventive and fascinating at the same time. One of the guards brought in what seemed to be a large plastic sack and carefully laid it down directly onto the carpet in the middle of the room. As the sack was unfolded, I realised that it was actually a large round plastic sheet, about one metre in diameter. And bundled in the middle of it was a huge pile of food. Chicken, rice, some vegetables and a hot chilli sauce to be exact.

No plates or cutlery were either offered or needed, as we simply all sat on the floor around the sheet and picked up the food directly with our right hand. It was a bit tricky for me with the rice as it was not sticky, but I still managed to shovel it into my mouth sideways. The best bit was when we had all finished eating, the edges of the plastic sheet were once more carefully gathered in together and the whole kit and caboodle was lifted away. Job done with no washing up or any carpet cleaning required.

The overnight guards thought it best for me to bed down in a workman's portacabin out on the edge of the apron. This suited me well as I was then left undisturbed by their regular security patrols during the night. I wearily rolled out my sleeping bag on a rickety camp bed and called it a night. Lying in the pitch-black dark I thought, "What a difference to that four-star stopover in Alexandria. This is proper pioneering aviation now." I then promptly dropped off to sleep.

11 April 2010: Al Ta'if, Saudi Arabia – Petrol station one, Saudi Arabia – Petrol station two (overnight), Saudi Arabia

The advantage of camping out on the apron was that it then allowed me to have a good early start the next morning, as I didn't have the usual hassles of getting in through security and passport control. As if staying on a real campsite, I just nipped into the terminal building to make use of the bathroom facilities. Though afterwards I resisted the temptation to stroll back through the VIP lounge while brushing my teeth, complete with my towel slung casually over my shoulder.

Happily, the airport was very quiet and I was left in peace to complete my daily pre-flight checks and to re-pack ready for departure. Compared to the frantic over-concern that I had faced from ground staff in Egypt, it was relaxing to be now left alone to prepare. Checks completed and engine warmed up, I called the tower and was given an immediate clearance for departure towards the east. There was no micro-managed flight path or strict altitude adherence here, I just had to keep the tower advised of my intentions as I took off. This wholly relaxed departure procedure gave me the distinct impression that there would be no other traffic to bother me once I was airborne.

This was to be another big day, the main flight over the bulk of the interior of Saudi Arabia and the scenery en route proved to be spectacular. I was struck by how varied it all was – I spotted everything from flat desert and towering sand dunes to surprisingly high mountains that, when viewed from a distance, gave an impression of being huge, isolated boulders sticking up in the sand on a beach.

I had initially worried about the remote isolation and what to do if I had to land out in the desert. I need not have been so concerned however, as every 10 minutes or so I seemed to fly past a small huddle of Bedouin tents pitched on the sand. They appeared so frequently that I soon realised that the desert in these parts was not in fact *deserted* at all, and I took a passing interest in each camp as I flew overhead. Typically, each one had an assembly of joined-up tents, a scattering of off-road pickup trucks and perhaps a camel herd that was sometimes tethered out in a long line to form a classic camel train. Last, but definitely not least, another essential item was a large road-going water tank sitting on a trailer. It could easily have been a desert scene from a *Mad Max* movie. If I did ever have a problem, I decided that my emergency plan would be to land as close in to one of these camps as possible and then just take it from there. At least with local people there, I hoped I might be cared for much better than trying to look after myself in the very unfamiliar desert conditions.

In the middle of the flight, compared to Egypt, I had little or no radio contact with anyone. I just reported my position and progress as and when requested en route, but information exchange was minimal and I was mostly left on my own. Unlike Egypt, where ATC had insisted that I remained up at 8500ft, I was now able to fly a lot lower between radio calls and really take a good closer look at the stunning desert scenery. I had also agreed a flight plan with ATC in Al Ta'if of simply maintaining a straight-line flight path directly towards Riyadh. In that way, if anyone had had to search for me, at least they would know whereabouts to start looking.

The weather was quite surprising, not the wall-to-wall baking sunshine that I previously imagined a desert climate to be. The visibility was decidedly patchy. Poor, hazy and murky conditions were then followed by a brighter patch. At one point, for almost 100 miles or so, I was slowly catching up a large thunderstorm cell moving along in front of me. I kept a close watch on it nervously. It was slap bang in my flight path and worryingly, wasn't moving off or dispersing any time soon. I shortly caught up with the back end of the storm and I then had to seriously consider my next options. At first, I put the brakes on so to speak, as I did not want to fly within even 20 miles of this towering monster. Being able to fly extremely slowly is one of the great advantages of a gyroplane – it allowed me to loiter and skirt back and forth at a respectfully safe distance behind the storm, like a sheep dog herding sheep. However, as I watched, the storm continued to build up in the afternoon heat, widening and darkening ominously at its base. I knew there would be no easy option to get past it.

What to do?

I tried to skirt around to the left of my direct track, checking to see if there were any chinks of light which might indicate an easier path, but it all appeared too solid. During this diversion however I did overfly a remote desert road, with a road junction, a few isolated buildings and a petrol station. A plan of sorts then hatched in my head. I had been creeping along for some time behind the troublesome thunderstorm cell and I was concerned that my fuel reserves would soon be running low. I had already been flying for five hours at this point. My new plan was to land on the desert road and taxi into the petrol station to fuel up as this would then extend my range for the rest of the flight. Once back in the air, I could then continue to fly slowly onwards toward Riyadh while waiting for the thunderstorm to eventually move off my track.

I scanned the layout of my improvised runway, deciding to land on a quiet side road that spurred off the junction. The road was deserted and as I touched down, I quickly stopped the rotor blades so I could then safely backtrack to the junction and enter the slip road for the petrol station. I turned off the engine early so I could then roll to a full stop close to the petrol pumps. I was most happy to see that 95 octane was available, so I jumped out and quickly filled up with 100 litres, an amount that would give me another five full hours in the air if I needed it. Unsurprisingly, the young garage attendant had been quite amazed at my sudden arrival, and whilst I was only on the ground for about 20 minutes, word quickly got around the local area that a weird vehicle had pulled into the garage. Half a dozen local youths, driving battered pickups, suddenly turned up from out of the desert to see this crazy flying motorbike at their gas station. I felt like an outlaw in a wild west movie. Fuelling complete, I quickly saddled up my pony again and taxied the short distance back out onto the road to take off before any traffic appeared. Making sure to avoid the powerlines running close to the roadside, I was soon up and on my way once again.

The troublesome thunderstorm from earlier in the day had now, at long last, begun to move off my track. This allowed me to again proceed at a reasonable speed on towards Riyadh. I flew for a further hour and 30 minutes in relatively clear conditions, but I could see there were still many localised thunderstorms dotted around on the horizon.

I doggedly pushed on.

Every 20 minutes or so, I passed by a desert road and the odd time there was also some sort of farm, pumping station or outbuilding. Subconsciously, for safety, I took to spotting all of these small signs of human civilisation as I flew along, a habit which soon proved to be very fortuitous.

About an hour out from Riyadh's King Khalid International Airport, I began to pick up their approach traffic on the radio. I was still only in range to listen to them and not able to call them directly, but as the radio signal gradually became stronger and transmissions less broken, I was really surprised by what I was beginning to hear. Riyadh was currently diverting all incoming traffic away from its runway. In effect, the airport was now closed for all traffic movements, due to a large Category 4 thunderstorm cell sitting right above it. Riyadh-bound large commercial airliners were being re-routed and sent off to land elsewhere or given lengthy holding patterns before the airport would reopen.

"Damn," I thought. "If heavy aircraft with all their automated landing technology were being turned away, then there was absolutely no chance that I would be permitted to land either."

For the second time that day, I was in a dilemma about what to do. Unable to continue towards Riyadh, I decided my best course of action would be to turn around and fly back 30 miles towards a small alternative airfield I had spotted alongside some sort of desert pumping station. It was in the middle of nowhere but at least I might be safe there, sitting on the ground. I swung the aircraft around 180 degrees and glanced down to plot a direct course to steer on my GPS for the airfield.

Finding my bearings, I glanced up again to check the horizon. "Oh no!" I thought. "Surely not another one!" The sight before me made me grimace and I immediately recognised the seriousness of my predicament.

I had previously been completely unaware of it, but a second large thunderstorm had been lurking directly behind me. It was now sitting about 20 miles away, but squarely in the path I now needed to follow to reach my diversion airfield. I was effectively sandwiched between these two huge thunderstorm systems, and unfortunately they were slowly converging towards each other. Feeling suddenly very exposed and alone over the open desert, the sky was closing in on all sides and leaving me with nowhere to run.

I now really, really, needed to come up with another plan. And within 30 seconds or so of gritting my teeth and wracking my brain, in a flash an idea came to me. Oh boy! The gods were surely watching out for me this day.

About 10 miles previously, I had passed over yet another remote desert highway and next to it, I had spied yet another petrol station, possibly a mile over to the right of my track. Normally I would have glanced over at it for a second or two and then flown on, but for whatever reason, on this occasion I decided to veer off my track to go and have a closer look at it. It was certainly an isolated spot on the highway, and I pondered on how it could make any profitable income in such a remote place. Interestingly, as well as the standard petrol pump forecourt it had several outbuildings and also what seemed to be a large, open fronted shed. It was just a brief casual observation and I then thought no more about it and quickly reverted back onto my original compass bearing, still heading for Riyadh.

Well, within those 30 seconds of urgent plan searching, I suddenly remembered that my GPS was accurately plotting my previous track as I went along. I quickly checked back along my route on the Garmin 695 GPS screen and sure enough, I came to a part of my reasonably straight-line track that showed a slight kink, or squiggle in it. I knew instantly that that squiggle was where I had diverted across to see the petrol station. Bingo! All I now had to do was fly back to that point on the GPS and it would take me directly back overhead of the garage. The only problem however was that that also meant flying directly *towards* the rear thunderstorm, which was already creeping up ever closer. I simply had to reach that garage before the advancing storm front beat me to it. With a huge surge of adrenaline pumping through me, I knew the race was on.

I dropped lower in the increasingly strong headwind and increased power to achieve 100 mph, which was the VNE (velocity never to exceed) figure for the aircraft. I may have only had to fly back 10 miles, but it felt like 50. I focussed on flying as fast as possible and could now plainly see the towering storm front looming closer and closer ahead of me. A wall of dust was being kicked up by the squalling winds, with a thick belt of dark rain-bearing clouds following on closely behind. This was a brooding, menacing monster and yet incredibly, here I was, flying directly towards it at full speed!

With barely a mile to go and with much relief, I finally spotted the garage. Now all I had to do was reach it. I urgently scanned the adjoining highway and thankfully the road was completely empty of any traffic.

"At least that's one less thing to worry about," I thought.

I now really had to be careful. The wind was extremely volatile, aggressively buffeting me about in all directions. A successful landing could easily have been scuppered just before touchdown by a sudden violent downdraught or side sheer hitting me at the worst possible moment. I just had to hope that I could arrive close to the ground smoothly enough to land and not be dropped forcefully onto the tarmac from 10ft up in the air. The turbulence was unnervingly bumpy, like riding an out-of-control rollercoaster, but I kept fully focussed and fluid on the stick, throttle and pedals. I was half flying under control and half just reacting instinctively to each squall as it hit me. Cautious of slamming into the tarmac, I held off slightly and then allowed myself to drop in for a little bounce from 2ft and I was down.

Phew! Certainly not my prettiest landing, but hey, that had been the least of my worries!

I quickly applied the rotor brake to stop the main rotor before taxiing briskly off the highway and down the slip road onto the garage forecourt. Glancing around, I saw the open-fronted shed to my right and two Arabian petrol pump attendants running out of their doorway to my left. As cool as a cucumber and with no time to ask for permission, I simply waved at the attendants and drove the gyro straight into the shelter of their big open shed.

I shut everything down. Momentarily it all went quiet while I took my helmet off and took stock of what I had just achieved. Then an almighty deluge of rain hit the tin roof. I estimated that I probably touched down no more than five minutes before the storm front arrived. As I stared in amazement out of the shed doorway, sand, litter and debris were now being blown all over the place and the whole sky had turned brown. Visibility was so reduced that I could hardly make out a highway road sign, now rocking in the gusty wind barely 50m away. I felt euphoric to be safely down in one piece, but I was literally shaking from the enormity of this close call. I did not give a monkey's hoot that technically I had just made an unlawful landing on a public highway, nor that I was now an illegal alien in a country that had been unwilling to give me an entry visa. At this moment, such details were merely artificial, man-made obstacles, as opposed to the very real and much more powerful one Mother Nature had just thrown at me. I slowly climbed out of the cockpit and turned towards the door as two heads popped into view around the side wall of the shed.

The garage attendant at the first petrol station earlier in the day had been amazed when I dropped in out of the sky for fuel, but that reaction was trivial compared to that of my two new best Arabian friends. From the sheltered doorway of their small garage shop they had witnessed my whole arrival sequence, followed by the sudden onslaught of the storm minutes later. They knew as well as I did that it had been an exceedingly close race. I must have suddenly appeared like some storm-battered bird, being tossed about all over the sky and fighting desperately just to get down safely on the ground. I smiled broadly at them as they both continued to watch me from the doorway.

"Salaam," I said. It was the only Arabic word I knew, meaning 'Hello, peace be with you.'

My new best friends spoke no English at all. They smiled and continued to be amazed, speaking excitedly to each other, as they came forward to inspect *Roxy*. I gestured to be aware that the engine would still be hot if they accidentally touched it, and they smiled back at me, in mutual recognition of the danger. We were off to a good start, and I instinctively knew that I would be OK with these guys.

Then I had an idea and reached for my mobile phone. I was very relieved to find that I still had a signal, and quickly dialled the number of my English-speaking flight handling agents in Riyadh. I had spoken to them briefly before departing from Al Ta'if to give them my ETA, but time was ticking on and I was becoming overdue for my still expected arrival at their airport. With the aircraft-diverting thunderstorm closing down all flight operations, my handlers had become increasingly concerned about my whereabouts and were therefore happy to hear that I was now at least safely on the ground. I told them that I planned to stay overnight at the garage to allow the storms to pass and apologised for having to land out on the desert road, citing that it was a force majeure event beyond my control.

Being caught between the two thunderstorm cells, I urgently had to land when I did. I had no other options available. Thankfully my handlers and other airport staff were sympathetic and also proved to be very resourceful, by opting to keep my active flight plan 'open' overnight. In effect it was simply kept *under the desk* until the following morning before being reinstated again after I was airborne and proceeding on to Riyadh, continuing on as if nothing had happened. Before signing off the call, I handed my phone to the older of my two new best friends. The Riyadh handler was then able to explain everything about me and my world flight in Arabic, and this was followed by a lot of knowing expressions and nodding in my direction. From a situation that 15 minutes previously had been pretty desperate, things were now feeling a lot more optimistic.

***

I now sized up the prospect of spending the night in the Saudi desert with two Arabs and a white camel who, I suddenly realised, was gazing at me from over the wall at the back of the big shed. It was looking on, somewhat non-plussed, as if an aircraft dropping in to say hello was a normal everyday occurrence in these parts, and then continued to munch away on its bale of green alfalfa.

My friends and I had no common language between us, yet through sign language alone we ended up having a great evening together, even if it was all a bit surreal. The older of the pair was probably aged in his mid-40s, while the other was 20 or so years his junior. The older one was the easiest to communicate with. He was a similar age to me, had experienced a lot of life already and therefore just knew, or could accurately guess, a lot of what we needed to 'say' to each other. I quickly covered *Roxy* with her dust cover in a valiant attempt to keep out the worst of the light debris and sand that was still blowing madly about. Waving goodbye to the camel, all three of us then battled our way across the garage forecourt to the shop entrance. I was invited to sit down on a seat at the doorway and was supplied with some lovely hot chai tea. It was extremely sweet, but after the flight I had just endured it was very welcome. I drank three cups, one after the other, before even removing any of my flying suit. I then downed another two cups after that for good measure.

I glanced around the small shop. Wholesale food boxes sat about in piles, waiting to be eventually opened one day. These were interspersed with equally large piles of the long-life products that each of the wholesale boxes contained. Tinned goods, packaged nuts and dried fruits were all in plentiful supply. I got the impression that the delivery truck probably didn't need to call by very frequently to restock the shelves here. What did catch my eye though was the refrigerated cabinet. It had certainly seen better days but appeared to be still working and carried a small selection of recognisable foodstuffs. With a knowing nod from my hosts, meaning 'help yourself', I proceeded to choose some yoghurt, several cakes, nuts and a long-life flavoured milk drink to have for my 'dinner' later on.

It was now late afternoon and the storm front had rolled off into the distance. Weak and diminishing sunshine now filled the sky, and the air was once again calm without any real ambient noise, apart from the very occasional faint rumble from the far-off storms; no trees rustling their leaves, no birds tweeting in the growing twilight. The three of us just sat in long periods of silence, and I enjoyed the peace and quiet after such a hectic day.

Passing customers for the garage were thin on the ground at this time of day. Occasionally however, away off in the distance, a vehicle engine could be heard approaching. We would all then glance at each other and smile. I knew as well as them what they were thinking. A potential customer! To make more of the simple humour, I would look up and down the road and gesture, as if trying to work out from which direction the vehicle was approaching. As the noise grew louder, we could be more certain of its origin and then our three sets of eyes would peer intently and expectantly off in that direction. As we shifted up to the edge of our seats, hopes of catching a customer would gradually rise. But time and time again, the passing vehicle would not slow down. It would just cruise on by at top speed, leaving us only to raise our eyes and shrug our shoulders in that universal sign of 'all hopes dashed'. We would then slump back down in our seats and return to the little calm oasis of our silent world.

Through our ongoing sign language, I established that the garage would shut at 10pm and open again at 6am. Although they were going to lock up the garage, I was going to be allowed to sleep in one of their outhouse rooms. I later found out that it is quite common in these more remote places for petrol stations to have some basic accommodation like this, so that road repair workers might stay close by their work. When I say basic, it was exactly that; simply a large, thick carpet on the floor to lie on and a rickety old air conditioning unit rattling away by the window. My room wasn't that bad though as numerous big beetles seemed to be quite at home and happily willing to share their floorspace with me. Out came my trusty sleeping bag again and I spent some time trying to process the day's events in my head while listening to light rain falling on the roof. Me, *Roxy* and a camel, all bedded down in the middle of the desert, miles from anywhere. How truly bizarre. As I drifted off into some well-needed sleep, I thought I could not have ever made up this scenario, even if I had tried. And who was it who said that it was never supposed to rain in the desert...

12 April 2010: Petrol station two (overnight), Saudi Arabia – Riyadh, Saudi Arabia – Doha, Qatar

I had slept very well again, as with other recent nights, through exhaustion as much as anything else. My two hosts were back and pleased to see me emerge, a little bleary eyed, from my workman's hut. Breakfast was a re-run of the same menu selection from last night and washed down with more hot chai. The weather was now bright and clear, putting me once more in a buoyant mood. I repacked *Roxy* and pushed her to the petrol pumps to top up again on 95 octane fuel. While parked up at the pump I ran out and took a few photos of the aircraft. It was such a marvellous scene, *Roxy* and my two Arab hosts at the pumps with the garage and desert in the background. We bargained in sign language on how much I owed for everything. We quickly reached agreement that a full tank of gas, dinner, bed and breakfast came to the grand total of US$20.

I put in a quick call to Riyadh and suited up. The road was now busier in the morning, but I soon found a long gap in the traffic and took off easily. I circled low over the garage to wave my goodbyes. My hosts waved back madly, but alas the chilled-out camel didn't even lift its head up from its breakfast. I was off and running once more.

A short time later, but unbeknown to me, my 2004 bowel cancer consultant oncologist, Mr. Harte, happened to be passing through a busy tube station in London. Amongst the throng of commuters, by chance he glanced over the shoulder of a man reading the daily *Metro* newspaper. He couldn't believe his eyes. The picture of the day printed large across the page featured a little yellow gyroplane parked up at a petrol pump in the middle of the Saudi desert. He smiled to himself, for he recognised instantly who that belonged to. I was only retold this story the following winter while attending Mr. Harte's clinic in Belfast for my routine annual cancer check-up. I was not actually scheduled to see the great man himself, as (thankfully) by this time I was no longer one of his main priority patients. I was to be seen by one of his junior consultants, but as soon as he heard I was in the building he came rushing in to tell me the story of the chance encounter. We were both quite amazed at the coincidence of it all.

But I digress dear reader, let's get back to the desert....

To my relief, the final completion flight over to Riyadh was uneventful, with a total flight time of only one hour and 30 minutes.

I was greeted warmly on arrival with a few knowing looks from the handlers. The stop in Riyadh no longer needed to be overnight, and I only really needed to pass through in order to officially leave the country via an international airport. Customs was a formality as I had never actually entered the country for immigration purposes (cough... ahem... say no more...), so I was only required to be on the ground for little over an hour. Even so, the landing fees and charges were still in excess of US$500.

Once again, I queried the steepness of the charges put on my privately funded, small-scale, charity flight, only to be politely laughed at by the admin officials.

"But Captain, for our country US$500 is such a small amount. It's like nothing!"

"Well, if you think it's 'like nothing', why don't *you* just pay it for me?" I retorted.

All went quiet. He had no answer.

Once again, as with Egypt, I found it quite a relief to be getting off the ground and flying onwards into a new country. Saudi had been very interesting, I had met some really nice, genuinely friendly people, but the strict rules, inflexibility and tight bureaucracy governing so many aspects of normal peoples' lives did make it difficult to remain positive and upbeat.

Just as I thought the dramas of the Saudi desert were finally behind me, I experienced another form of sandstorm as I headed towards the Qatar border. A light, hazy dust seemed to billow up and envelop the gyro, even while I was up at 1500ft. I was engulfed in the middle of what felt like an opaque fishbowl. I could still just about see definition on the ground below me, but visibility in all other directions was extremely limited. I considered, briefly, climbing to the clearer skies above but reasoned it was much better to remain with a constant visual sight of the ground, even if that view was poor. Thankfully I was still in radar contact with Riyadh control, so I took slight comfort that at least they could alert me of any conflicting traffic, if any happened to be heading my way. Flying was difficult, as my only sense of perspective was while I was staring directly down towards the ground and there were no other horizon references at all. Happily, the sensation was short lived and within 15 minutes the sky was clearing again. I then knew I was through the worst of it.

On reaching Qatar airspace, I was vectored on a very circuitous routing, right around the whole coastline, to reach Doha. It was blamed on *military airspace restrictions,* which in this region, as with many others around the modern world, could mean just about anything. Still, I was happy to be making good progress once again in fine weather, and after the recent testing time in the desert, I looked forward to reaching the much more comfortable surroundings of Doha's Hamad International Airport. I experienced a very fast landing at Doha, as for some reason (that was never explained) all traffic was being required to land down wind.

Doha is a major hub airport for the whole of the Middle East region and this was very evident immediately on my arrival. A 'Follow Me' car was sent to escort me in from the taxiway and led me on a lengthy, 20-minute circuitous route, seemingly around the whole airport perimeter to reach my allotted stand.

The terminal buildings were now miles away, but at least a few cargo planes were dotted about nearby, so I wasn't entirely on my own. It was such a contrast to the previous night sitting in the cosy confines of the Saudi petrol station. Like in Egypt, the local handlers then gave me their 'full service' treatment. Once again it felt very odd to be the only passenger on a 50-seat bus, when I could have simply jumped in the front passenger seat of the 'Follow Me' car that promptly arrived back at the terminal the same time as I did.

I was then processed as a normal international arrivals passenger. After the Saudi desert, it was such a contrast walking through an ultra-modern, well-equipped airport, with air-conditioned shops and cafés. A very helpful lady at the information counter assisted me with booking accommodation. She soon found me a budget two-star hotel (which after the desert felt more like five-star), and sensing I needed further help, she also proceeded to accompany me out to the taxi rank. She had a word with the taxi manager and emphasised that it was pre-arranged for the taxi driver to be paid directly by my hotel (and the charge to me was subsequently added to my hotel bill). I thought this was a slightly odd arrangement until she took me to one side and quietly explained that this would ensure that in order to be paid, the taxi driver would have to take me directly to *my* preferred, fairly priced hotel and not to *his* 'preferred' hotel, the one where he would no doubt have received a handsome backhander for delivering yet another unsuspecting tourist (along with my fare).

What a nice lady! My hotel-booking guardian angel had well and truly scuppered this frequent scam, and the sideways glaring glance that the taxi driver and the taxi manager exchanged with each other spoke volumes. Smiling to myself, I cheerfully loaded my bags onto the back seat.

13 April 2010: Doha, Qatar – Abu Dhabi, United Arab Emirates

My two-star hotel had at least the five-star luxury of hot running water, so I was able to do some much-needed washing to get the Saudi desert sand out of my clothes. Returning to *Roxy*, I spent the time needed for my daily pre-flight checks to also hang out my washing. I must admit that for any casual onlooker in the Etihad first-class cabin, who happened to glance out of their window while taxiing to the runway, it must have seemed like quite the bohemian scene. There *Roxy* was, flanked by a long-haul 747 cargo plane on one side and a short-haul turbo-prop business aircraft on the other, but she was the only aircraft in the entire international jet set fleet that had a very chic row of socks lined up over her rudder, a crumpled T-shirt over her starboard tail fin and several pairs of pants hanging off her propeller blades. The reality of flying around the world in your own aircraft was not always quite so glamorous as it sounds! At least on the plus side, the morning breeze was so warm that all my washing was bone dry in just 30 minutes.

I was able to pick up avgas after a short airfield taxi run to the flight training school compound. Had I been made aware of their presence on arrival, I would have requested to overnight with them instead of being put out on the commercial apron. A lost opportunity, as I am sure I would have been well cared for by the staff I met during refuelling. One of whom even gave me a very generous charity donation.

I was now mentally preparing to head back out over water once again, this time straight across the southern Persian Gulf for a direct-route, two hour and 30 minute flight to Abu Dhabi. However, almost immediately I encountered a serious problem on the climb-out from Doha. ATC had assigned me a squawk code to use on my radar transponder. This four-digit code would help to identify me on all the controller's various radar screens, but on this occasion, they were having difficulty spotting me. It appeared that my transponder unit was only working intermittently, so the controller requested that I 'squawk ident', which meant I pressed a button on the transponder to make my identity flash up more visibly on their radar screen. This helped, but it still seemed my signal remained intermittent as I continued to Abu Dhabi.

As I made my final approach, it was clear that the intermittency problem had not got any better, but fortunately Abu Dhabi ATC still allowed me to land, so that I could then hopefully get everything sorted out on the ground. This was a major issue as without a working transponder, I would simply not be permitted to fly in the very congested and tightly controlled airspace around any of the world's major international airports. The radar controllers could not afford to have a small, slow-moving aircraft become effectively invisible on their screens. I would now urgently have to find a workable solution.

Taxiing in at Abu Dhabi, I was allocated parking alongside the local commercial helicopters. *Roxy* attracted plenty of attention on the apron, especially when people heard I had just made the over-water crossing from Doha. Later, I was allowed to push the aircraft into the helo workshop hangar for the night.

A few days previously I had been emailed by Tony Cowan of the UK Civil Air Patrol Sky Watch organisation. He had a good contact in Abu Dhabi called Jim Martin, who was working as a helicopter pilot with the Abu Dhabi Police Air Wing unit. It was quickly arranged that I would be able to stay with Jim at his city apartment for a couple of days. After so many nights spent alone in quiet hotel rooms, I was glad of the opportunity to have some good company. That night we had a great chat together, along with Jim's mate Dave, when we all went out for dinner.

14 April 2010: Abu Dhabi, United Arab Emirates (non-flying day)

I enjoyed the chance to have a non-flying day and used the time to sleep, give a radio interview and meet up with Hussein, the local agent for Rotax engine spares. I needed to pick up spare oil and an oil filter so I would be ready to get an engine service completed whenever the opportunity arose in the next few days. Hussein was an incredibly easy-going, relaxed guy and we enjoyed a pleasant conversation over an extended lunch by the harbour.

15 April 2010: Abu Dhabi, United Arab Emirates – Al Bateen, United Arab Emirates – Muscat, Oman

With my batteries recharged, I was ready for an early start. Once back at the airport, with the heat of the day rapidly building, I re-packed *Roxy* in the shade of the hangar. My transponder had been checked on my arrival, but all that had been found was a slightly loose-fitting clip. I wasn't happy with the idea that nothing definite had been found, and my fears were confirmed on take-off. I was quickly notified by the ATC radar operator that I still had an intermittent fault when in the air. I simply couldn't continue my world flight without the transponder working perfectly, so I elected to quickly set down again, at a small executive jet airfield referred to as Al Bateen. It was only a 10-minute flight and Abu Dhabi ATC were kindly able to permit me to fly there without my transponder.

Safely back on the ground, I arranged to meet up once again with Hussein, who was quite unbelievable in his generosity. He had earlier organised refuelling for me, but upon now learning that my transponder was still playing up, immediately went on to offer me a working unit from one of his own aircraft. Transponders are very expensive, yet he refused to take no for an answer. He speedily arranged installation and testing of the swapped over unit, along with an impromptu lunch for both of us at a hastily set up table in the hangar.

With time ticking on, I became ever more concerned about getting airborne as soon as possible. The delayed flight across the Red Sea into Jeddah had warned me of the dangers of leaving too late in the day, and there was no way that I wanted to end up landing in the dark again. My worries were soon alleviated however, as Hussein's aircraft engineers had made short work of *Roxy*'s repairs. I thanked Hussein and his team profusely. Without his kind generosity, I would have been grounded there and then. Quite simply, he had kept the whole show on the road.

Just before departure, Jim dropped by to wish me a bon voyage through the perimeter fence. Some months later I would receive a cryptic message from him that he had found a lost sock of mine, which I'd misplaced while 'sofa surfing' at his apartment. A picture of the said sock was even posted online, and I was able to reply that I was still in possession of its twin.

The flight into Oman had the most dramatic scenery that I'd witnessed so far in the Middle East. Originally, I had planned to head up the coast to Dubai, but with all the unscheduled transponder delays, I opted to fly a more direct route straight towards Muscat instead. The dramatic topography of Oman's interior however posed a significant challenge. There were reassuring highways to follow, but on either side, these were flanked by rugged mountains with the most brutally jagged and sculpted terrain that I had ever seen. Rainfall erosion of the soft arid rock faces had certainly taken its toll, giving each peak a sharply defined edge. And each gully between the peaks was an equally sharply defined, deep V shape. If not for the roads, there would have been nowhere to land safely in this environment. The ridgelines were so sharp that it would have been impossible for *Roxy* to remain balanced atop of them, and the gullies were so steep that I feared the rotor would probably strike the side walls before my aircraft's wheels even touched down.

By comparison, the smooth, snaking tarmac of the desert highway looked much more friendly for use in an emergency, even though I would still have to take my chances with the busy convoys of trucks rattling and smoking along its length. Only when I reached the coastal plains of the Gulf of Oman, to the north-west of Muscat, did the scenery once more flatten out. Similar to some areas of the Saudi desert, I then flew over isolated hills that looked more like huge boulders scattered about on an endless beach.

On first contact with Muscat ATC, they opted to route me towards the airport in a very roundabout fashion, instructing me to fly a long, positioning loop out over the sea. I would have much preferred to continue along the coastline, but who was I to argue. This was a busy international airport, and I had no option but to comply and maintain the impression that I was happy enough with their instructions.

On landing I was put on a stand that was only a short walk into the terminal building, which was great news. Not so great however was my experience shortly afterwards at the aircrew desk, where I requested a free overnight visitor's visa. It should have been a painless formality, but instead I got hassled by the airport police chief.

"You cannot be a pilot. Where is your uniform? he stated.

"Yes, I am a private pilot. I have just arrived here in my own aircraft," I retorted.

"But where is your pilot's shirt and captain's stripes?" he quizzed.

"Not all pilots have to wear a uniform. My aircraft has an open cockpit, so I need to wear a special protective flight suit instead. Here are my documents, UKCAA pilot's licence and AOPA pilot ID. You can also see that my aircraft is sitting just outside the window."

Several minutes of heated debate later, the police chief finally relented. I was in the right and all the evidence was now stacked against him.

"OK, OK, you can have the overnight visa," he grumbled "but next time, be sure you are wearing a pilot's uniform."

As I smiled sweetly and thanked him for his understanding, I was muttering, "What a complete Jobsworth!" under my breath.

A couple of other pilots, who had also been waiting in line, sympathised with me and offered to give me a lift to a local hotel that gave good stopover aircrew rates. While we were all checking in, they were telling me that they had heard of a big volcanic eruption going on in Iceland. The volcanic ash plume from Eyjafjallajökull was disrupting air travel in wide areas of Europe, with many aircraft grounded. I wondered if it would adversely affect me in any way later in the flight.

5

Indian subcontinent: Pakistan to Bangladesh

16 April 2010: Muscat, Oman – Gwadar, Pakistan

I arrived back at Muscat Airport at 8am, however such was the lengthy bureaucracy that my actual departure ended up being at 1.15pm, right at the hottest part of the day. It was sweltering enough out on the apron, but as I was about to fly over the Gulf of Oman to Gwadar in Pakistan, I was also suited and booted in my full immersion suit. Sitting there, with all the zips and seals done up, I knew exactly how a boil-in-the-bag meal feels when it is immersed in a cooking pot.

Being incredibly cautious of the upcoming sea crossing, I initially thought I had a radio problem because my transmissions with the tower were weak and broken, but thankfully the signal strength greatly improved once the engine had fired into life. With a renewed dose of confidence and an equal dose of nervous adrenaline, I was off.

Next stop, Pakistan!

Having already crossed both the Mediterranean and the Red Sea, my psychological fears of lengthy over-water flying had decreased considerably. And by comparison, the flight over the Gulf of Oman was thankfully quite uneventful. The weather was kind, only some wispy high clouds above and a few light and fluffy cotton wool ones out on the horizon. Accurately following a compass course could often be quite hard going, especially out over a desolate featureless seascape, but having those slow-moving clouds off in the far distance (that were roughly in the right direction) proved to be ideal to aim at. I still regularly checked and updated my course heading with the compass and GPS every 20 miles or so, but for ease of navigation, I could rely for extended periods to simply point at, say, the third fluffy cloud from the left. It reduced my cognitive workload and yet still proved accurate enough for what would soon turn out to be one of the most tightly controlled sea transits I would make on the whole circumnavigation.

Whilst flight planning earlier in the morning with the tower staff in Muscat, I was instructed that I would have to fly a dog leg course across the Gulf of Oman. Marked on the charts and projecting like a shallow V shape down from the north, an international flight boundary cut right across the mid-point of my direct track towards Gwadar and denoted a highly sensitive block of airspace. I was told that under no circumstances should I try to take a shortcut across this zone. The airspace belonged to Iran, and I was informed that if I were to wander into this area unannounced, I could easily panic everyone in the region and possibly even end up being shot down. There was simply no other option, I had to fly a dog leg towards the south to avoid any potential *diplomatic unpleasantness.* To minimise the crossing distance, I used the southernmost corner of the block of Iranian airspace as my mid-crossing waypoint. Once past this point, I could then relax a little, turn further north again and set a direct course aiming for the relative safety of the Pakistan coastline.

Yet as I made my way across the Gulf of Oman, a slightly maverick plan formed in my head. There was absolutely no air or sea traffic anywhere in my vicinity. I had flown past a few container ships plying the seas below, but even these were very few and far between. I was effectively on my own. To stave off the boredom of sitting for three plus hours over the sea, I began to ponder on how finely tuned the resolution of the Iranian airspace zone would be on a radar screen and how that would look for an Iranian controller. At a range of over a hundred miles out over the horizon, flying low and hugging the ocean surface, I doubted I would be detected at all from any Iranian land-based radar stations due to the curvature of Earth. In theory, I could have still been detected by another aircraft or ship somewhere nearby, but even this would still have to be tens of miles away for me to not have seen it visually. On balance, I felt it was safe enough to implement my rebellious plan. Just as I approached my mid-crossing waypoint, I crossed the zone boundary line (as plotted on my GPS screen) into the southernmost corner of Iranian airspace and flew a little tight circle. This was then plotted on my screen as a dotted line trail behind my aircraft. It couldn't have been much more than 200m in diameter, a perfect little artistic loop; and then just as quickly as I had entered, I flew back out of the airspace again.

I figured any controller would not have had the screen resolution to be able to see my manoeuvre. In the grand scale of things, my little orbit, if noticed at all, was probably hidden by the thickness of the pixels plotting the airspace boundary line on the radar screen.

I had just busted unannounced into Iranian airspace (well, for about a minute at least) and had lived to tell the tale!

* * *

Other than it being ridiculously hot, I had really no idea of what kind of reception to expect upon arrival in the small, dusty town of Gwadar. I hadn't even heard of it prior to my flight planning, but it just happened to be the nearest Pakistani international airport that I could use after crossing from Oman. Being only a few miles from the Iranian border, it had understandably tight security, especially in and around the airport. Yet upon my arrival on the apron, I was greeted warmly, with smiling staff streaming out of their small terminal building to welcome me with open arms. I felt at ease right away, and it was clear that I was no longer in the Middle East. Although the people surrounding me were from another different culture altogether, it was one that felt strangely familiar to me.

For security reasons, it was decided that the only accommodation

I could stay at was a huge palatial mansion situated high up on a ridge, overlooking the town. I began to understand their decision more clearly when I was personally delivered to the hotel in the airport security chief's own pickup truck. I was strategically placed in the middle of the back seat, with a security guard on each side of me, while two more literally rode 'shotgun' (armed with rifles) perched up in the back on the tail gate. As we drove fast through the dusty streets, dodging and weaving about in the loose sand, I noticed we also had a second truck, acting as backup, following closely behind us. It was like we were in a mini-presidential motorcade. The downtown buildings were all only one-story high and looked to be of a mud/sandy brick construction. The roads, walls, roofs, backyards, everywhere was the same dusty beige colour. Wind-blown sand dunes on the streets, mixed with a scattering of cavernously deep potholes, made the journey as violently hard and bumpy as it was at times suddenly soft and sinky. The vehicles drifted and rallied around the bends at high speeds.

I couldn't quite believe the contrast. Barely an hour before I had been flying along, peacefully calm and dust free, out over the Gulf of Oman and yet now, it felt I was a passenger in the leading truck of the Dakar Rally. The *transporting Mr. President* high-security measures continued, right up to ushering me through an airport-style metal detector at the hotel. As at Jeddah, I was then told for my own safety, not to leave the hotel overnight. I instantly thought to myself "Don't worry mate, after that delivery ride, I'm not planning on going anywhere."

Later in the evening, it dawned on me while I was ordering food, why I had such a strange sense of familiarity for a country that I had never visited before. I was handed the menu at the bar and perused the dishes on offer.

"I hope the menu is OK for you to read sir," said the barman.

A quick glance of recognition, and I was able to cheerily reply.

"Actually yes, this menu is no problem at all. It's just like being back home!"

I went on to explain to him that about 80% of the dishes on the menu could have been taken straight out of a typical Pakistani curry house in the UK. Back in my student days, I lived for several years in and around Bradford in West Yorkshire, which has a large and vibrant ethnic Pakistani community. So needless to say, I was quite comfortable making my way around a curry menu. After that, the rest of the evening went very well, although as a reminder of where I actually was, we did also have two power cuts that plunged the whole hotel into darkness.

17 April 2010: Gwadar, Pakistan – Karachi, Pakistan

The next stage of the Dakar Rally (shotgun class) to deliver me safely back to the airport, got under way after breakfast. What did I eat? Yet another delicious curry. Well, why not? When in Rome and all that...

A similar route was taken through the streets as the previous evening, only this time we stopped briefly to pick up fuel for *Roxy*. I wanted to see the condition and quality of the petrol pumps first-hand, but I then quickly wished I hadn't. My motorcade was immediately drawing in a crowd and attracting a lot of unwanted, potentially dangerous attention, so the decision was taken to forgo the fuel and head directly back to the airport. I was told that the fuel would then be delivered to me there.

Sure enough, not long after I was safely back in the secure area of the airport, 50 litres of gasoline duly appeared in a battered blue plastic barrel. After some excitable discussion on the best way to proceed, it was eventually hoisted up onto a raised platform and siphoned directly down into my fuel tanks via my trusty water-separating fuel filter. This device, which automatically separates fuel from water and other foreign particulates, was essential, especially when dealing with any fuel sources of unknown providence or pedigree. In practice, evidence of water was extremely rare, though particulates less so; but *not* finding something was exactly the point. It gave a welcome boost of confidence and reassurance, that the engine wouldn't suddenly start to splutter and struggle soon after take-off.

While refuelling was underway and quite by chance, the British

Assistant High Commissionaire to Pakistan casually strolled up and introduced himself. He had travelled to Gwadar on other government business when he learned that a British registered aircraft was currently passing through. We had a pleasant, albeit quick chat, about my journey so far, and he offered any consular assistance that might be needed while I was in the country. We squeezed in a quick photo together and then he was off again onto his next appointment.

Because of the ongoing heightened political tensions in the region, the safest plan for my journey through Pakistan was to fly directly along the coastline until eventually turning inland to land at Jinnah International Airport in Karachi. As with nearby Iranian airspace, under no circumstances was I to wander off route and fly over any of the interior of the country.

The Pakistani airports were secure enough and I was fine while I was up in the air, the only slight uncertainty was if I had to land out somewhere en route. This could not be fully predicted of course, but in any event, sticking to the coastal region was deemed to be my safest route.

As it happened, I thoroughly enjoyed this four-hour flight. I had a nice tailwind to hurry me along, visibility was good and navigation was easy (just keep the sea to my right). Best of all, I had been assigned a specially arranged routing that would keep me away from all other possible traffic, so the sky was empty. As with the sharp, rugged mountains in Oman, here too were at times some extremely jaggy, highly eroded hills, but at least I often also had a flat beach or shoreline to aim for during any emergency. The heat of the day was building, so I elected to fly up at 5500ft to maintain a comfortable temperature. This worked very well, but there was no escaping the heat when I eventually came to my final descent into Karachi – it suddenly felt like I was flying down into a huge fan oven.

Approaching Karachi, I passed over the world's largest shipbreaking yard at Gaddani. I had previously seen some YouTube clips of ships that were brought here to be scrapped on the beach. After being rammed at full speed as far up onto the sand as possible, they were then unceremoniously chopped up into manageable pieces, largely by hand with gas-powered cutting equipment. It was an incredible sight to behold from the air. Ship after ship after ship, all lined up for miles along the beach, and all sitting at different stages of dismantlement. This nautical graveyard was also my waypoint to turn left and head a few miles inland directly towards the airport.

The destruction, however, continued.

Yet it was no longer the physical butchering of the ships themselves, rather it was an even worse kind of destruction, that of the environment. There was a clearly visible, heavily rust-stained contamination of the ground spreading for miles inland towards the scrap metal smelting plant. It was such a shame to see after the wild, remote and rugged natural beauty that I had witnessed on much of the coastline.

As I made a slow descent through 3000ft, I could already sense how uncomfortably hot it was going to be on the ground. It was the dry season and ground temperatures of over 40°C were regarded as quite normal at this time of year. Although this was a better time to cross the Indian subcontinent than during the upcoming monsoons, I was certainly now paying a high price for it – I was literally paying for it in sweat.

On arrival, I was put on a stand close under the Karachi Control Tower. Again, as with Gwadar, I had a welcoming reception, but I was also really melting in the heat. *Roxy* too was suffering as the glue holding some of the labels onto her instrument panel was starting to melt.

I hurriedly draped my yellow cover over the aircraft to provide at least some shade from the relentless sun. But while doing so I spotted, not 50m away, what looked like a lean-to shed.

"How about we all push the gyro over into the shaded area under that open roof canopy over there," I said to the gathered entourage. "That way we can all get out of this fierce heat and cool off a bit."

"Wait Captain. I'll radio the tower to ask if we can do that for you," came the helpful and optimistic reply.

"Sorry Captain. It is not possible. It is not allowed. Your aircraft has to stay here, exactly on the stand," came his apologetic reply.

The inflexible nonsense of petty bureaucracy strikes again!

"Fine, fine, no problem. We'll all just continue to boil out here until the sun goes down," I said to myself in defeat.

Why couldn't they just have made a one-off allowance, for one night only, for one highly vulnerable open cockpit aircraft to be pushed under a simple lean-to roof? It was hardly asking for much. After all, no other type of aircraft, other than a gyroplane, was even capable of such a feat. Those with *sticky out wings* simply wouldn't have fitted, while those other *whirlybirds* that sit on skids would simply have stayed stuck firmly to the ground out on the apron. It was a wholly wasted opportunity.

At least I had one piece of good luck. Rather than needing to go off foraging for fuel, Dakar Rally style, I was able to source what was loosely termed as 'high octane petrol' from the airport's own airside vehicle fuel station.

Fuelling completed, I was given a lift to a local hotel, and I had my first experience of the somewhat chaotic city streets. Cairo had been bad enough, and Gwadar felt like it was more off road than on, but Karachi turned out to be far worse. I saw an ancient passenger bus, already packed to the gunnels, with easily an extra 20 or more people sitting up on the roof. This was quickly followed by a mother holding a baby on the back of a motorbike, while two older kids were perched up on the handlebars and the petrol tank. The streets in this early evening rush hour were heaving with traffic of all shapes and sizes; huge trucks were belching smoke and blaring horns and overloaded motorbikes were squeezing through inconceivable gaps. To the uninitiated, it just appeared as uncontrolled mayhem.

Interestingly, while stuck in traffic jams, I could see that many of the trucks were hand painted with very intricate, brightly coloured coachwork designs. Even the rusty undersides of the trucks were adorned with ornate patterns, carefully painted right down to the very axles and the transmission bell housing.

In the evening, I was invited out to attend a university staff house party in an upmarket suburb of Karachi. It was a very pleasant evening, spent sitting around chatting. The calm, leafy suburban atmosphere made a lovely contrast to the jostling vibrancy that I had witnessed earlier in the city centre.

18 April 2010: Karachi, Pakistan – Ahmadabad, India

I tried to depart early from Karachi but was delayed while I waited for the airport manager to attend. At the last minute, I was told that he wanted to have his photo taken with me and to wish me bon voyage for the benefit of the press. I was not best pleased as for the past half hour, I had already been fully suited up in preparation for the flight across to India and I had also just been presented with yet another hefty bill for airport and handling fees. After a considerable further wait, he eventually turned up, not realising all the bother he was causing, and we all quickly lined up to take the required photos. Time was ticking on and I knew I still had a flight of some four hours and 30 minutes ahead of me.

The weather en route was changeable, and I encountered yet another form of localised dust storm. Over Saudi Arabia it had been dust and fine sand billowing up to reach quite a height. Here by contrast, the dust and golden sand, remained low and swirled over the surface terrain and features. From my high vantage point, it just looked like liquid gold flowing over and around the undulating ground. It was mesmerising and quite beautiful to look at. But I had to remind myself that a forced landing in these conditions would have been very tricky, as I would not have been able to gauge the depth of the swirling sands, nor the layout or makeup of the underlying terrain. Thankfully, the challenging conditions were short lived and soon enough I was flying with reasonably clear ground visibility once more.

As the flight wore on, the landscape began taking on a more and more whitish appearance. I tried to work out what was going on, but eventually a nearby salty lake gave me the best clue. Salt (or some other similar mineral deposit) had leached to the surface of the soil, and now gave the gently undulating hills a striking brilliant white, wintery appearance. It reminded me very much of flying over the Yorkshire Dales in the snow. For my amusement, I played with this idea a bit further in my mind. By squinting my eyes a little, I could easily imagine the scene below me to really be the snow-covered fells of the north of England. For added effect, I whistled the theme tune of the popular BBC series *All Creatures Great and Small,* featuring the charmed rural life of a Yorkshire vet, James Herriot. I loved reading the stories while I was growing up; they were full of real solid characters and creative observations on country living. Mrs. Pumphrey and her Pekinese dog, *Tricky Woo* were my favourite characters. Tricky Woo would send his 'Uncle Herriot' a huge food hamper from Fortnum & Mason every Christmas, so of course the dog was looked after very well all through the year.

* * *

Alas I digress yet again dear reader, I was not now in North Yorkshire, I was crossing the border between Pakistan and India.

The sun beating down every day was becoming relentless. I could fly at a comfortable altitude for ambient air temperature, but my face and especially my nose was becoming ever more weather-beaten with every flight. Despite slapping on factor 50 sunscreen, my nose had become quite red. So as I flew along, I fashioned a page of my notebook into an origami-style nose guard. This was then held in place by tucking it under my sunglasses, and it actually worked a treat. Admittedly it didn't look very *James Bond,* but hey, no one could see me up here anyway. All I had to remember was to take it off before coming in to land and no one would be any the wiser.

Landing at Sardar Vallabhbhai Patel International Airport in Ahmadabad in north-western India, I was directed across to a large maintenance hangar. The plan was to overnight *Roxy* here so that she could have an engine service in the morning. Luggage removed and dust cover on, *Roxy* was then safely tucked up for the night, but before I was eventually able to leave the airport, I was to get my first taste of Indian bureaucracy working at its best.

A full 45 minutes of form filling, by two staff members, was needed to ascertain that I was due to pay the grand sum of US$4 of tax to complete the entry customs formalities. With hindsight, I should have just given them US$10 at the outset and told them to keep the change, at least then I might have bought myself 45 minutes of much needed extra sleep. I was now in an odd time-zone, 5.5 hours ahead of UTC. Constantly flying eastbound, I was losing an hour of time zone every few days and invariably that often translated into an hour less sleep at night.

19 April 2010: Ahmadabad, India – Nagpur, India

Heading down for breakfast, I was greeted in the lobby by a journalist with a long grey beard. He had been waiting patiently to conduct an interview for his press agency so that he could report on my journey so far, flying from the UK to India. We sat and chatted as I had my meal. He was a lovely character and like many older people, I could read from his face that he must have reported on a rich tapestry of local events during his career.

Returning to the airport, I had the usual hassle of getting through the many layers of airport security. Each stage seemingly had several essential forms to complete before I was eventually allowed through to reach my aircraft in the hangar. Only then, once I had arrived, could the local Rotax engineer set about his important work of servicing the engine. About an hour later all was completed to his satisfaction, and we finished up by signing off the aircraft log books.

Taxiing out for departure I was given an option by ATC.

"Golf Yankee Romeo Oscar X-ray, are you ready for an immediate departure?"

I wondered momentarily what the sudden urgency was all about. And then I saw the issue. A large dust storm was encroaching towards the runway. If I was quick, I would be able to take off before it arrived. If not, it was going to be quite a while before I would get take-off clearance again.

"Tower, this is Golf Oscar X-ray. Affirm. I will expedite departure to clear the dust storm," I confirmed.

"Oscar X-ray, you are clear for immediate take-off."

I quickly lined up and got off the ground as soon as possible. ATC routed me away from the advancing dust cloud and I was once more on my way. Looking back, I could see the thick density of the dust and the sheer size of the storm from above. I was lucky to get away when I did, as it would not have been at all pleasant sitting on the taxiway waiting for it to clear whilst getting sandblasted.

* * *

I was excited about the prospect of flying right across the Indian subcontinent in the next few days. Apart from the constant hassle of getting to and from the aircraft at each stop-over, and no shortage of quite pointless paperwork, the journey proved to be fascinating. At times, the land was well cultivated, set out neatly in clearly defined fields and marked out with hedges and trees. Country roads and smaller tracks wended their way through the landscape, so much so that I could easily imagine I was flying over the rolling gentle hills of southern England. Only there was one main difference, everything here was brown.

It was nearing the peak of the dry season, about six weeks before the annual monsoons would begin, and all the vegetation had browned off. The soil had seemingly turned to dust and the air close to the surface was often hazy. I preferred to fly up at about 5500ft in these conditions, primarily to have a comfortably cool air temperature, but also to avoid flying through the worst of the murky air below me. From this vantage point looking down, I saw lots of perfectly round water wells dotted about in the fields. Their uppermost walls and rim were often painted white, giving the impression that they were hundreds of buried long-range missile silos planted in the landscape.

From time to time, I also saw the odd forest fire, adding yet more hazy smoke to the already soupy atmosphere. One fire I happened upon however, was noticeably bigger than all the rest. From 5000ft I could clearly see the long red ribbon of the fire's leading edge burning fiercely, even through the billowing smoke. The flames appeared vividly bright, almost like how a river of molten red lava might look, cutting through the grey-brown smoke.

I enjoyed a fabulous tailwind that stayed with me all the way across to Nagpur. By the second half of the flight, having burned off some weight of fuel, I was constantly tramping along at over 100 mph ground speed. On my VHF radio, I was monitoring 121.5 MHz when a call came through from the pilot of a passing airliner, flying high above me and no doubt whizzing past at five times my own groundspeed. He asked for my current position and an ETA update for Nagpur, the details of which I quickly calculated and passed back to him. He then relayed that information on to Nagpur ATC and then bid me farewell and good luck for the rest of my journey. It was always nice to receive these calls, often quite literally out of the blue. Each time it showed that somewhere at least, an ATC unit was keeping an eye out for me.

I was now flying well away from the cooler effects of the coastline, right into the middle of the country. The result was an even hotter landing in Nagpur, where the mercury was hitting 47°C. Help!

20 April 2010: Nagpur, India – Raipur, India

My overnight hotel had been quite close to the airport and this helped in my quest to be away as early as possible, thereby avoiding the hottest part of the day. My first task on leaving the hotel was to source fuel, so I arranged for an airport pickup truck to help me. We headed off into the local suburbs to find a petrol station, but the first one we tried looked a bit dodgy. It just sold 'petrol', and I wanted a bit more assurance of fuel quality than that, so we returned to the hotel lobby to ask about any better fuel stations in town. We were then directed to a slightly larger petrol station, which reassuringly displayed prices for three different fuel grades. The top grade was simply branded as 'Speed', and so this had to become my preferred fuel of choice. Safely back at the airport, the re-filled Turtle Pac was then offloaded onto a small tractor and baggage trailer. This was then kept in the shade for as long as possible before being loaded onto *Roxy*'s back seat just prior to departure.

I continued to get ready as quickly as possible. After repacking the aircraft, loading the fuel and completing all my pre-flight inspections,

I visited the tower to get my FAI forms signed and file my flight plan. With the heat from the sun steadily building, I walked briskly over from the aircraft to the airside fence and the guard on gate duty let me out to climb the steps up into control tower building, the entrance of which was only a few metres away. Shortly afterwards I came back down to the same gate, needing now to return back to the aircraft. With flight plan approved and activated, I was ready to fly and the clock was now ticking on my planned departure timeslot. The very same guard however, who had just witnessed me leaving my aircraft on the apron and walking through his gate a few minutes earlier, would not now allow me back onto the apron without ID.

Unfortunately, all my ID documents were already packed away in my emergency waterproof grab bag clipped into the front cockpit of *Roxy*, parked in plain sight not 50m away. Nothing had been said when I had gone out of the gate, but still he would not budge on the protocol of showing ID. I had to then wait, as many precious minutes ticked by, until a security supervisor was summoned. Only then was I able to argue for the logical, practical solution of simply being escorted back over to the aircraft to check as much of my ID as they pleased.

But even the supervisor was hesitant, so I had to further convince him that I was indeed the pilot of the small yellow aircraft that was sitting on the apron within sight of us all. For starters, I told him that I wouldn't normally walk around in a red flight suit, unless I was just about to get in my aircraft and take off. Eventually he relented and escorted me across to check the details. All very frustrating of course, but at least now I was gradually learning to accept such over-complicated red tape.

This added delay had cost me time that I didn't have to spare, and on engine start up I was given a hurry up call from the tower. Raipur would be closing at 1pm for about three hours, and if I didn't leave quickly, I wouldn't make it there in time. Thankfully, apart from the odd bump of turbulence from rising thermals, I flew the whole way in pleasant conditions at 6500ft. As it happened, I managed to arrive just in time at 12.55pm.

***

Raipur was *only* a mere 40°C, and I was instructed to park at the very farthest stand from the terminal. Compared to the interest that had been shown at the other Indian stopovers, here *Roxy* and I were left much more on our own. That said, two army helicopter pilots strolled over while I was unloading my overnight bags for a poke around the aircraft.

When they came close by, I could hear they were talking to each other.

"Wow! It's like a small helicopter!" said one of them.

"No, sorry guys," I chirpily replied. "A gyroplane is not *like* a helicopter at all. It's more the other way around, a helicopter is *like* a gyroplane."

Watching their puzzled faces, I explained further.

"At least it is when your helicopter has to try to become a gyroplane to save itself in the event of a total engine failure. If, during an emergency landing, your spinning helicopter blades cannot successfully achieve full autorotation (how gyro blades work all the time in normal flight) it's not going to end at all well when arriving on the ground."

The two helo pilots glanced at each other and graciously accepted my correction. They had no counterargument, as in such emergencies, becoming *like a gyroplane* was their only viable solution to landing safely. As the two pilots wandered off again, suitably enlightened, I smiled and thought they hopefully wouldn't make that wrong assumption ever again.

The airport concourse was deserted in the heat of the day. Everything had literally stopped. The local policeman on door duty called for a free shuttle bus to take me to a small hotel situated right in the centre of the city. Raipur was much more rural than the relative sophistication I had experienced in Ahmadabad or even Nagpur, and around every corner I was presented with a fantastic glimpse of grassroots Indian life.

The bus driver was very fond of using his horn, essential equipment as the streets near the centre were just a riot of colour and street-trading activities. Amongst it all, sacred cows were wandering about seemingly quite unfazed by the noise, pollution and traffic running haphazardly in every direction. The hotel, when we finally battled our way to its smart glass-fronted doorway, was surprisingly modern and minimalist. It looked quite out of place jammed as it was, right in the middle of a row of lesser, more shabby looking buildings. The main thing, however, was that it had clean rooms, free Wi-Fi and as I was soon to find out, very attentive waiters. At mealtimes, no less than four waiters were ready to serve my table, each gently vying with each other to swoop in every time I made the slightest move to pick up my napkin or reach for the pepper.

I was pleased to see that there were some lovely curries on the menu – it gave me the decisive excuse I needed to scrub any notion of flying the next day. I had been flying every day since Abu Dhabi on the 14th, so I figured one day off after a week of hard flying was now well deserved. It also gave me time to sleep, recharge the batteries and catch up with paperwork and clothes washing.

21 April 2010: Raipur, India (non-flying day)

After a morning of paperwork, emails and washing, a late curry lunch was followed by a stroll around the city just as the heat of the day was subsiding.

On most stopovers, I saw the airport, the taxi rank, a nearby hotel and a petrol station, which meant that I often witnessed precious little else of each country on the ground. So, it was now very interesting to have the chance to wander around a small, seemingly off-the-beaten-track place like Raipur. It was a scene reflecting real life in this vibrant, living and breathing country, not a potted or sanitised version provided for tourists 'doing' India by perhaps just visiting the Taj Mahal. It seemed I was *the* tourist in Raipur for that afternoon. A few small boys even shouted out "Hello!" or "Take my picture!" to me in the street, a good indicator that my presence was quite unusual.

Walking around town I was fascinated by the inventive industry of a population who seemed most happy and content in their existence. At one corner near the bus station, a man was busy crushing sugar cane in a very antiquated machine. His ancient cart sat nearby, piled high with cut sugar cane, no doubt gathered straight in from the fields. The sugary sap oozed out of the cane crusher to be collected in a small jug and sold in little paper cups to waiting bus passengers. A neat process, direct from the fields into the hands of the customer. No need for a big multinational company to manufacture, transport, market and sell their expensive bottled fizzy drink brands here. As well as the many food and drink stalls, there were a notable number of shops all seemingly specialising in pumping equipment (presumably for farmland irrigation) and blacksmith/metalwork shops.

One 'shocking' aspect of life was the very haphazard way electricity had been distributed around the town. Pole-mounted distribution boards, high-voltage switchgear and transformers were located in crowded public places, sometimes barely above head height, with virtually no health and safety provision at all. In some places, bare cables, high-voltage bus-bars and switchgear were clearly accessible in open fronted cabinets. In the UK all such potentially lethal equipment is locked away behind spiky anti-climb palisade fences and labelled everywhere with 'Danger of Death' signs. In rural India it appeared that there was a much more relaxed safety regime in place.

22 April 2010: Raipur, India – Village track, India – Jamshedpur, India

With renewed energy from the rest day, I was up early to battle the obligatory traffic back to the airport. The usual paperwork bureaucracy continued, including writing out my own boarding pass – I resisted the temptation to put down 'Surplus Airlines' as the aircraft carrier, though such was the reverence given to every scrap of official paperwork in India, they probably would have accepted it without any fuss. As it was, I wrote 'Private aircraft' and used 'G-YROX' as my flight number. I was now becoming quite used to the lengthy paperwork process.

On one occasion, I had been given seven separate bits of paper to sign, mostly just chits for small taxes and other scraps of handwritten invoices coming in all colours. I also had a dozen or so witnesses assembled, all closely leaning in around the small table where I happened to be sitting. Each of the scraps of paper were seemingly owned by someone in the assembled crowd, and even while sitting there, another anonymous arm would squeeze through the crush of bodies, to place a couple more forms onto my to-do pile. All wanted to witness that their own vitally important piece of paper would get signed by myself and then countersigned by the airport handler sitting across the table from me. He ranked each one in order of importance and handed them to me for signing. I had little idea what each form was saying, except that without them I would not be allowed to get back out to my aircraft, so I just signed them all as quickly as possible.

As I signed off on the very last paper with a theatrical flourish, I looked up at the handler and the sea of surrounding faces and proclaimed...

"All done, at last!"

Looking at the handler, I then posed a question.

"With all that joint signing, does that mean you and I are now married?"

With much laughter all around, he gave me a wide grinning smile.

"Oh no Captain!" he exclaimed, "But you are very funny, Captain!"

It felt so good to poke a little fun into their otherwise very dry, serious proceedings.

* * *

The day had warmed up considerably by the time of departure for Jamshedpur. It was now 22 April, exactly one month since I had left Larne. I had flown over 7000 miles in just over 100 hours of flying time. Things were settling down nicely and my daily flight routine was becoming comfortably familiar. I was also gradually becoming acclimatised to hot weather flying, something I could not prepare for much in advance. After all, an air temperature of 40°C is virtually unheard of in Northern Ireland and the rest of the UK. I was feeling good, in buoyant mood. I even flew along singing a few songs to myself.

And then it happened.

On the instrument panel, my 20-litre fuel warning light flickered on.

I stopped singing.

The warning light indicated that I only had 20 litres of useable fuel left in the main tanks. This gave me only one hour of flight endurance, but I still had at least another one hour and 30 minutes to run before reaching Jamshedpur airport. I couldn't understand the problem. I reached back to the rear seat and could feel that the Turtle Pac was still quite heavy with fuel. By my fuel calculations of flight time versus fuel burn, I estimated I should have around 50 litres of usable fuel on board, meaning 30 litres was somehow still stuck in the Turtle Pac and hadn't drained itself down into the main tanks.

"Houston. We have a problem," I whispered to myself.

I had a real problem. I reasoned with myself that a blockage must have developed in the fuel line feeding into the main tanks.

As I flew along, clock now ticking, I had to quickly decide on what to do. I certainly couldn't reach my destination on the fuel range I had in the main tanks, and yet I knew I still had plenty of extra fuel in the Turtle Pac if only I could get at it. What I really needed to do was find somewhere to land and sort out the fuel supply issue on the ground. If need be, I would simply disconnect the fuel line and then manually drain the Turtle Pac straight into the main tanks. I flew on, slowly allowing myself to descend to a lower altitude. The landscape was a mixture of forested hills and cultivated valleys. As each valley was crossed, I began to search for a suitable landing spot. I wasn't panicking over the situation as I had the luxury of knowing that by flying a gyroplane, I could at least set down in a much tighter landing spot compared to other types of aircraft. As a minimum requirement, I just needed to find a reasonably straight farm track, away from any obstructions, people or traffic. And in theory, I'd also then be able to take off again from the same spot. *In theory...*

I began to consider a couple of landing spots as they presented themselves below, but on closer inspection quickly rejected them. One for a hard-to-see overhead power line running close by and the other for an unsuitable climb-out profile. There was no point in making a successful landing if I then couldn't take off again, so I flew on. After more searching, I found a viable dirt track running between two small villages situated in a wide cultivated valley. The track looked to be made of a compacted hard clay surface and was completely deserted. Glancing around, all of the adjoining crop-filled fields were also empty. I checked my gauges and by this time, my five-litre fuel warning light (15 minutes endurance remaining) also began to flicker on. Command decision made, this roughly constructed dirt road was now suddenly my No. 1 runway of choice!

Smoke rising lazily from a nearby chimney gave me a wind direction to land into. I then made a slow controlled descent and my landing roll out was barely five metres. That was the easy part however, getting airborne again was going to be the real challenge. I had come down on the middle of a long stretch of straight unsurfaced road. It was indeed dry clay as suspected and rock hard. I noticed a few red half house-bricks sticking proud of the surface and surmised that the track had been constructed by including building rubble.

"Take-off might be a bit bouncy," I thought, "but nothing like as much as a deeply rutted cattle field back home."

I stopped the main rotor and shut down the engine. Taking off my helmet and sunglasses, I looked up to see a gathering dust cloud ahead on the track, about 600m away. Glancing around I also saw another dust cloud a similar distance away on the track behind me. What had been a completely deserted, quiet and peaceful stretch of countryside a few minutes previously was now rapidly filling up with people. About 200 local villagers were making their way excitedly towards me from the village ahead and another 200 were pouring out from the village situated behind me. Most were running, though some also had bicycles or small motorbikes. The noise level was rising along with the dust, as excited kids were shouting in glee at the amazing thing that had just happened.

I continued to unstrap my harness and climb out of the cockpit.

"This is going to be interesting," I thought.

Both groups of villagers arrived near to the aircraft at about the same time, but their next actions were most unexpected. As they approached, they also fanned out on both sides of the track into the fields on either side. Coming in from both directions they formed a great big circle of about 40m diameter right around the aircraft. The noise died away and then everyone just looked at each other for a moment. It was quite amazing, but I now know exactly what a space alien would feel like when they land in a UFO, the crowd half expecting me to step out from my spacecraft and say, "Take me to your Leader!"

I had to think quickly what to do. I needed about 20 minutes on the ground to drain the fuel manually from the Turtle Pac into the main tanks, so I thought I would have to keep everyone entertained for that long at least. I smiled and waved at everyone and shouted, "Hello!" Broad smiles of relief were given in reply by the crowd as everyone realised I was indeed a nice friendly UFO and that I had come in peace.

The crowd however took my friendly gestures as their signal to start edging closer and closer in, until the throng of people were all crowded in tightly around *Roxy*. I tried to communicate, but soon realised that no one in the crowd spoke any English. This was after all, a very rural part of India. I thought I'd keep everyone entertained by getting my camera out to take some pictures. I also had some *B9 Energy* sew-on patches that I had thought might be useful to give away on the trip, so I passed a few of these peace offerings out to the kids. They were a very friendly crowd and even though we were not speaking verbally, they still offered me bottles of local water that they had brought with them. I politely declined their offer as I couldn't have risked drinking any of it (running to the toilet at 6000ft was just not viable), but their thoughts and concern for my overall welfare were very touching.

As the fuel was still slowly draining into the tank, I was kept busy with more photos and laughter. However, what happened next caught me quite by surprise. As one particular man stepped forward out of the crowd, the rest of those gathered immediately reacted by stepping back a little. I realised this was something significant and important. I nodded hello to the man, and putting my palm to my chest I said, "I am Norman."

He did the same and said, "Dennis."

OK, so now I suddenly had a new best friend called Dennis. It was at this point that he then tried to explain who he was. He appeared to be saying that he was some sort of locally appointed policeman. In the style that a magician might bring out a pack of cards to show the audience, Dennis ceremoniously brought out and flashed a small, folded ID card at me, though not for long enough to let me see any details on it. He then grabbed a guy out from the crowd nearby and held him in a playful headlock, rasping his knuckles over the poor guy's forehead as he did so, perhaps just to show he was a nice playful sort of a guy. Next, he latched onto my hand to shake it. To diffuse the situation a little, I made a big gesture of handing my camera to a person in the crowd to take a picture of me and Dennis together. With arms around each other's shoulders, we both smiled broadly at the camera and this set the crowd off cheering excitedly. Now playing to the crowd, his next move was to grab hold of my head and he planted a big theatrical kiss on my cheek. The crowd loved this even more.

Enjoying the joke, I then retrieved the camera and snapped shots of the rest of the crowd enjoying themselves, a tactic which also helped to restore a little of my personal space back from Dennis. I also checked on the refuelling; *nearly there*, just a few more minutes needed.

It appeared that Dennis hadn't quite finished with me yet. He then proceeded to pull a wallet out of his back pocket. He showed it to me, opening it up as he did so. It was completely empty. Reading between the lines I sensed he was obviously hoping that I might be going to put something in it for him. My countermeasure in this game of charades was that I pretended not to see his wallet, keeping my eyes engaged with the rest of the crowd and simply ignored his action. Thankfully, after a little more wallet waving, he soon got the hint and put it away.

Fortunately, right at the end of the refuelling, an older man was ushered through the crowd to meet me. I think one of the motorbikes must have raced off to fetch him when I first arrived. To my relief he was able to speak some English, and so I was able to quickly explain that my aircraft flew more like a fixed wing plane than a Helicopter and that I needed to use the dirt track as a makeshift runway in order to take off. He then barked out instructions to the crowd, with much arm waving, for everyone to stand back and remain a safe distance away in the surrounding fields. The huge crowd scattered as quickly as it had formed, and I could once again study the layout of my soon-to-be improvised airstrip.

Planning in my head, if I pushed the gyro back to a curve in the road, I then had a good 50-70m of straight roadway to work with. After that, there was a small humpback bridge made of rough stone and the roadway then kinked 15 degrees abruptly to the right. I was loaded quite lightly with the remaining fuel on board so this would help for a short take-off run, but the hot dry air hung very still in the valley, so I was nervous on how quickly I would generate enough lift under the main rotor to get up and clear of the ground.

I planned to make an attempt, but if I subsequently had to abort the take-off, I would aim to hop over the bridge, jink to the right and land again on the further short section of straight road beyond. It sounded easy in my head, but the whole roadway was raised two metres up from the surrounding ploughed fields, so above all else, it was *crucial* that I stayed on the hard surface of the track and avoided running off onto the 45-degree sloping verges alongside.

Hey ho! All in a day's work for a solo, around-the-world adventure pilot, I suppose.

Still mulling over my safety tactics, I turned *Roxy* around and began to push her back towards the last bend. Willing hands helped to push with me, and excited, expectant chatter arose all around, as people speculated amongst themselves exactly how this strange contraption was going to get airborne. It felt like a scene out of the 1920s and the early pioneering days of powered flight, where getting airborne was always a great spectacle but never a certainty.

The main crowd followed, scampering excitedly over the rough fields on both sides of the track. A positive benefit of having virtually everyone from both villages already present, was that we could now at least be sure that there would be no other traffic on the roadway. Spinning *Roxy* back around 180 degrees on her main wheels, I lined up on the 'runway' and the remaining helpers scattered down into the fields to join the expectant crowd.

I fired up the engine...

Looking out and waving to everyone, the fields suddenly sprouted a *bumper crop* of phone cameras being made ready to record the take-off. If anything was now to go wrong, at least it would be well documented. I noted the half-concerned, half-excited faces in the crowd and realised that this was just as much an unexpected adventure for everyone on the ground as it was for me attempting to take flight. Even to this day, those two villages are still probably remembering and talking about the extraordinary time that that crazy, red-suited alien landed in his little yellow UFO.

I wound up the blades with the pre-rotator and then released the brakes. It was now all or nothing. I was fully focussed and fully committed to get off the ground before the bridge. The surface was uneven and bumpy, the odd half-brick causing a jolt that would instantly sap some of the aircraft's rolling speed. But I was still accelerating.

The front wheel came up and I was wheel balancing on the main undercarriage, getting lighter and lighter on the ground as the main rotor started to take the strain to pull me up off the ground. I was skipping and skittering along on the rough surface now very lightly on the main wheels. It was a good feeling, though I had to stay 100% focused on keeping myself literally on the straight and narrow.

A jarring bump on one wheel or the other continually threatened to knock me off course and all too soon that damn bridge was rapidly approaching. I was almost at flying speed. I reached a shallow rise leading onto the bridge and, as with a ski jump, I ran up the slope and then simply continued skyward as the ground dropped away below me. I was airborne!

For a few seconds I held my breath. Was it just a long optimistic hop or were the blades now holding their own in the tricky conditions? Thankfully I slowly continued to climb and gained normal flying speed. Shortly afterwards I circled back, low over the fields, to give the villagers a thankful wave and fly past. There was relief all round; I was waving madly at them, and they did likewise back at me. Both parties knew we had just experienced something quite special. Still buzzing with adrenaline, I climbed out to re-join my direct routing for Jamshedpur.

Phew! I breathed a long sigh of relief.

I had been on the ground for a total of only 30 minutes, but it had been such an extraordinary, unpredictable event. As with the thunderstorm incident in the Saudi desert, the concern for my welfare and the warmth and support I felt from the local people assisting me in my time of need was so life reaffirming and really comforting. There is so much basic goodness in humanity around the world, and thoughts of this kept me smiling for the rest of the flight. Though to avoid any awkward questions, I made sure not to make any mention of my unscheduled, precautionary out-landing, until I had flown a good distance out of India.

* * *

After mulling over what possibly could have gone wrong with the fuel line, I worked it out later in the day. When the fuel line had originally been installed, in one section near the on/off valve, the fuel delivery hose needed to loop back on itself before being discharged into the main tanks. This loop meant the hose was curved upwards slightly, before looping around to drain into the tank. Every part of the auxiliary fuel system had worked fine all the way to India, including during the significant water crossings in the Mediterranean, Red Sea and Gulf of Oman. The Turtle Pac had been full on each occasion over water and the head of pressure that that induced in the system (due to gravity) was such, that any possible air bubble that might have gathered in the loop was simply flushed on out through the fuel line. However, in Raipur I had not needed to refuel the Turtle Pac. I still had enough fuel in reserve from the day before to make the flight to Jamshedpur. So rather than carrying extra weight of fuel, I elected instead to wait and refuel in Jamshedpur, and this proved to give rise to the problem.

Overnight I had disconnected the partially filled Turtle Pac in Raipur and that action may have introduced a small amount of air into the fuel line. When the Turtle Pac was reconnected for the next flight, the system did not then have the raised fuel pressure that a full Turtle Pac would have had and so the stubborn bubble of air in the loop was able to resist the weak pressure of the fuel to rise and push around the loop. The end result was that the fuel remained stuck in the Turtle Pac. Once discovered, it seemed so obvious. It was quickly and easily fixed by simply turning the loop downwards rather than upwards, so that an air bubble could no longer ever exist in the system. I was incredibly fortunate to have discovered this over terra firma, where I had been able to quickly land and decant the fuel manually. If it had happened whilst out over the ocean, I would have had to either quickly find a passing container ship to land on, or much more likely, I would have been in for a very long swim.

* * *

Arrival into Jamshedpur was sublime. After all the excitement of the emergency landing and the good fortune to have discovered the potential showstopper of the fuel line issue, landing now on a regular runway (with no half-bricks to contend with) in a quiet, rural airport was just lovely. No one seemed to mind that I was running a little late and the airport staff made me feel very welcome.

A press conference had been laid on in one of the briefing rooms in the small terminal, and I was soon busy answering the many questions concerning my overall flight so far. During the Q&A session, a tray appeared on the table in front of me. On it was a pot of tea, milk, sugar, some biscuits and a bone china teacup. The tea was duly served up to me and between questions, I took my first sip of it. After all the trials and tribulations of the day just gone, it tasted fantastic. It was not how the Arab tea had been (after that other significant emergency landing), but it tasted just exactly like a good cup of tea would taste back home. For a moment I was amazed at this fact, imagine a cup of tea in a far flung, remote little town in India tasting *exactly* like a cup of tea back in the UK. It was only then that I realised of course, that most *'English' breakfast tea* has actually come from India in the first place and that it is we, in the UK, who are enjoying *Indian tea,* not the other way around! Anyway, it was so nice, I was quick to ask for a second pot.

Later in the evening, I was taken to find fuel in a small car manufactured by the huge Indian-based international company Tata. I was informed that Jamshedpur was an original home base of Tata and indeed they appeared to still own most of the town, including the airport. The best petrol we could find was only 91 octane, but it would have to do. I would just have to go easy and not push the engine too hard on climb-out the next morning.

23 April 2010: Jamshedpur, India – Kolkata, India

This was to be a day with special significance. By calculation, it was reckoned that by the time I reached Kolkata, I would have flown G-YROX farther than any other gyroplane in history.

Previously in 2004, during his own circumnavigation attempt, Barry Jones had successfully flown a Magni Gyro from the UK to an Indian Air Force base near Kolkata, but he had started his journey from Middle Wallop in England. As I had flown from Larne, Northern Ireland, I had approximately an extra 200 miles under my rotor and therefore, if all went well, I would now soon be able to lay claim to the world's longest-distance flight.

The day started well. I refitted the fully fuelled Turtle Pac and tested the now reconfigured fuel hose system on the ground. I would also monitor the fuel flow carefully during the flight to make sure the air bubble problem would not now reoccur. Many of the press who had turned up the previous evening reappeared again to witness the soon-to-be farthest gyroplane flown in history taking off. I was even presented with a bunch of flowers as a gift from the airport to celebrate the occasion. After some photos, I quickly presented them back to the girl who had given them to me, thanking her kindly but also explaining there was not enough space in the open cockpit gyro to carry them with me.

Shortly afterwards, I was taken across to the ATC tower to be presented to the controller on duty. He was quite an odd character who spoke on the radio with a clipped air of authority, which intimated that he perhaps thought of himself as *Lord High Commander* of the airwaves. His control tower desk held a solitary basic radio set and a microphone. No radar monitoring service was present in such a small airfield. In between managing what little passing radio traffic he had, he turned his attention to me and proceeded to 'hold court' over the proposed flight plan that I had presented to him.

Such was his caustic tone and condescending mannerisms that I was given the feeling of being an errant schoolboy in the headmaster's office. I quickly realised that it was best just to smile and humour him in this situation, if only that he might then allow me permission for a reasonably direct flight routing. The flight plan was eventually approved, but as I was taxiing to the runway a little later, I then asked on the radio for an impromptu permission to perform a flypast of the hangars. This would allow the press that had gathered there a final close-up shot of my take-off and subsequent climb-out. There was no valid reason not to give me permission. The airport was quiet, there was absolutely no other traffic to inconvenience. I expected the controller to show a little relaxed empathy and approve the request.

"Noooo..." was his immediately dismissive and wholly unhelpful reply. "Stick to your flight plan *X-ray*. On departure, climb straight ahead and report at 5500ft."

With a click of his microphone, the insensitive jobsworth had denied the expectant gaggle of press photographers (who had waited patiently several hours for this moment) any chance of a decent shot of the aircraft flying past. After the warm reception I had received on arrival, I felt I had let everyone down, seemingly sneaking away off into the distance without even as much as a cheery farewell wave. It would have taken all of an extra minute to perform a quick orbit over the runway. Climbing out, en route to 5500ft strictly as per the draconian instruction of my ATC master, I was not best pleased.

* * *

The flight to Kolkata was only two hours and 20 minutes, but unfortunately turned out to be quite murky. There was no definite horizon due to the haze, though happily the ground below remained quite visible at all times. I expected that the airspace around Kolkata would be once again much more congested, as it was a major international airport, however I had no other option but to land there and clear Indian customs before flying on to neighbouring Bangladesh.

With a sky full of international traffic, I needed to keep alert and to be constantly on top of my game. I would have to react professionally and immediately, to any instructions given by ATC, as they guided me and all the other aircraft through the highly choreographed arrivals procedure. In short, I had to be on my best behaviour and, as I had already successfully landed in several large international airports, I was confident that I knew how to conduct myself appropriately.

Soon enough, I made first contact with Kolkata Approach. After some initial vectoring to guide me closer in towards the airport, I was handed over to Kolkata Tower to make my line up on finals to land.

Kolkata normally has two parallel active runways, approached (from one end) on a bearing of 190 degrees. Assigned left and right, they were referred to as 19L (Lima) and 19R (Romeo). On final approach the tower advised me that 19L, the runway farthest away to where the tower was situated, was closed for heavy maintenance and that 19R was therefore now the only runway in use. Indeed, as I flew closer,

I could see that patchy resurfacing work was going on all along the length of 19L.

"Golf Oscar X-ray, make quite sure you are lined up for landing on One Niner Romeo."

"Affirm tower. I am on finals to land One Niner Romeo, Golf Oscar X-Ray," was my reply.

"Golf Oscar X-Ray, you are clear to land," they chimed.

"Clear to land, Golf Oscar X-ray," I replied and continued my calm and steady descent.

Then suddenly I heard...

"Oscar X-ray! Pull up! Pull up!" the controller was shouting.

"Go around! Go around!" He continued.

At first, I couldn't work out what was going on, but I decided ATC must know something that I didn't, so instinctively, I pulled back on the stick and applied full power to climb away from the runway.

I put in a quick circuit to bring me back once again onto final approach, where once again I lined up to land on runway 19R. I was on exactly the same approach as before and so I asked the tower for clarification.

"Kolkata Tower, this is Golf Oscar X-ray. Can you confirm you want me to land on runway One Niner Romeo?"

"Affirm. That is correct. Clear to land Golf Oscar X-ray," he replied.

I landed with no further problems and taxied clear of the active runway. I was still confused as to what had just happened and so I asked the tower for yet more clarification.

"Tower, I am slightly confused, that was exactly the same final approach onto the same runway that I was lining up for the first time."

"No," came the reply, "The first approach you were landing on the wrong runway. You were landing on One Niner Lima, which is closed."

This was a clear mistake on their part, but they were adamant that *it was I* who was clearly in the wrong and had now even broadcast the fact to me on the radio. However, I knew I was correct but after several more heated exchanges on the radio, they still stuck to their story of events. It was their word against mine and no doubt the tit for tat battle gave much amusement to the other international airline pilots who happened to be on frequency and listening in from their flight decks.

Evidence appeared to be stacking up against the oddball amateur pilot in that funny little helicopter thing. The professional ATC, masters of all they survey up in the tower, were bound to be correct, right?

Wrong...

And I was about to deliver the ace up my sleeve.

"Tower, I can assure you that I was lined up on One Niner Romeo on both approaches, as instructed. What is more, I have on-board video evidence that has recorded the whole event. And I can play this back for you later, if you would like."

Silence.

But they had certainly heard me alright and so had all the other pilots listening in, some of whom were then smiling out at me as I taxied past their aircraft. I knew that they knew and smiled back.

But I was still raging inside. It was yet one more example of where ATC, especially in India and Egypt, would be so self-assured, so over-bearing and commanding of their powerful position that even when they were clearly in the wrong, they could still believably argue *with authority* that they were right. This time however I now had them bang to rights, good and proper. I didn't say any more about it for the moment because I wanted to check later that I had actually caught all the events on my forward-view camera. I would have to go to the tower in the morning anyway to file my onward flight plan to Bangladesh, so I decided to keep my powder dry until then.

24 April 2010: Kolkata, India – Chittagong, Bangladesh

I arrived back at the airport at 8.30am, having battled through the morning traffic, but only got airborne at 10.51am. This delay was quite typical of the lengthy time everything took in India. I was often left waiting for this paper to be signed or waiting to see that person simply to allow me to do something else, which then involved yet another wait.

However, in amongst this tedium, there was one thing I was looking forward to and that was my visit to the tower.

First things first, I visited the ops room to check out my routing for Bangladesh. There was a NOTAM (notice to airmen) in force issued by the navy around the Bay of Bengal, which meant I had to be careful in some sections of the crossing. I certainly didn't want to suddenly become live target practise for some rooky navy gunners. Apart from that complication, my general flight plan was approved.

Next stop was the main ATC office. Walking straight up to the front desk, I brought my camera out and placed it on the desk. At first, the controllers in the office were a bit hesitant to watch the footage of my landing from the previous day. They did not of course want to be confronted with the evidence. They tried to tell me it wasn't necessary for them to see it but I wasn't taking no for an answer. I was furious that they had put me in such a position and I wanted answers. I showed the video clip. It clearly showed me steadily descending over the threshold of runway 19R, which had its name emblazoned on the end of the runway in huge numerals. Then suddenly, only 30ft or so above the ground, I made a sharp pull up and banked to the right as instructed by ATC. Why did they think I was on the wrong approach? And why, if they thought I was landing on the closed 19L runway, did they instruct me to make a right-hand circuit for my go around, which then had me encroaching on the active 19R runway? If they did think I was approaching 19L they should have given me a left-hand circuit to loop around the far-left outfield, safely away from both runways.

"Any answers?"

They had just seen my irrefutable video, and I pressed home my advantage.

"Yes, it was our mistake," they said honestly. "You can clearly see that from the video. On your first approach we thought your aircraft was larger than it really was. From our view point it looked like you were a larger aircraft landing on the farther away (19L) runway. The perspective and very steep glide path made it appear like you were just about to crash into the far runway!"

Leaning forward with hands on the desk, I softened and quietened my delivery.

"Admittedly it is an unusual aircraft type for you to have to deal with and yes, it happens to have a much steeper approach profile. I acknowledge that might well have caused you enough concern to ask me to go around and that's fine, I have absolutely no problem with always putting safety first."

They took some comfort from that statement, but I was not finished quite yet.

I continued apace.

"But that is not the issue. The issue I have is ATC having the on-going arrogance, after the event, to automatically assume that I must be some sort of rooky pilot just out of flight school. You assumed my in-competence would have me pick the wrong runway and then promptly crash headlong into it!"

I was really getting into my stride.

"Let me remind you that I have already flown this aircraft almost half-way around the world, in and out of several of the world's larger international airports. So you would think, would you not, that I should at least know a left runway from a right runway by now!"

And finally, time to light up the afterburners!

"You then proceeded to bully me on the radio by first assuming and then asserting that your decision had been correct; that I had made a gross error of judgement, when actually the gross error was in fact, all yours. And what's more, just to add to the problem, you then decided to send me on a right-hand orbit that could have easily seen me flying the wrong way back along the active runway (19R) and headlong towards any other aircraft that happened to be on final approach!"

Silence, again.

I then realised I had been shouting out the last part of my rant, such that the heads of all the other staff in the office were now turned and looking in our direction. I had made my point, so I quickly returned to my normal, gently spoken, easy-going self. I rounded off the conversation by hoping they could all learn from this experience and wished them all a good day.

Walking back out of the ATC building I was still shaking with adrenaline, but very thankful that, in the next few hours, I would be leaving behind the petty bureaucracy and the bombastic self-importance of Indian airport staff and airspace controllers.

I was leaving the country with a very similar, almost relieved manner as I had felt when departing Egypt.

* * *

Returning to the main terminal, the more mundane low-level type of Indian bureaucracy reined over general proceedings once again. At least by now I was learning to take some amusement out of it. At one stage I was led by a security guard through a packed queue of people waiting to go on a Kingfisher flight to Bangkok.

The queue was severely backed up; the main bottle neck being that everyone had to go through a single metal detector scanner near the departure gate. I was clutching my own handwritten boarding pass for flight number 'GYROX'. Approaching the back of the queue, the uniformed security guard who was escorting me proceeded to clear a direct path through the crowd so that I could be led directly up to the scanner. I could feel that the whole plane-load of tourists was now looking on at me, this slightly dishevelled, solo traveller, being marched through their ranks by a uniformed guard.

"They must either think I am some sort of poorly dressed VIP, or perhaps assume I am an international criminal being deported," I thought.

I resisted the temptation to start playing up to the crowd, snarling menacingly to them as a criminal in a superhero film might do. I just kept my head down, said nothing and got out to the aircraft as soon as possible.

Just prior to me suiting up ready for departure, the local flight handlers brought me over to sit in a minivan to go over my invoice and then presented me with a whopping US$1200 bill for their handling fees and overnight airport charges. And the payment needed to be in cash, immediately, if you please. No, I was not best pleased. They had waited until the very last minute to spring this huge bill on me, knowing I would have no available time in which to challenge it. It was clearly presented to me as a *fait accompli.* I tried to complain to the airport manager when she turned up a short while later but she was more interested in getting her picture taken with G-YROX and me as my story was in all the morning papers. Here I was, effectively being robbed, whilst at the same time they saw nothing wrong with getting me to pose for publicity pictures and expecting me to smile and appear happy. The big bill seriously depleted the last of my US dollar cash reserves. I would have to try to draw more money out in cash after I landed in Bangladesh.

The flight across to Chittagong sent me out over the sprawling mouth of the Ganges Delta, where the mighty river spills out into the Bay of Bengal. After the dry, dusty landscape of central India, the delta scenery was spectacularly green and lush. I tried not to think too much about the real possibility of there being a few man-eating Bengal tigers prowling in the swampy mangrove flood plains below, nor the fact that although the terra firma looked solid enough from a distance, if I had had to make an emergency landing on it, I suspected that the *terra* had very little *firma* about it.

I flew along at 5500ft and experienced very broken, white fluffy clouds scudding past me just below this level. The general visibility had much improved close to the sea and I was glad to get a sharp view once again of the horizon, rather than fumbling around in the hazy murk of the last few days. It was quite a short flight, only two hours and 30 minutes, but it was necessary to allow me to land and clear custom formalities in Bangladesh. My position was relayed to Dakar control a couple of times before I was handed over to Chittagong Tower with about 70 nautical miles to run.

Listening on the tower frequency during the last hour of the flight allowed me to build a good mental picture of any possible traffic movements in the area. Happily, there appeared to be very little going on, so I was able to relax a little in the cockpit and enjoy the scenery of arriving in yet another brand-new country.

Final approach was made from out over the sea. I began my initial descent from 5000ft and passed by about 40 bulk carrier ships, all at anchor, presumably waiting on orders for their next voyage. After the oppressive dry heat of India, as I dropped lower, I could feel a definite increase of humidity in the air, and it was also much cooler. After a straightforward landing (such a contrast to how my last arrival had been in Kolkata), I taxied the short distance to the apron. Here I could smell the sea, feel the cool breeze and see wild meadow grasses blowing around on the verges of the hard standing area. Bizarrely, it felt remarkably similar to the wilder parts of the west coast of Ireland. In particular, Achill Island in County Mayo, where we used to go to a beach campsite every summer holiday. A bright sunny day, fresh sea breeze, rough grassland and waving meadow flowers all combined to transport me back in an instant to when I was seven years old running around in shorts with my brother, David and sister, Norah on the beach.

The moment of nostalgia was short lived, as about 30 very excited faces rushed across the concrete to welcome me into Chittagong. After the usual post-flight checks and unpacking ritual, I was shown to the airport offices, where I discussed refuelling and the ever-sensitive issue of airport fees. As suspected, after the heavy demand for US dollars in Kolkata, I was now going to have to get more cash from somewhere ASAP.

I was given a lift into town and got my first close-up look at Bangladesh. We passed many ships berthed at the river wharfs, and everywhere seemed a hive of activity – it was positively bristling with marine-related industries. My driver was not afraid to sound his horn at every opportunity. I wasn't sure if that was just his normal practice, or whether I was deemed VIP enough to give him the excuse he needed to scythe his way through the rush hour traffic as if (as in Gwadar) he was carrying the president on board. In double-quick time

I was delivered to the best hotel in town, and seemingly the only one considered suitable for foreigners. It was locally rated as a *five-star*, but I suspect its rating had been awarded back in the 1960s with very little upgrading of the furniture and fixtures since. Mind you, if it was also still charging 1960s prices then I wasn't going to complain too much.

I soon realised why the hotel was singled out as suitable for foreigners. On checking in, I was taken in the lift to the third floor. As the lift door opened, I could see that two armed guards had been posted on duty in the corridor. Apparently, all foreign travellers were assigned rooms on this floor so that they could be minded by this 24-hour armed security. Trying not to be too alarmed at the extreme measures, I thought at least I could hope to get a good night of undisturbed sleep.

25 April 2010: Chittagong, Bangladesh (non-flying day)

I awoke for an early breakfast as usual in readiness for yet another onward flying day. Though unfortunately, the weather had other plans in store for me. Heavy thunderstorms with torrential rain interspersed with abrupt violent gusts of wind, battered the trees outside the hotel windows.

At least the conditions were so bad that it made my decision not to fly very easy. I contacted the airport from the hotel to say that there would be no onward flight that day. They had expected as much given the atrocious conditions. I felt badly for *Roxy* however, as I had not managed to get her a hangar the previous evening. She was left out in the open with only her lightweight cover protecting the cockpit. This cover was fine for the light drizzle of a summer rain shower back in the UK, but I was not sure how it would stand up to the car-wash strength deluge it was experiencing now.

So purely by chance, I was now presented with an unexpected non-flying day. As usual, it allowed me to catch up on admin and some washing, but my most important task for the day was to try and source more US dollars in cash. The airport management had insisted that, without exception, all their fees were to be paid in US dollars. No problem I thought, as I had already seen that the city centre had a good number of banks. I waited until early afternoon to allow the thunderstorms to clear and then ventured out to find a suitable international bank. After recently experiencing the sights and sounds of Indian city streets, I was also now keen to see how the Bangladeshi streets were by comparison.

My first impression was that there were many more bicycle rickshaws and hand-pulled carts rather than motorised ones. All the rickshaws had a roof for the rain, and I briefly considered catching a ride in one. But I wasn't that comfortable with the idea of asking someone to do all the peddling on my behalf and, as I didn't have an exact destination in mind, I decided to walk. After a period of wandering around, I came to a branch of the HSBC bank. I remembered their advertising slogan, 'HSBC: The World's local bank'. Great I thought, I am bound to be able to get some US dollars out of here quite easily.

"Sorry sir, it is not possible for me to give you any US dollar currency," was the reply to my request.

"But you are an international bank, supposedly the world's local bank. Why can you not just give me some US dollars?" I pleaded.

"It is against the law for any bank here to issue out hard foreign currency. We can happily *accept* US dollars and other currencies into the bank, but we cannot give them out."

"But that is crazy!" I replied, "The international airport has an official government policy that all fees have to be paid in US dollars, cash, yet at the same time the international banks have a conflicting official government policy that they are not allowed to issue any US dollars in cash over the counter?"

It was a nonsensical *Catch-22* situation.

"Can you tell me exactly how in this country, I am now supposed to gather enough US dollars together so I can pay my airport charges? I do not want both my aircraft impounded and myself arrested for non-payment of fees."

The bank teller helpfully replied: "Try asking the reception desk at your hotel; they sometimes have spare US dollars in cash that have been paid in by visiting foreigners."

NOTE: to international financiers… I hope this sage advice eventually reaches someone high up in the IMF and World Bank. For future international money trade deals in Bangladesh, don't bother speaking with the banks, just simply speak directly with the receptionist at the front desk of your local hotel instead.

***

Following the bank teller's advice, I returned to the hotel intent on buying up as many US dollar bills as they had in their strong box. Unfortunately, although they had some, it was still nowhere near enough to cover the airport handling fees.

What was I going to do?

I calculated I probably needed to source around US$1000 to re-inflate my contingency cash reserves. It wasn't just the airport fees I needed to cover, but also any 'what if' situations that might occur en route. I explained my lack of cash dilemma to the reception staff and it appeared that this was an all too familiar story. They did however offer a solution. I was sent to have a chat with the head of hotel security, and together we formed a cunning plan. It was to be acted out in three stages:

Stage 1 - Luckily, for situations such as these, I had prepared myself by taking four different bank cards on the flight. Using all four cards I was able to use the various local currency cash machines around the city to gather up 72,000 Bangladeshi taka (approximately US$1000). Thankfully the head of security escorted me in person while I withdrew the cash. By the time we were finished and had returned to the hotel, the wad of grubby taka bills withdrawn from the machines was sizeable; the pile of well-worn notes measured about seven inches high when stacked on a table in the lobby!

Stage 2 - The security chief then made a few phone calls, and I was told to sit and wait for a few minutes near the hotel doors. Suddenly a very well-dressed man appeared; mid-40s, neat hair, expensive tailored shirt, freshly polished shoes. He and the security chief exchanged a few words, and I was summonsed over to join them. On the chief's signal, I handed over the wad of taka notes in a brown paper bag and the man removed a much thinner wad of notes from his pocket. He proceeded to count off ten, crisp US$100 bills into my outstretched hand. Uncreased and presumably never in circulation until now, I hoped that they had not just been freshly printed that morning somewhere downtown.

I thanked the man but then realised that they were all large denomination bills. I needed some smaller bills if I was to avoid any airport ripping me off with the 'no change' scam, as we saw back in Aswan. The smartly dressed guy promptly took back one of my US$100 bills and made off out to the doorway. I was suddenly left standing, slightly confused, now holding only US$900, but the chief said not to worry, everything was going to plan.

Stage 3 - A few more minutes passed by and I was beginning to think I had just been robbed of US$100, when another man appeared in the lobby, just as quickly as the first. However, this guy was not so well turned out as the previous dealer; his hair was not quite so slick, his shirt was more creased, even with some grubby stains, and his shoes were worn and dusty. As with the first guy, he also had a few words with the security chief and then proceeded to produce and peel off ten, not so pristine, well-used US$10 notes. I quickly realised that while the first guy had been the local black market 'US$100 dollar man', this guy was now the 'US$10 dollar man'. It was fascinating to observe that the persona of each perfectly matched their financial trading status. I wondered whether there might have even been a 'US$1 dollar man' lurking somewhere close by, but alas, I never got introduced to him if there was.

It was amazing to think that because of the direct government policies imposed at the airport and at the banks, designed no doubt to pull in and then keep as much foreign hard currency in the country as possible, it was actually the local black market money exchange that ended up being the main trading beneficiary. I wouldn't have used the black market route at all, had it been possible to exchange the money by other more conventional, official means. But in this case, when needs must, there was obviously no other way to do it.

26 April 2010: Chittagong, Bangladesh (non-flying day)

I was up and ready to check out of the Hotel by 6am, hoping for an early getaway. But in the early hours a message had come through from Mike Gray from White Rose Aviation in England. Mike was assisting in some sections of my forward flight planning and was now organising my clearance permissions through to Myanmar. Because I had been delayed by the torrential rainfall the previous day, my entry permission had elapsed. The upshot of this was that I would now have to wait another day in Chittagong before once more having clearance to enter Myanmar airspace. While all the paperwork was re-submitted, I was forced to wait yet another day in my five-star (going on two-star) hotel. The only real luxury was that I now had plenty of extra time to appreciate how rundown the hotel décor really was.

The only internet connection was situated in the main lobby, so laptop in hand, I settled in to create my own workspace for a few hours. I decided to camp out on one of the rather too-easy, easy chairs near the reception desk. I didn't really sit *on* the red leatherette 'business lounge' sofa, for once sitting I simply continued to sink further and further *into* it. Getting up each time was always a very undignified manoeuvre, which saw me semi-crawling out onto the floor to get a firm footing before then being able to stand up.

Sanitised *Muzak* wafted around the reception area constantly; the small selection of tunes being played over and over again, engraining themselves into my brain. Rather amusingly, the theme tune to the film *Titanic* kept being played. Casually looking around the tired, dated fixtures and fittings of the lobby, I could see that perhaps they would have been worthy of a glorious first-class stateroom when first installed.

Now however, they were hardly worthy of even a steerage-class inside cabin. Clearly everything was well past its sell-by date.

Sitting there it was quite easy for me to imagine that the whole hotel could slowly tilt, start to fill with water and then gracefully slip off beneath the waves. And no doubt the relentless *Titanic* tune would defiantly play on through the loudspeakers to the very last. The hotel management can be thankful that not many icebergs have ever been spotted floating around in the Bay of Bengal.

I looked around the lobby from time to time between writing emails. People-watching was always a good sport in such places, and I gradually became aware that there was a hotel staff member present, who always seemed to be loitering near the lifts. After a while I became curious as to what his job actually was. But everything soon became clear when I needed to return to my room to pick up a cable for my laptop. I gathered my things, took five minutes to escape the sofa and headed across the open lobby towards the lifts. Immediately, our mystery staff member sprang into action. Seeing me approach, he pressed the call button for the lift. The doors opened as I arrived and with a nod of my head in gratitude, I walked in. The second I was inside, my mysterious assistant stuck his head around the open door and without a word of enquiry, pressed the 'floor 3' and 'door close' buttons in quick succession. His head then darted back out as the lift set off. As he hadn't asked me where I wanted to go, I was left standing somewhat bemused, as the lift launched skyward up to the third floor. On reflection, I suppose his orders were to send all foreigners to the third floor, as that was the only floor we were allowed to stay on for security reasons. I mentally named him the 'Lift Lurker' after that, as pressing one of the six buttons in the lift was the *only* job I ever saw him do in the hotel. That said, he did it with such pride and enthusiasm; he made the job his own and I simply couldn't deny him his rightful position in the hotel hierarchy.

* * *

The storm from the previous day had finally cleared away and so

I now had the chance to have a good explore around the immediate neighbourhood. As in rural India, concern for health and safety on the streets did not appear to be a high priority; there were plenty of opportunities for slips and trips on the very uneven or missing pavements and kerbstones. But that was OK, I was prepared for the rough terrain. What I was not so prepared for was the risk of imminent death by high-voltage electrocution. At one point I came across a very haphazardly guarded diesel generator set that had been shoehorned into a hole in the wall. As I approached along the street, there was so much blue-and-black smoke belching out of the generator enclosure that I thought it might actually be on fire. On closer inspection, I discovered that it was just running at full throttle, and the noise from the poorly silenced exhaust was horrendous. I could also see that it was supposed to be kept contained and housed safely away from the public behind some slatted louvered screens, however both of these were hanging off their hinges. I imagined that the lack of adequate ventilation in the tiny cubicle might have caused the gen-set to overheat when fully enclosed, so their solution was to simply remove the safety screens to let more air in. This meant that the high-voltage bus-bars and circuitry that were also supposed to be enclosed safely inside the cabinet, were now fully exposed, right next to the pavement and at shoulder height; just lying in wait and ready to give any unsuspecting passer-by, a deadly little *zap*!

I was constantly amazed at the amount of industrious work going on all around me, though not always in a good way. A little later, I passed a building site where small gangs of boys, some not even yet into their teens, were hard at labour breaking old bricks down with hammers to make piles of hardcore fill for future construction work. Everywhere bicycle rickshaws and traders' hand carts were being pulled around by some undoubtedly very fit people. I wondered how they would fare in a race against regular sports cyclists. Put a rickshaw cyclist on a professional racing bike, and with a bit of coaching, sponsored kit and the correct diet, they might even win the *Tour de France*. Or conversely, what fun would it be to take some professional race-winning cyclists, who are used to their hi-tech, streamlined, ultra-light gear, and to challenge them to compete instead on home-welded bicycle rickshaws made out of recycled parts. Oh, and why not also add in a couple of overweight tourists sitting in the back seat for good measure! Who, I wonder, might then be crowned 'king of the mountains' or get to proudly wear the *maillot jaune* through the streets of Paris!

The whole scene was one of extremes. Some people in society had the most gruelling, hard labour tasks such as hammering rocks, whilst others seemed to have an easy life, and plenty of cheap labour to make it even easier. Looking on from the kerbside, I didn't feel at all comfortable with either of these positions in life. It felt as if sheer hard work and sheer laziness were somehow co-existing, hand in hand, and that one extreme lifestyle needed the other for both to survive. Quite bizarre to me and yet everyone around me seemed to just accept it as normal.

Returning to the hotel, my thoughts quickly moved on to my imminent departure early the next day. As I had now been a resident for a few days, I thought I'd thank the hotel staff by handing out some tips. I quickly ran into a dilemma; who or more exactly, how many people should I tip in this situation? And how much should I give? In fact, where was the 'one dollar man' now when I needed him?

The conventional jobs such as room cleaner, waiter, bar staff and receptionist were all fine as each had clearly recognisable roles. However, there were many other jobs about the hotel that seemed either wholly oversubscribed, with too many staff, or simply appeared to be made-up jobs to give further employment. There were *three* doormen for example, but only one of them actually held open the door; the other two seemed to have the sole job of just saluting all guests on their arrival and departure. And then of course there was my 'Lift Lurker'. Could his job be counted as an essential service to me? Even if I had wanted to select and push a lift button myself, I would have immediately felt guilty of stealing the man's livelihood. I decided for peace of mind just to tip him along with all the rest. In fact, I ended up giving him a bit more than the others; he was well deserving of it for showing his unfaltering dedication to the job over the many hours I had sat in the lobby.

Returning up to my room, after struggling through an overly rich buttered chicken curry, I came across one final amusement. As usual, my lift supervisor (to give him a more befitting official title) sent me up to the third floor. As the lift door opened, I was once again met by a high-security, gun-wielding armed guard, keeping an ever-vigilant watch over the safety of all the foreign hotel guests. Rifle clenched across his chest, he would have certainly made a formidable first (and last) line of defence, were it not for the fact that, rather unfortunately, he was fast asleep, gently snoring while sitting in his chair. The loud 'ding' of the lift-arriving bell hadn't even woken him, so I didn't either as I walked right past him and on into my room.

6

Southeast Asia: Myanmar to Thailand

27 April 2010: Chittagong, Bangladesh – Yangon, Myanmar

I had the usual delays getting away from the airport. The fuel station I had been taken to was a ragtag outfit, without any of the usual forecourt niceties; it was more like a junkyard with a couple of pumps in the corner that were simply labelled 'Octane'. As to what specific grade it was remained a mystery, although the station manager had assured me it was "very good fresh fuel." I knew it definitely wasn't diesel or kerosene, but nonetheless I was still slightly nervous when introducing it to the engine. In the end, to my great relief, it ran very well with no problems.

My routing to Yangon allowed me to initially fly south following the coastline. Soon enough though, I needed to cut inland, across a long chain of coastal mountains, to access the broad and flat plain of the Irrawaddy Valley in the interior of Myanmar. I knew that once I picked up on the wide, meandering river, I could then find Yangon easily by flying downstream until the river met the sea.

Flying over the coastal mountain range proved to be interesting. It appeared to be only lightly forested, so one of my main concerns of having to make some sort of an emergency landing into dense jungle was not an issue, initially at least. Venturing farther inland, from the air I could see that dozens of forest fires were ablaze. They had haphazardly broken out all over the mountains, and evidence of previous fires had also left much of the landscape charred and blackened. I could not tell if any of the fires had been set deliberately or were accidental wildfires, set off by the oppressive heat. But the extensive patches of scorched bare earth, together with some areas of more obvious permanent deforestation, meant that in an emergency, I could have considered landing on the top ridge line of many of the hills. Although the only issue then would have been my inability to take off again. The rising palls of blueish white smoke indicated that I had a light tailwind, which helped push me along and raised my morale. Taking in the vastness of this incredible smouldering spectacle I thought, "Good job we are not prone to jungle wildfires back in County Antrim." Peat bogs can catch fire and burn in very dry summers, but our Atlantic maritime climate and resultant soggy summers, tends to equip Ireland with one of the world's largest fire prevention sprinkler systems.

Occasional flare ups in the fires created walls of bright orange flames that were visible, even from 2000ft above ground level. I was constantly wary that the rising heat would create a lot of unwanted turbulent air, which combined with the already mountainous terrain, could have made for quite a bumpy ride. However, my fast-spinning rotor blades, as usual, chopped through much of the air disturbance with indifference. "*C'est une formidable machine!*" as the Le Touquet traffic controller put it.

I flew along trying to avoid the worst of the rising smoke, but even at 2000ft I could smell the burning wood. Suddenly, I became aware of small dark objects in the air. Initially they startled me. I couldn't work out what I was seeing, but I soon realised that the objects flying towards and around me were actually charred leaves being plucked skywards from the forest floor with the flames; they appeared like black tissue paper or confetti fluttering in the breeze. I quickly established that being so lightweight, they would do the rotor no harm and marvelled at the spectacle for several minutes. Amazingly, some of the bigger leaves appeared to be fully intact and probably 10 inches or so in length. Soon enough the phenomenon then dispersed, just as quickly as it had appeared, and I was then thankfully back into clear air and heading away from the fires.

Once I had passed over the coastal mountains, the broad interior valley opened up and I could relax a little in the knowledge that I would now get a clear run right down the river flood plain into Yangon. Only things didn't go entirely to plan...

About an hour from Yangon, some four hours and 15 minutes into the flight, I hit a problem. In my haste to get away from Chittagong, I had only checked and noted down the radio frequencies that I needed for my departure. Now approaching Yangon, I soon needed to make an initial call to their approach frequency to update them on my progress and expected arrival time. However, I now discovered that I did not have their approach radio frequency noted down anywhere.

Suddenly I was in a very sticky situation. I couldn't expect to just fly into an international airport unannounced. No radio would effectively mean no entry. I flew on for a few minutes mulling over my next move, all the while getting closer and closer to my destination. I decided the only thing to do was to put out a call on 121.5 MHz, the frequency reserved for any aircraft in difficulties. I urgently needed to make contact with someone, *anyone,* who might then be able to give me the correct approach frequency for Yangon.

I keyed the mike, "All stations. All stations. This is gyroplane, Golf, Yankee, Romeo, Oscar, X-ray."

I waited, listening hard into the background hiss of the headset.

Nothing, no response. Wasn't anyone in the sky around me? Immediately I felt very lonely and isolated.

I waited a few minutes and tried again.

Silence again. Long seconds of nothing, and then quite suddenly I received a reply, loud and clear from a passing airliner.

"Golf Yankee Romeo Oscar X-ray, I have a relay message for you from Yangon control; they are expecting you, please free call them on the following frequency."

Yes! What a relief. I quickly noted down the frequency and thanked the anonymous pilot who was at that point flying high above me. A warm glow of belonging once more passed through me as I now had the means to re-establish proper contact with the outside world. Thank goodness for international radio protocols. I soon made first contact with Yangon and was then vectored in for a trouble-free landing.

***

A warm welcome party greeted me on the apron and the head of airport security appointed himself to take care of my welfare. He was a very friendly guy, his face and broad smile reminded me very much of Mr. Sulu from the original *Star Trek* series; he was dressed in a full length, silk woven, business sarong. This fact alone emphasised the sensation that I had arrived in yet another country, with many different customs and traditions to experience. In truth, I didn't quite know what to expect with Myanmar (formerly Burma). In 2010 the whole country was being ruled under a very strict military regime, and I needed to practise my best diplomatic behaviour. I had been advised to keep all cameras and recording equipment out of sight in the aircraft, which meant that I had little opportunity to take many snap shots of my surroundings.

The Buddhist influence was starting to become much more evident, Thailand after all was now just next door. The many people who I was introduced to were very polite and gracious, even though they were surrounded by heightened security. My allocated minder organised my accommodation to be in the airport hotel that was directly across the road from the airport entrance. As with the higher security situations in Jeddah and Gwadar previously, I was once again told not to leave the confines of the hotel until I was picked up again by the security team in the morning.

Hey ho… No city sightseeing for me then. At least the hotel felt calm and pleasant, though with the unstable political situation I, once again, appeared to be one of the only guests staying there.

28 April 2010: Yangon, Myanmar – Bangkok, Thailand

Obtaining fuel was going to be the trickiest part of my day; there was a government ruling in place that gasoline could not be pumped into any container apart from a standard car petrol tank. I think this was to prevent dangerous stockpiling of fuel, or perhaps to make it harder for anyone attempting to manufacture petrol bombs. I arranged to be taken by a local driver to a nearby petrol station, where I hoped to get my Turtle Pac fuel bladder filled. It's a highly unusual container to be refuelled on any forecourt, let alone in the nervous city streets of Yangon, so in true James Bond-style I knew some sort of subterfuge would have to be called for.

My first task was to be able to pay for the fuel. More draconian government policy dictated that all fuel could only be purchased using an official 'dollar equivalent' paper currency; which reminded me of the sort of pretend bank notes that you would see in the board game *Monopoly*, only these were much more serious and real. My driver quickly found a guy off the street who exchanged my real US dollars for the local government-issued 'Monopoly dollars' (US$83 bought $80 Monopoly). We then joined a lengthy queue of cars waiting at one of the few official petrol stations that were operating. The upside of using the official garage was fuel security. It was rumoured that the many little roadside garages dotted about were adding quantities of kerosene into their gasoline, in order to boost their profits, not exactly what you want to be using when taking to the air.

Soon enough it was our turn at the pumps. The driver went off to keep the forecourt attendant talking, while I stood at the rear of our vehicle. I smiled over the roof of the car at both of them and appeared to be innocently filling the regular fuel tank (situated behind the rear passenger door) with the required fuel. But what I was really doing was filling the Turtle Pac, that was lying on the back seat of the car covered over with some old clothes. Job done, we handed over the Monopoly money and headed back for the airport.

The little that I got to see of Yangon on the ground from this fuel journey was impressive. We passed some fantastic golden arches, and everywhere the streets were spotlessly clean. There were even no car horns blaring incessantly from the traffic, as had been the case in India and Bangladesh. It turned out that sounding car horns in Yangon had been banned completely. Perhaps living under strict military law had at least one or two benefits after all!

The flight out of Yangon was unfortunately highly contrived. Taxiing out, I was required to use runway 03 for take-off, despite there being a good 10 knot tailwind blowing in that direction. As I lined up for the downwind take-off, staring at the wrong end of the windsock, I suspected that the odd choice of runway direction was more to do with keeping me away from overflying the south and west of Yangon City, as this would have afforded me a great view of the golden Shwedagon Pagoda.

The authorities were still quite wary of my flight and thought it best to vector me a good 20 miles up to the north-east of Yangon before allowing me to resume a more direct line towards Bangkok. The result, just as the overly sensitive authorities intended, was that I saw virtually nothing of the skyline of Yangon during my climb-out, never mind take any tourist snaps of the famed golden pagoda from the air. The only view I got of it was as a whitish blob disappearing away off into the far distance.

I coasted out and flew about 80 nautical miles over the Gulf of Martaban to the north of the Andaman Sea. I settled into my daily cockpit routine and was now really enjoying this flight. Despite all its military security hang ups, Myanmar had also displayed a lovely, gently calming atmosphere, a big contrast from the noisy, clamouring mayhem and melee that had been India and Bangladesh. If the increasingly Buddhist influence on the people was to bring out a more serene, tolerant, gentle way of living, then I was all for it.

I coasted inland again only to be presented with yet another mountainous coastal region ahead of me. This proved to be a complex, technical terrain that I simply had to cross to enter into Thailand.

Shortly after entering the mountains, I was presented with a long line of thundery and angry-looking clouds. There was no way I could fly through them, so I opted to track further south to fly around the southern end of the whole cloud formation. After several skirting approaches to the cloud base searching for a decent gap, I eventually made enough eastward progress to cross into Thai airspace.

Crossing the border, my persistence paid off and I received my reward, flying across a fantastic lake in the Khao Laem National Park. The aerial views of this feature and the larger lake behind the Sinakharin Dam, which I also crossed soon afterwards, were breathtakingly stunning. A myriad of small islands were sprinkled about on the surface of both lakes, and these were silhouetted jet black in the shimmering silvery waters of the reflected sunlight. From the air, this appeared to be a truly pristine and unspoilt region of Thailand, and the surrounding mountains were lush and thick with jungle vegetation. Mountain tracks and trails snaked their way around the hills and were a comforting sight in case I had needed to make any sort of forced landing.

Approaching Bangkok from the north-west, it seemed everywhere was wet. The sky had turned very gloomy with heavy rain showers dotted about, and on arrival over the runway at Don Mueang International Airport I could see a lot of standing water from a recent cloudburst.

Curiously on my final approach, a bright patch of unusual colour caught my eye off to the side of my flight path. It turned out to be a huge crowd of Red Shirts protesters who had blockaded one of the main highways near the airport. As in Myanmar, security once again was in sharp focus, and I saw many police, soldiers and army ambulances posted out around the busy streets during the evening.

Passing through Don Mueang International Airport was a surreal experience. It had been Bangkok's main air hub until the recently completed and ultra-modern Suvarnabhumi Airport took over handling the huge volume of international tourist traffic. Don Mueang was still operating, as Bangkok's second airport, but it mainly now served cargo flights. This meant that my walk through the cavernous, but empty, airport concourses to comply with the various customs and immigration formalities, gave me the impression that I was passing through a *Marie Celeste*-type theme park. The passenger terminal was fully lit, the escalators were all running, and the airport appeared to be fully open and functioning, yet there were literally no people. All the lights were on, but no one was at home.

After completing arrival formalities, I was instructed to taxi G-YROX from the passenger terminal across to the other side of the airport runway to find overnight parking at a row of private aviation maintenance hangars. To add to the surreal experience of the deserted terminal, traversing the two active parallel runways also involved, somewhat bizarrely, crossing a golf course that had been squeezed into the long thin gap between the two strips of tarmac. People are certainly inventive in Thailand.

29 April 2010: Bangkok, Thailand – Nong Prue, Thailand

Localised thunderstorms delayed my departure, but I knew the flight to Nong Prue was only going to take me around 90 minutes, so I was quite relaxed in waiting for the weather to clear. It was nice to have everything packed and not be in a rush to leave, although I was also conscious that a lot of people were waiting for my arrival at Nong Prue, a small airfield located near the popular beach holiday city of Pattaya. Some days before, Ian Gilks, an expat from the UK, had got in contact via my social media pages and recommended a stop at this little microlight grass strip. He advised that the airfield had an extremely active group of expat pilots, who had been following my flight, and that they would all be very keen to host me as I passed by. Compared to the large, impersonal international airports that I had been required to use in recent days, the idea of spending some time at a small friendly grass airfield was very welcome.

Little did I know at this point that I would in fact get to know this airfield and its pilots very well in the days (and months) to come.

On climb-out from Don Mueang, I was in for a surprise. The thunderstorms that had delayed my departure had rumbled off towards the north-east, so the decision was made by ATC to send me on a low-level helicopter route south, towards the coastline and then allow me to continue at this low altitude down the eastern shore of the Gulf of Thailand. This all sounded fine, as did the instruction to remain under the traffic flying in and out of the nearby Suvarnabhumi Airport. This meant I would have to fly strictly at 500ft above ground level. Normally this would pose no issues as gyroplanes can operate at such low levels very competently, however the instruction to fly due south on climb-out also had me flying directly over Bangkok city centre. Again, this in itself was no big deal, apart from the fact that the tops of some of the tall buildings, a mile or so off to my right, were actually not much lower than I was. My defensive flying strategy was to follow the main Chao Phraya River as well as a major highway that appeared to scythe its way through the built-up areas. Both features were relatively open to the sky and would hopefully have allowed an emergency landing if it had become necessary. The over-city view was spectacular, a myriad of multi-coloured ramshackle buildings, mixed together and juxtaposed against imposing, modern concrete-and-glass skyscrapers. It amused me to see that a lot of smart shop fronts at street level belied the fact that often their hidden roofs were embarrassingly made of rusty old corrugated tin.

Soon enough, the brown river spilled out into the sea and I was able to turn south-eastwards to run down the coastline. North of Pattaya, I turned inland to be met by an aerial reception party of three flex-wing microlights that had flown out to meet me. Smiles, waves and thumbs up, they then led me into land.

My first impression of Nong Prue Airpark was that of overwhelming warmth and friendliness. Everyone had turned out to meet me and after brief introductions all round, I was handed a beer, and a fantastic hangar barbeque evening followed. After so many weeks of enduring the hassles of the Middle East and the Indian subcontinent, it was a real relief to stop in a place where one of my hosts, Tom Grieve, a Scotsman, was able to offer me both overnight hangar space and a freshly made bowl of porridge.

I was introduced to the airfield owner, a larger-than-life Thai man called Tiger. He was very enthusiastic to see visiting aircraft make use of his fine airstrip and kindly organised for me to stay in the nearby equestrian resort of Horseshoe Point. This was quite an amazing complex, combining a luxurious hotel with a state-of-the-art equestrian centre. Rather bizarrely a large indoor dressage arena was situated right in the middle of all the hotel rooms.

30 April 2010: Nong Prue, Thailand (local flying day)

I was up bright and early for some media interviews, followed soon afterwards by a fly out around the local area with some of the resident flex-wings. We flew past a huge image of Buddha depicted in gold that had been carved into a large slab of rock, and also buzzed along the main tourist beach before returning to the airstrip when local thunderstorms began to bubble up. We retired to Tom's hangar to enjoy that not-so-well-known Thai delicacy of mince and champ. After all, it was an ideal occasion to celebrate our joint Scottish/Irish Celtic connections!

1 May 2010: Nong Prue, Thailand – Nong Prue, Thailand

After taking a couple of new friends (Dan and Neet) for short flights in the morning, I repacked *Roxy* to be ready to depart by 2pm. The intended flight was a short one, just a hop across the Gulf of Thailand to the island of Ko Samui. The guys made sure I was fully fuelled and ready for departure straight after lunch.

The flight however lasted all of one minute...

As I bumped and trundled out over the baked-hard ground towards the grass strip runway, I was quite confident about the upcoming flight. It was relatively short and I had benefited from a good rest day. I was mentally ready to take on my next over-water crossing.

Holding on the taxiway, I discussed the wind direction with the local flyers over the radio. The light wind was very fickle; the almost limp windsock and various flags seemed undecided, swapping back and forth, momentarily favouring either direction. The rising heat of the afternoon was also not helping, especially as I was slowly melting inside my immersion suit, that had already been fully zipped up in preparation for crossing the Gulf of Thailand. It would be all fine, just as soon as I got airborne.

Out on the horizon, I could see a towering thunderstorm cell building in the heat, which would no doubt be bringing on heavy rain and possible lightning later in the day. But were its updraughts also now already having a local effect on the wind, I wondered? For a time, the wind favoured one direction for take-off, so I lined up with the Nong Prue Lake running parallel to my left side.

The take-off roll was fine, the engine and prop were pushing well, but in the heat of the day the air was thin. And the fickle headwind was perhaps helping me only part time, which meant the rotor blades were struggling to gain much purchase into the air and generate decent lift. I rose off the ground and as was normal, I stayed low to build up my airspeed. But still the aircraft felt sluggish. I was flying, but not with any great gusto. With hindsight, I should have dropped back to the ground and backtracked on the runway for another go, but I felt that at any moment the ground speed would build, and the rotors would pick up, as they would often naturally do.

So unfortunately, I pressed on with the take-off.

I was holding my own with altitude, but not climbing. The blades were struggling, well behind their power curve of maximum efficiency. And by the time the expected rotor lift failed to happen, I was unfortunately running out of both runway and possible options.

Normally in such a situation, as I was already now in the air, I could have simply extended the near ground take-off distance and climbed slowly straight ahead, beyond the end of the runway. Gradually building more airspeed and rotor lift before actively climbing away. But this was not a normal situation, as beyond the airfield boundary ahead were roadside powerlines that stretched right across my flight path. For whatever reason, the Thai authorities seemed to prefer their electricity poles and power lines to be perhaps 50% taller than in most other countries.

I quickly eyeballed the wires, and it was very obvious that I would not be able to clear them. For the briefest of moments, because the wires were so high, I thought I might be able to fly *under* them. But then I spotted it, a very thin additional wire had been slung, about 5ft underneath the main set.

Damn! I was suddenly caught between a rock and a hard place.

I couldn't now drop back onto the runway without stuffing the aircraft into the airfield boundary hedge. That was an unthinkable option, but in hindsight it was exactly what I should have done.

Scanning around quickly and trying to think even quicker, options were hard to find. I couldn't land ahead, that was certain. I couldn't bank to the right, as that would have taken me slap bang into a thick grove of Coconut palms. But I could possibly bank to the left slightly and head out over the Nong Prue Lake. That seemed the perfect escape plan, to continue the slow climb out over the flat, unobstructed lake and then clear the power lines later, once I had built up a better rate of climb.

Banking very cautiously to preserve the precious rotor lift I had, I managed to maintain a steady height and headed for the open water. Moments later, I cleared the shoreline of the lake...

Then it all happened at once.

Over the land, I had been maintaining height and flying (albeit not very well). Out over the lake however, everything suddenly became a vastly different story. Rather than holding its own in the air, the aircraft now started to sink. It was the worst sickening feeling that I have probably ever experienced as a pilot. I was low over the water in an aircraft that could not keep itself in the air for much longer. I was now just a passenger in my own plane.

But even in this dire situation, I continued to scan for any option that might help with damage limitation. I knew I didn't want to land in the middle of the lake, so very gingerly I used the little height remaining to bank around right again to try to make it back to the shoreline.

Travelling at about 20 knots forward airspeed, I didn't quite make it back to dry land and ditched into the water. Close to the shore, it was only about 2ft deep, but in a split-second after touching the water, poor *Roxy* pitchpoled, end over end, right over her nose, to land upside down. I was suddenly inverted, disorientated, still strapped in my seat and held completely underwater.

"I'm upside down!"

My aircraft was lying on top of me. I was submerged underwater. And I was in darkness.

Still in my seat straps, I could reach to feel the bottom of the lake above my head. It had an oozy muddy texture, the sort that I might normally feel squeezing through my toes when paddling in bare feet.

Only this did not feel normal, not normal at all.

My immediate thoughts: "What have I done to end up in this situation? Why am I not flying?"

Moments before, I had been saying my farewells to my new-found friends at the airfield and then, so suddenly, I found myself to be an uninvited guest in their lake.

Thankfully, there was no panic.

The violence of the impact was quite surprising. After a slow, inevitable descent towards the lake shoreline, I was instantaneously pitchpoled forward as the gyroplane tripped over its nose in the shallow water. Upside down, though not fully inverted, my aircraft was leaning slightly onto its right side, and this simple fact, as I shall explain later, would directly help to save me, the aircraft and ultimately the whole expedition.

But wait, I should correct myself; there was no panic, *initially*...

At first, I sensed an inner calmness in my head, and I attribute this to having already experienced many very violent crashes into water. Not from flying admittedly, but rather from windsurfing in high winds on rough seas. The effect of being thrown from my board, slammed into the water at 20 knots and being momentarily disorientated, felt very similar to my current tricky situation. When tangled up and held submerged under a large sail, made heavy with overlying water, the best course of action was always: to mentally control any immediate sense of panic; to take stock of my situation; to work out my orientation and escape route; and, finally, to simply float my way out from under the obstruction as calmly as possible to regain the surface.

Thankfully then, when it came to attempt my escape from a suddenly inverted, ditched and damaged aircraft, my body and brain thought instinctively that this was a fairly normal experience.

My next conscious thought was surprising:

"What a pillock! What did you go and do that for?"

Only then to be quickly followed by:

"Well, I suppose I'll have to try to get out now."

Being upside down and underwater was also similar to being sat in a capsized kayak, and fortunately in my earlier adventuring days I had additionally spent plenty of time dumped upside down in one of those. After a capsize, there was a technique I often used with my paddle, to allow me to roll the kayak back up again. The trick was to reach down, which was actually up, and tap the water surface with my paddle blade. This then gave my brain a solid reference as to which way was up. If on occasions I had lost grip of my paddle, then I was able to do the same action with my hand. And so this was what I did in the aircraft. Luckily my fingers tapped the surface only a few centimetres above the inverted cockpit, so I knew at least that the surface was not far away. Next, I released my seat harness buckle and while wrestling out of it, I managed to wiggle around in my seat to allow my face to break clear of the surface. Well, half of my face, but crucially just enough for my nose and mouth to be able to breathe again. At least I was alive and thankfully now breathing, but the rest of my body and legs were still wedged inside the cockpit.

The whole ditching episode to this point, had only taken around a minute. Fortunately, I was not physically hurt. But how to get out?

The next vision I had was of a tall, athletically built Thai lad bounding across the lake shoreline at full speed in my direction. Moments before, he had been waving me bon voyage with the rest of the airfield entourage, around 200m away. Being so fit, he was first on the scene to offer me help. Before he could reach me however, I shouted a crucial instruction to him.

"I'm OK! I'm breathing! But whatever you do, DO NOT run into the water to reach me!"

He was a little puzzled.

"Just walk in, nice and slowly," I continued, "The last thing I need you to do is set up a tidal wave and cover my face."

More people quickly arrived to help and within seconds I had been untangled and manually pulled out from the cockpit. I was then able to stand up in the shallow waters. Even though I had appeared not to panic and had stayed cool, calm and collected throughout, the adrenaline was still pumping through me and I exploded with frustration at the aircraft.

"Why didn't you fly!" I shouted, whacking the underside of the upturned hull with my hand as I was helped out of the lake. Moments later the shock kicked in and I sat down to process my thoughts, still fuming with myself for being so stupid as to have ditched poor *Roxy* in the lake. After checking I was unhurt, the onlookers immediately swung into action on their next task.

The next priority was to try to save *Roxy*.

She was upside down, but because of the stainless-steel rotor mast, which had now stuck in the lakebed mud, she was also leaning slightly over on her right side. Crucially, the air intake filter was located on the lower left side of the engine and this section had managed to remain clear of the water throughout the ditching. An extremely fortunate follow up photo taken of the scene, visibly showed the air filter to be sitting up high and dry and this proved to be pivotal evidence when dealing with the UK CAA some weeks later. The photo demonstrated that although the rotor blades, propeller and much of the fuselage had been severely damaged during the ditching and roll over, the engine itself had not actually ingested any water internally. After a number of further tests to ensure there was also no damage to the gearbox, the engine was eventually allowed to continue in service.

Incredibly, that one crucial photograph had saved the engine, which also helped to save the aircraft, which then saved the entire circumnavigation project.

But for now, *Roxy* was still lying helpless, upside down in the lake. Immediately, in an effort to save her, the inventiveness and industrious can-do attitude of the Thai people was combined with the true kindred spirit that is felt between fellow aviators. En masse, around a dozen fully clothed people waded in and gathered around the fuselage, and with human power alone they were able to roll *Roxy* back upright and onto her main wheels. Within 30 minutes, a flat-bed truck arrived, complete with a Hiab crane and promptly proceeded to reach out from the shoreline and pluck the very dishevelled, bruised and battered *Roxy* from the water. Soon afterwards she was carefully transported on the flatbed truck back to Tom Grieve's hangar.

In a flurry of activity within the next 90 minutes, the engine was checked over, a temporary prop was fitted, and the electrics were dried out. The engine was then turned over manually before finally being allowed to run for a short time. It was like witnessing a gravely ill patient suddenly being resuscitated after heart failure. Everyone cheered as the engine spluttered into life – it was a significant step, but I knew it was still very uncertain whether this was now going to be the end of the world flight.

Everything that had been in the aircraft was now soaked and covered in oozy mud, but again, within minutes of being back at the hangar, an army of Thai volunteers pulled everything out and cleaned off all the mud. The entire internal contents of the aircraft were then laid out on a tarpaulin in the hot sun to dry out completely. Still in shock, I looked on from where I had been seated and felt a tremendous sense of empathy, love and kindness for all these people who were now working tirelessly to help fix this disastrous situation.

As soon as I could, I borrowed a phone and called home. It was still early morning back in the UK but I wanted Celia and the family to hear directly from me before any other news of the ditching had circulated more widely. I reassured her that I was OK and physically unhurt, but that the aircraft had been badly damaged.

I was still at a loss to work out what went wrong with the take-off, but eventually, as so often is the case with aircraft incidents, it was thought to be an unfortunate combination of numerous small factors that conspired together with dramatic effect. Heavy with fuel, biting into thin warm air and with a variable, fickle headwind, these incremental effects helped to erode my overall performance and resulted in a very sluggish take-off. Sluggish, but perhaps at that point, still a wholly recoverable situation.

But the last piece of the jigsaw, the 'gotcha' moment as we later surmised, was the temperature difference between being over the ground and being over the lake. While over the ground, I was airborne and maintaining an adequate (albeit sluggish) climb-out rate. Yet as soon as I crossed over the lake boundary, I then lost height rapidly. One theory was that there was possibly a local rotor effect going on in the air; that the air was *rising* over the hot ground (aiding lift and keeping me airborne), but then it was *sinking* over the relatively cooler lake surface (and bringing me down with it). Such small, innocuous details in themselves, but when they all conspired together to create a chain reaction of events, the end result sadly proved quite cataclysmic.

There was now great uncertainty as to what could be done to save the aircraft, and for the next two days, I continued to think that this was very likely to be the end of the whole project.

7

Thailand: A different adventure

2 May – 31 July, 2010: Repairs in Thailand

Immediately after the ditching, Tom and his partner Mae put me up at their house for a few nights. In part, it was to ensure I was still OK mentally after the sudden trauma of having just survived a plane crash. I was extremely fortunate to not suffer any physical injuries, but any possible mental effects were not so visible. The support from Tom, Mae and all the Nong Prue flying club members proved vital in the weeks that followed, as it gave me a tremendous sense of friendship and belonging in what otherwise would have been a very lonely, daunting, and almost insurmountable situation.

Within the first few days, I had been lent the personal use of a car, a motorbike and even, with kind thanks to expat microlight flyer Steve Butcher, a 15th floor condo apartment to live in. The expat community of flyers at Nong Prue Airfield, along with Tiger and his partner Moe, gave me an instant support network of likeminded friends to spend my time with. Simply put, if the ditching had happened in a less friendly country, one with a less positive and optimistic attitude than that of Thailand, any thoughts of aircraft repairs could easily have been dismissed as being a totally impossible challenge.

My immediate practical concern then, was whether there was any chance of *Roxy* being saved. Over the next few days numerous technical emails and phone conversations went back and forth between me, Gerry Speich of RotorSport UK and John Hereward (my regular aircraft mechanic in the UK) to assess the damage, and to work out if a repair plan could be put in place. Gerry in turn, was also then in contact with the main factory headquarters of Autogyro in Germany.

Slowly a plan of action emerged. An aircraft rebuild in Thailand could indeed be possible, as long as some replacement parts could be shipped in from the UK and Germany, and if John could be brought in to do the strip down and rebuild in situ. Once rebuilt, Gerry then needed to flight test and sign-off on the rebuild, which in turn would allow the UK CAA to permit G-YROX to return to service. It was all logistically feasible, but it also required a monumental effort from all those involved.

There was still however, one loose spanner in the works. The nose section of the carbon fibre fuselage had been severely damaged during the pitchpole into the lake. It now resembled a cracked and broken bright yellow eggshell; still holding its shape, but without any structural strength. The question remained, how could this carefully crafted, aircraft-quality, carbon fibre construction ever be repaired at a small grass airstrip in Thailand to the complete satisfaction of the UK CAA? Help was to come from a very unexpected alliance.

After driving one hour north from the airfield, rattling around in Tiger's big pickup truck, we arrived at a neat, well-appointed factory. In the back was *Roxy*'s stripped-down carbon fibre bodywork. The owner of the Thai factory was a German entrepreneur involved in the aviation industry. And as serendipity would have it, he already knew the German owners of the Autogyro factory back in Europe. Even more coincidental was that the industrious little factory we were now visiting, specialised in the manufacture of *Helix* carbon fibre propeller blades used for powered parachute engines! A conversation between the two German bosses soon opened the door to allow *Roxy*'s carbon fibre bodywork to be repaired, to an aviation grade quality, in Thailand, and barely an hour's drive away. Fantastic!

And what was more, as the icing on the cake, the repair was also completed absolutely free of charge!

One slight technical difficulty however remained. Carbon fibre needs a high temperature to properly cure, but the factory only had small kilns that were used to manufacture the *Helix* propeller blades, not the huge curing oven that was normally needed for an aircraft fuselage. As ever, a work around was found; after the nose was strengthened and repaired internally, with a patchwork of supporting carbon fibre matting, the bodywork was just left outside for a few hours to cook in the intense heat of the Thai mid-summer sunshine. Job done.

After a complete strip down back at the Nong Prue hangars, the myriad of assorted parts that ultimately combined to make up a fully functioning gyroplane were laid out neatly on an old table tennis table. The strip down and rebuild process was relatively quick (around three weeks in total) but alas, the red tape involved with the UK CAA trying to make a decision on allowing the re-build to go ahead, added a further *nine weeks* of delay to the start of the process. They had needed convincing that the aircraft could be rebuilt in Thailand to the same exacting standards as if it had been shipped back to RotorSport UK for repairs.

It was nine full weeks of added frustration that I simply couldn't afford in the flight schedule, and ultimately it meant I then lost the brief summer window of opportunity to make the permitted flight across Russia and the Bering Strait. Had the Thailand repairs taken say only six weeks (instead of 12 in total), I could have continued in mid-June and reached across to Alaska easily by mid-July. Unfortunately, with all the protracted delays and stalled decisions, I only got going again in early August, having spent a full three months on the ground for repairs.

8

Southeast Asia: Thailand to the Philippines

1 August 2010: Nong Prue, Thailand – Trang, Thailand – Hat Yai, Thailand

I was up for 6am to remove the last of my luggage out of my apartment and set off to the airfield for the last time. I was the first to arrive but over the next 30 minutes or so everyone appeared in order to give me a good send off, and Tiger phoned through my flight plan. I had decided this time to bypass Ko Samui; I felt I had lingered enough in holiday destinations and really needed now to get some serious miles flown. My plan was to fly about 80 nautical miles over the Gulf of Thailand and then, by early afternoon, make a precautionary stop at Trang. This would allow me to double-check the aircraft and stowage on the ground, as I hadn't flown many miles since the comprehensive rebuild. I then planned to make a shorter hop to Hat Yai International Airport, to clear customs and immigration, before flying south to cross the border into Malaysia.

The wind was calm for take-off, and I knew the cooler, denser air of the early morning would help to give me additional lift. Fully loaded for the first time in three months, with all my circumnavigation kit back on board, I wanted to build in as many safety margins as possible. With no wind factor to consider, I elected to take off in the opposite direction to my 1 May departure – I definitely didn't want history to repeat itself! Reassuringly, the climb out in this direction had no overhead wires, only a few low farm sheds. With some trepidation, I lined up quite close to the spot where *Roxy* and I had gone for our swim. I wound up the rotor and gave the engine full power. Rolling down the bumpy grass surface I was determined to get off the ground as quickly as possible, but it still felt like a long time. I passed the line of spectators at the short taxiway marking the approximate halfway point still feeling the aircraft to be very heavy. But then, in one glorious moment, the wheels became light on the ground as the rotor took up the full weight of the aircraft. I sensed that I was nearly flying, still had plenty of runway left and a clear climb-out path ahead; smiling to myself, I knew that this time, I was good to go. I heard later that everyone on the ground was clapping and cheering as I finally rose into the air. A big relief all round. I continued my climb-out to get well clear of the ground and made a single, high-level overhead pass to give a final wave. It was quite an emotional moment as I said my farewells over the radio, exactly three months to the day since I had ditched in the lake.

Suddenly I was on my own again, coasting out over the sea, but I quickly fell back into what had been my usual routine. The cockpit was my familiar office space and it felt very much that I was once again, back at work. The miles passed quickly as I reflected on my time spent grounded in Thailand. There were so many interlinking factors during the repairs, that had to combine and dovetail together to eventually get the whole show back on the road. Looking back, I never could have imagined how this whole adventure would end up taking so many twists and turns of fortune. You simply couldn't make it up!

I was in a reflective mood but was also feeling very relieved to be up and running again. As if to gradually ease me back into the daily hazards of circumnavigation flying, I experienced heavy cloud bursts of rain as I coasted in towards southern Thailand. Thankfully, they remained isolated and didn't organise themselves into more complex weather, which enabled me to dodge around most of the worst showers to remain in clear visibility.

Trang was noticeably quiet when I arrived. It was a small regional airport and had a very calm atmosphere. The staff even had time to chat and made me most welcome with a cup of coffee. It was a gentle introduction back into my special world of being something of an aerial nomad. I was only on the ground for a short time to check the aircraft but one of the heavy tropical cloud bursts caught up with me and so we pushed *Roxy* temporarily under a covered area that held the baggage carousel. I was once again very thankful of the manoeuvrability and versatility of a gyro to be able to squeeze into a tight space when required. The flight from Nong Prue to Trang had taken me 6hrs 5mins. After a quick splash of fuel, the short onward hop to Hat Yai took only a further 1hr 25mins.

In the evening I met up for dinner with Ian Gilks, who had first recommended I stop at Nong Prue back in April. By lucky coincidence he was attending a week-long motorbike rally nearby. I expected this to be my last evening in Thailand before moving onto Malaysia, but alas bureaucracy once again had other ideas.

2 August 2010: Hat Yai, Thailand (non-flying day)

During the rebuild process in Nong Prue I had imported a good number of new aircraft parts. Customs at Hat Yai insisted that these had to be inspected to confirm that all imported parts were now in effect being exported again as part of the aircraft. It seemed quite ludicrous to imagine that I had somehow planned to ditch the aircraft in the lake, just so I could use it as a cover story to import and presumably sell on smuggled aircraft parts in Thailand. But this was indeed what the local customs officers needed to clarify. All I could do was smile nicely and comply with their requirement to visually check that any replacement parts listed on my import shipping documents, were now permanently affixed to the aircraft. I set about laboriously taking them through the complete list and I am sure that with half of the specialist items, they wouldn't have known if I was pointing to the correct part or not. Still, it was the easiest way to get around the problem. Unfortunately, it took ages to complete, so much so that by about half-way through, I slowly realised that I was no longer going to have enough daylight to complete my next flight to Malaysia.

Knowing the best part of the day was now lost, I decided to have a bit of fun with my 'captors' when they called me into their office to complete the final paperwork. They stated that they were now happy that all the parts on my list were indeed being exported again from the country.

"Good!" I exclaimed, "In that case, can I now reclaim back all the *import tax* that was applied to the parts when we shipped them in? You have confirmed to me that all these parts are not staying in Thailand; they are not for domestic use in your country, and they have been attached onto a foreign registered aircraft, which is now leaving the country. I should therefore be able to claim back all the domestic import tax paid."

I put on my best, winning smile and waited for their response.

They did not know if I was joking with them or not, and so for my own amusement I maintained that I was indeed serious about reclaiming my money, even though I knew full well that I was asking for the impossible. I just enjoyed watching the customs officers trying to talk themselves out of the situation, struggling to justify why it was not possible to return my import taxes, whilst trying desperately to appear that they were not in the wrong.

3 August 2010: Hat Yai, Thailand – Kuala Lumpur, Malaysia

The previous day's customs delays had at least allowed me to be ready for an early start. I was finally leaving Thailand and flying south into Malaysia. A few days previously my GyroxGoesGlobal online team had discovered a fantastic contact called Captain Siva from Kuala Lumpur. He was (and is) an extremely well known and accomplished commercial airline pilot, and along with his wife Rani, proved to be terrific local guides and fabulous hosts as I navigated my way around Peninsular Malaysia and across into Borneo.

My initial instructions were to fly down the western coast of Peninsular Malaysia and rendezvous with Captain Siva in the air, over a prominent lighthouse on the shoreline. True to plan, as I approached the meeting point, the Captain appeared in a light fixed-wing aircraft. Establishing radio comms, I was then instructed to follow him closely as he led me through the congested airspace around Kuala Lumpur. This was a great help as I could relax on my navigation and simply concentrate on being a good wingman alongside his plane. Flying in close formation, we passed straight by Subang International Airport, which was to be our final destination. In doing so, Captain Siva explained that he had been able to arrange permission for an extra photo-shooting opportunity. Little did I realise at the time, but here was a man with many contacts and connections in all the right places. The skyline of downtown Kuala Lumpur loomed large in the late afternoon sun, and it soon became apparent that our photo op was going to be flying around the world-famous Petronas Twin Towers.

On a previous visit to Kuala Lumpur, I had stood below the towers, gazing up in awe at their incredible construction. Never would I have imagined back then that one day I would be flying in my own aircraft around these twin marvels of engineering. We circled five or six times around the mid-section, with Captain Siva flying a wider orbit than my own to enable him to take air-to-air photos. It was all quite an amazing and surreal experience, it must be said. We eventually peeled off and landed line astern on the runway at Subang, where after taxiing into the flight school, I was finally able to get out and shake the captain's hand. Meeting Rani, she generously offered me overnight accommodation for the evening at their house, and on the drive home we went for a very convivial Chinese meal near the airport. Rather bizarrely, I remember there was a huge glass fish tank set into the back wall of the gent's urinal. It was an impressive design but also somewhat unsettling with all the fish staring back at you! Back at the house, we sat up discussing future flight plans and retelling various earlier adventures until nearly 1am. After such a momentous day of flying I was ready for much needed sleep.

4 August 2010: Kuala Lumpur, Malaysia – Johor, Malaysia – Kuching, Borneo, Malaysia

Despite the late previous night, I was up early as another big day awaited. I was aiming to fly to the island of Borneo, the first island I would visit since leaving Crete in the Mediterranean Sea. Islands have always had an additional appeal for me as they often retain a strong sense of their own independent character. They are harder to get to and therefore often feel more culturally separate. Flying across the South China Sea, the large island of Borneo marked the start of a chain of island hopping that hopefully would see me safely all the way up to Japan.

Within this phase of the circumnavigation, I knew that I was going to spend most of my time flying over water. On the positive side, this would mean smoother air, less congested airspace, beautiful tropical islands and interesting island cultures. On the downside, it could potentially also mean dealing with the risks of man-eating sharks instead of man-eating tigers.

Departing from Subang, I was again personally escorted by Captain Siva's light aircraft. He had arranged another fly around the Petronas Twin Towers to gain some more air-to-air shots before I was sent off on my merry way towards Johor. The total flight time, with extra sightseeing, ended up being 2hrs 50mins, and ever conscious of the precious daylight time ticking away, I had to make the lunchtime Johor stop very brief. Fortunately, *the captain* had already phoned ahead to organise a fabulous Formula One-style pit stop.

A reception committee was on hand, and as soon as I rolled to a stop I was quickly topped up with fuel. In the meantime, I took a drink, ate some buns and had a quick pee. Not quite as glamorous as Formula 1 perhaps, but an hour after touching down, I was already saying my farewells and was off again.

* * *

I now headed due east towards the South China Sea for the second flight of the day, one that would take a further 5hrs 25mins. Tracking just to the north of Singapore, this flight also marked the southern-most point that I would reach on my entire circumnavigation, as I made the open water crossing at exactly 1 degree north of the Equator. I briefly contemplated detouring slightly and crossing into the southern hemisphere but soon decided that this day was already going to be plenty long enough. Totalling 8hrs 15mins of flight time, with most of it flown over water, I reasoned that flying a lengthy southerly dogleg, just to see the *degrees north* change to *degrees south* on my GPS screens perhaps wasn't worth the additional risk.

Crossing the South China Sea was one of the three longest over-water stretches I had flown so far, along with the Mediterranean and the Red Sea. Thankfully the weather en route was quite favourable, with clear blue skies followed by fluffy broken cloud in the middle section and heavier layered clouds nearby the coastline of Borneo. I had 300 nautical miles of open water to cross, which took 4hrs 35mins, shore to shore, as I was lucky enough to also have a helpful tailwind. Approximately halfway across the open water, I received a relayed message from a passing airliner above me. Singapore Control were asking for a flight update after they had been in contact with Captain Siva. He was definitely still looking after me, right across the country and beyond and this gave me a warm glow of encouragement to know that I was not entirely on my own out there. The final part of the flight, coasting in over the western shores of Borneo, was through Indonesian airspace. The landscape here was much less intensively managed compared to that of west Malaysia. Tightly packed rows of houses, backing straight onto the rainforest, were strung out along roadsides for miles. This jungle backdrop looked very dense and offered very few opportunities of any rough tracks to land on, so I tried to stick close to the principal roads as much as possible.

There is an aviation saying that if you have to make an emergency landing and fall into a jungle canopy, it's actually the second fall, the one from the high treetops down to the ground, that is the most dangerous. Peering down at the wildly tangled web of treetops and vines, I certainly didn't want to try testing out that theory. After many further miles of Jungle flying, my eventual arrival over the smooth, flat runway at Kuching Airport felt especially welcome and I had a trouble-free landing.

Later on, while searching for some shelter from the now frequent tropical downpours (and to add to my growing list of unusual hangar spaces), I managed to persuade the airport to allow *Roxy* to be parked up overnight under a carport awning.

In the evening I was picked up and taken under the wing of three local flying enthusiasts who had made contact through social media. They brought me to a street restaurant, where I enjoyed a local noodle dish and soya milk and later organised the most accurately described *economy hotel* accommodation I was to experience in any country, for just US$6 a night. A small standard room had been partitioned down the middle, so that my somewhat spartan accommodation now only had half a window frame, half a set of curtains and a 'wardrobe' comprised of one screw affixed to the wall with a singular, well-used wire coat hanger hanging on it. Oh, and there was no need for a bed-side table or lamp either, as I could easily reach to turn off the main light switch operating the single bare bulb in the ceiling, without even getting out of bed. Still, the bed was at least clean and after such a long, exhausting flying day, I found it perfectly comfortable.

5 August 2010: Kuching, Borneo, Malaysia – Miri, Borneo, Malaysia – Kota Kinabalu, Borneo, Malaysia

The Sarawak region of Borneo was lovely to fly through. I had a hassle-free flight to the north-east up along the coastline to Miri, where I made a quick stop-off for fuel. As with Johor, I needed a fast turnaround, so one of the security guys at the airport very kindly gave me and the Turtle Pac a lift to the nearest fuel station. Flying again in the afternoon, I passed many small, classic desert islands of the type often drawn in cartoons. One island in particular was little more than a patch of brilliant white sand with a solitary palm tree growing on it. A coconut must have been washed up on the beach and was now growing into a full-sized tree. Resilient nature helping to colonise an otherwise barren island, it was evidence of evolutionary survival at its best.

After skirting around the sovereign state of Brunei, I arrived at Kota Kinabalu (aka KK). Just in time, as it happened, as only 10 minutes later a heavy cloudburst of rain descended from a blackened sky. Rain in the tropics really knows how to put on a show; it was an absolute deluge. Happily, there was a very handy lean-to shed situated next to the main commercial hangars and I pushed *Roxy* under it for shelter. As I unpacked my gear and put the dust cover on to keep her safe and cosy from the deafening rain pelting down on the tin roof, I wondered if this might be a proud moment for the shed. I doubt it had ever been called upon to house an aircraft before, let alone one on a pioneering worldwide flight.

It could now at last and forever more, rid itself of having an inferiority complex about being *just* a shed. It had now made it into the big time; it had morphed into becoming an aircraft hangar.

6 August 2010: Kota Kinabalu, Borneo, Malaysia (non-flying day)

Word came through from the Philippines, my next destination country, that my handler for the island of Palawan was not quite ready to receive me, so I had to wait another day in KK. This was welcome news as the last three days had involved a lot of quite intense, multi-leg flying. I caught up on some sleep and walked around the local area of my small motel accommodation in the afternoon. Soon enough I found a barber shop and decided on getting another haircut, the third one on the trip so far. I was pleased that the barber understood what a 'number three' cut was, and he went to work with his clippers. While I was in the chair, the guy in the next seat recognised me from reading the previous day's Malaysian newspaper *The Star*. Apparently, my trip around the Petronas Twin Towers in KL had been widely reported.

We had a great conversation, which continued into the late afternoon as we sat in the small local square just outside the barber shop. I treasured this social interaction, even though it was nothing extraordinary. Just hanging out with a few local people on the island of Borneo, who were busy doing ordinary things. It felt remarkably similar to my time at the Saudi desert garage. It was wholly spontaneous, random even, only with the added bonus that here at least we could communicate more easily in English.

7 August 2010: Kota Kinabalu, Borneo, Malaysia – Puerto Princesa, Palawan, Philippines

I had been in Malaysia for four days now. Fully rested, with a fresh haircut, I was ready to reach out for my 16th new country, the Philippines.

Departure from KK was under a bright blue sky, with nothing but a few high wispy clouds on the horizon. Initially at least, the flight was idyllic. I left the north coast of Borneo and was soon flying over more stunning tropical islands. Some appeared quite rocky and deserted, others seemed to be luxury exclusive resorts built beside pristine beaches and coral blue seas. One in particular caught my attention – it had a lovely sandy cove beach resort surrounded on three sides by towering mountains covered in an impenetrable tropical jungle canopy. It appeared to be such a juxtaposition between the ultimate luxury of refined modern living and the utterly wild wilderness beyond. I half imagined that this would be the perfect place for King Kong or lost dinosaurs to be lurking. I kept an eye out as I passed overhead but sadly didn't see any huge creatures rampaging through the trees.

Further north the dramatic mountainous island of Palawan came into view. It was a fantastic sight, roughly 250 miles long, yet only around 20 miles across at its widest point, and with a backbone of high mountains running along its length. I was heading for the main settlement on the island at Puerto Princesa, situated about halfway along its length.

I had a terrific tailwind while skirting along the south-eastern shoreline. My GPS was indicating my ground speed as 137 mph for an indicated airspeed of 98 mph meaning my tailwind was a good 35 knots.

For the last 50 nautical miles that I ran along the coastline of the Sulu Sea, I encountered very heavy cloud. The damp humid maritime air was colliding with the high mountains of Palawan and forming a dense hanging cloud formation that then sprawled out and down from the mountains to reach the shoreline. On several occasions I was compelled to make lengthy dogleg diversions well out to sea, to allow me to fly around the worst of the weather. All the time to seaward, the sky remained blue, with clear visibility. This was fine, for now at least, as I could theoretically stay out to sea as long as my fuel reserves would allow. I also knew however, that in order to eventually land, I would have to fly inland of the shoreline to reach the airport runway. By skirting around the flanked edges of the clouds, I managed to stay out of any hazardous flying conditions right up until the last ten minutes of the flight.

"Right then, here we go!" I thought as I psyched myself up for the challenge ahead.

Having contacted the ATC tower and established that there was no other traffic expected to affect my final approach, I orbited a couple of times out at sea to weigh up the weather. Because of the strong sea breeze, the low cloud was very changeable and active. This was useful, as it created breaks in the overall cloud base, which at times was reaching down to only 300ft above the sea. Curtains of heavy tropical rain also periodically extended down from the cloud base. These were too heavy to see through and were certainly to be avoided if at all possible. As I watched for a few minutes, time after time what initially appeared like a promising gap opening in the cloud base would suddenly and rapidly close up again. This was not ideal.

Eventually after what seemed a long wait, but was probably no more than about 10 minutes, I had worked out my best option and decided to go for it. Flying into the squally tropical rain, I would have to dive down low under the cloud base and skim the surface of the sea in towards the runway.

As I dropped under the cloud base, heavy drops of rain spattered on the windscreen obscuring my forward view, but thankfully in the distance I could also at last make out the bright lights of the runway stretching away off into the murky gloom. I ducked lower in my seat to avoid the worst of the deluge that was now battering poor *Roxy*. The clever design of the screen meant that although I was in an open cockpit, I was not actually getting that wet. As long as the aircraft kept moving quickly forward, the rain was hitting the screen and flying right past me horizontally through the air. Fortunately, the end of the runway threshold was positioned almost on the beach, and within a couple of minutes I was down and safely on the ground.

However as soon as I landed and slowed to taxi onto the apron, I was no longer shielded from heavy rain and was soon soaked. Oh, the joys of flying a roofless aircraft!

Despite no let-up in the heavy downpour, the tower sent me to park at the far end of the apron, alongside a big Cessna already parked there. Given the deluge, with the rain hissing and bouncing off the concrete all around me, I chose to ignore the tower and made directly for the nearest part of the apron next to the small terminal building. Several ground handlers came running out to meet me, and thankfully one of them also brought out a large café umbrella that helped keep the rain off until I managed to get permission to keep *Roxy* in the nearby maintenance hangar overnight.

Yet again, this was an example of the detachment of the tower from what was actually happening on the ground. No doubt the official instructions were to put *all* visiting aircraft on the far end of the apron without a thought as to any practical difficulties this may entail.

Thankfully, what the tower lacked in sensitivity and common sense was more than made up for by the helicopter maintenance company in the hangar. John, who was a Canadian but had worked in Shannon Airport in Ireland for two years, was immensely helpful. His time in

Ireland had given his voice a slight Irish twang, which was great to hear, now that I found myself so far removed from the Emerald Isle. In the maintenance shop, I was even able to get a running repair done on my rudder trim tab. This small piece of bent metal was affixed to the rudder and allowed the aircraft to fly in a straight line with the minimum of applied rudder pedal. Unfortunately, the trim tab stuck out slightly from the rear of the aircraft and had been bent nearly to breaking point by some overzealous local ground handling earlier in the journey.

As I was now entering the Philippines from an international flight, there was a lot of paperwork to complete. Adrian, my local flight handler had arranged for all the necessary people to be in attendance. We had the normal customs and immigration procedures as well as additional checks by agencies concerned with agriculture, food, plants and animals (as Palawan was home to some very rare and unique species).

Soon enough, with paperwork completed, Adrian and I readied ourselves to pick up some fuel. To my surprise we were met outside the terminal by a fantastically unusual form of transport. On Palawan it was called a *taxicle*, and it basically comprised a motorbike and side car, which were both fully enclosed inside the external bodywork of the vehicle. Half taxi, half tricycle, hence the name. With such heavy and frequent tropical rain, it was a very practical form of cheap transport on the island. I sat on the small side car bench seat with the Turtle Pac while Adrian rode pillion behind the taxi driver. It was quite surreal to be sitting inside the taxicle with the motorbike engine roaring away right alongside my seat, but great fun all the same.

8 August 2010: Puerto Princesa, Palawan, Philippines – Magalang, Luzon, Philippines

With clear skies compared to the previous day, I was close enough to walk back to the airport terminal from my hotel accommodation. It was refreshing to take a stroll along the road and stretch my legs for a while; there would be no chance to do that whilst airborne.

I decided that my best routing was to immediately fly across the width of the island, while the weather was clear, towards the north-west coastline. From there, I then planned to skirt up the western fringes of the Philippine archipelago to reach the country's biggest island, Luzon.

Fortunately, I was able to pick a reasonably low-level cloud-free route, directly through the mountains and soon enough I was on the opposite side of Palawan and continuing my flight along the South China Sea coastline. Once again, I picked up a favourable tailwind, but the forward visibility steadily deteriorated. In the high humidity, a low cloud base gradually developed over both the land and the sea, so much so that while crossing the Mindoro Strait, I came to a point where two very low-level cloud masses were conspiring to converge together at just 200ft above the sea. I carefully considered the gap of clear air between them, as it was directly on the route I needed to follow. I could see that beyond the gap the sky was clear, but even as I looked on, the gap appeared to be slowly closing up like a giant set of theatre curtains. If I carried on, I estimated that I would arrive at the point between the two clouds at just about the same time as they fully converged. But conversely, to avoid this route and make a detour around the smaller of the two clouds was going to mean a considerable diversion off course.

After weighing up the options for a few moments, I decided to go for the gap and flew as fast as possible aiming for the centre point between the two clouds. Sure enough as I arrived, the fist wisps of water vapour were forming on each side of me but I could still see ahead that the sky was opening up again, clear and blue. I charged through the crack in the clouds, cheering to myself as once again, I emerged into bright sunshine on the other side. It felt like some fancy manoeuvre that the *Star Ship Enterprise* might have pulled off while narrowly avoiding a couple of colliding asteroids. Though thankfully, I was only dealing with water vapour and not solid rock and ice. As I glanced behind me a short while later, I could see that the gap had completely closed up.

The weather continued to deteriorate, so that I had to fly at under 1000ft all the way up through Manila Bay. I had one military training area to cross over, but a quick call on the radio confirmed that it was not currently active (not that surprising I thought, considering the murky visibility). Persistent rain showers were everywhere, but I managed to weave my way around the patches of heavier rainfall and this afforded me the comparative luxury of just having to fly in a constant light drizzle. Lovely! Coasting in over Luzon Island I continued fumbling along at a murky low level, over huge areas of flooded rice paddy fields until I finally made radio contact with Clark Air Base and was directed into the neighbouring Woodland Airpark near Magalang.

On arrival overhead, I made a quick flypast to get my bearings of this lovely grass strip and then landed as soon as possible, to get out of the rain. Similar to Nong Prue in Thailand, I was met by a great bunch of expat flyers, only this time rather than being predominantly from the UK, they were more international: Americans, Australians, British and Germans. Everyone was passionate about their flying and there was a great eclectic mix of light aircraft, from a bright yellow Stearman biplane to an amphibian ultralight.

Soon after arrival, Jay Cook, who was a retired engineer from Australia, sorted me out with hangar space and gave me a lift into town. Fortunately for me, Jay's good friend and fellow Aussie, Chris 'Ding Dong' Bell was out of town for a few days, and I was allowed to stay in his apartment, which was right next door to Jay's place. It was great once again to be in the company of fellow aviators, sharing a few beers and comparing flying adventures.

9 August 2010: Magalang, Luzon, Philippines (non-flying day)

With Jay's expert assistance we were able to utilise a non-flying day by giving *Roxy* a 25-hour airframe inspection, as this was now due after the aircraft rebuild in Thailand. I was also given a tour of the Stearman biplane, which was in its final stages of a two-year rebuild and restoration. It was yet to take to the air but was very nearly ready to do so.

In the afternoon I took 'Stearman Bob' (the biplane restorer, who was in charge of the rebuild) and Jay for short flights around the local area. It was very gusty in the heat of the afternoon, but *Roxy* thrived in the lively crosswind conditions that would have grounded many other light fixed-wing aircraft.

In the evening, over a couple of tins of Guinness that Jay had kindly sourced locally (a rarity in these parts, hence a price tag of US$6 each) there was much discussion about another gyroplane, which had recently been on a very secretive flight...

From emails received during the day, I had heard via one of our online sources that a 29-year-old American, Matthew Hayduk, had now finally come to a very abrupt halt after landing some weeks previously in a rice paddy field in Cambodia. This proved to be a very significant psychological relief for me as for the past two and a half months, Matt had been on a somewhat covert mission. Seemingly unannounced to most of the world's media and the general public, he was also attempting to be the first person to fly a gyro around the world. Along with Barry Jones and myself, Matt had now become only the third person to ever attempt a gyroplane circumnavigation.

He was flying an Italian-built Magni M22 Voyager gyro and had departed from the Magni factory in Italy in late May, only a few weeks after my ditching in Thailand.

If someone was forensically analysing his timing, they might well imagine that he had been watching my ongoing attempt from the sidelines and as soon as I ditched into the Thai lake, he then triggered his own attempt. Though this, of course, was only pure speculation.

Off and running, initially Matt appeared to be covering some huge distances. Reportedly flying with a 200+ litre capacity fuel tank (some 25% more capacity than G-YROX), this gave him the ability to make some ambitiously long endurance flights.

Flying eastbound, he quickly passed through Europe, the Middle East and India in a broadly similar routing to my own. However, on reaching Myanmar, rather than heading south towards Malaysia as I had done, it appeared that he had been aiming to fly eastwards towards Vietnam, presumably to 'cut the corner' and avoid the longer routing down towards the equator and then up through Borneo. My sources indicated that as he attempted to gain access to cross into Vietnamese airspace he had been turned back, for whatever reason, whilst airborne. Ultimately, he then ended up at an airfield in Siam Reap, Cambodia.

Towards the end of June, he presumably replanned his forward route and then prepared for a challenging, lengthy diagonal leap right over the Gulf of Thailand from Cambodia, directly across to Malaysia. Reportedly he was attempting to take off for this flight from Siam Reap, presumably very heavy with fuel, when for some reason he was unable to sustain flight and had to resort to making a heavy emergency landing in a paddy field close to the airport.

Initial photos taken after the event, appeared to suggest that the forced landing had not significantly damaged the aircraft. Seemingly it had not rolled over, so the front wheel, forks and main under carriage probably took most of any apparent heavy impact damage. At the time we assumed that it would be only a minor setback for him.

It was quite a bizarre coincidence to think that while I was grounded with repairs underway in Thailand, Matt had now found himself in a similar situation, just over the border in neighbouring Cambodia. After each aircraft had successfully flown a good third of the way around the globe, they were both now stuck on the ground barely 200 miles apart!

So at that point, the race was still on (or so I thought) to get our respective aircraft back in the air and flying again. However, as the weeks ticked by through July, it became apparent that there was little news to report coming out of Cambodia. I finished my repairs in Thailand and managed to get flying again in early August, and yet Matt's machine still appeared to be firmly grounded.

Finally, after several more weeks of apprehensive waiting, I learned that Matt had had to abandon his circumnavigation attempt in Cambodia. I then began to wonder why his aircraft had not been easily repairable. The damage after all, had not appeared to be too severe. It was certainly a lot less than *Roxy* had suffered during our impromptu gyro swimming lesson, and yet she was now fully repaired and up flying again.

I could only come up with one very speculative conclusion.

His flying tactics right from the get-go had been to fly very stealthily. Few people were made aware of his flight, except for his small team of supporters involved with monitoring his record-setting attempt. Looking in from the outside, there appeared to be no mainstream media engagement, no network building of social media contacts, or no publicly visible online tracking system for people all around the world to enjoy. Matt also appeared to have no online social content that allowed followers to freely contribute comments and share ownership of his whole flight experience live, as it unfolded. All these aspects had been actively promoted and encouraged during my flight through my GyroxGoesGlobal social media pages and website. Instead, Matt's plan seemed to be to fly around the globe almost in secret, sharing information with no one, and to then (presumably) suddenly pop up on the media radar screen only whilst crossing the USA and the Atlantic Ocean during the latter stages of the flight.

In short it was the direct opposite approach that I had taken.

Of course, this stealthy strategy in itself was fine; there are no set rules to say you are obliged to involve anyone outside your own team. The only real difficulty that I could see was that it gave one of our two circumnavigation attempts a distinct tactical advantage over the other. Had it come down to a close finish, tactically Matt's team would have been able to see all my cards laid out on the table whereas, we would have been quite unaware of what Matt was up to. It could have been as unfair a race as say between a surface ship and a submarine.

The stealthy tactic had served Matt well so far, as it had after all kept us guessing. We had to search hard for contacts, who had seen his recent whereabouts as he passed through various airports en route, and as such, our information was frequently delayed by a few days. However, where the stealthy tactic became a distinct *disadvantage* was when he finally landed out in the Cambodian paddy field.

In Thailand, I had become stuck, but I had a host of new-found friends gathered about to help with all aspects of the aircraft salvage and repair. I had the physical support of all these people, and most importantly I also had their psychological support. In the immediate aftermath of the ditching, I was quickly sorted out with hangar workspace, free accommodation (thanks always to Steve B for his generosity on this), a car to use and even a small motorbike to ride. But most importantly, I had a whole network of light aircraft savvy buddies to help work through the huge task of organising an aircraft rebuild programme and at the end of many a long day, to still go out and share a beer with me.

Put another way, if it had not been for all the huge support, goodwill and warm genuine friendship that I received in Thailand, I would simply not have been able to get the whole show back on the road.

By contrast, Matt had arrived in Cambodia largely unannounced and no doubt due to his team's self-imposed secrecy, appeared to have made very few, if any, local contacts. As such he then effectively found himself stuck, alone with a damaged aircraft, in Cambodia, with seemingly precious few friends to call on. I was not therefore surprised to hear some years later that Matt's aircraft was still languishing at Siam Reap, albeit now minus the engine and other more valuable parts that had been removed for salvage.

Given that there were (at that point) only three people who had ever attempted the gyroplane circumnavigation, I hold no personal grudge whatsoever over Matt's tactics during his considerable achievement. With no formally set *rules of engagement,* we were both having to make up our strategies as we went along. Some of his flights were phenomenally ambitious, far more daring than I would have considered comfortable or even achievable. In these flights he showed a level of bravery and commitment to pioneering aviation that went well beyond any normal expectations. He pushed the flight envelope for expeditionary gyroplanes to its very limits, perhaps sometimes beyond, along with stretching his own personal endurance.

I have met and spoken with Barry Jones many times during and since our global attempts. We are good friends and forever linked by our truly unique experience of pioneering long-distance gyroplane flights. Matt is also one of this extremely rare breed and yet (so far) we have never managed to meet up with him in person. I do look forward to hopefully meeting up with him someday and hearing his own side of the story.

10 August 2010: Magalang, Luzon, Philippines – Laoag, Luzon, Philippines

With *Roxy* returned to service, the next flight was a relatively short hop of some 200 nautical miles up to the City of Laoag at the northern end of Luzon. The flight was pleasantly quiet. I had really enjoyed the company at Woodland Airpark and I was pleased to be now once again making fast progress across the globe. Little did I know then however, that international bureaucracy would soon enough rear its head again, conspiring to keep me on the ground for some considerable time to come…

I flew a low-level route up the western coastline of Luzon in clear conditions. On arrival into Laoag International Airport I was met by a TV crew and about 20 onlookers, who immediately surrounded the aircraft. It took a good 10 minutes to finally get out of my seat. My local handler introduced himself as B.J. Abadilia, and he turned out to be my key man in this whole region of the Philippines.

I took to B.J. instantly. He was friendly, kind, unassuming and passionate about all things aviation. With his assistance, we quickly worked our way through the crowd that had gathered, allowing me the space to answer all the usual questions:

"Where had I come from?"

"Where was I going next?"

"How high do you fly?"

"How fast do you fly?"

"How far can you fly?"

We then managed to organise permission to taxi *Roxy* to the fire station building. With no hangars available, this was the next best thing. The firefighters were just as friendly and as curious as the office staff had been out on the apron.

The fire station was an open-fronted affair, a bit like a glorified carport and so not really all that secure. B.J. quickly came to the rescue and organised for two local guards to come and act as night watchmen for the aircraft. Initially everyone thought this arrangement would only be needed for a couple of days, but doubts on the permissions for the upcoming legs of the journey – towards Japan and onwards through Russia – quickly rose to the surface. I would end up leaving *Roxy* at the fire station for the next 10 days while emails flew back and forth regarding the onward journey.

11–20 August 2010: Laoag, Luzon, Philippines (non-flying days)

With B.J.'s fantastic local contacts and assistance, I was billeted in a staff house of the Northwestern University campus in Laoag. It was a spacious and grand residence, complete with its own golf cart that B.J. and I could use to commute ourselves around the grounds. The university had its own sports ground and for a time I considered relocating *Roxy*. But on further reflection, I thought the grass infield was a little too short for a comfortable subsequent take-off. While waiting for various diplomatic responses via email, B.J. and I took an overnight bus trip south to Manila to visit with his family. I spent a very pleasant, relaxed afternoon, sitting out on the roof terrace chatting with B.J. and his mother.

We later returned north again to Laoag, only to find that gaining entry into Japan, the next destination country, was proving to be a much more difficult problem than first expected.

21 August 2010: Laoag, Luzon, Philippines – Magalang, Luzon, Philippines

With little prospect of permission to fly onwards into Japanese airspace arriving any time soon, I made the decision to return the aircraft back down south to Woodland Airpark near Magalang. The set up there had been fantastic – it was the only airfield I had ever visited that had its own outdoor swimming pool in the grounds, and local flying club members had been exceptionally welcoming during my last visit. There was a very real prospect, now looming large, of having to temporarily halt the circumnavigation and leave the aircraft hangared over the coming winter months.

It was now mid-August and getting very late in the season for venturing north toward the Arctic Circle. Even if I suddenly did get permission to hurry on through Japan in the last few weeks of late summer, I would be then cutting it very fine to make a successful crossing of the Russian Far East and the Bering Strait before the oncoming winter would, somewhere, stop me in my tracks. Far better, I thought, to be approaching the Russian section at the start of next summer, with ever-improving weather and daylight, rather than at the tail end of this summer and running the very real risk of becoming snowbound and stuck in a remote Russian outpost, in the grip of a long and dark Siberian winter.

Despite the frustrations of the lack of onward permission, the flight back down the coast of Luzon was relaxed and enjoyable. It was very unusual to be heading backwards like this and especially over terrain that I now already knew. The other fun aspect was that as I was backtracking my route, this flight did not really form part of the circumnavigation. I would again, at some future point, have to fly back up this same coastline to Laoag before continuing onwards with my circumnavigation.

With no records being set on this flight, I didn't need to fly solo and so I enjoyed the novelty of being able to take a passenger along in the backseat. B.J. jumped at the chance to hitch a ride with me, albeit having to share his rear seat with a very slender 'girlfriend' (aka the Turtle Pac). B.J.'s date contained just the small amount of additional fuel required for the flight, so I rolled her lengthwise to form a long cylindrical tube that could still be cosily strapped into the seat alongside her man. After an hour or so in the air, and following several affectionate squeezes from B.J., his girlfriend alas became a shadow of her former self and completely devoid of any substance.

It was great to have some companionship on the flight, and a real treat to be able to discuss the landmarks and fantastic natural sights that we passed along the way. I hadn't realised how much I missed this social aspect after previously flying solo for so long.

One of the most notable sights we passed on the shoreline near to Laoag was a huge, red brick building complex. It was now a lovely hotel, one that B.J. and I enjoyed eating in earlier in the week, but in a former life, it had been a grand residence of the notorious ex-Philippines president Ferdinand Marcos and his shoe-loving wife, Imelda.

Further south as we approached Woodland Airpark, we ran into heavy rain showers though thankfully these were isolated and easily avoided by flying around them.

Although surprised at my sudden return, I was made very welcome once again by all the resident pilots at Woodlands. Yet internally, a growing sense of unease had also crept into my thoughts. Having decided to turn back and retrace my route south, I now had to contemplate revising my onward journey over a longer timeframe than I had originally planned. But halting things for the time being was still my only practical solution, even though it meant I would have the added complexity of trying to arrange the annual re-permitting of G-YROX (for its Permit to Fly certificate) while positioned in a non-UK airfield. I was feeling a long way from home, but the camaraderie of the flying club members ensured that any upcoming logistical problems didn't feel quite so daunting and that any issues could no doubt be resolved with a bit of local help and guidance.

9

Philippines: a winter's wait

22 August 2010 – 17 July 2011: Magalang, Luzon, Philippines

In the end, by late summer I had made a command decision to pause the circumnavigation flight over the winter months. Although this was a major upset to my schedule, it had become a relatively easy decision to make. The Bering Strait acted as a natural barrier, one that I could only contemplate crossing within a very narrow summer weather window. By late August, and still sitting only 15 degrees north from the Equator, all hope of reaching 65 degrees north to cross the strait was now firmly out of the question. With such a certainty in place, it came as a relief to not only pause the flight, but also to pause the constant uncertainty that surrounded it. I could now physically relax in the definite knowledge that I would not be expedition flying for at least the next six months.

Mentally however, in the background, there was still the ongoing diplomatic wrangling to sort out before I could gain entry into Japan. Another long-burning issue was that the whole circumnavigation flight would now spill over into the next year, which gave me further technical challenges. Not only did I need to keep G-YROX fully insured, but also fully legal as far as the UK CAA were concerned.

Another key issue was keeping the aircraft well maintained,

exercised and generally fit for the onward flight. Unlike a lawnmower that might be kept mothballed and gathering dust in the shed for six months over the winter, an aircraft cannot be treated in such a cavalier fashion. Ideally *Roxy* needed regular maintenance and flying hours to keep her healthy come the springtime.

Local flying helped, and I enjoyed exploring the local airspace around the Woodlands airfield. The terrain was variable, providing low-level flights through the paddy fields or skirting around the edges of wild tropical jungle, coconut palms and mango trees. These all became my new backyard playground, and were a far cry from the chilly winter-time, sheep-grazed, rain-soaked fells of the Cumbrian Lake District. To help maintain my basic aircraft handling skills, I would sometimes tightly manoeuvre to follow the twists and turns of meandering rivers or circle up around the peak of a local dormant volcano. There, I could soar and hover on the uprising thermals, and often exchanged a friendly wave with the scientists based in the summit research station.

Right through the winter months, while I periodically travelled back and forth home to the UK, I was extremely fortunate to be able to count on the ongoing expert help and local guidance of Jay Cook. As a similar character to Tom Grieve back in Thailand, Jay now played a fundamental and vital part in maintaining both my morale, whilst being temporarily halted on the ground, and helping to keep *Roxy's* whole circumnavigation show on the road with his brilliant electrical and mechanical expertise. Between us, and especially with Jay's seasoned knowhow of maintaining light aircraft engines and airframes, we were able to work with the UK CAA, to allow the aircraft to remain legal for the next flying year.

A major obstacle had been how to re-permit the aircraft from such a remote location, as normally a UK aircraft surveyor was required to make a physical inspection on behalf of the UK CAA to show that everything was in order. Clearly, this was not so easy to do while sitting in the Philippines. However, as luck would have it, in mid-May 2011, a UK CAA surveyor had been sent out to the Philippines from his headquarters in Gatwick to visit Manila on aviation business. And fortunately for us, as he was visiting for a few weeks, he also agreed to drive out and visit Woodland Airpark to perform a full annual inspection of G-YROX on his day off. I was so grateful to him for voluntarily giving up his own free time in that way as it also meant that I could subsequently also renew my insurance documents and remain legally permitted to fly for another year.

It was at times like these, when the sheer enormity and complexity of what I was trying to accomplish, really struck home. Time and again I would have to struggle with the vagaries of international diplomatic relations, ever present bureaucracy and the highly uncertain logistics that constantly surrounded the pioneering, first circumnavigation flight of this unique type of aircraft. These were mostly indirect, consequential difficulties, but still they often far outweighed the perhaps more obvious constant challenges of just climbing aboard, relentlessly day after day, and then trying to actually fly the thing around the world. I was now really discovering, first-hand, some of the same difficulties that the historic early aviators of the 1920s and 30s must have endured.

Obtaining permissions for some countries was frustratingly slow, and at times a highly tedious process, requiring the writing of countless convincing emails. There were many knockbacks, refusals, ignored requests, unhelpful negative comments and 'know it all' condescending opinions to contend with along the way. And yet through it all, I had to keep smiling, appear positive and 100% optimistic. In the end, if I didn't believe I could do it, then no one else out there would have believed I could do it either.

Attempting to become the first gyroplane circumnavigator was shaping up to be 1% trailblazing and 99% sheer bloody-minded hard work.

10

Far East Asia: Philippines to Japan

18 July 2011: Magalang, Luzon, Philippines – Laoag, Luzon, Philippines

Finally, after much last-minute packing and weighing of luggage, I was once again good to go. Similar to my extended stay in Thailand, I had made many good friends here over the winter months, which made my onwards departure all the more significant. I had experienced many mini-adventures during my stay, some highly enjoyable, some not so much. Scuba diving with Jay, Maracel and Lyn to explore a ditched DC-3 aircraft in Subic Bay was a notable highlight, as was occasionally attending Ding Dong's celebrated Monday lunchtime wine tasting club. Less recreational visits were spent repeatedly attending the Russian, Japanese, Chinese and British embassies in Manila, in numerous stalled diplomatic attempts and negotiations, before my onward flight was eventually allowed to continue.

The flight back up to Laoag was quite relaxing by comparison to many of my other flights so far. I had flown the route before so knew in advance what terrain and hazards to expect en route. It was great to be finally moving forward again.

I had had a solid winter break from the circumnavigation flight, and although I had spent time in the air recreationally, I now needed to prepare for serious expedition flying once more. I had come to realise that flying *Roxy* around the world required a completely different approach than that employed when simply flying around a local airfield or setting out on an afternoon cross-country jaunt. Take-offs felt slow, heavy and cumbersome when I was fully loaded, fully packed and fully suited. It often felt like I was clawing my way up into the sky. Additionally, on expedition flights, I frequently had complex navigation, tricky weather, patchy radio comms, conflicting traffic and restricted airspace issues to deal with. On an emotional level, I keenly felt both fantastic support, yet also a burden of expectation from my online followers, who were flying 'virtually' alongside me in the cockpit. Coupled with constant attention from the mainstream media, these external sets of watchful eyes and caring hearts actually led me to adopt two very divergent personas as I prepared to take flight. On the outside I'd be all smiles and waves, but on the inside I would already be intensely focussed on trying to second guess the unknown battlegrounds that could so easily be awaiting me in the sky.

Arriving in Laoag, I was once again reunited with B.J. We spent an enjoyable evening together as I briefed him on the diplomatic manoeuvrings that had been employed on my behalf, in order for me to fly within Japanese airspace.

Despite historically having many examples of gyroplanes flying in their airspace, over half a century on, the Japanese authorities had become unfamiliar with the modern type of factory-built machines that were now coming out of Europe. Indeed, the attitude of the aviation authorities in general towards all microlight and ultralight aircraft flying in the country had evolved to become much more restrictive than in most other advanced technological nations. In many small airfields these types of aircraft could often be restricted to conducting flights only within a 3km radius of their home base runway. In such a risk-adverse country, there had been very little precedent set for the type of adventurous cross-country flying that I was now proposing and the idea of flying a small, relatively unknown type of rotary aircraft across the entire Japanese archipelago from south to north was unthinkable. Incredibly, the fact that I had already flown my aircraft halfway around the world to reach Japan, did little to help influence their thoughts. Simply put, there were no rules in place to allow such an unusual aircraft to fly through Japan, and to allow something to exist in Japan without following a set rule, proved to be extremely difficult.

After much protracted discussion, a breakthrough finally came courtesy of Captain Andy Edney, the defence attaché of the British Embassy in Tokyo. Fortunately, Andy had a very good working relationship with the American Embassy's defence attaché, as both had worked closely together assisting in the international relief efforts made after the 'Great East Japan Earthquake and Tsunami' of 11 March 2011. Collaborating together, they both now cooked up a highly ingenious plan. I would fly north-east from Laoag in the Philippines towards the Japanese islands, but then technically land in America, not Japan. Yes, really.

With a special security clearance given from the Pentagon, I was permitted to fly directly into the USAF Kadena Air Base on the Japanese island of Okinawa. By landing at the American base first, I could then clear customs and subsequently enter Japan formally in a more controlled way. The Japanese authorities were happy with this *halfway house* arrangement, and so, with much diplomatic relief all round, I was then also granted permission to fly onwards through the rest of the country. Permission was on the strict condition that I skirted around the Sea of Japan coastline (rather than flying directly through the mountainous interior of Japan) to reach my intended crossing point to fly onward to Vladivostok in Russia. A further condition was that I had to select my route from a list of Class III airfields only, which meant I could only use the smaller regional airports, which were the sort that I much preferred anyway. The obligation to avoid at all times, large, expensive, busy Class I and II airports with complex airspace procedures, was just fine by me.

19 July 2011: Laoag, Luzon, Philippines (non-flying day)

The logistics of the upcoming flight to Okinawa were daunting. The expected flight time from Laoag to Kadena Air Base was approximately 8hrs 30mins, 98% of it over the western Pacific Ocean (Philippine Sea). If that wasn't challenging enough, my maximum fuel endurance was an hour shorter than the proposed flight. It looked as if it just couldn't be done in one hop. I spent hours scouring Google Earth for possible alternate routes before a rather creative plan finally emerged.

Two hours north-east of Laoag was a small cluster of Philippine islands called the Batanes. Rather conveniently located there, clinging to the side of a steep Volcano, was a small regional airfield called Basco, which was normally used for domestic flights only. However, the only way I could make the long flight to Okinawa was to somehow organise briefly landing at Basco and replenishing the two hours of fuel that I had used to get there. With fuel tanks topped-up and again containing 7hrs 30mins' worth of fuel, the onward flight to Okinawa, some 6hrs 30mins distant from Basco, then became physically achievable. It all sounded possible in theory, but strictly speaking, once cleared for an international flight from Laoag, I was not then supposed to land again at a domestic airport. But when needs must…

A few phone calls later and I was all set.

20 July 2011: Laoag, Luzon, Philippines – Basco, Batanes, Philippines – Kadena Air Base, Okinawa, Japan

Wind direction and speed were crucial on this flight. Thankfully while in the Philippines I had kindly been given a wind prediction software package by a retired live-aboard sailor from Subic Bay called Terry Sergeant. This allowed me to accurately forecast the wind strength along the whole route to Okinawa. Over such a long distance, I could not afford to have any headwind component, and fortunately the forecast gave a steady tailwind of 15 knots, that picked up to 25 knots at altitude.

After a slow and heavy take-off, Laoag ATC instructed me to climb to 5500ft, set a squawk code of 2777 on my transponder (so I was identifiable on their radar) and to report when 10 miles out of Laoag. Thirty-five minutes later I was coasting out over the sea, on a heading of 033 degrees, knowing that ahead of me, for hundreds of miles, lay precious little in the shape of dry land. Laoag handed me over to Manila Control, which for a while at least, gave me further comfort that someone was still listening, until I finally went out of VHF radio range, and I was on my own, with only the vast Pacific Ocean for company.

Since turning to fly north-eastwards near the equator at Johor, the GPS latitude and longitude readings were now both steadily counting upwards, marking off the position, 19 degrees north and 121 degrees east. It was at this moment that I suddenly realised I had now flown over one third of the way around the globe from the Greenwich prime meridian line. All this way, with so many adventures already, yet I had still two thirds of the world to go! It was at times like this that I realised that the sheer size and scale of the Earth's surface was truly mindboggling.

After 1hr 20mins of flight time, the constant chatter of Manila Control in my headset now became very faint. I still had some 40 nautical miles to run before reaching Basco, but I suddenly became aware of a dramatic change in the sea colour all around me. No longer was I seeing greenish turquoise coastal waters; the sea below was now a deep, dark velvety blue. I was to find out later that the seabed here dropped to a depth of 10,000ft. No wonder the surface looked so dark, despite the bright sunlight reflecting off it.

The white caps on the wave patterns indicated a good Force 4 wind (on the Beaufort scale) blowing at sea level, still thankfully as a tail-wind. Cruising up at 4000ft, I was making a reassuring 105 mph over the water for an airspeed of 80mph. I was going well, all I had to do now was pull off the ruse we had put in place to pick up my extra fuel in Basco.

Calling Basco Tower I made a request for a precautionary landing, with the gist of the conversation as follows:

"I need to check a luggage strap in the rear seat that has come loose. It's now flapping about in the wind. I will need to sort it out before heading on to my destination in Okinawa. My intention is to be on the ground only for a few minutes and I will remain on the airside apron."

"G-YROX, you are clear to land. Runway in use is 06," came the much-welcomed reply.

Relieved at gaining landing clearance, I now faced my next challenge with Basco's very unusual runway. It was situated on the lower slopes of the island's 3310ft volcano, meaning that the whole runway length inclined at an angle of about 10 degrees. Typically, fixed-wing aircraft were expected to land *uphill* on 06 and take off *downhill* on 24, regardless of the wind strength and direction. But in a gyroplane, things were slightly different. The wind was gusting at 18 knots from the sea directly up the runway towards the volcano. To land into wind, my best option was to line up and touch down on runway 24. It meant landing down slope, but more crucially for me, also safely into the stiff breeze, much like a seagull floating down to land on a beach. The controller initially questioned why I was making a final approach on 24, but they then realised that my approach was so slow that my landing, almost now a descending hover, was going to be made at a walking pace. I quickly taxied to the small apron area and shut down the engine.

For the next few minutes, I busied myself checking the aircraft and 'fixing' the loose strap. A few of the airport staff came out of the picturesque little terminal building to take photos and to see *Roxy* close up. Then, as if by pure magic and with perfect timing, a small motorbike rode up the hill from town. Strapped onto its pillion seat were two 20-litre cans of unleaded petrol. Oh, how fortunate! And wow, what a coincidence. Just what I needed! Our clandestine phone calls of recent days had clearly worked a treat. I quickly paid the delivery rider and swiftly re-filled *Roxy*'s tanks. Then it was a few last-minute selfies with the airport staff and whoosh!... I was off again, high tailing it back into the sky.

Job done!

* * *

Climbing out from Basco, grinning from ear to ear and once again with a full payload of fuel, I quickly turned downwind to focus on the long run to Okinawa. I flew past the western flank of the Island's huge volcano, which was a truly awesome sight. It climbed straight out of the sea at a steep slope and continued upwards in this manner to about 3000ft until it disappeared into its own mountain top cloud base.

Back in Northern Ireland we have a lovely, lilting Irish folk song that includes the lyrics "Where the Mountains of Mourne sweep down to the sea" and so for my own amusement I changed the lyrics around to "Where the volcano of Basco dives down to the depths", which now seemed so much more appropriate. I had to have something to lift my morale, the GPS was giving me an initial ETA for Kadena of over *seven* hours. Though I also had to remind myself that this estimate would hopefully shorten considerably as I burned off fuel weight and gradually picked up speed later in the flight.

I pulled out my camera, but while concentrating on catching a picture of the volcano, I made a big mistake. I had set a direct course for Okinawa, which unfortunately took me close by the downwind side of the island. Without any warning, the aircraft suddenly started to heave up and down quite violently, even with the full load of fuel onboard. I immediately felt very nervous for *Roxy's* poor rotor blades, having to undergo the additional stresses of supporting a heavy load while being bounced around all over the sky. I quickly realised what had happened and cursed myself for not being more alert. The strong tailwind that I had experienced earlier in the day, was now being severely obstructed by the island's volcano, and I had inadvertently placed my aircraft right into its downwind wake. With gritted teeth and over-tensed muscles, I hung on and tried to dampen the effects of this turbulent rollercoaster ride that Mother Nature had now so generously provided for me, *free of charge*. As I moved farther downwind the effect gradually subsided, and with much relief, I knew I would soon be in clear smooth air once again.

Crisis over, I tried to calm my adrenaline level and settle back into my normal cockpit routines. Glancing at the GPS, I could see that the update on my estimated flight time for Okinawa was still going to be a leg-cramping, bum-numbing, and mind-wandering 6hrs 30mins. But to keep me focussed, 99.5% of the whole flight was above water, out over the Philippine Sea and the amazing depths of the Ryukyu Trench; which while not quite as deep as the Marianas Trench (at 36,000ft), was still deep enough for me to pass over a point where the seabed was some 23,500ft below the surface. Retrieving a ditched aircraft at these depths would certainly not have been as easy as from the shallow lake in Thailand! It was interesting to consider that as I was flying about 4500ft above sea level, it meant that at this point I was actually flying at 28,000ft above the Earth's crust, the highest 'altitude' above solid ground I have ever flown!

For safety, I elected to fly a slight dogleg to stay closer to the Japanese island chain Ryūkyū-ko (the Ryukyu Arc), which stretched out to the north of my track. En route I had good communications with Naha Control and also with Miyakojima Approach as I passed by that island. I received permission to cross their airspace zone at 3000ft, however on arrival I had to request a revision of the crossing height down to 1000ft due to murky, low cloud conditions. Thankfully my request was accepted, and as I scudded low-level across the island, its urbanised areas of buildings, radio masts and powerlines immediately felt very complex and busy, compared to the vast emptiness of the ocean. It was comforting to be closer to civilisation for the few minutes it took to overfly the island, but it actually came as a relief when I returned back out to sea heading on towards Okinawa. Clear of the island weather, I again had much improved visibility and climbed back up to 3500ft as I passed oceanic navigation and reporting point TORII.

According to the GPS, I now had 1hr 51mins still to run, after having already been flying for almost four solid hours. But with the tailwind starting to drop and extra time needed for USAF Kadena Air Base approach procedures, I estimated that the final total flight time would likely still remain around 6hrs 30mins.

* * *

My approach to Kadena was very interesting. On first contact with the tower, it was quickly established that unlike their usual military customers, I hadn't already been given a reporting point. Unsurprisingly, fast jets and gyroplanes have quite different requirements, but the duty controllers, ever the professionals, took it all in their stride. They vectored me towards a VFR reporting point over a nearby lighthouse, and from there vectored me in to land on runway 23R. It felt so calm and simple on a very quiet frequency, but on final approach, as I expedited for the runway at my maximum permitted speed of 100 mph, a movement caught my eye over on the parallel left runway, 23L. Glancing over in that direction, I was most surprised to see that a Harrier jet was also landing with the same approach speed as me.

I was caught completely unawares, as there had been no mention of it on the radio, but I then suddenly realised that although it was all very calm and peaceful on my VHF frequency, the airfield was actually very busy with other traffic on other (presumably military) frequencies. I quickly regained focus on my own landing as it would not look good if I messed up and dropped or barrel rolled the aircraft onto the tarmac here of all places! All went smoothly thankfully, and I was instructed to exit the runway at taxiway Delta. The runway was huge for my small aircraft, (it needed to be, to accommodate the 210-knot take-off speed of the iconic SR-71 "Blackbird" aircraft that were once based here back in the day), and I trundled along searching for the turn off, only to find that up ahead the runway seemed to be blocked by an obstruction. Drawing closer it appeared that someone had stretched a long line of fishing floats out across the whole runway, blocking my path. I was puzzled for a few seconds until, drawing closer still, I realised what I was looking at and then grinned to myself.

"Well, this is going to be a first," I thought.

What I was now inspecting close-up and in-person was an arrestor wire for US Navy pilots to practise their landing technique onto an aircraft carrier flight deck. Never in a million years had I thought I would encounter such a thing in a gyroplane. My next problem was how to get over it. Up close, it was quite big. The wire was 40-50mm thick and held up off the runway surface by the 'fishing float' deck raisers.

It meant the wire was some 150mm above the surface, which for a gyroplane, with wheels the size of a wheelbarrow, presented quite an obstacle to climb over. I double-checked with the tower that it was safe for me to cross, and they gave me the reassuring advice:

"Sure, it will be fine, just take it nice and slow."

"Easy for them to say", I thought, "they're not driving the wheelbarrow!"

So, with a committed lunge and a hop, skip and jump, I bumped my way over the wire and taxied up to the Kadena Aeroclub GA apron where about 30 base personnel were waiting to give me a warm welcome. I was amazed to discover that the huge US Air Base, home to over 25,000 personnel, had established its very own 'on base' light aviation flying club, coordinated by Scott, the aeroclub manager and his support team.

Corey Martin, 18th Wing vice commander and his family welcomed me as the acting base commander. I was mightily relieved to have made the flight safely, but even though I had had a very long day in the cockpit, a total of 8hrs 30mins, I was not allowed to climb out of the aircraft for yet another 20 minutes. Protocol dictated that as I was an international arrival, the local Japanese customs officers would have to complete their CQI (customs, quarantine and immigration) checks first. With the forms finally completed I was at last allowed to climb out onto terra firma and meet up with everyone properly. They all showed great interest in my journey and my numerous adventures to date.

However, as we stood chatting in the late afternoon sunshine, a funny situation arose.

A number of military jets had been out on manoeuvres over the Pacific and were returning to their hangars along the same taxiway that I had used. As they passed us by on the apron, all the 'Top Gun' pilots raised their canopies and gave us a salute. I would like to imagine that they were making a tribute salute to a fellow daring, Pacific-conquering pilot and his fantastic gyroplane steed. The reality I suspect was much less grandiose, in that they were most probably saluting their acting base commander who was standing right next to me.

Still, I gave them all a wave back, just in case!

21 July 2011: Kadena Air Base, Okinawa, Japan – Fukue Island, Gotō Islands, Japan

I was up at 6am, picked up from the accommodation at 7am and aimed for an engine start time of 9.45am. It was going to be yet another challenging day of open ocean flying, clocking up a further six hours in the cockpit, on top of the arduous 8hrs 30 min flight from the previous day. I had actually landed after the long flight from Basco with 30 litres of fuel remaining, thanks to the strong tailwind, so I only needed to fuel up with a further 120 litres. The airfield had two fuel bowsers: octane 91 mogas and avgas. With the latter costing US$20 a gallon, a fill up would have cost me more than US$500. Fortunately, they took pity on me and very generously filled *Roxy* with avgas for the mogas price (about US$90). Little did I know it then, but I would be very grateful for that avgas later in the day.

G-YROX had spent the night in a maintenance hangar, directly opposite a fast jet that was ready for deployment. In the morning, just before my departure slot, I sought special permission to get a photo of *Roxy* and the jet, side by side. The gyroplane was dwarfed by the jet; it always surprises me how big they actually are when you get to stand next to one. I often make the comment that while both aircraft only have two seats, I easily know which one's fuel bill I would prefer to pay.

As I departed into clear skies, it felt much less daunting to be flying out from the airbase than it had felt flying in towards it. Ground taxi and tower comms with ATC all felt very calm, and soon I was vectored out into a quiet piece of sky that was well away from any of the more regular military traffic. I flew north-east along the northern shoreline of Okinawa, studying the distinctive landscape unique to Japanese islands. The houses, the fields, the fishing boats, even the rural roads wending their way through the steep mountainous forests, miles from anywhere, all had their own neat and orderly Japanese style.

Soon enough, I was heading out to sea again. Initially at least, the seascape views were spectacular. Three classic cone-shaped volcanoes appeared, dramatically pushing skyward out of the ocean about 10 miles further to the north of me. Real live volcanos! I wondered if any had been active recently. It was a pity I hadn't spotted them a bit earlier as I could have diverted my course slightly to pass close by.

The clear skies of my take-off gradually deteriorated. Two horizontal layers of cloud appeared in my path, and I became increasingly wary that I didn't want to get caught in between them. All was fine while the base layer continued to be very broken and patchy, as I could easily remain in sight of the sea surface below. However, as the base layer then gradually thickened, I found myself at one point having to turn 180 degrees to backtrack out of the situation. Finding a suitable hole in the cloud, I ducked down through the gap to have a look at the conditions underneath it. It was raining steadily, but definitely appeared brighter off into the distance, so I decided to push on, scraping along just under the cloud base. I thought it much better to suffer a few raindrops than to be the reluctant filling of a *cloud sandwich* up above.

* * *

My strategy for this flight was unusual as I realised the Japanese archipelago was not a straight line. The island chain gently curved as I flew up towards the mainland, so my most direct route to reach Fukue Island (pronounced *foo-koo-way*... my destination within the Gotō group of islands) was to cut directly across the bend so to speak, which resulted in taking me far offshore. For safety however, I decided to opt for a dogleg route closer to the islands that afforded me the comfort of multiple alternate landing sites as I flew past them. On the airways chart for the area, I found a useful reporting point called BOMAP, which was roughly in the right position out over the East China Sea, and so I planned to use that as my turning point. The flight from Okinawa to BOMAP took just over three hours with a 15-knot crosswind blowing in from the north-east. This was fine, but I knew that when I turned to fly northwards at BOMAP, heading directly for Fukue, I was going to encounter a partial headwind. As a rule, I always looked to avoid headwinds as much as possible, especially over the sea and even more so on a long flight. Unfortunately, this flight was shaping up to be both – it was wholly over water, and still had another three hours to run.

To compound the difficulty, the expected light headwind at the turn had strengthened and was now at 20-25 knots. I was clearly going to have a battle on my hands, so I got organised and settled in for the long haul. Windspeed aloft generally increases with altitude and so I trimmed the aircraft to fly as fast and as low as I could comfortably maintain, often flying at 90-100 mph only 250ft above the rough sea surface. Periodically I allowed myself a rest, rising up to 400ft for a short while, before trimming back down to resume lower-level flight again. This took a lot of concentration, but I knew that I had to conserve as much fuel as I could whilst still making landfall as quickly as possible. I made flight time, groundspeed, distance to run and remaining fuel calculations in my head constantly. If at any moment I felt that I couldn't make the distance to Fukue on the remaining fuel available, then my emergency plan was to turn southwards and run downwind for about 70 miles to reach the nearest alternate landfall. This backup plan was valid until I passed the point of no return, where my actual destination then became the closest point of land.

That point came about one hour's flight out from Fukue. Ten minutes after this point, my 20-litre fuel level warning light started to flicker on. Twenty litres would give me another hour in the air, and I had another hour to fly. It was going to be tight. Flying so low to the surface my radio comms were also a concern. Commencing the flight, I had reported my original ETA to be 07:05UTC, but the stronger headwind had slowed me considerably en route and now my revised ETA was going to be 07:55UTC, a full 50 minutes later than expected. Fortunately, I was able to make radio contact before I became 30 minutes overdue. Had I not done so, it was quite possible that ATC would have reported me missing and commenced search and rescue procedures, which wouldn't have been the best way to introduce myself to a new country.

At flight time 6hrs 7mins, I still had 15 minutes to run. The 20-litre warning light was now solidly lit, and the very low fuel warning light had also started to flicker on. As witnessed in India, this warning light indicated about 20 minutes of useable fuel remaining. It was always a concern when this light came on, but as the minutes slowly ticked by, a glorious moment came when I knew that I was going to be OK; I had landfall now well within sight and finally crossing over the rocky coastline towards the airfield, I was awash with relief.

"Hallelujah!" I breathed to myself as the shoreline passed below me, I could now land in a field if needs be and not get my feet wet. A few more minutes and I arrived on finals to land.

The total flight time had been a gruelling 6hrs 30mins, more than half of which was flown at just 200-400ft above the East China Sea. I was mightily relieved to get on the ground.

Checking the tanks later, I had just seven litres of useable fuel remaining. I was extremely glad that I had been fuelled up with avgas at Kadena. For the same volume of fuel, but using regular lower octane-rated mogas, I wondered could I have still flown a similar overall distance...

I was warmly greeted at Fukue Regional Airport by the manager who spoke very good English. This was my first proper Japanese stopover, as the USAF Kadena Air Base had really felt more like landing in America.

After some discussion, I was able to persuade the fire crew to allow *Roxy* to overnight in their garage, and one of the fire trucks was duly brought out onto the apron to make room. Accommodation for the evening was in a small business hotel, and the airport manager took me out to a local restaurant for my first real experience of rural Japanese cuisine.

Lots of little dishes were served up: sea bream *sashimi* (raw fish); skewers of chicken, pork and beef; small vegetables and *onigiri* (a sticky rice ball). These were washed down with a large glass of local beer and *shōchū*, a Japanese distilled liquor that I felt had a remarkably similar taste to Irish poteen. Evoking such thoughts of home, it at once reminded me of the tremendous distance that I had now flown since first departing the old Emerald Isle with its 40 shades of green.

22 July 2011: Fukue Island, Gotō Islands, Japan – Dōgojima, Oki Islands, Japan

Still feeling relieved after the previous day's long flight to Fukue, my morning pre-flight inspection now flagged up a new problem. I found that the end of a spring on the pre-rotator arm had broken just where it hooked onto the gearbox casing. Luckily the spring itself had remained intact, but I now needed to find a way to re-attach it. After a few enquiries, the airport staff were able to produce some suitable locking wire and I was able to bind the end of the spring back in place. It was a temporary fix, but on a part not required whilst airborne, so the field repair would just have to suffice until I could get a replacement.

The wayward spring gave me a slightly delayed start to the day, but I was soon refuelled with 140 litres of mogas that was brought to the apron in fuel cans. With both warm air and high humidity drawn in from the sea, the weather was best described as *claggy*. My much-anticipated flight towards the Oki Islands led me along the coastline of mainland Japan for the first time, but the clinging low clouds hung around the coastal mountains of Kyushu like a thick, ragged blanket. In the open cockpit, I could actually feel the warm humidity in the air against my face, reminding me of landing at Chittagong on the Bay of Bengal. Flying in or near such conditions would have normally caused some concern, but I could see that the effect was confined to the landmass and that out to sea, as often the case, the sky was much brighter and clearer ahead. I reassured myself that if I were to encounter any *obstacle clouds* along the way, I could easily bypass them by flying a few miles out to sea.

The landscape below was now considerably more populated than on the outlying islands. The steeply sloped mountainous interior was heavily forested but in stark contrast, every valley floor seemed to be fully developed and built upon to maximise the use of any available flat land. Gently sloping foothills were utilised likewise, being sculpted into vast staircases of terraced land. Small fishing harbours and villages were squeezed into the bays between prominent headlands. Rock faces near roads and railway lines, had been wire-meshed to prevent rock-falls, and in places, whole rocky outcrops had been clad in a concrete skin, wrapping and following the contours of the rock structure below. The surface pattern was akin to the hillsides being wrapped in a giant waffle. I was curious to know why this natural landscape had been so pinned down and over-engineered like this, until I remembered that I was now flying alongside the Pacific's *ring of fire*, which made the whole region prone to frequent and sizable earthquakes.

The miles passed by quickly, the coastline features being so much more interesting than when flying out over the featureless ocean. The cloud base established itself at about 2000ft and I settled into a happy sightseeing altitude of 1000ft.

Arrival at Oki Islands Global Geopark Airport on Dōgojima was glorious. To assist with language translation, contact had been made with an English teacher called Elizabeth, and she was waiting with her companion Rika as I taxied in. They were holding a huge banner that read:

"Welcome to Oki – Go around the world!!!"

The whole airport staff had come out to greet my arrival and there was much warm welcome and celebration that I had made their beautiful island one of my overnight stops. In the evening I was taken to a sushi train restaurant before overnighting in a lovely small hotel surrounded by a huge cedar forest.

23 July 2011: Dōgojima, Oki Islands, Japan – Sakata, Yamagata, Japan

Departure from Dōgojima was spectacular. The far end of the runway was perched directly above a dramatic cliff face that plunged down vertically into the sea. So abrupt was the drop off that my take-off and climb-out over the sea felt as if I had just been launched from the flight deck of an aircraft carrier. (Which was appropriate, after feeling I had recently landed on one at Kadena Air Base!)

Having spent the last three stops on outlying Japanese islands, I was finally now going to make landfall on the Japanese main island of

Honshu. Initially, I continued my course over the sea to the north-east, skirting along the southern edge of the Sea of Japan. Out to my right, I was gradually converging my course with the Japanese coastline and out to my left, but far away over the horizon, the next landfall was North Korea and the Russian Far East. As time passed, Japan's coastline features gradually grew larger, with steep coastal mountains and dense forests stretching off into the interior as far as I could see. The hillside slopes intersected and overlapped each other, gradually fading off into the distance. It was an iconic sight, depicted on countless landscape paintings and drawings that illustrate a classic Japanese mountain scene. I had truly arrived in *Nihon* – meaning *origin of the sun* in Chinese, but more frequently known to the rest of the world as 'the land of the rising sun'.

I made landfall and tracked along the shoreline, following the coastal road as it snaked along the edge of the rugged landscape, sometimes disappearing entirely from view as it tunnelled through the more obstructive basalt headlands. I was most surprised that the scene initially appeared very similar to the Antrim Coast Road back home, but the impressive sea defences here spoke of a very different climate. Dominating what were otherwise small, quaint-looking fishing villages were high-concrete-walled harbours, indicating that this Sea of Japan coastline was definitely more exposed than the shores of the North Channel of the Irish Sea.

My navigation to Shonai Airport was made easy as it was located right on the shoreline, with my final approach to land made over the sea. From this vantage point, I was treated to an impressive view of the whole Shonai plain stretching out before me, an area of rich farming land surrounded and protected by the interior mountains of the Akita and Yamagata prefectures. Mount Chokai, a snow-capped 2236m (7336 ft) semi-dormant volcano that last saw activity in 1974, dominated the horizon.

Taxiing in from the single runway to the modest, but neatly maintained terminal building, I was still unsure of how long my stay here would be. Deep down inside, I remained apprehensive that Russia could so easily withhold my entry permit for any number of reasons. However, one thing remained a certainty, until I received onward flight permission from Russia, I was now going nowhere.

11

Japan: the long wait

I was met on the apron by a fantastic welcoming committee of airport staff. Cutting a fine figure amongst them, and officially dressed in his tropical whites, was the British Embassy defence attaché Captain Andy Edney, who had travelled out from Tokyo to welcome me. Andy had been instrumental in diplomatically negotiating my permission to fly in Japan and it was great to finally meet him in person. I was also introduced to Mr. Muraoka – a charming and generous-natured man with responsibility for development and promotion for the airport – who greeted me warmly with an infectious beaming smile.

Over each of the following days, Mr. Muraoka enthusiastically enquired if I had any news regarding the Russian permission to allow my onward flight to Vladivostok. Alas, sadly, after several weeks of anxious waiting, word came back to the effect that although I had had outline permission with the Russian authorities during 2010, it was now 2011. I was glibly informed that "there were all new people here now" and that I would have to re-apply for the permission. This was submitted immediately, with an expected 14-day wait for the reply.

Mr. Muraoka became one of my main airport staff supporters along with his colleagues Mr. Igarashi and Mr. Nagasawa. Together, they helped me liaise with the Japan Civil Aviation Bureau (JCAB) head office when I needed to perform essential maintenance flights to keep *Roxy* fit and healthy during this lengthening incarceration.

Other staff also proved to be a great support, such as Mr. Kanda – the regional manager for ANA (All Nippon Airways) – who assisted me greatly in essential maintenance tasks on the aircraft, and Kato Yusuke (Kato San) who, outside of office hours, also became a great local guide and companion while taking me on sightseeing trips to many local landmarks of interest and for home visits with his charming family.

But it must be said that I was looked after extremely well by *everyone* I came into contact with. Early on, Mr. Igarashi generously provided me with the use of a brand-new bicycle and this proved to be a fantastic way for me to get about. I could easily commute between the airport and the town and spent many happy hours in the saddle, exploring the backroads and by-ways of the whole Shonai plain area. I'd stop occasionally for homemade blueberry ice cream or *onigiri* (rice balls), perhaps washed down with some iced coffee from a vending machine (which in the colder months also served hot coffee...in a tin). A favourite ride was out to the coast and past the Kamo Aquarium, which houses the largest Jellyfish collection in the world – it's an amazing attraction and well worth visiting to see how these incredibly diverse creatures have evolved in the natural world.

As the days of patiently waiting turned into weeks and months, I remained positively optimistic that the Russian permission would eventually be given. I stoically sat it out, assuming the numerous repeated flight permission applications would finally result in the desired outcome.

Diplomatically, I had to also keep the Japanese authorities onside as time rolled on, with crucial British Embassy support from Andy Edney and his endearing and ever-resilient assistant, Rebecca Wells. On various occasions when I had to visit Tokyo, for embassy meetings with JCAB and Russian visa applications, I had the great pleasure to occasionally stay with Andy and his family at his official residence at the embassy or with Rebecca and her welcoming family in their ultra-modern Tokyo townhouse. Over mugs of British tea, toast and marmalade, these visits became like a *home from home*, a welcome morale and psychological boost during the ongoing uncertainties hanging over the Russian permission.

JCAB had originally been persuaded to allow my flight through Japan on the understanding that I would pass through quickly and would soon be exiting out to the next country on the circumnavigation route. They (and I) had not expected that I would then become stuck by a sudden U-turn of cooperation by the Russian authorities. My only saving merit, I think, was that the Japanese authorities must have liked my patient, but dogged, perseverance. They appreciated that the issue was not of my own making and that I was continually trying my best to resolve it. In that attitude they saw me as a trier, someone who didn't give up easily, and therefore they resolved to support my efforts as best and for as long as they reasonably could.

The local airport ground handling staff were also very supportive. As in previous stopovers, where there were no hangar facilities, *Roxy* was accommodated in the fire station building, where the fire crew immediately took charge of ensuring her ongoing safe keeping and comfort. Thankfully, amidst all the other uncertainties surrounding the flight, at least I didn't also have to worry about *Roxy's* wellbeing for a while.

* * *

With potentially a long wait ahead of me before permission might be granted, I based myself in the nearby city of Tsuruoka. There, I was both relieved and pleasantly surprised to find that the 'salaryman hotels' were very moderately priced. Catering for travelling local businessmen, they were basic but comfortable, though not brimming with the luxurious trappings of the more upmarket tourist hotels. I was actually very taken with the efficient simplicity and functionality of the décor and ambiance. That said, after a few weeks the first one I selected became a little overbearing, as the same piece of soothing piped Muzak was being played relentlessly on a short continuous loop in the breakfast lobby. Day after day after day it became a sort of slow torture. Delivered in a gentle instrumental style, akin to the *Medication Valse* soundtrack from *One flew over the Cuckoo's Nest,* the music eventually had so much of an influence that one morning, I started to imagine myself waltzing serenely with a chair around the breakfast tables; it was at that point that I knew I would have to move home. Thankfully my second pick, the *Alpha 1,* was much easier both on my eardrums and my sanity.

The rural nature of the Shonai plain, for centuries naturally cut off from the surrounding country by its imposing interior mountains, gave the impression that not many international travellers ventured this far away from the Shinkansen bullet train network and the more well-trodden tourist hot spots around Tokyo and Kyoto. Walking around town, I could easily go a whole week without seeing another Westerner. In the supermarket and shopping malls, I would often have Japanese students plucking up courage to say hello to me; we'd go on to have a simple, yet very polite, English conversation. It was fascinating to develop an everyday real-life impression of Japan rather than experiencing the tourist stereotype-packaged versions of the bigger cities.

Psychologically I was now in a very different place. The Russian delay created an unpredictable ongoing vulnerability around the whole flight that was completely out of my control. I was feeling extremely frustrated, lonely and abandoned. Why couldn't the Russian authorities just play ball like all the other countries I'd already encountered? Thankfully, Tsuruoka and its wonderful people soon rallied around and came to my aid.

I was introduced to the staff and English-speaking volunteers of the Kokusaimura International Centre, which provides services to assist all non-Japanese visitors and local foreign residents alike. The office staff – Sachi Sato, Ayako Sato, Konno Shizuko and Yongli Yang – all brought a friendly and relaxed style to their work. The same can be said for the volunteers that I also spent time with – Atsushi Noguchi (Guchi San), Aki Takano, Yui Meyer and Dan Meyer – who also assisted the centre in a variety of supporting roles from time to time.

Dan (an American teaching English in a local school) was very kind to allow me to stay with him for a few days shortly after my arrival.

It was here that I also met with his circle of fellow JETs (Japanese exchange teachers). One memorable ice-breaker event that I attended for newly arrived JETs was a *noodle chute* party. The idea was to chute some cooked noodles in soy sauce down a long bamboo half-pipe, with the idea of catching the noodles with chopsticks at the far end. Timing was critical, as was a good sense of humour when, invariably, it all went wrong.

English was a useful common language for many different visiting ethnic minorities, especially on first arrival when perhaps their Japanese was very basic. There was a surprising variety of nationalities making use of the centre for everything from helping to translate and interpret official Japanese residency documents to assisting patients attending hospital appointments or maternity clinics.

Kokusaimura also hosted an annual International Bazaar, where all manner of international cuisine and products were set out on market stalls to purchase. It was here that I first overheard, and then subsequently met, Dr. Dougie Murray and his wife Miho. A towering Scotsman, Dougie was a university research lecturer, and we became good friends. On various occasions, we drank beer, sung karaoke (very badly!) and attended local baseball games together, chatting about all things Celtic from our shared cultural heritage. It was yet another example of a little bit of familiarity from home helping to lift my morale.

As time passed, I was assimilated into the local community. I made great friendships with my main contact at Kokusaimura, Sachi Sato and her extended family. Sachi's mother Kikui, sister Tomo, cousin Hidero Shoji, and his wife Yuki all welcomed me into their family circle, which was a great privilege. Hidero's family farm business meant he was kept extremely busy throughout the year with rice and vegetable production along with an annual cherry harvest. I relished the opportunity to help out as his occasional farm hand whenever required. Harvesting cherries was a completely new experience for me and as I moved around while up a ladder in amongst the cherry trees, I reflected on the fun I had flying low-level over the olive groves of southern Italy.

"Don't fall off the ladder!" I thought to myself.

Other highlights included helping with the planting and harvesting of Hidero's rice crops, and I was honoured when given the task of operating his rice harvesting machine. It was a tracked vehicle, about the size of a mini digger and its cutting blades out front looked remarkably like a giant set of hair clippers. Starting at the outer boundary, I diligently worked my way into the middle of the field in ever-decreasing circles. Hidero had warned me to look out for any small creatures that might break cover at the last minute, but happily I had not disturbed any on this occasion. Though I did later spot a large snake hunting for frogs in one of the surrounding water ditches – not a sight I would see while helping with the haymaking back home!

On another occasion, I volunteered to help Hidero make his annual delivery of the rice harvest to the local agricultural cooperative grain store in town. It felt good to be usefully employed and to help where I could during my enforced downtime, even if only in a small way.

From Hidero's farmyard, we loaded large sacks of rice onto the back of his small flatbed utility truck and lashed them down with a large tarpaulin and rope. It was very early morning, and we were one of the first farm trucks to arrive at the grain store. Hidero literally *showed me the ropes* on how to untie the cargo and fold up the tarpaulin in a particular way, so we were ready for the grain store merchants to unload, inspect and grade our wares for quality and moisture content.

The grain store was massive but as yet cavernously empty. First load safely delivered, we then scooted our way back to the farm to pick up our second cargo of the day and returned once again to town. This time however, a sizeable queue of white farm trucks had built up, all waiting patiently and we decided to play a little prank on everyone. It appeared that Hidero knew all the other local farmers, so he busied himself chatting and standing around with them while we queued. As our turn came (and on Hidero's signal), I then hopped confidently out of the cab and began to expertly remove all the lashing points. I then folded the tarpaulin, without the need for any words of instruction or guidance, as if it was something I had been doing for years. All Hidero's farming buddies looked on with expressions of disbelief. How had wily old *Hidero San* managed to find himself such an *expert* Western farm-hand who was already so *au-fait* with the ways of Shonai rice farming that he needed no assistance whatsoever? It was hard for us to keep a straight face at the time, but we certainly laughed about it afterwards all the way back to the farm.

Another highlight was climbing Mount Gassan 1984m (6509ft). While not quite as high as *Chokai San,* it still proved to be quite a trek. I tackled it along with Sachi and her close friend Saiko Fukuta. Most of the rugged parts of the trail were laid out in carefully arranged steppingstones, whereas heavy wooden running boards spanned many of the more boggy areas. During several hours of continuous hiking, these both proved to be a great help on our way to the summit. Being one of the *Three mountains of Dewa* holy sites (along with nearby Mount Haguro and Mount Yudono), Mount Gassan attracts many traditionally dressed pilgrims. They all make their way towards a very compact and weather-resistant Shinto Shrine, which had been constructed on the summit, along with a cluster of more modern buildings nearby.

On our way back down the trail, we met a figure running up towards us, who I can only describe as being the most extreme food delivery courier I have ever seen. Decked out as if he were an extreme endurance runner, complete with a sweat band around his forehead, he carried a huge polystyrene insulated box on his back as he jogged up the steep mountain towards the summit. It turned out he was making the daily delivery of raw fish so that the hungry souls at the top could still order up their favourite sushi and sashimi dishes! I didn't enquire about the prices charged but I can well imagine that the cost of fresh seafood, delivered by foot after a three-hour mountain climb, could well be as high as the mountain itself!

Given the choice of sushi up a 6000ft mountain or good old fish and chips served in yesterday's newspaper down by the harbour, I know which one I would be buying!

* * *

Out of all the diverse regions that I travelled through during the world flight, Japan had one aspect of life that I found most unusual to experience – earthquakes. Hailing from Northern Ireland, which happens to sit well *inland* on the Eurasian Tectonic Plate, I had never experienced the sensation of an earthquake before. So it was with great surprise that my first tremor was felt in the middle of the night up on the 8th floor of the Alpha 1 hotel. It was a most odd feeling, like someone was silently but forcefully nudging my bed from side to side. It stopped quite abruptly, and I thought for a moment that perhaps it had all been just a dream until, turning on the light, I saw that the *Do Not Disturb* sign hooked onto my room's inside door handle was still rocking to and fro… The movement had been amplified by the fact I was so high off the ground.

I experienced many more of these small tremors throughout the late summer of 2011. Unfortunately, many were probably still the aftershocks of The Great East Japan Earthquake that had tragically occurred on the 11 March 2011 on the opposite (Pacific) coastline of Japan's northern Tohoku region. The largest regional city directly affected by the earthquake and resultant devastating tsunami was Sendai, which lies only some 106km (66 miles) as the crow flies from Tsuruoka, across the interior mountains. In September 2011, I visited Sendai and was able to travel out to the nearby coastal towns of Matsushima and Shiogama. Although situated in a bay and partially protected by outlying offshore islands, they had both suffered significant damage from the tsunami, which was still clearly evident some six months on from the disaster.

On arrival in both towns, I was immediately taken aback at the extent of devastation and physically damaged infrastructure that had occurred below the level of the wave surge, much of which had remained unchanged since the tsunami. A large commercial fishing vessel that had been previously tied alongside in Shiogama port, was now lying on its side up on the pier. Everywhere I looked, pontoons and marina walkways were twisted and broken or lying semi-submerged with no longer any boats to support.

Most striking of all were the metal clad warehouses in a low-lying trading estate some 300-400m inland – it was as if someone had taken a giant can opener to the cladding and ripped off the entire walls, exactly up to the high-level mark that the surging water had reached. Above this line, the buildings still looked perfectly untouched, but below...it was devastation. From the street I peered into one of the interiors, where, like some macabre movie set, the full and complete contents of a former busy office building lay mashed, jumbled and chewed by the dreadful force of the water. Broken furniture, office equipment and paperwork were all scattered randomly and untouched. Most poignant, was a bundle of promotional advertising leaflets that perhaps had been printed up that very day back in March, now left to be forever unused and unclaimed. First-hand evidence of the many thousands of people who had tragically lost their lives and whole communities that had suffered so badly at the hands of Mother Nature.

The extent of the devastation was both a sobering and humbling experience. But at the same time, I was incredibly impressed by the sense of stoic resolve that the local people displayed while beginning to slowly rebuild their communities. Many people who had lost virtually everything were now being cared for and housed in temporary accommodation. Local market traders, whose communal building was now deemed unsafe to enter, had set up makeshift market stalls in another less damaged building nearby. Wanting to show my support and solidarity for the relief and recovery efforts being made, I bought numerous items from the stalls, including two fundraising stickers that were later added to each side of *Roxy's* fuselage and a fundraising T-shirt printed with the slogan *Ganbaro Tohoku* – broadly translated as "we are with you, Tohoku". It was a message of support and solidarity from all of Japan to its victims of the 2011 tsunami.

For many years, the Japanese have become well prepared and trained for living with the continual threat of earthquakes. On one occasion, I had the opportunity to take part in one of their earthquake readiness exercises. It was in a purpose-built earthquake simulator, a mock-up living room, which could be shaken with various degrees of magnitude. It allowed people to learn how to react in each scenario, knowing what to do and what to avoid. The first few simulations were of comparatively mild tremors, such as those I had already experienced in reality, but as the shaking became ever more violent, it was incredible to experience how everyday inanimate objects within the room could suddenly become a dangerous threat as they began moving, falling loose or even launching themselves across the room. I could easily see why many open shelves, cupboards, bookcases and the like, really needed to be firmly secured to the walls rather than to be left free-standing. It was a consideration that I had never thought of back in the *rock steady world* of the British Isles, where even if a slight earth tremor does happen to rattle someone's teacup, it makes the evening news headlines.

Over these uncertain and unstable months, the one thing that unfortunately held firm was the Russian *stonewalling* – absolutely nothing was forthcoming. The authorities there, although generally supportive, were obliged to request an official response from their security services before flight approval could be granted... but no response was being given. The FSB (Federal Security Service) were neither saying yes nor no, rather they appeared to be intentionally just saying *nothing*. This assured that I was not able to move without permission, yet by withholding their response, they remained clear of any potential criticism of making a wrong decision. Unfortunately, this diplomatic impasse and ongoing tactical silence from the Russian Authorities concerning my repeated applications (submitted regularly every few months) dragged on for the next *three years...*

12

Russia: visit to Vladivostok and the impasse

23 October 2012: Tokyo, Japan – Khabarovsk, Russia – Vladivostok, Russia

During the middle of the impasse, in October 2012, I made a short trip (via commercial airliner) from Tokyo across to Vladivostok. My hope was to rally some local support to help get me on my way to Alaska. I flew with Vladivostok Air, which routed me via Khabarovsk Airport. It was my first ever visit to Russia and right from the get-go, I was fascinated at the same-but-different feel that I experienced everywhere.

Passing briefly through Khabarovsk Airport, I saw a surprising mixture of new and old security technologies. At one level, they employed a modern X-ray security scanner set up in the voluminous (yet very empty) Soviet-style concourse, but at the same time I was bemused to find that in their wisdom, they had also thought to employ an airport cat. It busied itself freely strolling around the concourse, while displaying an air of self-importance seldom seen in humans, as it confidently greeted various passengers on their arrival. Presumably employed to help prevent any local rodents from becoming unwanted travelling companions, the cat certainly had its work cut out in the huge expanse of the worn-out old building, one that had clearly long since seen the last hurrahs of its former glory days.

These contrasting technologies seemed to be working in perfect harmony, that is until the cat's meandering patrol route reached the security scanner's desk. At this point, in a fantastic display of technology misalignment, the on-duty security guard promptly leaned down to stroke the cat rather than keeping a close watch on his screens. Looking on, I smiled to myself as several passenger bags then swept through the hi-tech scanner, completely unobserved. I had spotted a loophole in the system! Would-be smugglers take note – to evade detection at an airport scanner all you need to do is equip yourself with your own remote-controlled *robo-cat-3000* and then quietly set it to work...

My main objective was to build up relations with local aviation contacts, who hopefully could then lend their support to my cause. My main contact was Dmitri Igrushin, who guided and looked after me extremely well throughout my stay. Dmitri worked at Vladivostok International Airport, but he actually lived in the small outlying town of Artem and so I took up residence at a local hotel just down the road from his home. This proved to be a terrific experience. Unlike the internationally famous city of Vladivostok, a favourite stopover for passing cruise ships and the end-of-the-line destination for the Trans-Siberian Railway, Artem, with its utilitarian apartment blocks and Soviet-style architecture was way off any regular tourist trail. On several days, I was let loose to wander around the town by myself for a few hours to soak up the atmosphere.

Unlike many of the other foreign countries I had visited, it was quite surreal that here, I was completely ignored. The prime reason for this was that I looked very similar to the local population. In places such as Japan, India and the Middle East, I always looked different and stood out in the crowd as obviously not a local. But in Artem, many of the people buttoned up in their warm jackets against the biting wind looked very European, similar to me. As long as I didn't have to speak, they just assumed I was another local and treated me accordingly. I therefore quickly became an *invisible tourist* and could freely wander about the market and through shops without drawing any attention to myself.

On the surface, things looked similar to any small European town, but occasionally I was suddenly taken aback by something that clearly wasn't. At one point there was a crowd gathered around the back of a car in the main shopping carpark. I went forward to have a look at what was happening only to find that the car's owner was selling the roughly dismembered parts of a whole butchered pig from his boot (trunk). Perhaps this could have been normal enough if it had been some sort of sterilised mobile butcher's shop, but it wasn't. It was just a battered old hatchback car with a grubby tarpaulin spread out over the spare wheel and other tools in the back.

In the local supermarket, things were not quite as they seemed either. I was admiring the plentiful array of goods, set out on the heaving shelves along with the myriad brands of vodka, when I suddenly became aware of some 'shoppers' who were clearly not shopping. Two burly, unsmiling and unflinching minders were standing, one at each end of the narrow aisles and they remained unfazed by any shoppers who were trying to squeeze past them. I later learned that they were likely connected with various local protection racketeering gangs – making their presence so obvious that the shop would not be easily targeted and ransacked. Normality, it seemed was perhaps only a thin surface veneer in these parts.

By contrast, I found the city of Vladivostok to be much more cosmopolitan. Its fantastic mixture of grand architectural styles reflected its colourful history as being the long-time principal trading post and sea-port of this region. That said, at one point when Dmitri and I returned to his parked car on one of the city streets, he made a point of walking right around the car before getting in. I thought this was slightly odd behaviour until, after we drove off, he explained that it was not unusual for parked cars to have their passenger side wheels stolen and replaced with bricks. Their absence perhaps going unnoticed until the owner jumps in and tries to drive away...

Continuing our whistle-stop sightseeing tour of the city (thankfully with all wheels still intact), we visited the mightily impressive heavy shoreline fortifications that are still preserved (now in museum form) from the time that the port served as a stronghold strategic base for the Soviet Pacific Fleet. The port was so well guarded by its comprehensive array of shore defences that it is proudly stated that no attempt has ever been made to conquer it from the sea.

***

Being an undercover tourist (incognito or otherwise) was not of course my main purpose of the visit. I was here to meet with local contacts, airport officials and flying club members of the Primorsky Flying Club, who I hoped might be able to host my flight after I crossed the Sea of Japan. Therefore, instead of being received merely as a tourist, I experienced an authentic flavour of Russian Far East hospitality from my newly established hosts at the flying club.

This hospitality included a small gathering of club members and rapid drinking of at least(!) five toasts of very fine Cognac, along with some snacking on local sausage, cheese and chocolate. This in itself would have been fine but immediately afterwards, esteemed and revered ex-military pilot Valeri Tamarovski, came bursting through the door and announced that it was my turn next to be strapped into his fabulous Yak 52 Aerobatic aircraft for a surprise 10-minute sortie above the runway. Thankfully he had of course not been drinking! Numerous stomach-churning dives, loops and barrel rolls followed, with a low pass and a wing-waggle to finish for the club members watching and cheering below.

As I climbed out of the aircraft onto the lovely, flat and stable concrete apron, I was informed by Valeri that we had just pulled around 6.5 Gs in the high-speed loops and turns. By comparison, a high-speed roller-coaster only ever reaches about 3 Gs. Thankfully, now safely back on the ground, I was most grateful that my insides had just about coped with the onslaught, without spilling their contents.

"Anyone for another smoked sausage?" came the cheeky question. To which, with a big grin, I politely declined.

The hospitality carried on into the evening and after I had presented a clubhouse talk on the circumnavigation, I was further hosted by the chief of the air club to a fine supper. However, this time I lost count after about 10 Cognac toasts, but thankfully the drive back into town afterwards at least didn't involve any further impromptu aerobatic manoeuvres.

Another highlight of the trip was to make contact with the local language school in Artem, where I was asked to give my slideshow talk to a number of their English-speaking classes. To have a native English speaker was seen as quite a rare event and so I was again treated to a great welcome.

A regional tradition on the arrival of any traveller was to be presented with a gift of some salt and heavy black bread. The latter is broken and then dipped into the salt and eaten. With great ceremony, we enacted this tradition with the young students at the beginning of my first talk, but I then had to try to start my slideshow presentation with a big mouthful of very hard to swallow dry bread, much to the amusement of everyone in the room.

Diplomatically, the trip had been a great success in building connections with all the wonderful people that I met. From everyone who I spoke to, I was met only with kindness, empathy, and a genuine concern for my ongoing situation. If it had been up to the people on the ground to decide, I would have been given permission to fly into Russia immediately. As far as I could tell, the military had no issues, nor the aviation authorities or even the ministry of foreign affairs, who were tasked with coordinating the permission. Only one agency – the FSB – remained steadfastly quiet on the issue and simply continued to ignore any and all appeals to give their (required) opinion. Without it, as they were no doubt well aware, permission could not be granted. In the autumn of 2012, I had no idea that the FSB would ultimately continue with this long-arm tactical silence, all the way through to 2014...

13

The Pacific Ocean: Japan to USA (by ship)

The conflict and regional political turmoil caused by the annexation of Crimea by Russia in March 2014 rumbled on throughout that summer, and consequently diplomatic relations between Russia and the European Union became progressively ever more strained. Looking on at this situation from halfway around the world in Japan, I found the late summer diplomatic mood music about Russia not sounding pretty. I had already been held at arm's length by the Russian authorities for three long years, without any sign of being allowed permission to fly onwards through their country. With the deterioration of relations over Crimea, it felt that permission was now even less likely to ever be granted. It was clear that I could easily be left sitting in Japan and ignored for another three years, or six years or forever.

I had to do something. The Japanese authorities too felt they had stretched their hospitality to the limit. Over the three years, they had shown great sympathy for the predicament that Russia had placed me in, through no fault of my own, and had been extremely generous and supportive of G-YROX's enforced stay at Shonai Airport. But enough was enough.

The Crimean issue thus proved to be the final straw. Without overflying Russia, there was simply no other viable route to fly *Roxy* across to North America and so I had to make the difficult decision to physically transport the aircraft over the Pacific Ocean by container ship to the US West Coast. My continuous flight around the world had been interrupted.

With a heavy heart, I arranged road transport for *Roxy* on a small flatbed truck. Once loaded up, many airport staff gathered to wave farewell to the plucky little aircraft that had by now become a familiar part of their airport community. She would be especially missed by the airport firefighters, who had adopted her under their protective wing from day one.

It was a 30-minute drive to reach the nearest container terminal at Port of Sakata. On arrival, *Roxy* was unloaded again into a shipping agent's warehouse. A last logistical challenge remained, and that was to squeeze a nearly 10ft-high gyroplane into an 8ft-high shipping container. A standard 20ft-long box container was fine for both length and width, but the height remained the issue. However, I had a plan. I was able to source some small load-bearing trolley wheels (as you might see on a supermarket shopping cart) in a local farm supply and DIY store. I replaced *Roxy*'s chunky main wheels with these much smaller ones and also unbolted the whole rotor head assembly from the mast. Thus, by reducing height from both the bottom and top extremities, the overall height of the aircraft was just about right to fit through the doorway of the container.

With a makeshift ramp and the manual help of the warehouse stevedores, we pushed the now squat and decapitated airframe forward, nose first towards the open doors.

It wouldn't fit! The top of the mast was still a couple of millimetres too high for the doorframe. Damn.

We rolled it back out. Then I thought to try it the other way around, tail first. It looked likely that the same issue would reoccur, but we soon realised that if the nose was held up really high in the air, the top of the mast would lean back and also dip down slightly. Held at this peculiar angle, and with the tail scraping the floor, we rolled the airframe back in again and the mast now cleared the doorframe by just a few millimetres. Once past this constriction, the actual roof height inside of the box was considerably higher, allowing the airframe to be levelled again and to be strapped down securely to the floor. It was in!

We all cheered. Me especially, as those precious millimetres had just saved me about US$1000! If the airframe had not fitted in, my only other option would have been to hire a more expensive 40ft 'high cube' shipping container instead, with a higher door clearance, but also 20ft of extra (and totally unneeded) length.

With the airframe and de-rigged rotor blades securely held in place and strapped down, all my other expedition equipment was also stuffed in. We then closed the doors, and I ceremoniously attached a security seal on the doorhandle.

The next time I would see *Roxy* would be in Oregon, USA.

11 September 2014 – 20 October 2014: Port of Sakata, Japan – Busan, South Korea – Tacoma, Washington, USA – McMinnville, Oregon, USA

After the decision had been made to up sticks in Japan, I had needed somewhere to ship the aircraft to once it had arrived in the USA. I had long thought of the idea of crossing the States between Portland, Oregon and Portland, Maine, and so the Evergreen Aviation and Space Museum in McMinnville became an ideal logistical base – it was just 30 miles south-west of Portland. Numerous exploratory emails then flew back and forth across the Pacific to the museum, and I was very relieved when Larry Wood (executive director) and Stewart Bailey (museum curator) informed me that the museum would allow *Roxy* to become a temporary exhibit over the upcoming winter months.

Roxy was initially transported south-west, over the Sea of Japan to Busan in South Korea. More containers were then picked up, before the ship steamed across the Pacific to arrive in Tacoma, Washington, USA some six weeks later. The final leg of the journey to McMinnville in Oregon was then completed by road on the back of a container truck.

Initially, I was hopeful of keeping the *expedition team* together and I'd asked if I could accompany *Roxy* on the sea voyage across the Pacific, by becoming a passenger on the container ship. But unfortunately, the shipping company quickly came back to say it was not logistically possible on this occasion. So instead, I followed on, flying by commercial airliner on 7 October from Narita Airport in Tokyo to Vancouver, Canada. An onward connecting flight then delivered me on to Portland, Oregon.

By 9 October I was settled into a motel in McMinnville and had had a face-to-face meeting with Larry Wood, Stewart Bailey and Terry Naig at the nearby Evergreen Museum.

On the 14 October, in preparation for *Roxy*'s imminent arrival and to provide some background information on my flight so far, I gave a PowerPoint slide show presentation to the museum docents (museum guides) and other staff in their huge IMAX screen auditorium. It was slightly unnerving, however, when at one point I caught sight of myself projected in enormously large detail on the big screen behind me.

20 October 2014 – 30 May 2015: Evergreen Aviation and Space Museum, McMinnville, Oregon, USA

Roxy's arrival day at the museum was a big milestone. At the Japanese Port of Sakata I had been assisted by the local stevedores in packing the shipping container. For our convenience, the container had been placed down on the ground, so it allowed us relatively easy access to roll, tilt and squeeze the airframe into it. However now, at journey's end, the much-travelled container had arrived atop a flatbed truck and was waiting to be unloaded at the huge hangar doors near the museum's rear parking lot. This then presented our next challenge. We had no crane on site, no unloading bay and no ramp or lift to help unload *Roxy*'s container.

But we did have Terry.

Terry Naig was our secret weapon. He was the 'go to guy' for all things maintenance at the museum and possessed a very practical sense of how to get things done. As the saying goes, 'Necessity is the mother of invention.' And it was certainly necessary for us to get *Roxy* out of the container and safely down onto the tarmac. We didn't have a crane to lift the box off the truck, but we did have Terry's forklift truck and a small flatbed trailer at our disposal. So thinking out of the box (excuse the dreadful pun), we used the forklift to lift the small trailer up to the height of the container and rolled the aircraft out onto that. We then lowered the trailer to the ground and replaced the main wheels on *Roxy*'s undercarriage. Finally, we simply tilted the trailer and rolled her off and down onto the tarmac. Happy Days.

Unloading the rotor blades and other parts from the container, we then rolled the airframe through the hangar doors and into the museum, ready to take up temporary residency during the upcoming winter months. Over the following few days *Roxy* was reunited with her rotor and returned to flying condition once more.

The Evergreen Aviation and Space Museum holds a fantastic collection of aircraft. Most notably, it is the home of the Hughes H-4 Hercules flying boat famously known to all as the *Spruce Goose*. Constructed from wood, its huge size was a marvel of ingenious engineering, and its presence dominates and fills one of the two enormous exhibition hangars.

Roxy had the honour of being given a temporary berth under the tail of the massive aircraft, complete with her own roped off area. Close by, was the very shiny fuselage of the Boeing B-17 Flying Fortress that was used in the 'skyhook' pick-up closing scenes of the James Bond movie *Thunderball.*

It made for quite a surreal experience when I soon found myself acting as something of a *pilot in residence.* Often, I would be busy working away on background maintenance tasks within *Roxy's* roped off area, when visitors to the museum would wander past and stop for a chat. After many such encounters, I began to feel like an exhibit in a zoo, with everyone looking on and studying my day-to-day activities. Unfortunately however, despite me always using my most winning smile, no one ever thought to throw me a bun.

On occasions, through the many months of waiting for the summer to return, I was allowed to take *Roxy* out of the museum and fly around the local area. This also provided a most unusual additional attraction for the visitors. Many of the museum's curator staff and docents were highly knowledgeable volunteers who often either had a background in the aviation industry or were retired military personnel. *Roxy* was quickly adopted by these docents as one of the aircraft in their care, and so on those occasions when I was preparing to take her out for a flight, I quickly had a whole ground crew willing and able to help coordinate my take-off and landing sequences. Depending on the wind conditions, I could typically roll out of the hangar doors and either use one of the access roads or part of an empty rear car park as my make-shift runway. The docents skillfully stopped the traffic and cleared the area in readiness for my departure.

This high-level of coordination with my *flight deck crew* felt like I was being launched from an aircraft carrier each and every time I took off. I flew on some lovely local jaunts out around the vineyards of the Willamette Valley, along the fantastic Pacific coastline and over the heavily forested coastal mountain range, where at one point I was both amazed and privileged to share a few moments of flight with a magnificent bald eagle. We were both occupied in soaring along the same ridgeline when I spotted him below me. I looked down warily, not wanting to scare him in any way, but as a top predator and presumably with no known enemies, he didn't even flinch at my presence.

The museum closed at 5pm every day which also happened to be 00:00UTC (midnight). On my GPS clocks, I maintained the standard practice of always keeping time in UTC, as I was changing local time zones so frequently. So when I was out flying, I kept an eye on the UTC time and I often felt a bit like Cinderella on many afternoon sorties; I could head out and fly all over the place, just as long as I returned back home before midnight! Unfortunately however, on one occasion I was late, as I had been delayed by an unexpected headwind. I arrived back about 00:10UTC to find the rear hangar door already open and all the docents lined up to welcome their wayward overdue pilot (now sitting in a flying pumpkin) back home. It was a lovely Museum family to be part of and I thank all the staff and volunteers who made my stay so welcoming.

14

North America: Coast-to-Coast, USA

1 June 2015: McMinnville, Oregon, USA (local flying day)

It was time to restart the circumnavigation, again! Thankfully the process was now slightly easier as I knew, almost instinctively, where and how best to stow all my luggage and equipment. As my journey progressed around the world, the mental challenge also became slightly easier, as I was able to tick yet another country off the list. I was now on the US West Coast, with relatively simple flying ahead of me to cross to the East Coast and then turn northwards up into eastern Canada. I expected the flying on this next section to be the easy part, but as to what lay in store after that – crossing northern Canada, Greenland and then the open Atlantic Ocean – well for now, I just had to keep all that mentally on the back burner.

The logistics of my departure were slightly convoluted. I took off lightly loaded, from the rear access road at the museum and made a two-minute hop across to McMinnville Municipal Airport positioned just across the highway. I was then met there by Tom Halvorsen and Terry Naig with all my additional fuel and luggage. The weather was grey, drizzly and dull, so we used a lean-to shed to shelter in while I stowed everything away. There were fond farewells on the ground and waving from the air as I took off and climbed away. I was once again up and running, though on this occasion it proved to be short lived.

As I wanted my flight crossing the US to be 'Coast-to-Coast', my plan was to initially head west and fly out to a small airport called Tillamook directly on the coastline. It involved flying about 30 miles or so over the heavily forested mountain peaks of the Oregon Coast Range, but I had already flown the route several times in training flights, and I knew in advance that there were wide logging roads of perfectly graded gravel criss-crossing the whole area. Having these gravel roads to act as potential emergency landing sites within the trees, was very reassuring.

The mountainous terrain was therefore not my biggest issue, but the poor weather skulking around the treetops was. As I flew higher towards the main ridgeline peaks, ground-hugging mountain mists slowly closed in around me. The cloud base was ragged yet contained holes that gave tempting, but potentially deadly glimpses of bright weather ahead. I could sense that the worst weather was being held in the mountains, so I knew that if I could somehow break through to the coastline, I would most likely then have blue skies and clear conditions near the ocean. I dodged about indecisively for a few minutes looking for my best routing, but as quickly as a glimpse of a clear horizon appeared, the swirling clouds rapidly closed in again to block any hope of flying through. Pulling back on my airspeed, I orbited and backtracked several times, probing and testing various valleys and ridges to see if any other path through them might be more promising. But time and time again my progress was thwarted. All the while, I was extremely aware that I didn't want to be enticed into a half-promising situation, only for my escape route to close up behind me. If that happened, I could easily be engulfed in cloud and left with no way out. I shuddered at the thought and decided, after 20 minutes of fruitless searching, that perhaps living to fight another day was the best plan. Relieved with my decision and with a renewed sense of purpose, I turned tail and flew back out of the foothills to return to McMinnville.

I think I was as surprised to see Tom Halvorsen upon my return as he was to see me. After he had gone home, he had watched my progress on the SPOT satellite tracker and saw that I had had to turn back. He immediately returned to the airport and was there to greet me. With no sign of any improvement in the weather forecast, we then scrubbed flying for the rest of the day.

2 June 2015: McMinnville, Oregon, USA (non-flying day)

With the weather conditions remaining very similar to the previous day, it was an easy decision to stay grounded at McMinnville for at least another 24 hours. However, instead of taking *Roxy* back over to the museum, we arranged storage in a small vacant hangar at the main airport. I kept most of the luggage and the Turtle Pac fully loaded, which then allowed me a much faster turn-around time as and when the flight conditions next improved.

3 June 2015: McMinnville, Oregon, USA – Tillamook, Oregon, USA – Scappoose, Oregon, USA

The onward flight finally got underway again. Thankfully, the weather was much improved, and I headed once again for Tillamook. Following my same route, I smiled to myself when passing the mountains that had caused me so much delay two days previously. With settled weather they now looked much less threatening, and visibility was clear all the way out to the Pacific.

Tillamook was to be a significant stop on the circumnavigation, but not as I had first imagined. I had planned for it to mark the start of an FAI 'Coast-to-Coast' record for crossing North America, which would finish over on the Eastern Seaboard of the States. But I soon learned that if the record was to be set *wholly* within the USA, then it would have only been regarded as a US national record, not an international one. It would also have required me to work under the guidance of the US FAI records coordinator instead of the UK FAI equivalent, Geoffrey Boot, who was already looking after all my international records. So, in order to continue to set an international record it was an easy fix:

All I had to do was adapt my Coast-to-Coast record routing to be from Tillamook, Oregon, USA on the west coast, to Sept-Îles, Quebec, Canada on the east coast. Within this routing however, for my own sense of completeness, I still flew between Portland, Oregon and Portland, Maine (wholly within the USA), but I subsequently didn't claim it as an FAI national record.

Tillamook was almost deserted when I landed. The only person on hand was the airfield manager, who was able to officially record the flight on my FAI landing and take-off certificates. When I explained that I would use these forms as the basis of my record claims across America and eventually over the Atlantic, he was suitably pleased that he had played a small, but crucial part in the whole expedition.

With this one solitary witness to my departure, I was quickly up and away again for the short flight north-east over to Scappoose Industrial Airpark.

I arranged to overnight there in a lovely wooden-cladded B&B guesthouse, the Scappoose Creek Inn and met with Jim Vanek for dinner in the evening. His Sport Copter gyroplane manufacturing business was based at the airport, and he kindly hosted *Roxy* overnight in his maintenance hangar. We chatted for several hours about the shared history and future of gyroplane development in the US and Europe.

It felt great to be back in the saddle and making progress eastwards once more.

4 June 2015: Scappoose, Oregon, USA – Hermiston, Oregon, USA

Over the previous weeks, I had flown out on several repeat day trips to both Tillamook and Scappoose from the museum. As a training strategy, I wanted them to already feel as comfortable, friendly and familiar locations for when I would next be calling by, in full circumnavigation mode. Today however, I would be leaving behind that comfort zone. Once more I would constantly be flying into new, unfamiliar territory, and I quickly had to regain my expedition mental resilience, in order to cope with the continuous uncertainties that such a pioneering flight presented. In the back of my mind, I now had yet another new continent to cross and still the ever present, ever daunting mighty Atlantic Ocean to conquer.

As ever, my best coping strategy was to focus all my efforts on making one safe and successful flight at a time.

Bidding Jim and his Sport Copter team a fond farewell, I tracked up the mighty Columbia River Gorge and skirted around to the north of the city of Portland. Thanks to earlier recce flights, the landscape was still reassuringly familiar to me until I passed the small airstrip at Cascade Locks. I had landed out at this lovely little strip a few weeks earlier, spent about 10 minutes on the ground, saw no one and then took off again. It was a real pleasure (after the paperwork complexities of flying in Japan, Egypt, India and other places) to just be able to drop into an almost random, quiet airstrip somewhere, totally unannounced, as if I was simply pulling into a layby at the side of the road. A quick stretch of the legs and perhaps a snack on a handful of nuts would then see me up and on my way again, all within a few minutes. I found that the whole of my US crossing was punctuated with similar small community airstrips. Every regional town or even smaller settlement seemed to have one nearby. The constant and plentiful supply of these alternative emergency landing sites was continually reassuring.

The natural scenery in the Columbia River Gorge was tremendous. Flying at about 800-1000ft, I felt I was flying *within* the scenery rather than *above* it. I stayed to the northern side of the river to avoid the turbulence caused by the downdraught on the other bank, as the wind was blowing from the south. I passed over the city of Hood River, where a wide section of the Columbia River is well known to be popular for kite surfers, and I could see that the warm wind was certainly assisting them to scoot back and forth across the water. Even though I knew I had a good 500ft of clearance below me, I still was wary of the collective damage that a large kite getting tangled in my main rotor would make.

So I climbed up another 200ft, just to make sure.

It must be said that planning the US Coast-to-Coast flight was a piece of cake compared to other countries. Having a suitable small airstrip every 20 or so miles along my route allowed me to select a comfortable flying distance, scope it out onto a chart and then look to see what settlement was suitable for me nearby. It was a bit like route planning using the childhood game of sticking the tail on a donkey; it allowed me so much freedom to choose a very flexible route as I went along.

Some destinations picked using this *pin on the map* technique proved to be excellent, others not quite so as we shall see...

I wanted these first flights to be leisurely, to ease myself gradually back into circumnavigation mode and to get back into my regular flying routine. I aimed to build up progressively longer distances each day and so, after only three hours in the saddle, I arrived at my first previously unvisited airport, Hermiston.

I was pleasantly surprised (and slightly bemused) to be warmly greeted at the Hermiston FBO (fixed-base operator) by a chattering gaggle of senior citizen ladies, who I think had been using the airport building for one of their regular meetings. As they spilled out of the offices to inspect my aircraft, they were keenly curious to find out the full story of my journey so far and followed up with many questions.

I had forgotten a little bit of the unusual nature of what I was trying to achieve, and some of the ladies were in disbelief at what I was hoping to do, especially crossing the Atlantic to get back to Europe. But all of them were supportive and wished me the best of luck and good fortune for the rest of the flight. A few even wished that they could have done something similar when they were many years younger.

I thanked them all for their enthusiastic and encouraging words as it meant a lot for my ongoing morale. I was off to a great start.

My familiar arrival routine now also kicked in once again: find hangar space, unpack luggage, check fuel requirements and put *Roxy* to bed. Next, sort out transport and nearby food and accommodation for the evening. All this would then be repeated in reverse order the next morning, often combined with a trip to the nearest petrol (aka gas, we were now in the USA after all) station for fuel.

5 June 2015: Hermiston, Oregon, USA – Caldwell, Idaho, USA – Glens Ferry, Idaho, USA

Navigation through the Rockies was something I had to consider very carefully. There was no avoiding the geography; to fly through from the Pacific Coast to the Great Plains, I was obliged to cross over some pretty high, remote and extremely mountainous terrain at some point in the journey. After many hours of pondering over Google Earth, I hit on the most practical route possible for my lightweight open cockpit gyroplane.

I decided I would fly an *IFR route,* but not in the usual sense of the phrase as used by commercial airlines, which is 'instrument flight rules'. In my case it stood for 'I follow roads'.

My plan was to pick one of the few interstate highways that would cross the Rockies by the least complicated terrain. I soon spotted that I could follow the course of the Columbia River up to Hermiston then continue to follow Highway 84 south-east. This would allow me to fly up the Snake River Valley towards West Yellowstone, Montana. Crossing over Yellowstone National Park, I then planned to exit the park on its eastern side, via US Route 20 and continue to climb over the Sylvan Pass to briefly reach 10,500ft. After reaching that highest point, I could finally then drop down towards Cody, Wyoming, and the relatively lower flat lands to the east of the Rockies. It was a routing that would allow me to fly below 10,000ft for most of its length and provide me with the comfort of a reasonable width of highway nearby, should I have needed an emergency landing.

So, on leaving Hermiston, although I had the overall flight strategy worked out for the Rockies, I only had a vague plan of where I would end up by the end of each day's flying. I wasn't overly concerned however, as this was one of the luxuries of General Aviation flying in the USA. In the vast tracts of unrestricted airspace, I could afford to go a little *off grid* and make it up as I went along. Imagine the horror that would have caused in places like Egypt!

"No Captain, you must stay *exactly* on the air route at all times..."

My rough plan was to reach and then broadly follow the path of the Snake River Valley. I would subsequently just see how far I would get, though I also had to factor in a short stop for a local TV interview, that had been arranged for me at Caldwell Airport. Happily, I planned that this would also coincide with lunchtime. And depending on how long I was on the ground filming, it would then dictate how far up the Snake River I might reach before quitting time for the day.

As it happened, somewhat predictably, the interview filming took quite some time and it was well into the afternoon before I finally got going again. Back in the air, I assessed my options. I decided to plump for a small town called Glens Ferry, Idaho. As is my preference, I liked the idea of dropping into lesser-known places that perhaps get by-passed by most other air traffic. I was curious to see what adventures a small, randomly picked, rural settlement in Idaho might bring. The airfield facilities proved to be even more spartan than I had imagined. The runway was fine, the taxiway was OK, but it led only to a small cluster of tin shed hangars that were completely deserted. I taxied to the side of the nearest one and went to unload my gear.

Usually in such circumstances, as in the small Italian grass strip in Pescara, a few locals would spot the strange craft now landing at their local airfield and jump in a car to race down to see me. Here in Glens Ferry, no one came.

I waited for a while longer, still no one came.

I started to query my decision on landing here. The town was probably a good half hour hike, a daunting endeavour seeing I had all my luggage and fuel bag to carry, so I decided to wait even longer still. Then joy of joys! A pickup truck hove into view in a cloud of dust.

Huzzah! The Cavalry had arrived!

The truck drove right past my position and headed for a slightly larger shed. I mentally gathered up my best scrounging chat-up lines and headed for the now opened hangar door. Interestingly the hangar was not for aeroplanes at all, instead it was a storage base for aerial crop sprayers who could drop in to replenish their payload before heading off to buzz more local fields.

Soon enough, after a bit of friendly chit chat, I was given a lift into town and dropped off at a small roadside motel. Perfect for my needs, it even turned out that the motel owner's husband was a local pilot who was glad to help me with picking up fuel and getting me on my way again the next morning. Happily everything worked out just fine in the end!

The only downside that I quickly realised was that I had to share my room with the empty Turtle Pac. After a while, stored in a confined space, the fuel bag often had an antisocial habit of slowly infusing the room with a petrol perfume. Usually if I was lucky, I would be able to store it outside on a balcony or in a shed, but in this place the motel rooms were all on the ground floor and opened straight onto the street. The best I could manage was to confine it to hanging in the shower cubicle of my small adjoining bathroom, opening the even smaller window and keeping the interior door tightly shut.

Yet again I was reminded, 'Necessity is the mother of invention'.

6 June 2015: Glens Ferry, Idaho, USA – West Yellowstone, Montana, USA

Fuel pickup so far had been a truly varied operation, sometimes by taxi, regular car or security truck, other times by hand cart, luggage trolley or even a taxicle. However, this process had now become more difficult since leaving Japan, as while waiting there I'd received a new Turtle Pac from the company's owner Laszlo Torok, which was able to hold an extra 60 litres of fuel. This gave me the added flexibility of being able to pick up a full 140 litres at a time from local gas stations and bring it all back to the aircraft in one go. As a result however, the additional volume proved a bit more unwieldy to handle when full. So much so that while unpacking it for the first time in Japan, I'd nicknamed my new 'sumo wrestler'-sized friend the *Saki Barrel.* But a discovery in Glens Ferry would ease this refuelling process for the rest of my journey across the States – to the rescue came the ubiquitous pickup truck, and its handy tailgate.

It was such a fine vehicle for a number of reasons, not least that I could refuel the Turtle Pac directly from the gas station pumps and then manoeuvre the tailgate of the truck close in beside the back seat of the gyro once back at the airfield. The height was usually perfect, such that I could then connect the full fuel bladder into the aircraft fuel line and begin to refuel the main tanks while the Turtle Pac remained perched on the pickup's open tailgate. This enabled me to effectively halve the weight of the full Turtle Pac before we then wrestled it onto the back seat of the aircraft to be strapped in. It greatly eased what had become potentially the most physical task of the whole flight preparation.

* * *

The flight to West Yellowstone was full of anticipation. I was gradually gaining altitude toward the highest point of my whole circumnavigation and the scenery was becoming ever more mountainous all around me. Along the way, I made a small diversion in order to overfly an amazing geological formation at Craters of the Moon National Monument and Preserve. The scenery was dominated by a blanket of recent (in geological time) lava flows, which from the air appeared quite bizarre, especially as it was dissected by a black asphalt road snaking through its middle. I felt like an aerial tourist as I zigzagged across the extremely rugged terrain, though I was careful not to stray too far from the lovely smooth road as it was my only viable emergency landing option. I therefore followed the sweeping curves in the road much like a motorbike, though remaining a few hundred feet above the surface, I got to enjoy a much wider view.

On arrival, West Yellowstone was a surprisingly busy little airport. Being close to one of the main access points for Yellowstone National Park, it was a prime go-to stopover for many touring aircraft. The FBO gave me a warm welcome and were incredibly surprised to see such a small G-reg aircraft travelling so far from the UK. Gladly accepting a lift into town to find accommodation, I was given an impromptu guide of the townscape. I was surprised to learn that a huge new hotel had recently been established downtown, though at first I thought this was perhaps not so unusual, given it was located in such a tourist hot spot. However, on closer inspection, what did make it unusual was that the hotel had been financed and built *exclusively* to cater for legions of Chinese package tourists. Who, no doubt due to their sheer numbers, must have had to be bussed in and out of the park each day, with almost military precision.

7 June 2015: West Yellowstone, Montana, USA – Cody, Wyoming, USA

My main mission today was to safely overfly the world-famous Yellowstone National Park. The vast wilderness areas within the park are home to a wide variety of wildlife and amazing geological features, such as boiling mud pools, deadly acidic lakes and renowned geysers, including of course the most photographed and internationally recognised geyser of them all, *Old Faithful.* The fantastic natural, sometimes dangerous, environment of the park however gave me one further profoundly serious concern. Primordial forest. Unlike the more managed forests of the Oregon coastline, where logging roads and firebreaks criss-crossed the hillsides and helped to break up the tree blanket density, the forest in Yellowstone has always intentionally been left largely untouched. This was of course all well and good for the natural, unspoilt ecology of the park, but it was not so handy for any risk-averse, solo gyroplane circumnavigator who wished to pass by overhead. No logging activity meant no emergency logging road landing strips to follow and so my only safe option was to stick closely to within landing range of the main tourist highways. This was fine as a strategic plan, but it later proved to be a little tricky in its execution.

Approaching the main entrance gate to the park, I felt I was in a scene from *Mad Max 2.* Below me was a long convoy of cars, trucks, SUVs, motorhomes and buses. Like a mass exodus in reverse, all vehicles were heading into the park for the day, with no one coming out. Joining the cavalcade, I flew along over the top of everyone exactly like the *Gyro Captain* character did in his beat-up Benson B-8 Autogyro in the movie. And best of all, while the vehicles at the head of the queue were stopping at the park ranger station to pay their entrance fees, I gleefully blasted past overhead.

"No fees for me!" I thought as I gave the tourist traffic a cheery wave.

What a great way to travel.

Soon afterwards, I came across a stunningly mesmerising sight. Initially, the road rose into some foothills and I climbed along with it until I plateaued up and over a sharp arête of rocky cliffs. There, from my lofty vantage point as I cleared the ridgeline, the whole enormity of Yellowstone suddenly opened up right in front of me. I could see that the ridge was not an isolated feature, but actually part of a continuous ring of mountains that stretched out 35-40 miles or more in diameter. I was seeing with my own eyes an incredible natural feature that I had last studied in A-level geography, some 34 years ago.

This was the great Yellowstone Caldera, the crater ring of a super-volcano that is so large and complex that the normal simple term of volcano does not do it justice. I felt so privileged to be able to see its vast, yet intricate structure all at once, in its entirety, without any of the on-the-ground scenery getting in the way. (Although it is odd to think of the spectacular national park scenery merely as being view-spoiling 'clutter'!)

Off in the near distance I could see Yellowstone Lake, my next waypoint, and I remembered reading that over time, it had gradually shifted slightly due to the upswelling or bulging of the interior of the caldera. More recent studies however have suggested that the caldera has been in fact simply *breathing*, swelling and contracting over many years and so I took this as reassurance of the supervolcano's ongoing stability. This was comforting to know because should it ever decide to erupt, predictions are that it will be around a thousand times more powerful than the Mount Saint Helens eruption of 1980.

"Don't blow just yet," I thought, "at least not for the next few hours."

* * *

I followed the park's highway as best as I could. The road, unlike a regularly maintained highway, had many twisted sections and disappeared from time to time, hidden by the lush tree canopy on either side. Thankfully though, enough open sections were still visible to give me some chance of finding a landing spot. From time to time, I saw a bottleneck of traffic. Vehicles were pulled up haphazardly on the roadsides and I could then see people clustered in small groups looking off into the trees. It was a sure sign that some large wildlife, such as an elk, moose, bison or even a bear had been spotted nearby. Unfortunately, as interesting as it was for people on the ground, for me everything remained hidden and unseen overhead.

Wildlife aside, my main focus while passing through the park was to view the geysers. In the FBO office at West Yellowstone, I had made a note of the eruption times for Old Faithful. The legendary geyser originally earned its name because it was expected to faithfully erupt every hour or so, though in reality this natural geological phenomenon has often been much less predictable, erupting anywhere between every 35 minutes to every two hours. And so, armed with the best prediction time the FBO could offer (and a healthy dose of optimism), I flew in the direction of Old Faithful. On the way I managed to witness a different geyser erupt, and although I was still some distance off, it was quite spectacular to see the gushing mass of brilliant white water and steam shoot into the sky. From the air, the eruption gave a clear indication that the earth's crust really was seething and boiling just under its surface layer. I approached with a renewed wariness of the potential dangers of Old Faithful.

"No place for an emergency landing here," I mused.

After all, in the areas immediately surrounding the geysers, if you are not safely standing on the boardwalks, the ground can be so hot in places that your shoes could quite easily melt. I didn't want to imagine what would happen to the tyres of a gyroplane.

Alas, as I approached the famed geyser, I could see a mass of tourists slowly drifting away from the semi-circle of viewing platforms next to it. It was a sure sign that Old Faithful had just blown. The geyser had erupted slightly ahead of its predicted time but unfortunately, I couldn't afford the time to hang around for the next blow to occur. I still had a long flight to complete.

Picking up once more on the park roads, my next objective was to skirt around the edge of Yellowstone Lake. Yet on approaching the lake shore, I was immediately presented with a new dilemma. The weather to this point had been scattered cloud but I retained good visibility. Now there was an ominous darkening and thickening of a nearby cloud, which heralded the imminent arrival of a sudden heavy shower burst. Anywhere else this was not a problem, as I could often just tiptoe around the cloud fringes to stay dry, but here if I detoured to avoid the rain, it would put me way off course from the relative safety of the highway. I decided that I would just have to grin and bear it to remain in touch with the thin black line of reassurance and civilisation below me. Though as if to add insult to injury, as soon as I flew into the weather, the cloud burst intensified, and the rain turned to hail for a time. All I could do was crouch lower in my seat to allow my windshield to take most of the impact.

"Thank you. That's lovely flying weather you're giving me for June!" I hollered above the rattle of the hail bouncing off my helmet.

Soon enough the intense rain passed and thankfully, I could fly on again unhindered. By way of an apology perhaps and as something of a silver lining, the precious black ribbon below had now turned to a silvery strip of wet tarmac, glistening in the returning sunlight.

* * *

Beyond the lake, as I climbed out of the park, I reached the highest point of land that I had to cross during my entire circumnavigation. The highway at Sylvan Pass summited at 8500ft and so I crossed the mountain ridge at about 9100ft. It felt surreal to see that level of elevation on my altimeter, when I was physically only about 600ft above the ground. Occasionally, in other parts of the world, I was to fly higher for short periods due to airspace or traffic restraints, however this remained the highest physical barrier I would encounter anywhere.

Snow and ice topped the peaks all around me as I flew across the highest point. I had not flown in such chilly mountainous conditions since I had followed the A66 road over the Pennines after the Duxford press launch back in February 2010. These however were not now the gentle rolling hills of northern England, but rather the mighty, rugged, unforgiving, Rocky Mountains. Due to the high altitude, the air temperature had dropped considerably, and I was immediately wary of the turbulent air that was bouncing off the various jagged peaks around me. After around 20 minutes of significant buffeting, I was relieved when I was finally able to commence my gradual descent, following a long, ever-widening valley towards the infamous cowboy town of Cody. As I throttled back and flew leisurely down through more gentle slopes, the warm summer air returned and I was feeling quite elated to have crossed yet another major hurdle in the circumnavigation. Having successfully negotiated my highest point in the Rockies, it was now going to be 'all downhill' from here, out onto the Great Plains and onwards over to the Atlantic coast.

Cody proved to be a great stopover. My childhood knowledge of frontier cowboy country and the wild west was shaped by old Saturday TV matinee shows such as *The High Chaparral, Bonanza, The Virginian* and *Alias Smith and Jones.* Real life cowboy heroes such as Davy Crockett and Buffalo Bill with his Wild West rodeo shows were also part of this culture, and so to find that Buffalo Bill Cody actually had his own hotel (and these days even his own brand of beer) in the town that bears his name was a great treat. After booking into a local motel, I *moseyed* along the sidewalk intending to *go git me one of those fancy beers* and also had myself a *miiighty fine dinner* at Buffalo Bill's Irma Hotel. At any minute I half expected a cowboy to come crashing through the saloon window after a drunken brawl, but thankfully the local sheriff must have already locked up all the outlaws for the night.

8 June 2015: Cody, Wyoming, USA – Devils Tower, Wyoming, USA – Custer, South Dakota, USA

Hey ho! Another day, another dollar. I packed away my overnight bedroll on my aerial pony, suited up and climbed back in the saddle to continue heading eastwards.

After the drama of navigating the high Rockies, I expected the next few flying days to be much less taxing and was in a relaxed mood. But alas this assumed tranquillity soon proved to be a little premature... On climb-out, after a suspiciously long take-off roll, I experienced a very severe and unpleasant bout of 'stick shake'. Through the stick vibrations, the main rotor felt as if it was shaking and flapping quite violently. I was receiving my very own form of a *bucking bronco* ride as I fought to counteract the shaking, which thankfully was short lived. It was only after things smoothed out as I gained speed and started to climb away successfully that I was able to work out what had been going on. I had suffered from a combination of heavy fuel load, thinner air at high altitude (Yellowstone Regional Airport at Cody has a ground elevation of 5000ft) and hot ambient air.

Trying to coax a heavy object up into thin and hot air, had resulted in *Roxy* putting in a formal complaint to the management.

The terrain, although still high, was now much gentler; rolling hills rather than jagged peaks, which allowed for much less confused turbulence and much more singing in the cockpit. A main objective on today's flight was to overfly the Devils Tower in Wyoming's north-eastern corner. This introduced a considerable dogleg into the direct routing towards Custer (my next stopover destination), but it proved to be well worth the diversion. Ever since my teenage years I had known of the Devils Tower. Geologists are still debating the origins of its unusual structure; it was either formed from an igneous laccolithic intrusion into the surrounding sedimentary rocks, or as the inner core plug of a long extinct volcano. One thing was certain though, the tower forms a strikingly dominant feature in the landscape as I was easily able to spot it from the air about 20 miles away.

I knew of its existence (as did many kids of the 1970s' era), thanks to the ground-breaking Steven Spielberg 1977 film *Close Encounters of the Third Kind*. The movie used the Devils Tower as the rendezvous point for meeting an alien spaceship, and it formed a crucial part of the storyline. Being such an iconic and unusual geological feature, it rated highly on my must-see list when I first sketched out the routing for my aerial road trip across the USA. As with Yellowstone National Park, I was allowed to overfly the monument and I took the opportunity to circle it a couple of times to truly appreciate its grand scale and structure. The top, usually seen only by the rock climbers who have successfully scaled its curtain-like sides of vertical igneous columns, was surprisingly flat for such a natural phenomenon. Besides thinking that it would be a great place for a picnic, its sheer columns reminded me greatly of formations seen at the equally famous Giant's Causeway back home in Northern Ireland, and of Fingal's Cave on the Isle of Staffa off the Scottish west coast.

Souvenir selfie photos taken, I hummed the five-note communication sequence played in the movie to myself, just in case any visiting UFOs were wanting to make contact with me while I passed by this intergalactic meeting point. In case you needed reminding, the sequence of notes was: G, A, F, F (lower octave) and C.

Alas nobody replied or materialised in front of me, so I just turned south and flew on towards the next stop on my aerial tourist trail, the famous Black Hills of South Dakota.

I was aiming for the town of Custer as it was my closest suitable airfield for another iconic American landmark, Mount Rushmore. Weather permitting, I was hoping to see the huge granite heads of four US presidents – Washington, Jefferson, Lincoln and Roosevelt – which were famously carved in the rock face there.

I landed into Custer in the late afternoon feeling tired but happy. I had been flying every day since leaving McMinnville on 3 June, as I had not wanted to linger anywhere while crossing the Rockies, just in case the mountain weather had suddenly taken a turn for the worst. Now, after six long flying days, and with the bulk of the difficult high ground behind me, I felt I needed (and had earned!) an off-day to do some washing and catch up with some much-needed rest.

I checked into the Rocket Motel, a delightful, freshly painted and immaculately kept place that looked as if it was straight out of the 1950s. Ever mindful of my empty Turtle Pac's lingering scent of petrol perfume, the motel was also able to provide me with access to their gardening tool shed in the backyard, which proved to be a perfect bedroom for my flexible friend. A little later on and to my further delight, I discovered just across the street, the very appropriately named laundromat The Lost Sock.

For now, at least, my rest day looked to be all sorted.

9 June 2015: Custer, South Dakota, USA (non-flying day)

A pleasant day, largely spent sock washing, enjoying a lovely coffee house and sightseeing around town.

10 June 2015: Custer, South Dakota, USA – Wall, South Dakota, USA

Feeling greatly rejuvenated from my rest day, I headed back out to the airport early to work on a special mission. My plan was to make a short sightseeing flight to Mount Rushmore, then return to Custer County Airport, load up my fuel and luggage, and depart onwards to the east. I also kept my final destination choice flexible, depending on how I progressed throughout the day.

I made the short flight across to the Mount Rushmore area in good time, though unfortunately I was disappointed to find that the hills were shrouded in parts with low hanging cloud and mist. I flew a few passes to see if the swirling clouds would afford me even a short glimpse of the presidents, but alas it was not to be. Flying in such conditions over unfamiliar terrain, there was the very real potential of finding a hidden rockface lurking within every cloud. Another nagging thought in the back of my head was that many sightseeing helicopters also frequented the monument. I definitely didn't want to find myself making for the same gap in the clouds as one of those coming the other way, so I made the command decision to retreat and head back to the airport. The flight wasn't a complete washout though, as close by a new sculpture has slowly been emerging from the rockface of Thunderhead Mountain. Created to honour the Native American culture, a huge effigy of Crazy Horse, one that dwarfs Mount Rushmore's presidents, has been gradually taking shape since 1948. Although still a long way from completion, happily the memorial was clear of cloud as I made my flypast, and it looked to be an enormously impressive undertaking.

I made my somewhat truncated return to Custer County Airport after a total sightseeing flight time of only 30 minutes. It was still early in the day, but as I then began to plan out my onward routing and destination, a new and quite serious problem arose.

For the whole circumnavigation, I trusted my two main GPS devices: my primary-use Garmin 695 knee mounted unit; and a secondary smaller, and older, backup Garmin 496 unit mounted on the instrument panel. The 695 was fantastic. It was all singing, all dancing, had global charts, IFR air routes, detailed worldwide airport information (held on three interchangeable SD cards), and essentially allowed me to confidently fly in and out of any big international airport across the globe.

Only on this day, for some unknown reason, it just stopped working. Try as I might, I couldn't get the 695 to fire up and this now became a major problem. There was no way I could continue with the more technical sections of the world flight without an operational 695 unit. Thankfully, I still had the 496 working as a backup and reasoned that at least while I was crossing the USA, I could make do with this smaller unit, until I could source and replace the faulty 695. I was after all, crossing North America, the birthplace of Garmin, so was confident of finding a replacement soon.

I lost about three hours of prime flying time while I tried initially to fix the 695 followed by time taken to upgrade and reconfigure the 496 to take its place. By the time I was packed up and prepared to depart, it was already mid-afternoon, which reduced my list of potential onward destinations considerably. To make matters worse, unsettled cloud and heavy rain were forecast overnight and for the next few days around Custer, so I didn't want to linger and possibly become grounded by weather.

I had to make my escape.

I discussed my limited options with the Custer FBO manager, and he very helpfully suggested that I might head for Wall, only 60 or so miles away. It would take just over an hour to fly there in the late afternoon, and most importantly it would get me out of the weather uncertainty of the Black Hills and allow me to reach the wide-open flatlands of the prairies. From Wall it would then be plain sailing all the way across to the Great Lakes, or so I thought at the time. A quick phone call to Wall Municipal Airport and it was all arranged.

I was off and running again, well limping at least, with only the 496 for company.

My routing to Wall saw me skirting the northern edge of the famous Badlands National Park, a bit of a misnomer as the land was actually very scenic. I cleared the last remaining foothills of the Rockies and then, stretching away off into the distance ahead of me as far as the eye could see, lay the flattest landscape you could imagine. It took me by surprise, with a highly defined edge-line, the complex hilly terrain just suddenly ended and was immediately replaced by flat prairie lands that commenced in quite the same abrupt manner. Wall's airport, although small, was used like Glens Ferry's for crop spraying operations. Unlike Glens Ferry however, it had a lovely big secure hangar, and so was just perfect for me. I was warmly greeted both at the airfield and later at Ann's Motel on the edge of town. The railway ran immediately behind the motel and this was flanked by four enormous, galvanised grain silos that dwarfed Ann's two-story building. This was proof indeed that I had now well and truly arrived in the mighty Corn Belt of America.

11 June 2015: Wall, South Dakota, USA (non-flying day)

The weather that had chased me out of Custer became more widespread overnight and had now caught up with me in Wall. Looking out at the drab and heavily overcast sky it was an easy decision to scrub another flying day, but I took solace in the fact that at least I was now out of the hills and could fly on as soon as even marginal weather picked up again. So I suddenly had another free day, which allowed me time to go sample whatever delights Wall had to offer.

I didn't think it should take very long to look around, but I was pleasantly surprised to find a magical oasis of entrepreneurship and quirkiness lying in wait. It was such a stark contrast to the miles and miles of somewhat bland, orderly and uniform landscape that stretched out all around it.

Situated with access directly onto Interstate 90 (I-90), Wall in its early days became famous as a stop-off and watering hole for tourists heading west to visit Mount Rushmore and Yellowstone National Park. Since 1931 the Wall Drug Store capitalised greatly by enticing these long-distance travellers to pause their journey, especially for free 'ice water' in the days before air-conditioned vehicles were commonplace. Over the following years, Wall Drug grew in popularity as it added to its stop-off appeal by creating all sorts of quirky attractions, such as a huge sit-on sculpture of a 'Jackalope' (a mythical jackrabbit with antelope antlers) and a life-size animatronic T-Rex dinosaur that roared at visitors every now and then.

A large restaurant was festooned with cowboy country artwork and a huge collection of old branding irons (as each wild west ranch would have had their own unique mark). So popular was this rest stop that it soon became a major tourist attraction in its own right. It remains the only place that I have seen to date where I could pick up a pair of US$500 cowboy boots, a genuine Stetson branded cowboy hat, and a plastic frisbee moulded in the shape of a cow pat, all in the one shop.

Its '**Wall Drug of South Dakota**' car bumper stickers have become infamous and apparently are now posted all over the world. For such a small, unknown, insignificant town way out on the far western edge of the prairie, Wall certainly punches way above its weight in international marketing exposure!

Alas as my aircraft stowage capacity was extremely limited, the boots, hat and cow pat frisbee all had to remain on the shelves. I did however pick up the bumper sticker, which quickly found a home for itself on *Roxy*'s tail.

12 June 2015: Wall, South Dakota, USA – Mitchell, South Dakota, USA – Worthington, Minnesota, USA

The I-90 stretches all the way from Seattle to Boston, some 3020 miles in length. The mid-section cuts clean across the US Midwest, roughly along the latitude of 43 degrees north. From Wall, my next go-to destination was to be Oshkosh in Wisconsin, home of the Experimental Aircraft Association. The EAA Aviation Museum at Oshkosh is home to a wonderful line-up of iconic and historically significant aircraft, and I was keen to see some of its prize exhibits, especially two very different gyroplanes: *Miss Champion* and *Woodstock*. As Oshkosh lies at 44 degrees north, I soon realised that the I-90 could act as a perfect aid to my ongoing navigation and I could now basically follow it all the way across the country.

Looking for a point roughly equidistant between Wall and Oshkosh to stay overnight, my cursor landed on the town of Worthington, Minnesota. I had also been asked to call in to the town of Mitchell along the way for a local press and TV interview, and so that was quickly designated as my convenient lunch stop. How I loved the ease and spontaneity of flight planning in these more spacious parts of the USA. I thought back to the hassles and reams of paperwork involved in arranging to just get off the ground in places like Egypt, India, Myanmar and Japan. In those countries, the idea of taking the gyro up for a quick spin around the airfield, just for the simple joy of flying, was almost unthinkable. In such places each and every flight had to have a clear purpose and a good reason. All flights had to be tightly controlled, monitored and thoroughly planned, often days in advance. With so many restrictions, it was easy to see why there was little room for any spontaneity whatsoever.

Setting off from Wall flying east along I-90, I settled into what would soon become a very familiar landscape for the next two days.

The highway stretched off to the horizon and I positioned just off to the right-hand side of it, at about 800ft above ground level. International *Rules of the Air* for navigation dictate that for any two aircraft that are approaching each other head on, both should alter course so as to safely pass each other 'port to port' (ie left side to left side). Interestingly, these same basic rules also apply for two vessels passing each other at sea (as flight rules were largely adopted from the pre-existing rules for maritime traffic). By flying slightly on the right-hand side of the highway, I allowed for the chance that another aircraft could be approaching me in the opposite direction, following along the same linear feature. If so, the hope (and expectation) was that the other aircraft would also fly on *their* right-hand side of the highway, so that we could then both safely pass, port to port, with no further risk of collision.

***

I settled in for the long haul. The flat, repetitive scenery was a bit like one of those scrolling backdrops seen behind a car driver during a scene from a 1950s' B movie. Huge crop fields were interspersed with farmsteads, which would typically include a big farmhouse and barn, a clump of trees, a large feedstuff silo and various other farm sheds dotted about. From a distance, every farmstead looked remarkably similar. This rolling loop of scenery scrolled along until every now and then, a road intersection with possibly a truck stop, fuel station and a small town nearby, helped to briefly break up the monotony. Sometimes the crops changed, providing a passing interest of a different colour or land use, or at other times a heavy, but isolated, cloud burst would descend out from the overcast sky. These at least offered me some welcome distraction, as I would alter course slightly to fly around them rather than get the windshield wet.

Arriving at Mitchell for my lunchtime stop, I was greeted by a TV crew for my interview. A few minutes later, three National Guard medical helicopters also landed and proceeded to take on fuel. Chatting with the pilots a while later, it appeared that they had been following close behind me for some time as I progressed along the I-90. The drivers on the highway must have looked up curiously to see a tiny bright yellow gyroplane being chased (or escorted, whichever scenario you care to choose) across the sky by three khaki military helicopters in hot pursuit.

I was soon on my way again and quickly returned to my same long-haul routine. A steady three hours of I-90 piloting in the morning and two hours in the afternoon, all very workmanlike. Again, occasionally a noteworthy sight passed by, such as a line of five John Deer tractors, with their distinctive green and yellow paintwork, working together in tight formation across a huge field – I marvelled at their skilful unison of purpose. Similarly passing over a massive open-cast quarry, I was fortunate to see some of the gigantic trucks labouring away in the depths of the workings, though they just looked very much like big Tonka toys from my viewpoint. The most bizarre spotting, however – the one that left me smiling for the rest of the flight – occurred late in the afternoon, when by pure chance I flew over a group of four naked people relaxing with their beers in a hot tub. With my sudden low-level appearance over their barn roof, in the middle of nowhere, I don't quite know who was surprised the most, me or them!

Arriving in Worthington I was warmly greeted by the local FBO staff, as well as by a couple of special guests. One was Ivan Pollock, a fellow 'Larne man' from back home in Northern Ireland, but who was currently living in nearby Austin and had been tracking my progress online. The other follower was more local, Dwaine Dewey Higgins from Iowa, who previously worked for B9 Energy, a renewable energy company that I co-founded with my brother and three others in 1992. B9 had helped pioneer the early development of commercial windfarms in both Ireland and the UK, before also making a foray into business in North America. A great early evening was spent at the airport and a nearby restaurant catching up with them.

Later on, I was graciously hosted for the night by a local journalist Justine Wettschreck and her husband Eric, who lit a huge bonfire for us in their back garden. It must be said that the pile of logs we had available would probably have kept my wood burner going for a whole winter! We then enjoyed a fantastic evening of campfire hospitality, with a few beers and storytelling thrown in for good measure.

13 June 2015: Worthington, Minnesota, USA – Brennand Airport, Wisconsin, USA – Oshkosh, Wisconsin, USA

Refuelling *Roxy* was the first priority of the morning and involved a very nifty solution to the often awkward (if doing it single handed) task of getting the full 140-litre Turtle Pac (aka Saki Barrel) manhandled up into the rear seat. Firstly, a luggage trolley was commandeered to get it from the car in the parking lot to the aircraft hangar. Then came the *pièce de resistance.* I spied a small mobile crane hoist used for removing engines from airframes in the hangar, and it was soon employed as the perfect tool to lift the heavy bag up off the trolley and onto the seat. If only I could find such handy equipment at every stop!

I was now making great progress across the Midwest. The flying since leaving the Rockies had been both uneventful and relaxing, and I hoped it would continue that way right across to the East Coast. But as I arrived overhead of the mighty Mississippi River, alas things did again turn *eventful* and also proved to be anything but *relaxing.*

I had aimed to cross the Mississippi near La Crosse, on the state boundary between Minnesota and Wisconsin. Even here, some 1000 miles north of where the river finally meets the sea down in the Gulf of Mexico, it was still *half a mile* wide in parts. Such a mighty river indeed!

For me, it was the first over-water crossing I had made so far in North America. But unfortunately the river was creating its own local weather, and a low-lying humid mist hung over its muddy brown flowing waters. I had to fly low in order to remain in sight of the surface, but this also meant that if anything suddenly went wrong with the engine, I would not have had much height for gliding back to safety on either shoreline. For about a minute in the middle of the crossing, I thought how frustrating it would be to have to ditch into the water here, so far inland from the actual sea. I suppose I could have used my life raft at least, and as always, I was wearing my full immersion suit and lifejacket (yes, even 1000 miles from the sea!) so I would probably have been OK. It would have been a tragedy though for *Roxy*, as she would have surely been lost at the bottom of the murky and fast flowing river. Maybe, as with Huckleberry Finn and Tom Sawyer, I would perhaps have had to finish my whole American adventure in a different way, by just lazily floating on my life raft all the way downstream towards Louisiana and the Gulf of Mexico...

As it turned out, crossing the Mississippi was only the start of my problems. The bad visibility created by the low cloud and mist continued over on the Wisconsin side of the river, where the terrain abruptly became much more undulating, with steep gorge-like valleys cut into the heavily forested hillsides. Over a few short miles, the local weather conditions had now deteriorated considerably, and I still had over 100 miles to fly to reach Oshkosh.

The visibility fluctuated haphazardly but thankfully remained flyable, for now at least. That said, it was mentally challenging to navigate in such conditions, especially as I had already flown for four hours up to this point. I was constantly trying to pick out the routing that had the least cloud and/or the kindest terrain. At some points the mist and the hills touched, and I was left looking for gaps in the valleys with brightness and clearer skies beyond. It felt like I was flying through a constantly shifting maze and proved to be extremely tiring indeed.

Although I was in radio contact with the airport as I approached Oshkosh, the visibility close to the shores of Lake Winnebago became even worse. It was becoming very marginal for flying VFR without instruments. To further complicate matters, there were several high aerial masts in the vicinity, which I knew were often hard to see even at the best of times. I became increasingly uneasy about the prospect of continuing to fly deeper into the murky gloom ahead and so began to look for my nearest alternative airfield. Conditions looked slightly brighter to the north, so I made a beeline for a small airstrip called Brennand Airport, only 10 miles from Oshkosh. As it was a small private strip, I made some unanswered blind radio calls on my approach but knew that in reality no one else would probably now be up flying in these conditions. I had to get on the ground quickly.

Landing in on the short and narrow tarmac strip felt similar to my Saudi desert touchdown, like I was a ragged, storm-tossed seagull that had just gratefully landed on the beach, *any* beach. I was mightily relieved. I taxied to the small main office building but found it to be empty. I made a quick call to my EAA contacts, who were expecting my arrival over in Oshkosh, to learn that they had already seen from my tracker that I had diverted into Brennand and were sending a car over to meet me. A few minutes later it arrived, and I was immediately reassured that the claggy weather conditions were only very localised and would improve soon. Forty minutes later, in clearing skies, I was back in the air to make the short 10-minute flight across to Wittman Regional Airport, Oshkosh, and the home of the Experimental Aircraft Association.

14 June 2015: Oshkosh, Wisconsin, USA (non-flying day)

Overnight, I had kindly been accommodated by Chris Henry, a real fun and larger-than-life character and EAA membership services staff member. Chris gave me a guided tour of the extensive airport grounds that would soon play host to the annual EAA AirVenture Oshkosh convention and fly-in event, which regularly sees upwards of 600,000 visitors from all over the USA and beyond. Attendees converge with their tents, motorhomes and light aircraft for a solid week of trade exhibitions, air shows, and spectacular firework displays every year in late July. The show was still some five weeks away, but the preparations were already well underway. A stone's throw from the airport, I also spent a few hours touring around the EAA Aviation Museum, which displays an excellent collection of over 200 historic aircraft. Most notably (for my interest) were the resident gyroplanes on display:

1931 Pitcairn PCA-2 Autogiro, *Miss Champion*
1941 Pitcairn PA-39 Autogiro, *N3908*

1970 Brock KB-2 'Gyroplane' Autogyro, *N2303*

2000 Herron/Keetch Little wing LW-5 Autogyro, *Woodstock*

There was also a notable collection of highly innovative and experimental Burt Rutan designs, which I thought fitted very well into the overall EAA's *spirit of aviation* philosophy.

In the evening, with a full day of touring and sightseeing under my belt, and as something of a grand finale, Chris took me to visit a classic drive-in diner in town for some food. Like something straight out of the 1950s, Ardy and Ed's Drive-In was such a surprise. All the waitresses on duty were expertly zipping about, with loaded trays of food held high, between all the parked cars. Not so unusual perhaps - until you realised that they were all gliding around on roller skates!

15 June 2015: Oshkosh, Wisconsin, USA – Lansing, Illinois, USA

It was time to head south. The direct routing across to the East Coast would have been to continue east over Lake Michigan and the rest of the Great Lakes, but I had some other ports of call to make on the way. In America, the Popular Rotorcraft Association (PRA) acts as a national coordinating body for gyroplane clubs (chapters) that are dotted all over the USA, and I was keen to make contact and meet up with fellow gyro pilots and enthusiasts whenever possible. Lansing Municipal Airport lies just south of Chicago and acts as the home base for the Greater Midwest Rotorcraft Club (PRA Chapter 18). The club has about 15 resident gyroplanes representing examples of various gyro designs and function. I was invited to call in on my way past by the club members and most notably by one of the club's most stalwart supporters, Tom Milton. They all made me most welcome and Tom's son Mike also kindly put me up in his house during my stay. By happy coincidence, Mike's dog was also called *Roxy,* which led to us staging a delightful photo of *Dog Roxy* wearing a red T-shirt 'flight suit', proudly sitting in *Gyro Roxy's* cockpit. Together, **Team Roxy** certainly appeared ready to take on the world...

A little later, I was interviewed for local press within the very historic Ford Hangar building, built by the Ford Motor Company to house their Tri-Motor aircraft in 1927. G-YROX was then given special permission to overnight in this iconic building, and I was honoured to be sharing the very same hangar space that Charles Lindbergh and Wiley Post made use of during their 1920s' aviation promotional tours.

16–17 June 2015: Lansing, Illinois, USA (non-flying days)

I had been navigating solely with my Garmin 496 for the best part of a week, after my 695 GPS unit had experienced problems in Custer. I now had a plan in mind to remedy that situation and Tom kindly gave me a lift (twice, on two consecutive days) into downtown Chicago to visit the Garmin store in the city centre. Once I had told the staff there about my plight, they offered initially to take a look at it for me, but upon quickly establishing that it was unfixable they decided to give me a replacement unit, free of charge. This came as fantastic news; Garmin to the rescue! Many thanks for innovating and sharing with the world such incredibly useful products.

It was such a relief to have a working 695 again, and very timely given that I was now approaching the busier skies and congested airspace of the eastern States, not to mention the looming prospect of attempting to make the first ever gyroplane crossing of the Atlantic Ocean in a few weeks' time.

18 June 2015: Lansing, Illinois, USA – Port Clinton, Ohio, USA

Seagulls do exist hundreds of miles from the sea, and today I was going to find some.

I had a great send off from Lansing. It had been invigorating to meet with so many of the local gyro community and spending a few days with them really felt like I was now saying cheerio to some old friends. My destination was Port Clinton on the shoreline of Lake Erie, just to the west of Cleveland, Ohio.

All through my flight across the USA, I was keenly aware of a sense of travelling back in history. The early European settlers had pushed out west and I was now seeing all of their pioneering efforts, only in reverse, and now that I had reached the industrious north-east it became ever more obvious. The western states had been full of relatively newly established pioneer, frontier towns whereas the further east I flew the older, more elaborate, more established these townscapes became. Heavily organised industry now took over as the dominant feature on the skyline rather than agriculture. Red brick-built buildings rather than wooden barns. Iconic cities such as Chicago, Detroit, Cleveland and Pittsburgh, all popped up nearby on my GPS screen, each an industrial powerhouse that helped to springboard development, trade and commerce out to the rest of the country.

And the seagulls? On arrival at Port Clinton, I was given a ride downtown from the airport, where the waterfront area immediately reminded me very much of a regular *seaside* town. But even though Lake Erie is freshwater its vast navigable surface area warranted a sizeable coastal shipping fleet, which further backdropped the overall seaside ambiance. The waves were splashing on the beach and the flocks of seagulls were squawking overhead as ever. If I had been at home, I would have been looking out for the ice cream parlour and the fish and chip shop. Walking along the shore front I suddenly realised that I hadn't actually *seen* a seagull since leaving the Pacific coastline over two weeks ago. It really brought home how far I had travelled to cross the States and just how incredibly huge the country is.

19 June 2015: Port Clinton, Ohio, USA – Zelienople, Pennsylvania, USA

On departure from Port Clinton, I had quite a delay sitting on the apron due to the amount of ground traffic waiting their turn to taxi. I had become spoiled with virtually no traffic and empty runways over the past days, so this came as a timely reminder that I was now back to operating in more congested skies. The lengthy wait, however, wasn't all bad, as it turned out the main cause of the delay was for the take-off of an old P-51 Mustang warbird. I thought perhaps it was heading out to practise for the *Wings & Warbirds Over Port Clinton 2015* air show that was due to take place the following month. I was sitting at the holding point on the taxiway, engine running and with my headset on, yet still I could hear the tremendous roar from the Mustang's engine as it shot off down the runway on take-off.

On climb-out, I headed south-east to avoid the congestion around Cleveland and then headed directly south for a sightseeing landmark that I had wanted to see right from the earliest days of my circumnavigation flight planning, the iconic airship base in Akron.

Akron, Ohio is the home of the gigantic Goodyear Airdock, which was built in 1929 to accommodate the US Navy rigid airships of the time. It was instantly recognisable from the air as a long black half cylinder with rounded ends. I flew close by for a few photos but was slightly disappointed to see that there were no airships or blimps to be seen in the vicinity, and that the huge hangar doors appeared to be firmly shut. My disappointment was short lived however as about six miles farther to the east at Wingfoot Lake (named after the Goodyear winged foot logo of the Roman god, Mercury) another huge hangar served as the home base of the latest version of the Goodyear Blimp, which was attached to its mobile truck mast close by (at time of writing there are now three such 'new generation' semi-rigid blimps, operating out of Ohio, Florida and California).

As I flew past, it was nice to think that both the gyroplane and the airship were both born at the beginning of the 20th century. Although they were at times often regarded as being on the fringes of the aviation world, both were hailed as aerial wonders of the age, back in their 1920s' and 1930s' heydays. It was great to see that both types had now been reimagined, remodelled and reworked so that they have remained relevant into the 21st century.

In the previous few days, Eddie Gould had given me details of another adventurous long-distance UK pilot, Ross Edmondson, who he had been assisting with international flight planning logistics since 2010. As luck would have it, Ross happened to be living close to

Zelienople in Pennsylvania, which was not so far off my planned route. I decided to call in with him for a visit and similar to Lancing, I was given a great reception by all the local flyers who gathered to welcome me in. What could be better than landing, taxiing to a hangar reception and being given a cold beer in my hand, as soon as I'd shut down my engine. Ross and I then spent a relaxed evening at his place, comparing notes and sharing tales of our past flying adventures.

20 June 2015: Zelienople, Pennsylvania, USA – Niagara Falls, New York, USA – Brockport, New York, USA

Zelienople had been a slight diversion south of my general coast-to-coast routing, but now I made yet another diversion, up to the north-east to overfly my next must-see visitor attraction. I was not quite sure what to expect as I made my approach, but I must say it certainly became very easy to spot, even from quite some distance off. The great plume of mist seemingly rising out from the forest ahead was, of course, Niagara Falls.

The ease by which numerous iconic landmarks could be ticked off as I flew across the country was a real luxury. The only disadvantage was that even though I enjoyed my very privileged and unique perspective from above, I always felt a little isolated and cut off from getting up close and personal with whatever the attraction was down on the ground. I couldn't just land in the car park and wander into the tourist souvenir shop (unless it was at the Evergreen Aviation and Space Museum in McMinnville of course!). Niagara was no exception. While researching my routing, I was pleasantly surprised to find that General Aviation aircraft were permitted to fly over the Falls, albeit under strict safety rules. Numerous commercial helicopter rides operated locally, giving their paying passengers a spectacular close-up view. Meanwhile, General Aviation aircraft had to stay at around 1000ft higher than the commercial traffic, to keep the two sets of aircraft movements completely separate. The GA procedure was quite simple (as it had to be for safety, the simpler the better), a one-way circuit pattern had been created in the air over the Falls. It was marked out by several reporting points, and rather like an aerial roundabout, all traffic flew in the same clockwise direction. Everyone announced their arrival and departure from the circuit on the radio, so throughout my sightseeing flight I had a good idea of how many other aircraft were also sharing the circuit with me at any one time. The whole circuit, at my leisurely pace, took me about 20 minutes to complete, which was ample time to have a good look at the Falls from all directions.

Flying on, I only had a rough forward plan on where to stop for the night. I was heading towards Rochester on the southern shore of Lake Ontario, but decided to choose my destination airfield whilst airborne, depending on how long I had lingered at Niagara. This introduced an interesting surprise element of where I would actually end up. As it was, Ledgedale Airpark at Brockport, about 12 miles east of Rochester ended up being my airfield of choice for the night.

Initially on landing, Ledgedale looked deserted. I wandered around the various buildings, but I still couldn't find anyone. I briefly considered firing *Roxy* back up again and trying the next airfield on down the road, but then suddenly a pickup truck hove into view along the access driveway. It turned out to be an exceedingly kind lady behind the wheel, and after introductions were made, an explanation of my trip duly followed. She inspected G-YROX with both much curiosity and concern in equal measure. On hearing a brief outline of where exactly I had come from and where I'd be heading to next (the North Atlantic), I was quizzed further regarding my ongoing sanity. With a slightly bewildered and bemused shake of the head, she then helped me to sort *Roxy* out for overnight hangarage, and also gave me a much-appreciated ride to the local motel. From initially being something of a spontaneous but uncertain, *roll-of-the-dice* stopover, happily Ledgedale worked out very well in the end.

21 June 2015: Brockport, New York, USA – Glens Falls, New York, USA

Flying across upper New York State was surprisingly wild in parts.

Previously I had just imagined, having never ventured this way before, that it would somehow be an extension of the urban landscape of New York City, only a lot more sprawling. I hadn't appreciated the vast stretches of wilderness that I would encounter on the southern flanks of the Adirondack Mountains. Over the past week or so of flying across the Midwest prairies, I had been lulled into a false sense of security by the flat, open, land-anywhere terrain. But now, similar to the Oregon Coast Range, the undulating foothills were again becoming heavily forested. Although here they were without the useful addition of any logging roads for emergency landings. Some occasional highways did snake back and forth through the trees, but they were often partially obscured by overarching tree canopies that at times and for long stretches, seemed to engulf the road completely. It meant that any forced landing would have been quite a challenge.

During the flight into Glens Falls, whilst staring down into all those unforgiving trees, I had started to feel a creeping sense of foreboding as to the serious journey that still lay ahead. The bulk of my flying in the States so far had been relatively easy. After all, there had been plenty of time for singing in the cockpit. But now, upon encountering much more technically challenging terrain again, I was reminded that my US 'road trip' singing days would probably soon be coming to an end.

On arrival, I was pleasantly surprised to be met by a lovely group of well-wishers; some of whom had travelled a considerable distance just to meet up with me. After we had paused for photos and I had unpacked *Roxy*'s luggage, we sat chatting and eating snacks for quite a time in the late afternoon sunshine at some picnic benches just outside the FBO office. Psychologically it served to give me a great boost. It was a very welcome and a timely reminder to feel the warm enthusiasm, excitement and encouragement that my flight was inspiring in my many supporters around the world. It reminded me that although I was physically flying alone in the cockpit, I was definitely not alone in sharing the adventurous spirit of this pioneering flight.

It was the same spirit that was later captured brilliantly when a local pilot/photographer took some glorious air-to-air shots of *Roxy* and me during my departure the following day overhead of nearby Lake George.

22 June 2015: Glens Falls, New York, USA – Biddeford, Maine, USA

Arriving into Biddeford Municipal Airport was a great feeling. Situated just a few miles south of Portland, Maine, I had now successfully completed my original 'Coast-to-Coast' goal. I had linked Portland to Portland and Pacific to Atlantic, in just 20 days since leaving Tillamook on 3 June.

It had felt like a mini expedition in itself, one that was both easy to organise and could avoid the worst aspects of bureaucracy that so deadened the experience and spontaneity of flying in some other countries. Reaching the US East Coast was a milestone, but it also signified that I would now soon be taking on the most challenging part of the whole circumnavigation, attempting to make the first-ever gyroplane crossing of the Atlantic Ocean. The thought was never far from my mind and would resurface periodically. Such a crossing was a completely unknown undertaking and yet, somehow in the back of my mind, I maintained a stoic self-belief that *Roxy* and I were both capable of achieving it.

But these thoughts were all for the future. Returning to the here and now, I had completed the US continental crossing and my immediate goals were now turned to other things.

15

North America: USA to Canada

23 June 2015: Biddeford, Maine, USA (non-flying day)

This was my first non-flying day since Lansing, Illinois, and it was so nice to rest up. I had generously been given accommodation overnight in a beachside apartment belonging to the Ocean Walk Hotel, which was a real treat, especially as it was situated right on the fabulous Old Orchard Beach front. My hosts were also incredibly welcoming, which made it a rather memorable stay. I spent the morning catching up with admin and then hiked south along the beach as far as the classic seaside pier in the centre of town. It was my second 'seaside' town after Port Clinton and again, the seagulls were in fine voice overhead.

It was interesting to see how the Americans in Maine do 'quaint seaside town'. There was none of the brashness and razzmatazz of Miami or LA's muscle beach, no roller blading keep-fit fanatics or new age travellers here. Old Orchard Beach was just a peaceful, family-friendly seafront adorned with an abundance of neat, wooden clapboard buildings. The main concession to big time showbusiness was the fun fair at the pier, but even that was on a modest scale, harking back to a much more genteel era. Shelia's General Store, a few blocks south of my accommodation, had the same bygone charm when I called in to replenish my 'in-flight catering' requirements for the next day.

24 June 2015: Biddeford, Maine, USA – Nantucket, Massachusetts, USA

Before flying north into Canada, I had decided to make a detour in order to visit Betsey Sanpere on Nantucket Island in Massachusetts. I had been invited by Betsey to present a talk to a group of young aviation enthusiasts at the annual Aviation Career Education (ACE) Camp. Betsey was a real go-getter. Her zest for life and her enthusiasm for all things aviation was contagious, so it was a given that I would make time to visit the island. The benefit was mutual though, as after the talk I was going to leave the aircraft in storage for a week, while I flew by commercial airline back to Northern Ireland for an important family rendezvous. I would then return to Nantucket about a week later to be in time for the 4th of July celebrations on the island, before heading north again the following day to reach Belfast Municipal Airport in Maine.

Chatting at the reception building as I prepared to leave, I sketched out a provisional idea to return past Biddeford and Old Orchard Beach on, or around, 5 July. I wouldn't be landing, but I would hopefully overfly the Ocean Walk Hotel on my way north and give everyone a wave. Given I would then be commencing the most precarious part of my journey, I felt any luck-giving support was going to be much appreciated.

Bidding Biddeford a biddable bon voyage, (sorry, I just had to say it) I had a superb flight along the chocolate-box scenic coastline to the south.

I had really missed my coastal flying and it was exhilarating to be back among the rugged cliffs, hidden coves, white sandy beaches and rocky outcrops. In the afternoon sunshine the vivid colours of it all seemed greatly enhanced and what's more, this was now the Atlantic, my 'local' ocean back home. Ireland was now the next closest landmass, albeit still thousands of miles away beyond the horizon.

Passing down the coast, I overflew many picturesque coastal settlements including Kennebunkport, made famous as the summer residency of George H.W. Bush and his family when he was the 41st president of the USA. The family compound is on a promontory called Walker's Point and it was easily spotted on my way past. No one seemed to be in residence, so I didn't need to give any cheery waves. Perhaps I'd have the chance on the way back up north.

I passed by Cape Neddick Light, a lighthouse that's rather quirkily known as just 'the Nubble' thanks to the name of the island it sits on. Coastal towns rolled by, such as York, Portsmouth, North Hampton, Salisbury, Newbury and Ipswich. It was an easy guess where the early European settlers of these places hailed from.

Approaching Boston, I elected to head well out to sea across Cape Cod Bay; it was the more direct route towards Nantucket and it also meant I avoided the exceedingly busy airspace around Boston Logan International Airport. As I coasted out near Manchester-by-the-Sea, it felt a little odd to be out over the ocean again. I hadn't flown any long over-water stretches since I had landed at Shonai Airport in Japan on 23 July 2011, almost four years earlier.

It didn't take long for me to settle my nerves and I soon eased back into my familiar and comfortable oceangoing mindset. I focused as ever on two main mental reassurances: I was well prepared for sea survival should I have had to ditch into the drink; and as usual, *Roxy*'s engine didn't know that I was flying it over water. It was only a relatively short hop over Cape Cod Bay and Nantucket Sound to reach the island, but psychologically it gave me a welcome boost. It was valuable over-water practice for when I would take on the North Atlantic in just a few weeks' time.

Air traffic around Nantucket Memorial Airport was surprisingly busy; it was peak holiday season and lots of private aircraft had taken to the skies. The airport is in reality one of the busiest in Massachusetts, often logging more aircraft movements than Boston Logan in the busy summer months. The ATC staff were kept extremely busy, actively coordinating everyone, but I was eventually slotted in for a landing.

After the good number of quiet, sometimes almost deserted airfields that I had opted to use crossing the USA, Nantucket suddenly brought me right back into the 21st century. Private aircraft littered the tarmac, though it was surprising to see that most of these planes were not General Aviation light aircraft but were private jets. This was perhaps a reflection on the fact that an average price of a family house on Nantucket (as of 2015) was in the region of US$2.3 million.

I was greeted warmly on arrival by Betsey and a swarm of excited summer schoolers; they had been busy making brightly coloured welcome posters for me. It was a lovely gesture. There were many photos taken and questions asked even before I got to deliver my talk and slide show presentation in the lecture room. I was hosted by Ed and Sharlene Rudd (and son Ben) and I was given a tour of Nantucket's historic Old Mill, a wooden windmill that had been lovingly preserved by Ed and other local historians. We also enjoyed a delightful garden barbeque in the warm evening air, and I reflected that the last such American-style barbeque I had attended on an island had been at USAF Kadena Air Base, Okinawa; similar great US hospitality, but half-way around the world on a different Ocean.

25 June – 4 July 2015: Nantucket, Massachusetts, USA (non-flying days)

With *Roxy* safely hangared, I was off again, but this time I was on a special surprise mission. I was given a lift by car down to the harbour, where I boarded the Hyannis ferry as a foot passenger for the short crossing of Nantucket Sound to the mainland. When leaving the harbour the ferry passed by a small lighthouse on the shoreline at Brant Point, and tradition has it that you should throw a penny or two into the water at this point for good luck and to ensure a safe return to Nantucket one day in the future. I therefore lined up with the other passengers on the stern deck to do exactly that.

On arrival in Hyannis, I hopped on a bus to Logan International Airport where I flew via Newark to Belfast International Airport in

Northern Ireland. The following day, Saturday 27 June 2015, I joined a large group of my relatives by climbing on my bike.

Exactly 60 years previously, in 1955, my Aunt Isabel Woods (née Clements) had set a women's long-distance cycling record for the 'End-to-End' of Ireland, pedalling from Mizzen Head in West Cork to Fair Head in County Antrim. This was a distance of 386 miles and was completed in a record time of 23hrs 3mins. The record stood unbroken for *52 years*, which was quite an incredible feat when you consider the huge improvements in both cycling technology (bikes, clothing, sports diet, training etc.) and the upgraded quality of modern road surfaces. Even when Aunt Isabel's record was finally beaten by Rose Leith in 2007, the overall route was now some 18 miles shorter due to road enhancements made during the intervening years.

Incredibly, if the time taken to cover those extra road miles had been added onto the new record holder's overall time, Aunt Isabel's record may well have remained unbroken!

I was joining in on the last day of a 60th anniversary cycle, which saw 11 of my relatives finish their commemorative end-to-end ride. Split into three groups, they covered the entire route of nearly 400 miles, in much more leisurely time frames of eleven days, six days and four days respectively. Those who weren't able to participate on the full end-to-end ride were still able to saddle up and join in on the final day's ride to Fair Head, where Aunt Isabel (then aged 86) and Uncle Peter were waiting to cheer everyone over the finish line. Aunt Isabel's tremendous achievement and legacy had been marked in an exceptionally fitting way. My late-notice (best make that no-notice!) participation had been a complete surprise to everyone, as they had all assumed that I was still on the US East Coast. My whistle-stop visit home was well worth it just to see the surprise on all their faces and to join in on the post-ride celebrations.

I quickly started to retrace my steps and by 1 July I was back on the ferry again, this time heading from Hyannis to Nantucket. Passing Brant Point lighthouse at the mouth of the harbour I remembered casting my penny into the water barely a week before. It had worked! For I was indeed safely returning once more to the island.

* * *

For my second stay on Nantucket, I was billeted with Chris and Corrine McLaughlin, both highly experienced pilots. Among their notable exploits, was a return trip flying themselves from Cape Cod all the way down to Cape Horn in South America and then out to the Falkland Islands off Argentina. An amazing voyage in a light aircraft. Needless to say, we had a lot in common to chat about.

Another surprise was that a fellow-circumnavigator from the UK suddenly turned up on the airport apron. Colin Hales had been in communication with our mutual flight planner Eddie Gould and had arranged that our paths would cross in Nantucket. Colin was flying westward from the UK in his own home-built aircraft, a Rand KR2, and had recently crossed the Atlantic to reach the USA. Given this impending crossing was looming large in my own thoughts, I was keen to find out how he had fared. With such a spontaneous mix of long-distance flyers gathered together, we had a most memorable evening of chat around the dining table in a local restaurant.

Spending the 4th of July holiday on the island was a happy coincidence and Colin and I spent time looking around the harbour at the enormous influx of superyachts that had ventured in from all over the Eastern Seaboard. We also took time out to visit the well laid out Whaling Museum, learning how the booming 18th Century whaling industry shaped both the wealth and history of the island. Nantucket's fine leafy avenues of wood-clad homesteads were originally created by ship owners and wealthy captains, and the whole island has maintained an aura of a genteel, prosperous society ever since. Though a thought must be given to the countless thousands of poor whales that were hunted to near extinction to fund it all.

There was of course the human cost as well, with work on the old whaling ships being an extremely hazardous occupation. Walking around the town, it was easy to see this precarious way of life reflected in the architecture. Many of Nantucket's houses have a 'widow's walk' structure on top of the roof. This open, wooden balcony or lookout platform was said to be used by the wives of mariners to keep watch for the safe return of their seafaring loved ones. But such were the hazards of going to sea during the great age of sail, that many ships foundered and never returned to their home port.

In the 21st Century however, these lofty rooftop perches are now used for much more recreational pursuits. Indeed, later in the evening, I was extremely fortunate to be invited to watch the fabulous 4th of July fireworks from one such widow's walk vantage point, on top of a house that overlooked the whole harbour.

5 July 2015: Nantucket, Massachusetts, USA – Belfast, Maine, USA

After everything had paused for the 4th of July holiday, it was now exodus day. I was heading up north, back into Maine, but it seemed most of the executive private jets at Nantucket Memorial Airport also had plans to make a quick getaway. During the taxi out to the runway, I had to jostle for position with long queues of multi-million-dollar aircraft. This was fine, the holiday mood of the holding aircraft was polite and good natured, and ATC was doing a great job on what was probably its busiest day of the whole year. As soon as I was airborne, I was directed to route out at a low level along the eastern shoreline. This suited me just fine as I immediately flew into empty airspace and kept well clear of the busy departing traffic.

Soon I was coasting out past long spits of sandy beaches and the brightly painted lighthouses of Sankaty Head and Great Point. Once more across Nantucket Sound, I retraced my coastal route north. Passing by Cape Cod, I spotted huge colonies of seals on some of the more remote sand bars. At other points, closer to more inhabited areas, there were similar huge colonies of holiday beachgoers. From the air and from a distance, the two did not look so very different. As I drew closer however, the main differentiator was the overall colour, the seals being a rather uniform dark greyish brown, whereas the humans appeared as a jarring kaleidoscope of unnaturally bright colours.

The seals basking in the sun displayed minimal movement within their ranks, while the humans were much more animated, running around expending energy with frisbees, kites and beach balls. These divergent behaviours extended into the shallow waters nearby. The seals were lolling gently, seemingly meditating and being 'at one' with nature. In contrast, the humans were thrashing noisily about on all manner of watercraft: jet skis, paddleboards, sailing boats, inflatable rafts and speedboats. In an increasingly stressed and hectic world, where we are encouraged to take time out, relax and conserve energy, we could all certainly learn a few things from the chilled-out seals.

Passing by Old Orchard Beach once more on the way north, I was hopeful that the flypast arrangement that I had made with my hosts nearly two weeks before could now be realised. I flew parallel to the beach until I reached the Ocean Walk Hotel, where I slowed down to scour the parking lot for any sign of life below. Alas, all seemed deserted with no sign of a welcoming party. I wondered if they had simply forgotten as we'd only made a loose arrangement and after all, any manner of pitfall or weather could have easily intervened in the meantime to alter my flight schedule. Despite having quite a distance yet to fly up to Belfast, Maine, I thought I'd just take one more loop around to double-check that it was indeed a no-show. At that moment, I saw the side door of the reception lobby burst open and excited figures pour out of it and into the rear carpark. They were waving madly, and I did my best to match their enthusiasm waving back. We knew I wasn't able to land, and we couldn't even speak to say hello, but just the idea of being able to still communicate using this most basic of sign language felt fantastic as I flew by. I put in another loop above them, and with a big final wave and a pointed hand, I gestured "Northwards ho!", and I was off again.

* * *

Passing by overhead of Biddeford, I began flying again into new territory and, my word, what spectacular territory the coastal fringes of Maine turned out to be. I had heard that it was the lobster capital of America and within minutes I could tell exactly why. The topography of the rocky rugged coastline was festooned with densely tree-lined coves, creeks and inlets. These provided amazingly sheltered, natural deep-water lagoons where the sea could remain relatively calm, regardless of the raging Atlantic breakers that were crashing and foaming around the exposed bays and headlands nearby.

Amidst the deep dark calmness of the protected inlets, thousands of small, colourful dots shortly started to appear on the water's surface. Initially I was puzzled as to what they were but as I flew closer it became much more obvious. Each bright dot was a vividly painted lobster pot float and from the air, this colourful array had evolved into a most glorious work of art.

In order to keep tabs on individual lobster pots within this riotous sea of colour, each owner had adopted their own vibrant paint scheme, like the uniquely patterned jerseys worn by racehorse jockeys. The predominantly wooden marker floats were personalised with all manner of distinguishing features, some painted with stripes and dots, others perhaps decorated with contrasting rings, hoops or checkerboard patterns. Even on land the artwork continued, with old markers, long retired from their marine purpose, proudly put up on display on garden sheds or fishing shacks in the coastal communities. I imagine they were certainly a lovely way to brighten up any Maine seascape on a cold foggy day.

Arrival at Belfast, Maine was an emotional moment for me as I had pencilled in this stopping off point *six years* previously, back in 2009 during my pre-flight planning phase. Back then, I needed to find a starting point somewhere on the east coast of North America, which I could use in my attempt to establish an FAI point-to-point world record for the first crossing of the Atlantic Ocean by gyroplane. I knew the finishing point would be back in Sandy Bay playing fields in Larne,

Northern Ireland but I still needed to locate somewhere appropriate stateside for the start. This was when Google Earth came to the rescue.

Browsing the coast of Maine, I soon happened upon the small city of Belfast (population circa 6000). Even better, it had a small municipal airport, so it was an easy decision to set the course for my Atlantic crossing as being "Belfast to Larne – via the North Atlantic". For those unfamiliar with Northern Ireland geography, our own local version of *Belfast to Larne* is only about 22 miles by road.

Arriving at the quiet airport, I wondered initially if I would be able to find anyone to speak to. I needn't have worried, as finding one of the hangar doors open, I quickly fell into conversation with a local pilot, Peter Webb, who was also a highly skilled professional boat builder for the exemplary Belfast custom boat building company, French and Webb. I found it ironic that we too, back in Belfast, Northern Ireland, had a similar company that was world renowned for building boats, going by the name of Harland and Wolff… who of course built the most famous luxury boat of them all, the *RMS Titanic.*

Peter kindly offered not only hangar space for *Roxy*, but also arranged for me to stay for two nights at his home nearby. His fantastic house was set out in the woods, largely hand built in timber (just as you might expect from a master boatbuilder!), with a sizeable lookout deck that gave the sense of being held suspended out into the forest. Easing back on the veranda with a beer in hand, I had a great chat with him and his lovely family over dinner. It certainly made for a special end to the day.

6 July 2015: Belfast, Maine, USA (non-flying day)

Arriving back at the airfield, I had an unexpected surprise. Colin Hales, who I had first met in Nantucket, had turned up late the previous evening and had slept over in the FBO pilot's lounge. It was going to be a busy day as I was scheduled to do some filming for an upcoming Discovery Channel Canada programme. The short format six-minute documentary had been arranged by award winning broadcaster, Koula Bouloukos, who I had last spoken to whilst I was in Wall, South

Dakota. Between the camera interviews and filmed flying sequences, I managed to get Colin up for a brief passenger flight around the town. It was great to introduce him to *Roxy* properly before he saddled up his own pony and shot off towards the west.

Before I had left my hometown in Northern Ireland, I had been given some souvenir gifts from my local government office, Larne Borough Council, to present to the city council officers of Belfast, Maine. I called in at the mayor's office in Belfast City Hall and had a great chat with some of the city officers on duty before the mayor himself eventually appeared. After introductions, he then gave me a guided tour around the various public rooms, and proudly showed me the Belfast, Maine coat of arms displayed on a wooden plaque in the council chamber. As luck would have it, for the occasion I was wearing a Belfast N.I. T-shirt from back home, which also had that city's coat of arms printed on it. We noted with some surprise that the two coats of arms were exactly the same. The mayor then remembered that they had hosted a delegation from Northern Ireland's capital around 10 years previously and that the Northern Irish contingent had actually given *them* the wooden plaque. So it seems that Belfast, Maine had over the years adopted the original Belfast crest and coat of arms as their own. No harm done of course, as Northern Ireland's capital was the namesake of this lovely settlement after all. Walking around after my meeting in Belfast City Hall, I was impressed with the thriving community that had grown up in this place. Several stores had adopted the Belfast moniker, Belfast Bicycles and the 'Meanwhile in Belfast' pizza shop particularly caught my eye.

7 July 2015: Belfast, Maine, USA – Houlton, Maine, USA

As previously mentioned, the State of Maine is well known for its lobsters. But as I continued my flight north, up the coast towards the Canadian border, I became aware that the busy fishing industry was slowly being outmatched by farming. And one crop easily outnumbered the rest – potatoes. Fields and fields of spuds, stretching out as far as the eye could see, which was a long way given my elevated position.

Flying over it all, it was fascinating to see how the multi-coloured polka dot landscape of the lobster pots gradually and seamlessly transformed itself into the green monochrome of the humble potato plant.

My last stop before entering Canada was Houlton. I picked it strategically, as it was a big enough settlement to allow me to clear US customs and gain entry into Canada, but yet small enough to remain uncomplicated. As luck would have it, there was a roadside motel, a large supermarket and a gas station all close by. As I strolled about in what would be my last US supermarket for quite a while, I wondered what would now lie ahead. I knew that my next stop, Sept-Îles in Canada, would still be relatively urbanised, but what of the rest of the country beyond that? There would be no connecting roads to and from the places that I was going to visit. I was both apprehensive and excited in equal measure at the prospect of being the first person to fly a gyro up into the desolate and frozen northern reaches of this vast country.

8 July 2015: Houlton, Maine, USA – Sept-Îles, Quebec, Canada

An interesting sight greeted me when I returned to Houlton International Airport. While I was busy decanting fuel from the Turtle Pac into the main tanks from the tailgate of a pickup truck, I noticed nearby that a US National Guard helicopter, from US Customs and Border Protection, was also pre-flighting for a local training sortie. We nodded a friendly acknowledgment to each other but little else, as the unwritten rule between aviators was that you didn't interrupt each other during an aircraft safety check.

I thought nothing more of it, and after my own pre-flight checks were complete, I was up and away, departing from my last US port of call. The flight was quite scenic as the fields of potatoes slowly thinned out and I began to cross more densely forested areas once again. Good weather was helping the rather uneventful flight, and I mentally relaxed a little, preparing myself for the upcoming over-water crossing to reach the northern shore of the Gulf of Saint Lawrence.

Soon enough, as I flew along a river wending its way through the now heavily wooded landscape, I spotted a flag fluttering high on its mast over the treetops. Red and white with another little smudge of red in the middle, as I got closer, I recognised the red maple of the Canadian flag. It was confirmation that I had reached the border and was now about to cross into Canadian airspace. Just then however, as if from nowhere, a cheery voice chirped up on the radio. It was the pilot of the National Guard helicopter that had been pre-flighting back in Houlton. They had taken off shortly after I had, but unbeknown to me, during their training exercise they had then followed along behind me, tracking me all the way from Houlton up to the Canadian border.

It was all very friendly and good natured, and they wished me good luck and a safe onward journey as they peeled off to return southwards. It was a genuinely nice gesture to see me safely over the border, but at the same time it felt like they might have been simply *escorting me off the premises*!

South-east Canada, on first appearance, looked much like the north-east USA that I had just left; vast swathes of trees and the odd river. The subsequent crossing of the Gulf of Saint Lawrence went smoothly, and as I approached Sept-Îles (Seven Islands) Airport, I was amazed at the huge scale of the nearby railway sidings alongside the docks. The surrounding earthworks were heavily tainted a rusty red colour, a sure sign that this was the port railhead for the railway line that I would soon follow northwards, to reach the industrious iron ore mining town of Schefferville. The strangely familiar rust-stained landscape suddenly gave me a fleeting recollection of overflying the heavily contaminated land near the ship scrapping beach in Pakistan.

Sept-Îles is located in the French-speaking province of Quebec and hosts a curious mix of colonial French and British cultures set in a modern North American townscape. Its whole identity therefore felt oddly neither one thing nor the other, but it was a very welcoming place all the same, as personified by Karen who warmly greeted me on arrival at the FBO office and was on hand to sign my 'Coast-to-Coast' FAI paperwork. I was acutely aware of this being my last night of relative luxury, so I soaked up the relaxed atmosphere as best I could while dining out in a local sports bar in the evening. I watched the wall-to-wall TV sports channels along with French cuisine and a glass of red wine in hand (well, I felt I was now in France after all).

9 July 2015: Sept-Îles, Quebec, Canada – Schefferville, Quebec, Canada

This was it - the relaxed ambience of my flying road trip across the USA was now at an end. From here on things were going to become ever more arduous, and the pressure wouldn't let up until I had successfully crossed the Atlantic and arrived back the UK.

My only thin thread of connection to humanity now was a single-track railway line up to Schefferville, but even that would then disappear a few short miles north of the town. From there onwards there would be nothing... no visible sign of human effort, intervention or endeavour. Just a vast wilderness opening up in every direction. I was going to be very much on my own, often out of radio contact and having to rely on my own inner reserves of confidence and fortitude. I needed to remain positive and upbeat in the face of the great unknown challenges that lay ahead. In effect, I would be 'island-hopping' from now on, flying from one completely isolated settlement to the next, across an extremely *hostile sea* of forests, swampland, tundra, bare rock and ice. I could only hope now that each settlement might act as a little oasis of normality within the otherwise harsh and barren landscape.

To successfully fly a light aircraft around the world, I simply had no choice but to endure and overcome the unique challenges that some pretty 'out there' places would constantly throw at me. Emotionally, I was often well out of my normal comfort zone and perhaps at times even physically forced out of my regular safe-flight envelope. But by the very nature of the task in hand, it was the only way to do it. There was no tried and tested easy route, no pre-established bureaucratic protocol or helpful precedent of a prior flight to follow; this was after all, a path-finding maiden flight. I had to prepare mentally, as best I could, for the expected hardships ahead and just hope that those difficulties would not then prove to be too extreme, or dare I say, even impossible to overcome.

Crucially, both the remoteness of north-eastern Canada and the ever-present uncertainty of what would hopefully become the first gyroplane Atlantic Ocean crossing, were going to be the biggest test of the whole circumnavigation. And so, with these thoughts buzzing around my brain, and all the considerable trepidation of a would-be-pioneer, I tentatively headed north out of Sept-Îles and quickly picked up the railway line.

My plan was to follow the rail tracks all the way to Schefferville some 317 miles away, as it was my only route of comparative safety. In the event of an emergency landing, I would aim to set down (as best I could) near to the railway. I then hoped that at some point in the day, a train would eventually pass by and be able to give me some assistance. It was a sketchy contingency plan, but the only one that was available to me.

Happily, no such worse case scenarios occurred, and I arrived on the outskirts of Schefferville in a relieved and buoyant mood. I had seen some tremendous scenery on the way. Initially, as I was climbing up from the coast towards the higher interior, I caught sight of several incredibly powerful waterfalls. I had seen many picturesque rivers and waterfalls before in the Scottish Highlands, but what I was seeing now was definitely on another level. To witness the spectacle of such a wide, fast-flowing torrent of water suddenly surging over a jagged cliff face was phenomenal. Although from above I couldn't hear it, I could just imagine the thunderous noise it must have been making as, with a great cloud of spray, countless tonnes of water crashed onto the rocks below.

It was an odd feeling to be given such rare and close-up access to these splendid sights. Mother Nature was performing at her most magnificent and yet it was all going on, unseen and unnoticed by anyone else out here in the impenetrable wilderness. I immediately felt humbled and privileged to be flying so far off the beaten track that I could witness such spectacular forces of nature first-hand. My only disappointment was that flying solo, I had no one else there to share the experience with.

Another remarkable natural feature that caught my attention was the strange surface patterns that often appeared in areas of swampland. Highly deceptive, from a distance they resembled lovely smooth clearings of greenery within the trees, like large, manicured golf greens and I initially imagined them to be covered in moss, short grass or some other surface vegetation. They looked to be temptingly safe and ideal for an emergency landing spot in between all the unforgiving trees. But on closer inspection I suddenly realised that these patches of solid 'ground' were invariably either static pond water or soft bogland, with a thin covering of weed or green algae floating on top. These deadly camouflaged water traps would have caused immediate disaster had I attempted to land on one. So much for being safe havens!

Schefferville was, like the dockside in Sept-Îles, completely covered in the rusty brown hues of iron ore. But here, the colour had managed to extend its influence right around the whole town. After landing, I managed to obtain the last available room in the local hotel, the Rodeway Inn, which conveniently was only a short walk from the airfield. Given its remoteness, I was surprised that the hotel had full occupancy. But when I arrived to see the line of quarry workers' trucks parked outside, I quickly realised that the hotel's main clientele were, of course, not tourists.

The unique nature of the place was carried on inside the front door, where a prominent sign strictly instructed that 'ALL' outdoor footwear was to be removed in the front porchway. Such was the pervasiveness of the all-smothering iron ore dust outside, that such drastic measures were the only way to protect the hotel's interior. If it wasn't for the fact that most guests were then seen padding around everywhere in their socks, it all would have felt rather normal.

Maybe when we earthlings finally colonise the Red Planet Mars, all the hotels there will need to be just like this one.

"ALL boots and spacesuits off at the front door please!"

Looking out of the window of my room, the red dusty landscape outside certainly gave the impression of being on another planet. But after a hard day filled with isolation and a constant feeling of trepidation whilst flying alone into the unknown; to then find a clean, warm and cosy hotel on my arrival was most welcome indeed.

With long evening daylight, I ventured out to eat at the only restaurant I could find in town, which was about a 10-minute stroll away. Walking past the houses dotted about, it was clear to see that urban gardening was not high on the agenda. Ageing rusty snow-mobiles and sleds were the garden ornaments of choice, haphazardly scattered about on scrubby patches of overgrown grass that had most likely never seen a lawnmower. The ski-mounted machines, so vitally essential in winter, were seemingly now just left randomly abandoned exactly where they had last stopped. Brought to a grinding halt as the brief summertime thaw set in, they now appeared to be of as much practical use as a chocolate teapot. It was easy to see that for most of the year this place was covered in a lot of snow.

While gardening was definitely not on anyone's priority list, house insulation most certainly was. I observed that many of the properties had been externally clad in additional insulation, pinned over the exterior walls in large sheets. However rather bizarrely, it seemed that some residents had then not bothered to cover over these insulation panels. The result was a hotchpotch townscape of weather-beaten silver foil- and foam-cladded houses. Many even had the manufacturer's name emblazoned all over the exposed panels, giving the whole place an appearance of being a half-finished building site. Obviously, as dictated by the harsh winter climate, *functionality* rather than *aesthetics* was always given top priority.

10 July 2015: Schefferville, Quebec, Canada – Kuujjuaq, Quebec, Canada

Just three miles north of Schefferville Airport is a small lake called Lac de la Squaw. Flying over it I could see it was nothing out of the ordinary, much like all the other thousands of lakes that dotted this wild landscape. But to me it was a significant lake, as it happened to be at a latitude of 54 degrees and 51 minutes north, the exact same distance from the Equator as Larne Harbour back in Northern Ireland.

All my other flying adventures, spanning the past five years since *Roxy* and I had departed Larne, had taken place to the south of this latitude. The most southerly point had been crossing the Java Sea at 1 degree north of the equator, but I was now venturing northwards of my original starting point for the first time. Having finally re-crossed the 54th parallel I was now on my way (albeit very briefly) up into the Arctic Circle. Leaving the lake behind, I reflected that the next time I would see 54 degrees north again, would be on my eventual arrival back home. It was a sobering thought.

I was bound for Kuujjuaq and I knew I was heading into a vastly different region, both culturally and geographically. These northern lands are controlled and influenced by the traditions and cultures of the native Innuit population, a people that I had never previously encountered. Flying ever northwards, I noticed that the trees, previously lush and densely forested, were slowly becoming much more stunted and sparsely spread out. Tundra and low ground-hugging vegetation was slowly taking over where it could, but more often great patches of bare open rock and small lakes took precedence. The whole region was a victim of the last ice age, when thick glaciers, descending from the Arctic, managed to scrape off a lot of the rich fertile surface soil and dump it into the Atlantic Ocean to the east of Newfoundland. This erosion helped to form the Grand Banks, a relatively shallow underwater feature, which boasts some of the best fishing grounds of the North Atlantic. Below me, the resultant eroded landmass was increasingly rocky and barren.

Approaching Kuujjuaq, I could see that the whole town had a neatly laid out conventional road system, complete with a scattering of regular vehicles dotted about, but the roads then just abruptly ended a few miles out of town. Arriving from the south, I made a straight-in approach to runway 07 and taxied up to the surprisingly busy hard-standing area. Air Innuit was the main airline carrier that serviced these small outlying settlements, and Kuujjuaq acted as one of its maintenance bases. After some pleasant meeting and greeting with the Air Innuit staff, I was very grateful to the airline for taking me under their wing (quite literally) and allowing me to store *Roxy* overnight in a small corner of their large maintenance hangar. Even better, they also allowed me to stay in their crew accommodation block, where I was hosted by resident aircraft mechanic Kyle Marcoux. This proved to be a godsend considering what would be discovered the next day.

11–20 July 2015: Kuujjuaq, Quebec, Canada (non-flying days)

What was originally supposed to be only a one- or two-night stop-over, was soon to become something much more protracted.

When making my early pre-flight daily inspection of *Roxy* I spotted something amiss. The mounting bracket that supported the pre-rotator shaft drive just ahead of the propeller, had developed a crack across one of its main struts. It was a serious problem. If, during take-off, I now risked applying full pre-rotator loading to the weakened bracket, it could easily cause a much more catastrophic failure of the surrounding parts.

In short, I was now grounded.

I was unable to fly until I could work out a solution. Thankfully it was still morning time in eastern Canada, which meant the UK had not yet gone to bed, so some urgent phone calls and emails back to RotorSport UK followed to establish what to do next. I would now have to wait for a spare part – a whole replacement bracket – to be sent out to me from the UK. This was going to take some time and effort to organise, not least how to get the new bracket delivered to such a remote location as soon as possible. Thankfully, on hearing of my technical difficulties, Air Innuit once again stepped in to help me out.

Luckily, the replacement bracket was neither too big, nor too heavy, which meant it could slide easily into a small, padded Jiffy Bag. Rotor-Sport UK then air-freighted the part from England to the international hub airport of Montreal. From there, Air Innuit staff forwarded it onto their next Kuujjuaq-bound flight and it was finally hand delivered to me by the arriving air crew. Thankfully the package arrived within days, whereas I had feared it would take weeks.

During my enforced downtime, I was able to catch up on admin, sleep, maintenance chores and laundry, though not necessarily in that particular order. My new flatmate, Kyle, turned out to be an extremely resourceful guy. On being posted to the Kuujjuaq servicing base, he had managed to put his creative skills to good use. In these extremely remote settlements, all imports and exports were eye-wateringly expensive. So as a general rule, what arrived into Kuujjuaq, stayed in Kuujjuaq. This resulted in the growth of a sizable scrapyard on the outskirts of town, and it was here that Kyle was able to salvage himself the rich pickings of an old quadbike. Being a highly skilled mechanic, he made short work of fettling up a rough repair to get the old quad running again and this now acted as his rather magnificent, *Mad Max*-style personal steed.

With a few non-flying days ahead of me, I had no problem jumping on board Kyle's rickety quad to take a run downtown with him on his night off. It took all of five minutes along a loose gravel road and after a quick guided tour (another five minutes) we arrived at the bar. Being pretty much the only watering hole in town, it had a lively atmosphere and felt very frontier-like. Although we hadn't ridden in off the open trail on a couple of horses, we did still have to dust ourselves off after arriving on Kyle's quad. I was just a little disappointed that there were no swinging saloon doors for us to burst through.

We made our way up to the bar counter and ordered a couple of beers. A short time later, while we chatted, I spied a particularly welcome sight on the bar shelves – a bottle, that was now approximately 1959 nautical miles from home.

It was a bottle of Bushmills Irish Whiskey, from the oldest distillery in the world (dated 1608, it predates most Scottish Whisky by over 100 years). The small town of Bushmills is only about 50 miles up the road from Larne, so Kyle and I were able to celebrate the happy coincidence with a wee dram each. Strictly for medicinal purposes only you understand, just to help wash down the beer.

Kuujjuaq was different from any other place I had visited. The road infrastructure, streetlights and telephone wires all gave a sense of regular normality, but on entering the supermarket that illusion all changed. It was well stocked with all the standard foodstuffs, including fresh fruit and veg, but this was all just lulling me into a false sense of security. As I turned a corner, I was met with a supermarket display like no other: canoe paddles, fishing rods, rifle carrying cases, and even an off-road Yamaha motorbike and a Honda quadbike; the latter two haphazardly wedged between the display stands for T-shirts and bananas. I spared a thought for the poor shopper who might have only gone in for a pint of milk but came back out with a boat hook under his arm.

Walking down to the small pier, I learned that the nearby fuel storage facility was able to supply the whole town's needs by receiving only one or two fuel deliveries in the whole year. I also discovered that getting the fuel delivered to such a remote place was often only possible by boat or fuel barge during the short ice-free summer months. And because it was so much effort to deliver, the fuel was always of the highest grade so that everyone's gasoline needs could be satisfied. It meant that although the fuel at the pumps was very costly, at least I had the comfort of knowing it was of the best quality as I later poured it into my tanks.

On one of my maintenance days, a buzz of activity suddenly erupted from one of the offices. A local light aircraft had suffered an engine failure and had made an emergency landing on the gravel sandbank of a river about 12 miles away. Mercifully all the occupants were safe, due in no small part to the expert bush flying skills of the pilot. Raising the alarm, the occupants were soon recovered by the highly professional, locally based helicopter operator Nunavik Rotors. In many other parts of the world that would be that; ensure the people are safe and never mind about the aircraft. But this was an ever-resourceful Innuit community, and so within a few short hours a rescue plan was hatched with a salvage crew being dispatched by helicopter to prepare the aircraft for its recovery.

A short time later, in what looked like a well-practised procedure, I could hear the sound of the helicopter returning to the airfield. Upon going outside to scan the horizon I was greeted with a fantastic sight. The small white and red aircraft had been slung under the helicopter on a lifting strop. It hung in the air about 100ft below the helo to avoid the worst of the rotor downwash, and it flew along surprising well. I also noted that an interesting trick had been used. Before being extracted off the sandbank, both wings of the plane had been wrapped in some heavy-duty cargo netting. Apparently, this technique was to avoid the wings from acting aerodynamically while it was being dragged through the air, as the nets prevented the generation of any over wing lift.

With precise skill, the aircraft was gently set down right before us on the hard standing area, and once it was unhooked and safe to approach, we all had a closer inspection of the damage. The fuselage was virtually unscathed, which was a tremendous testament to the pilot's cool level headedness during landing. But alas the same could not be said of the engine. The initial assessment pointed towards the engine throwing a piston, and this had shot clean through the casing and had also ripped the engine cowling clean off as the rogue piston exited skywards.

That said, upon inspecting the damage himself, the pilot thought that it "wasn't that bad," and he fully expected to have the old bird back up and running again in a few months' time.

Fortunately, my own wait to get up and running again didn't take quite so long. The replacement pre-rotator bracket finally turned up, and after fitting and a quick check ride I was all set to carry on northwards once again.

21 July 2015: Kuujjuaq, Quebec, Canada – Iqaluit, Baffin Island, Canada

I was now facing the first open sea crossing since leaving Nantucket, only this crossing, 80 nautical miles over the Hudson Strait, was going to be significantly chillier. For safety, I elected to initially hug the coastline north from Kuujjuaq, joining the dots of the smaller Innuit settlements that lay in my path. Gone though were the familiar sounding place names from home that I had passed by down in Maine. I now had places such as Aupaluk, Kangirsuk, Quaqtac and Kangiqsujuaq popping up on my GPS screen. Names that certainly weren't familiar to me, but they would have made a great score when played on a scrabble board.

The terrain was now absolutely barren. The trees had slowly petered out, so too the tundra moss and low shrubs. All that was left was a rocky landscape littered with small pockets of lakes. Snow and ice were slowly encroaching also. Soon enough I noticed the lakes had a layer of thin ice on them, and there were winter snow drifts that had not yet melted away. Frozen water replaced open water, in a brutal and unforgiving terrain that I had never experienced before.

I was certainly a long way now from the hot and dusty sands of the Middle Eastern deserts and the steaming, lush jungles of Borneo.

Huddled in behind my windshield, I tried to conserve heat as best I could. The air was cold yet also parchingly dry, and the visibility was perfect. I could easily see 100 miles or more in every direction. But in all that landscape there was not a single sign of humanity, not one dog sled track across a frozen lake nor a solitary quadbike trail. I was very alone. I pondered on whether anyone would regularly ever fly in these parts? Probably not was my answer – it was too far off the beaten track and on the road to nowhere. Any Air Inuit passenger flights or enclosed cockpit helicopters that happened to pass by would all remain at a much higher flight level to maintain better radio contact. They wouldn't need to be skirting a few hundred feet above ground level in an attempt to keep that little bit warmer. For posterity, I took a few selfies as I appeared to be the only living thing out here to photograph.

As I flew along, I mused that maybe I would suddenly come across a crashed UFO out here in the frozen wilderness where no one was looking, and then I thought:

"Well, what would I do, if I did see one?"

I would note its GPS position obviously, but then the question would be:

"Would I report it on landing or not?"

If I did, would the world's media descend and have a field day, or would secret government officials rush in first to hide away the evidence. It was an odd debate to be having with myself, but it perhaps illustrated the state of my mind having been on the road for so long. The only important thing was that this internal debate certainly helped to take my mind off the oppressively real ongoing concerns of flying over such a hostile and inhospitable landscape. Effecting a search and rescue mission to any downed aircraft, be it a UFO or not, in such an inaccessible place would certainly not have been an easy task.

Despite me being apprehensive, the Hudson Strait crossing happily went without a hitch, and soon enough I was making my final approach into Iqaluit. I could see from miles out the bright yellow control tower building that this airfield is famous for. In 2009, whilst initially planning for the circumnavigation flight, I had noticed that this distinctive building had cropped up many times in research photographs of other earthrounder aircraft that had passed by this way. It was hard to miss due to its unique colour (but that's the point, I suppose!) and I was very moved to be actually now here, some six long years later. After all the trials and tribulations that *Roxy* and I had endured all over the globe in the intervening years, I had finally made it. It also marked the end of the Canadian leg of the journey, or so I thought at the time, as from here the plan was to strike out eastwards once more, towards Nuuk in Greenland.

On landing after my chilly flight, I was warmly received at the FBO office. Slightly unnerving however was the huge stuffed polar bear that was on display to greet me. Standing on its hind legs, it reared up to be around 10ft tall. Quite sobering given that I was soon to be overflying the land of the polar bear. I hoped that I would not encounter one, up close and personal as they say, any time soon.

I had the good fortune to be put up in a fantastic house overlooking Frobisher Bay, apparently the same house that Leonardo DiCaprio had stayed in when filming locally. It gave a terrific view out over the bay, where huge chunks of broken pack ice, some the size of trucks, lay strewn about on the rocks at low tide. At high tide, a few hours later, the ice then refloated and continued slowly bobbing around at the mercy of the wind and currents. I found watching these forces of nature fascinating and much better than watching TV! Though unfortunately, that same ice would end up giving me some real headaches the next day.

22 July 2015: Iqaluit, Baffin Island, Canada (non-flying day)

After an interesting evening, where I was taken to a local social club for a beer, I awoke without the ability to see anything.

Overnight, that stunning view from my window had suddenly disappeared completely.

Fog, the bane of seafarers and aviators alike, had formed above the chilly covering of sea ice in the bay and had then rolled in to form a thick blanketing layer over the shoreline. On arriving early at the airport, it was obvious that there was no way that I was going anywhere in these conditions and certainly not to Nuuk in Greenland, 444 nautical miles across the icy waters of the Davis Strait.

All I could do was wait to see if the fog would burn off later in the morning.

Around midday, the fog did indeed clear away to leave a sparkling blue sky with near perfect visibility. It should have been fine to attempt the crossing to Nuuk in the early afternoon, as I was at 63 degrees north (just below the Arctic Circle at 66 degrees 32 minutes north) and there was still plenty of long evening daylight left to make the crossing. Only there was one problem – Nuuk Airport would shut at 5pm local time, and as Greenland was two hours ahead of eastern Canada, that meant there were not enough hours left in the afternoon to make the flight before closing time. It appeared I would have to wait for conditions to hopefully improve the following morning and stay another night. To pass the time, I was taken on a tour of the town and to see a local pack of husky dogs. They were proper outdoor working dogs, well used to pulling sleds and battling blizzards, but now seeing them lolling about and basking in the afternoon sun, it felt like they were all on their holidays during these short summer months.

23 July 2015: Iqaluit, Baffin Island, Canada – Qikiqtarjuaq, Broughton Island, Canada

I awoke early to check the visibility outside, but the sneaky fog had crept back in overnight. I worried that I was going to be trapped here for some days, with the fog clearing too late each day for me to reach Nuuk before it closed. There were also hefty charges to pay if landing out of hours at Nuuk, so that possible option was really a non-starter.

What to do?

I contacted my flight planner Eddie Gould to explain the tricky situation. It was then that Eddie came up with a brilliant plan, one that really did literally save the day. Overnight he had been looking at alternative options for me and had focussed in on the small Innuit settlement of Qikiqtarjuaq, 255 nautical miles to my north-east. It appeared to be a viable option as an intermediate stop, and crucially it was still in my same Canadian time zone.

At first the logic of flying further north to help with flying east felt a bit odd, but soon the benefit of Eddie's creative plan became clear. The cartographical quirk of how two-dimensional maps are drawn to represent the three-dimensional globe, tries to show a round globe on a flat map. This causes a distortion in measurements and the resultant distances at both poles become stretched. To look at a regular map surrounding the Davis Strait, you would easily be mistaken to think that Nuuk must be closer to Iqaluit than to Qikiqtarjuaq, as it physically looks that way on a flat map. And yet, when it is properly measured correcting for map distortion, it turns out that Qikiqtarjuaq is some 80 nautical miles closer to Nuuk.

I was thrilled to realise that I could both extract myself from foggy Iqaluit *and* knock 80 nautical miles off my Davis Strait crossing in one fell swoop. After that conversation, I thought Eddie was in the wrong profession. He should really have been a magician, especially after pulling a flight-saving rabbit out of a hat like that!

I re-planned my route while the fog was once more steadily lifting, and I was all good to go.

That afternoon flight, taken in glorious sunshine and gin-clear visibility, took me across and through some of the most spectacular scenery that I would see on the entire world flight. And to think I very nearly missed it out in my haste to fly on directly to Nuuk.

The now familiar wilderness of barren rock, ice and snow continued northwards. Before I could overfly the relative safety of my flight's only alternate landing airstrip at Pangnirtung, I had to cross Cumberland Sound, a broad sea inlet which spanned about 60 nautical miles shore to shore. After the thousands of miles of open water, sea and ocean crossings that I had already traversed during my global flight, I assumed that this would be just another comparatively easy short hop. However, I soon discovered that it had something else to distinguish it from all the other crossings so far – pack ice.

As I approached, I could see that the entire inlet, maybe 100 nautical miles long, was covered in ice. Not the regular and uniform sort of ice that I had sometimes seen on frozen ponds and lakes back home. No, this was definitely not the smooth, 'get your skates on' type. This ice was rough, haphazardly broken sea ice riding confused on top of bitterly cold saltwater with riptides and currents that helped to smash it all about a bit; the pack showed all the signs of a violent recent history.

There were lots of large flat rounded slabs, like frozen lily pads, maybe 20 to 30 metres across, but these were then interspersed with a crushed soup of smaller ice chunks infilling all the gaps in between. It appeared that the whole pack had then refrozen and broken apart many times over. It was fascinating to see, though also quite menacing; the ice looked reasonably thick, but I wondered just how load-bearing it would be during an emergency landing. Would 500kg of gyroplane simply crack a large piece in two or even tip it to one side causing the aircraft to slide off its back and into the icy water below?

One answer was certain however: this was an infinitely more dangerous surface to cross than flying over open water. At least with the fully wet stuff, I knew that I could ditch and (hopefully) make an escape into my life raft. With this sort of thin pack ice, the greatest risk would have been *not to land*, but to fall straight through and then become submerged underneath.

With all these not so jolly thoughts running through my head, it is easy to imagine why the 60 nautical miles seemed to take an exceedingly long time to cross. Needless to say, I was so glad to reach the opposite shoreline and went on to pass by overhead of Pangnirtung without incident. I thought I had now had my most dramatic episode for the day, but as it turned out, there was much more to come.

The onward route to Qikiqtarjuaq was only another 95 nautical miles, but it still involved navigating a path through numerous high mountain peaks across the interior of Baffin Island's Cumberland Peninsula. During my hastily rearranged flight planning before take-off, I had spied a fantastic gorge, the Akshayuk Pass, cutting right through the towering mountains of the Penny Highlands. Fortunately, this now gave me a comparatively low-level, sheltered route to follow, with the added safety of having the airstrip at Pangnirtung to double-back to if I encountered any poor weather issues along the way.

For the next hour I was truly enthralled at what I was witnessing. The whole pass was a huge glacier-carved ravine, a classic U-shaped valley like the ancient ones we have back home from the last ice age. But the valley here was starkly more raw and recently formed. Smaller side valleys ('hanging valleys' as they are known to glaciologists and geographers) joined at intervals from either side, and as I peered up along their length, I could see in the distance the terminus or leading edge of the resident glaciers that formed them. It was like flying through a glacial version of *Jurassic Park*. The scale of it was awesome. I felt like a small insect, buzzing along in the middle of a huge gulley.

I thought I was completely remote and alone, but then down below I spotted a brightly painted hut, and then some miles farther on, another hut and then another. I quickly realised that these were emergency refuges, placed all the way through the valley for the added safety of the courageous mountaineers and climbers who visit here every summer. I mentally logged the position of each hut as I flew past it so that I knew which would be the nearest if I urgently had to find one in a hurry. Midway through the valley, I was left astounded as I turned a bend and was suddenly presented with a huge, towering wall of rock on my right-hand side. I found out later that this was Mount Thor, a 5495ft monster. What I was witnessing was its sheer vertical face as it dropped down into the pass. I was further amazed to learn that, at 4101ft, it is in fact the Earth's highest vertical drop. And here I was, a small insignificant yellow bumblebee, scooting along merrily beside it, at barely a third of its height up from the valley floor.

Very soon after passing this spectacle, I crossed into the Arctic Circle at the latitude of 66 degrees, 33 minutes and 46.3 seconds north. I was only planning to stay this far north for one night, but it was very satisfying to have reached this significant milestone, nonetheless. The next day I would head south again and leave the Land of the Midnight Sun behind as I passed down by Cape Dyer, en route towards Nuuk.

Breaking out from the northern end of the Akshayuk Pass, the broad valley continued seaward and transformed itself into a steep sided fjord. Unlike the jumbled up and re-frozen pack ice that I had experienced earlier in the day, these narrower inlets were surprisingly much more ice-free, perhaps because of the time of year or slightly warmer melt waters. Only the occasional large chunk of flat-topped ice floe remained in place for me to photograph.

The descent down through the bare rocky foothills to the coastline felt quite odd. In all other warmer parts of the world, such a flight from a high mountain pass down to the sea, would be accompanied by a marked increase of ground cover, trees, vegetation and human infrastructure. Here there was very little of these things, just barren brownish grey rock leading down to an extremely deep and dark, almost black sea surface.

Rounding a bend in the fjord, Qikiqtarjuaq village suddenly hove into view, its light grey gravel runway laid out nearby just at the edge of the bay. Unsurprisingly, in such a location there was no other traffic to affect my final approach and I came straight into land. I taxied up to the small airport building and shut down. Removing my helmet and headset, I was struck as to how absolutely quiet it was. Given there was almost no wind, there was no sound to be heard. There were no trees to rustle their leaves and no birds to twitter. Just silence. I then heard the airport office door squeak open and was soon being welcomed by the Airport staff and local residents.

A tall, solidly built, weather-hardened Innuit man approached and offered out a hand that showed all the signs of at least 50 years of hard manual work. Something of a gentle giant, he politely introduced himself as Billy, and it soon transpired that Billy Arnaqaq was now going to act as my fixer for sourcing fuel locally. With that, he instantly became my number one most important person in town. He was astounded that I had managed to arrive in this hostile place in such a fragile looking aircraft.

I really liked Billy and his quiet, unassuming, easy-going nature. After some gentle persuasion, I coaxed him to have a go at sitting in *Roxy's* pilot seat and imagine how it might feel to fly out over the wild Atlantic Ocean in such a tiny open cockpit. His disbelief at what I had accomplished so far only deepened even further!

Shortly afterwards, gathering fuel turned into its own mini-adventure. After assuring and then reassuring Billy several times that I only needed regular unleaded gasoline for my Rotax 914 engine, we gathered up the empty Turtle Pac and headed off in his truck for the settlement's fuel dump. Presumably for safety reasons, this was located about a mile out of town, on an elevated position halfway up a mountainside. We bumped along the rough stony track that served as a road, but as soon as we reached the fuel compound and got out of the truck we were literally swarmed by a big cloud of black flies. They were not biting thankfully, but they were still highly annoying little critters. I thought the smell of the fuel being poured into the Turtle Pac might have driven them away, but alas no, we only regained our sanctuary when back in the truck and bumping back down the road again.

Fuel was sorted, so now only food and accommodation were needed. Surprisingly there was actually a small hotel in the settlement, the Tulugak Hotel Inns North and I was able to find a room there. Accommodation is thin on the ground in these parts, and so it was quite normal that on arrival, I might have been expected to share a room with another guest. Fortunately I was in luck, they had a twin room that had previously been used by a single occupant the night before. They asked me if I would be OK taking the unused bed in this unmade-up twin room, if they just charged it as a single.

"No problem," I said. To be honest, I could have slept anywhere. I was that tired from the adrenaline of the flight.

The food was *one size fits all* in the style of a school dining hall, but it was quite tasty and filling. Compared to elsewhere in Canada, the food and accommodation proved to be exceedingly expensive. But considering the effort needed to keep such a remote place fully supplied and operating, it provided a great haven of relative comfort in the wilderness. That said, considering the substantial cost, I wouldn't have wanted to spend too many nights there.

Lying in bed, I reflected back on the day's awesome flying and of the serious journey I was about to embark on the next morning.

Crossing the Atlantic would be the crux of the whole expedition. I would be very much out on my own, flying over some of the world's most isolated terrain and inhospitable waters. Mentally, only my own courage, self-belief and sense of fortitude would carry me through from this point. Physically, the rest of the world flight had simply been *training* for what I was about to undertake. It was a daunting task that hung over my consciousness with a dark sense of foreboding.

The vagaries of the weather were always my greatest adversary, my greatest worry. The weather in the North Atlantic, even in the summertime, is notoriously restless and fickle as many pilots had already found out to their cost. Any flight greater than say, 100 miles, could easily start off with benign weather conditions, but then perhaps deteriorate mid-flight into a much more challenging sort of experience at the other end. I was realistic, I could only plan so far ahead, and I certainly couldn't dictate the weather. All I could do was mentally prepare myself, to be ready for *anything* that might happen, and then just hope for the best.

16

The Atlantic Ocean: Canada to UK

24 July 2015: Qikiqtarjuaq, Broughton Island, Canada – Nuuk, Greenland

During the night I happened to wake to the sound of an outboard motor on a boat. I looked out of my window and the sun was streaming in. I could see three huge icebergs floating out in the bay, shining a brilliant bluish white in all their glorious sunlit detail.

What time was it I wondered? Had I slept in? People were already up and going about their business. I had been very tired the night before, but I didn't want to miss my time-zone window for crossing over to Greenland, so I quickly checked my phone. Panic over. It was still only 3.30 am. The Arctic's midnight sun was certainly living up to its name.

After my hearty breakfast at a much more reasonable hour in the morning, I was able to stroll across town to return to the gravel air-strip. I was pleased to be able to stretch my legs for some exercise and had plenty to see while walking through the settlement of about 500 people. All the buildings were tin clad and constructed from sectional prefabricated panels. Most were raised on blocks above the ground, and many were further anchored down to the ground with steel cables.

Although I was fortunate to be experiencing lovely calm, sunny conditions, the fortifications of the buildings suggested the climate here was normally much more violent. It probably felt like quite a different sort of place in the dark depths of winter.

Considering I was now going to fly internationally between Canada and Greenland, which is under Danish sovereignty, the departure formalities were all quite relaxed. After all, it wasn't like I had any space on board my aircraft for smuggling any type of contraband.

Roxy had sat out on the rough gravel overnight and I had been slightly concerned that if the wind had picked up, dust and grit could have been blown up everywhere. Mercifully, it had been a calm night with the *overnight sun* (wow, how odd does that sound!) still shining brightly. Thankfully there was also no sign of the troublesome fog that had hindered my progress out of Iqaluit. I had an excited and optimistic feeling about the day ahead, but at the same time I sensed a nagging self-doubt about coping with such a hazardous journey.

Coasting out to traverse the Davis Strait marked the starting point of the Atlantic crossing. Whatever actions and decisions I would make, good or bad, in the coming days and weeks ahead would no doubt be noted and recorded for posterity. And whatever the outcome of this first pioneering attempt, would certainly influence the progress of all future attempts. If all went well, others might follow. If all went badly wrong, then others could possibly find themselves prohibited by the authorities from making any further attempts.

At this moment I felt a real burden of responsibility for the global gyroplane community. I sensed it even more now than I did before I embarked on the whole adventure, for this was where the flight would get truly serious. The rest of the flying around the world up to this point, with all its trials and tribulations, was just a dress-rehearsal for these upcoming flights. If I came unstuck in any way during this precedent-setting first crossing, then the risk was that *all gyroplanes* might then equally be considered and confirmed as 'less than capable', 'not a proper aircraft', or 'just a toy for local flying within sight of the home airfield'. Any failure would surely be fuel for the fire of those armchair pilots, who would seek to scorn or belittle something different, something outside their narrow, blinkered conventional experience of what was a *proper* light aircraft.

But in order to achieve a successful circumnavigation, the plain fact was that the Atlantic crossing was unavoidable. It had to be done, or attempted anyway, and so I would just now have to *bite the bullet* and get on with it.

***

Thundering off the hard gravel, I hoped the prop was not getting too damaged. There was little wind to assist me, but at least the morning air was cool and so I had good positive lift on climb-out over the bay and past the three icebergs that I had seen from the hotel. The sea inlet around Broughton Island was ice-free, apart from the odd rogue iceberg here and there. But as I turned south-east to fly down the coastline towards Cape Dyer, some 80 nautical miles away, I saw quite a different spectacle. Running for tens of miles ahead and hugging the rocky shoreline, was a huge ice floe.

Flat as a pancake on the top and stretching for several miles in width, the floe eventually dropped in a sheer 100ft-thick ice cliff down into the water on its seaward edge. It was easily the biggest lump of ice I had ever seen. Enthralled by its sheer scale, I chose to fly along its vertical cliff face and studied it closely. I realised that it would have been relatively easy to land *Roxy* on the top, given that I could normally land at not much more than a walking pace. It would have been easy enough to plump down onto the surface, even with a soft layer of new snow lying on top of the pack ice. Relatively easy to make an emergency landing perhaps, but definitely *not so easy* to take off from again.

Still, as a potential escape strategy, it was a much better option than landing in the sea, so I continued to use the edge of the ice wall as my flight path. There was a particular reason that I kept to the edge rather than flying farther inland over the floe and this was to maintain my peripheral vision by using the contrast of the sea against the ice. Had I not done so, I risked getting disoriented by flying over the completely featureless, blinding white surface of the ice. This was a strategy I would also later use when crossing the southern tip of the ice sheet in Greenland. Occasionally, parts of the ice wall edge looked to be very unstable. Huge crevasses cracked the perfectly smooth, pristine white surface, in preparation for calving a huge chunk of ice off into the water below. But alas, although I kept a close lookout, I unfortunately didn't see the awesome sight of any icebergs being born.

The scenery nonetheless continued to be stunning, as it had been throughout the Canadian wilderness.

Soon enough, I closed in on Cape Dyer, my last point of land before coasting out across the Davis Strait. From there, I anticipated crossing some 285 nautical miles of open water to reach Nuuk, which equated to nearly four hours of flying. For the first third of the crossing, the sea was littered with the broken debris of the iceberg maternity wards further north. Unlike my previous experience of thin ice, some of these thicker chunks were now substantial and probably could have been suitable for landing on in an emergency. However, as events unfolded, little did I know then, that the very next day just such an emergency would befall another circumnavigating pilot in the Davis Strait.

As I approached the mid-channel point, the ice slowly dispersed. The number of larger icebergs dwindled, to be replaced by much smaller growlers, which gave the whole surface an appearance of semi-melted slush. For a while I was back in the worst-case conditions for ditching. I was dealing with a surface that could both cause my aircraft a lot of physical damage and also end up being too weak to support its weight. Fortunately, this growler phase didn't last too long, and I was then mightily relieved to be flying over completely open water once again.

The weather continued to be clear with good visibility, but as I approached the coastline of Greenland, I could see that the landmass was causing its own localised effect. Thick blankets of multi-level cloud were hanging around menacingly, shrouding the jagged coastal mountain peaks around Nuuk. I pushed on closer, constantly trying to make sense of the dynamically changing picture ahead. Layers of cloud were forming at different levels and most worryingly for me, a band of much lower cloud was forming right across my route.

I dropped lower to remain under the cloud base, and I levelled out at about 500ft above the sea. This was manageable, as long as conditions didn't deteriorate further. Only they did. Now I was at 400ft… then 350ft. Up ahead I could see land, the rocky shoreline of an unoccupied peninsula that protects Nuuk from the open sea. Coasting in over the shore, the bare rock surface was perhaps only 100ft above the sea, but gradually rising. I had already learnt, whilst flying over the coastal mountain range in Oregon, that descending cloud coupled with rising landmass was never a good combination; and to add further to my problems, I still had about 12 miles of peninsula to cross.

With the swirling mist and low cloud base at times engulfing the highest ground of the peninsula, I had to carefully pick and choose my route to find a visible path through. But within a few miles of the airport, I eventually crossed over to open water once again. Removed from the land, the clouds lifted again considerably and to my surprise, the approach and landing at Nuuk was completely standard. Taxiing to park, I was extremely relieved that I had completed this crossing without incident, though those last dozen miles, in reduced visibility with a constantly undulating landscape below, had certainly proved the most challenging part of the whole flight.

* * *

I was warmly greeted on arrival by Dan Rasmussen, who worked at the airport. On learning that I hadn't yet sorted out any accommodation, he very kindly offered me a place to stay with his family in Nuuk, which I was most grateful for. To visit such places and experience the hospitality of a local host is so much more meaningful than to stay in yet another local motel or hotel chain.

On the short drive into town from the airport, Dan pointed out many local points of interest, my favourite being Nuuk's very own golf course. As you can imagine, creating acres of gently rolling, lush green fairways and carefully manicured tees and greens was exceedingly unlikely in such a harsh environment. The hardy Greenlanders however did not let the challenging conditions deter them and they had adapted accordingly. Liberal use of all-weather AstroTurf helped the club members both tee off and putt out, while the nine 'fairways' had to make do with scrubby tundra, interspersed with bare rocky outcrops and small lakes. Even the old wooden hut that served as clubhouse had to be securely lashed down with steel cables, presumably to stop it blowing over in an arctic gale.

Driving through Nuuk, my first impression was how surprisingly European it appeared to be. A strong Danish influence was reflected in the architecture and the population, and I certainly felt that I was no longer in North America. I had felt this sudden cultural change before of course, especially when it involved islands, but each time it happened it always took me slightly by surprise. Take-off from one culture, land in another. True international travel. And psychologically at least, Europe now felt so much closer to home.

I took some time out to explore the town. There was an excellent museum down by the shoreline, which gave a fascinating insight into the history and traditions of the Greenlanders through the ages. They were certainly an impressively resourceful and hardy people; they had to be just to survive in such a place!

Perhaps in a gesture towards the *Little Mermaid* statue that sits on a rock in Copenhagen, Nuuk also has its own version, known as *Mother of the Sea*. By clever design, the human statue also incorporated a whole range of local animals and fish, some of which I would have liked to meet. Though one of which, of course I wouldn't – the polar bear.

25 July 2015: Nuuk, Greenland (non-flying day)

Overnight I received news from Eddie that another eastbound circumnavigator, a Russian pilot called Sergey Ananov, was hoping to catch me up. Like me he was flying solo, but in a small Robinson 22 helicopter, and he was aiming to be the first person to fly a light helicopter (weighing less than one tonne) around the globe. He had been making good progress through Canada and while I had been overnighting in Qikiqtarjuaq, Sergey had arrived in Iqaluit, just behind me.

Soon an idea emerged, that if he was able to catch up with me, then we could perhaps look to fly around Greenland and even on over the Atlantic together in company. It would certainly be safer from a search and rescue perspective to have two aircraft crossing such hostile terrain together and so, I decided to wait for him in Nuuk, so we could discuss the logistics.

With no flying to worry about, Dan and I went out to the airport, in good time for Sergey's expected afternoon arrival. He had elected to fly the direct route from Iqaluit to Nuuk. We made our way up to the tower to check on Sergey's progress, but immediately Dan and I were stunned at the news that Sergey's satellite tracker had suddenly stopped working, mid-crossing. This was not good news, not in these parts. Ditching here was not like ditching in the Caribbean. We soon heard that the Canadian authorities were commencing their search procedures. Sitting in Greenland we felt quite helpless, but there was not a lot more we could do except hope that he would soon be found, safe and sound.

With nothing to do but wait for any update on the search overnight, we drove back into Nuuk. Heavy fog offshore had hampered the initial aerial searches of the area, but what they didn't know as yet was that Sergey had already made it safely onto an iceberg.

With still no news on Sergey's whereabouts, I had truly mixed feelings. I felt perhaps in some way that I was partly responsible. If he hadn't been rushing to try to catch me, perhaps he would have delayed his crossing by another day or put in the same dogleg as I had up to Qikiqtarjuaq, where the current crossing conditions were much less foggy. But he was flying his own flight, determining his own actions and having to live therefore with his own decisions. It was exactly the same for me. I had to now decide, even with Sergey still missing overnight, whether to press on with my own continued flight the next day.

I reasoned there was no point in further delay; it would just not help in such a changeable climate. Sergey would hopefully still be located and rescued as fast as possible, with or without my waiting for any news in Nuuk. I decided that if the weather was looking reasonable in the morning, I would look to fly down the west coast of Greenland. I wanted to move past this hostile, unpredictable landscape, as fast as possible if the local weather permitted.

26 July 2015: Nuuk, Greenland – Narsarsuaq, Greenland

The day started fine; the murky fog that I had encountered on arrival seemed to have dispersed so I was, physically at least, good to go. Mentally however, it was a different matter. We still didn't know the whereabouts of Sergey, only the presumption that he had definitely ditched and that the search and rescue operation was ongoing. All we could do was to hope for the best. It reinforced the idea that flying in a light, single-engine aircraft in such extremely remote places was certainly not for the faint-hearted and there was definitely no guarantee that any flight would necessarily work out 100% as intended. And yet, here I was, about to face one of the most intimidating flights of the whole circumnavigation. The plan was to follow the rugged coastline of western Greenland south, for some 265 miles, before making an 80-mile dogleg into the interior and skirting around the southern tip of the ice sheet to reach Narsarsuaq. I was certainly apprehensive. Alternate landing sites were exceedingly few and far between on this storm-ravaged coast, with only one usable airstrip possible, at approximately half distance at Paamiut. I had also been given details of one other landing area, a gravel river delta on the coastline that had last been used during World War II. I could probably have landed on it in an emergency, but taking off again would have been very unlikely.

While bidding Dan a fond farewell, he informed me that his father was based on the Faroe Islands, and he would let him know that I was en route to see him in maybe a week's time. It was nice to know in advance there would be some further warm hospitality waiting for me there.

The flight commenced quietly, and for the first 25 miles or so I navigated out of the sheltered fjords that protected Nuuk's microclimate. All was well, until I reached the Davis Strait coastline and then conditions deteriorated dramatically. It seemed that the low mist and intermittent fog banks that had plagued my arrival at Nuuk, had since moved on down the coast a bit and were now once more lurking in my path. Trying to remain optimistic, I reasoned that the toughest conditions might only last a few miles, maybe 20 miles at most; yet little did I know then that they would actually persist with me for the next *230 miles.* This flight was to become one of the most gruelling challenges of the entire journey.

The conditions were barely flyable, a 300-400ft ceiling of low mist clung stubbornly to the shoreline, and at times extended out to sea for a couple of miles before returning to hug the coast again. Thankfully, farther out to sea I could see there was a much higher cloud base, so I adopted the same tactic I had employed flying along the coastline of Palawan Island in the Philippines. If the swirling mist got too low for comfort close to the shore, I just headed out to sea to remain in reasonable visibility for a few miles until I was able to again return to relative safety over the shoreline.

Given the low flying altitude however, I had sparsely few options of quickly finding a spot to land if needed. A lot of the terrain was sheer jagged rocky headlands, ravines and inlets, complete with crashing waves thrown in for good measure. With so little height to work with, I constantly knew that I would be in serious bother if I had either elected to try a landing on shore, *or* a ditching into the sea. Caught quite literally *between a rock and a hard place,* I figured that staying as close as possible to the shoreline was still my best policy. This was the route that I was *expected* to be flying, so it would also have been the first place search and rescue would come looking for me if there was a problem.

I persevered, continually hoping that conditions would improve farther down the coast. Unfortunately, they didn't, and so the whole flight was a mixture of heightened awareness, adrenaline surges and controlled anxiety. Flying constantly so low to the rocks and surf, with occasional added turbulence thrown off the cliffs, required both extreme continual focus and precise control to remain safe throughout the flight. It proved to be incredibly wearing to concentrate for so long and keep the aircraft exactly on course and altitude. I continued to endure this mental and physical combat for about three hours, until the worst conditions mercifully started to ease. The oppressively low cloud base lifted to around 1000ft as I passed over Paamiut airstrip, and with brighter skies ahead to the south my own spirits were also lifted; I knew I had finally battled my way beyond the roughest patch of poor weather.

Turning onto my dogleg course towards Narsarsuaq, visibility further improved. It was only then that I began to catch glimpses of a brooding, deadly monster away off to my left-hand side. This was my first sighting of the edge of the Greenland ice sheet, and as I got a closer look, it was like nothing I had ever witnessed before.

Imagine a typical mountain scene such as the jagged 7000ft peaks of the Alps. Now plonk a thick all-smothering ice blanket on the top of that, one that reaches up to *11,000ft*, and you would begin to get an idea of how massively imposing and all-consuming the ice sheet was, sitting on top of the regular landscape. It was an incredible sight to witness first-hand. Both menacing and forbidding in its vastness, no wonder it commanded high caution and complete respect from anyone who ventured near its blinding white surface. Fortunately, I was able to remain flying over the low foothills, south-west of the ice sheet; hills which now helped to put the 'green' back in Greenland by beginning to sustain scrubby vegetation in their more sheltered valleys.

I had been given information that a local reindeer herder operated in this area, and sure enough I was soon able to locate his farmstead. I was particularly interested in him because I was also told that he flew an enclosed cockpit, two-seat gyroplane, an Autogyro Calidus. This was a modern descendant of my Autogyro MT-03 machine and I was intrigued to learn that he regularly flew it here in southern Greenland to check the whereabouts of his wide-ranging reindeer herds. Alas there was no sign of life as I passed overhead, so instead of popping in for some *kaffemik kalaallit kaagiat* (Greenlandic coffee and cake) I flew on towards Narsarsuaq.

Approaching the last fjord to cross before the runway, I overflew the carefully preserved ruins of an ancient settlement. I learned later that this was the Viking settlement of Erik Thorvaldsson, better known as Eric the Red, a pioneering first settler in Greenland. The fjord, complete with half a dozen enormous resident icebergs, was also appropriately named Ericsfjord.

The runway at Narsarsuaq was surprisingly enormous. Constructed in 1941 over a period of just six months, it had been urgently required as a stop off point to assist in the numerous transatlantic ferry flights and new aircraft deliveries that were desperately needed to help the war effort in Europe. On landing, I felt a huge wave of relief wash over me that I had successfully managed to push through such a mentally intense and physically challenging flight. Although delighted to be once more reunited with terra firma, I was also absolutely exhausted.

As I arrived outside the terminal, I was greeted to some most welcome news; Sergey had finally been located. Information was patchy, but I eventually heard the full details.

About halfway into his six-hour crossing, disaster struck. His helicopter suffered a catastrophic failure of its drivetrain system, and Sergey immediately knew he was in deep trouble. Without rotor lift he was no longer able to sustain level flight and was forced to make a controlled ditching down into the Davis Strait. To add to his troubles, the sea surface was blanketed with the same thick sea fog that had hindered me a few days earlier. The aircraft had sunk pretty quickly, but he was extraordinarily fortunate as he managed to swim towards and then clamber up onto a nearby iceberg. After a bitterly cold wait of some *36 hours,* he was eventually located and picked up by the Canadian Coast Guard Ship, *CCGS Pierre Radisson.* During his enforced stay on the iceberg, Sergey had had to endure bone-chilling temperatures and on three occasions scare off curious polar bears, but at least he had survived to tell his story.

Although he had lost his aircraft, I was pleased and greatly relieved about Sergey's successful rescue. Likewise, I was also pleased to have made it all the way to the southern tip of Greenland. But at the same time, I was constantly worried by the thought that to move on from here, I still had to fly up Greenland's eastern coastline. This was as equally hostile as the terrain I'd just struggled over, with the added element of being brutally exposed to the full forces of the North Atlantic Ocean.

Still, those jolly thoughts needed to be put aside for another day; for now, I was just glad to be safely on the ground.

The first-ever attempt to cross the mighty Atlantic Ocean in a gyroplane had truly begun!

27–29 July 2015: Narsarsuaq, Greenland (non-flying days)

Having just had such an anxious and physically taxing flight, I was quite relieved to learn that I was now going to have to wait in Narsarsuaq for a few days. Bureaucracy had once again reared its head, this time I had to wait for some necessary permits from Denmark to allow me to continue my flight through Greenland and the Faroe Islands. I looked forward to a few days of exploring the area by foot as considering its remote location, this could perhaps be both my first and last opportunity to do so.

On first arrival I had been directed to find accommodation at the Hotel Narsarsuaq, which was just a short walk from the small airport terminal. Having recently spent the night in Qikiqtarjuaq, where the ambiance was of a remote, comparatively spartan, shared bunkhouse, I was pleasantly surprised with what I found here; it felt just like a conventional hotel, and was easily as comfortable as anywhere else in northern Europe. On checking-in, I surmised that the price would probably reflect the more opulent surroundings, but again to my surprise, it was the same as any regular mid-range hotel back home.

I realised later however, while watching one of the few weekly scheduled flights arrive and disembark its passengers, that Narsarsuaq acted as the hub airport for many Greenland sightseeing tours, visiting TV documentary film crews and scientific expeditions. This presumably explained how the moderate sized hotel was able to maintain its profitably high occupancy rates, even in such a remote location.

The arrival of a big plane full of European passengers was the highlight of the day (or even week) for everyone involved with the airport. For me, it was a fascinating process to watch. All morning, Air Greenland helicopters had been ferrying passengers into Narsarsuaq from various pick-up points in surrounding settlements. Each helicopter would spill out a motley bunch of regular tourists, adventurers and scientists. Dishevelled and weather-beaten in appearance, they all looked to have been *out there* and roughing it for quite some time.

Huge piles of expedition kit were also unloaded and then, like a busy city taxi rank, the helos were quickly off again to pick up their next fare.

'People-watching' in such situations was often entertaining and I soon picked out the real stars of this particular show – Greenland's expedition guides – turning up to meet the newly disembarked passengers from the big plane. I was already familiar with the roles of mountain guides, climbing instructors, ski guides and outdoor pursuit leaders the world over, and they all clearly possessed an aura of complete and utter expertise in their various fields. For the students or beginner groups in their care, they would consistently make difficult things look easy, and challenging things look simple.

Guides that I'd often seen in the fashionable parts of the Alps or Rockies had adopted a certain dishevelled, outdoor-hardened look to project a level of expert prowess (think permanent sunglasses, rough hands and weather-beaten faces). This subtly fuelled the assumption by their students that they must have presumably achieved a lot of *extreme adventuring* to get themselves in that state, therefore they must also be *really expert* at what they do.

But here, while sitting on a low wall and looking on in Narsarsuaq, I realised that all those outdoor heroes I'd seen before actually now seemed a bit mediocre and second-rate, when compared with these Greenland guides. As with Darwin excitedly discovering his new variants of Galapagos finches, I now studied this new-found subspecies of the genus *Homo-adventurus* in finer detail.

The distinctive 'signature plumage' of both the males and females displayed a high degree of sun-faded, rugged, ripped, repaired and generally extreme-weather ravaged clothing and equipment. Their craggy facial features had knowledge of hurricane blizzards, frostbite and snow blindness written all over them. If the surrounding icy fjords had not been absolutely freezing, they could probably have added *shark wrangler* to their impressive CVs. Most were aged in their mid-30s, though their windburned faces and gnarly, beaten up bodies (no doubt scored and scarred by years of harsh rope handling and polar bear tag team wrestling) made them appear much older. But to look at them, these really were the top people at the pinnacle of their most extreme game.

And befitting the uber-harsh, challenging climate that was the Greenland guide's domain, I have little doubt that, just like a hungry polar bear, they could probably have eaten a whole suave and sophisticated Alpine guide for breakfast...

* * *

With no prospects of further flight for a couple of days, I took a stroll around the settlement. A small museum explained the wartime history of the runway construction and gave the buildings much more context as I wandered around. The sky was blue and the visibility crystal clear, allowing me stunning views towards the surrounding mountains. There was no sign of the misty murk and fog that I had battled with the previous day. "Perfect for flying," I thought, and then quickly put it out of my head. There was no point in having such thoughts with the spirit-sapping, time-eroding grip of government bureaucracy currently in charge.

As I walked down a dusty gravel road towards the small harbour, the afternoon sun beat down with surprising heat. It was amazing, here I was at the southern tip of Greenland, just a few hundred miles outside the Arctic Circle, and I was actually at risk of getting sunburnt. The wild grasses and colourful spring flowers all danced in unison in the light sea breeze. And as had happened in Chittagong, it again reminded me very much of childhood caravan holidays on the west coast of Ireland. Though I never imagined then, while as a child looking out west over the deep blue Atlantic, that I would one day, a full 50 years into the future, get to stand on one of its most beautiful opposite shores and be able to reflect on such things.

In that moment, looking out over Ericsfjord with its resident icebergs floating in the bay, I felt exceedingly happy and privileged to be in such a special and remote place. It had been a mammoth achievement to reach this far, but deep down I also knew there was much more difficult flying still ahead before I would be fully done with crossing the Atlantic.

The small pier and rocky harbour inlet looked as if it hadn't changed much since its creation. I thought of its rich history: the number of resupply ships it must have received during the war; fishing boats that had sought shelter; and scientific expedition ships that had tied up at the dockside so their crews could tinker and calibrate their hi-tech instruments.

It currently had a visiting yacht berthed alongside, one that had sailed all the way across from Denmark. It appeared to have just arrived, judging by the amount of clothing and sleeping bags that had been strung out around the rigging to air in the sunlight and drive out the damp. I chatted with some of the crew, quizzing them on how they had found the ice conditions offshore and how they had tiptoed their way through the clumps of pack ice that littered the coastline. A sailing yacht at least had the advantage of having a tall mast, one which could be climbed to allow a better view of finding a clear path through the small, low lying growler icebergs. I suppose these days, a camera drone sent aloft might further improve the view.

They were equally curious about my journey and gawped in disbelief when I showed a photo of how small *Roxy* was. They struggled to believe that a craft of her size and apparent fragility, could even contemplate crossing the Atlantic and be capable of transiting the world. And yet here I was, living proof!

30 July 2015: Narsarsuaq, Greenland – Kulusuk, Greenland

Eventually after days of waiting, the Danish paperwork was finally resolved, and I was free to move on. Fuel had been easy to source; there was a small petrol stand just across the road from the airfield that allowed me to push *Roxy* directly to the pumps to fill up. On arrival I had managed to find hangarage, but on opening the doors I was quite surprised to find an Autogyro Calidus parked up inside. It apparently belonged to the reindeer herder whose farm I had buzzed on the way in. Rather conveniently, it seemed that he could commute to the airport in his gyro before heading off on a commercial flight elsewhere. A rather novel, jet set life, Greenland style!

Considering the extremely poor visibility I had endured down the west coast, the weather up the east coast could not have been better. Blue skies and visibility of 100 miles plus, allowed me to relax a little as I trundled down the runway. To add further to my optimistic mood the cold, crisp conditions at sea level provided plenty of air density for *Roxy*'s rotor and propeller to bite into. I hoped it was going to be a good day in the air.

My first priority for the flight was to safely clear the southern tip of the Greenland ice sheet and reach the east coast. I could have elected to fly completely around the southern shoreline, but to do so would have added considerable total distance onto the already lengthy leg up to Kulusuk. So instead, I decided on a corner-cutting compromise, to fly directly over the extreme southern edge of the ice sheet.

It sounded OK in principle, yet I knew the ice reached up to 11,000ft in the interior of Greenland. Conveniently however, especially for my open cockpit, the southern tip of the ice sheet tapered down to a much more manageable 7500ft. Furthermore, by planning to overfly near the edge of the ice, I could also remain constantly in sight of the surrounding ice-free rocky peaks. This was essential to maintain my sense of spatial awareness. There have been many past instances where pilots have become wholly disorientated while attempting to make a transit of this ice sheet. The brilliant white surface of its unique landscape can appear to be totally featureless and blinding. In such conditions a pilot could easily lose their sense of depth perspective and no longer perceive at what height they are actually flying. Some have even reported crashing down onto the ice when they had thought they were perhaps still 500ft above it. To avoid such a calamity, I ensured my route always gave me a peripheral view of a non-ice horizon, or at the very least, a discernible local feature such as a rocky ridgeline or outcrop.

I was amazed at how quickly the mountains climbed skywards from sea level. Within 20 minutes I was clearing jagged 6000ft peaks, yet still I had to look up even higher to see the summit of the ice sheet. Incredibly, it was *that* massive. As I eventually reached and flew on over the top, I was able to scan the full horizon off to the north for the first time, brutal yet beautiful in equal measure and like no other place on Earth. The smooth white frozen snow and ice stretched away off into the distance as far as I could see. Momentarily I suffered the unsettling sensation of a full whiteout condition as there was literally nothing for me to directly focus on. Fortunately, it was only a fleeting disorientation as I quickly glanced southward to reset my spatial awareness, focussing in on some deep dark crevasses in the ice and a rocky ridge beyond.

Soon enough I was dropping down the eastern side of the ice towards the deep blue Atlantic Ocean that sparkled on the far horizon. Descending through the saw-toothed foothills, each of the valleys was home to a wide and comparatively dirty-looking glacier. I followed one down to the coast and marvelled at the long lines of eroded rubble and debris formed on the glacier's surface and especially along its edges. Its texture reminded me rather oddly of striped toothpaste or a stick of candy. At the point where the glacier terminated and met the sea in a long fjord, there was an impressive iceberg factory. Unfortunately however, as had happened in northern Canada, I was again unable to catch sight of any icebergs calving, despite there being plenty of shattered icy evidence floating around in the water, to show that some had done so very recently.

It was sobering to think that the infamous iceberg that went on to sink the *Titanic* probably began its fateful journey after being calved from one of these very factories.

With the ice sheet safely negotiated, I was relieved to be once again down at a *slightly* warmer altitude of 1500ft. The flight northwards along Greenland's east coast was absolutely stunning. I crossed numerous fjords and enjoyed witnessing the ultra-slow motion traffic jams of massive icebergs haplessly careering into and past each other on their way to the open ocean. Sometimes there were big pile ups where perhaps a barren, storm-ravaged island had got in the way of these restlessly shifting isles of ice. Other times, a few solitary icebergs appeared to be trapped and helpless in some backwater inlet, no doubt pushed that way by the wind and tides. Their only final means of escape was perhaps to slowly melt their way out.

Overall, the whole scene looked chaotic, with big blocks of ice strewn about the shoreline in a most haphazard way. Very occasionally, a reasonably flat gravelly beach area might appear, but it too was then littered by big blocks of ice that had been washed ashore. I was acutely aware throughout the whole flight of where, if anywhere, I could possibly attempt an emergency landing. As with the west coast, I was very uncertain of setting down successfully anywhere, and that once down, I'd have absolutely no chance of taking off again.

As if my constant background anxiety level wasn't high enough, I was now also in prime polar bear country. I kept a close lookout for any signs of them down below, but in such a chaotic icy landscape, I could plainly see how evolution had equipped the great white bear with the perfect camouflage. Peering down, ever hopeful of a sighting, I was often tricked into thinking that every other ice block was bear-shaped. I think the only way I could have positively identified a *real* bear would have been if one of the ice blocks had stretched its limbs and had started to prowl.

Fortunately, the rest of the flight was uneventful, with the worst hardship being the extreme cold. After a bone-chilling flight time of 6hrs 5mins, I was certainly glad to finally touch down on the rough gravel strip of Kulusuk. As was becoming a familiar reaction in these northern latitudes, there was local amazement that such a small open cockpit aircraft was capable of flying in such a challenging environment.

* * *

The hotel in Kulusuk was similar to the comfortable set up in Narsarsuaq, however a consignment of Japanese tourists had, alas, already booked it out solid. Though as luck would have it, I was soon given a much more interesting alternative, as one of the Innuit airport staff very kindly offered to put me up overnight as a B&B guest in his family home. The family spoke very little English but, as with my Saudi Arabian garage friends, we were able to communicate just fine with a few common words and sign language. Kulusuk village was a short drive from the airport and consisted of maybe 60 or so brightly coloured, prefabricated houses, all perched above the ground within a boulder-strewn landscape.

We dropped off my bags and I met my Innuit host family. While hot tea was being poured, several pre-school kids checked me out cautiously from behind the furniture. The atmosphere was a curious mix of traditional Innuit hospitality blended with a subtle Danish influence. A selection of foods came to the table, everything from dried fish to sliced cheese. I mused that the cheese, complete with hand slicer tool, *must* have been a direct cultural import from Denmark; there were definitely no cows to milk in this part of the world!

Fed and watered, I was then asked a question.

"Would you like to go out on a trip in the family boat?"

Keen to experience as much local Innuit culture as possible, I immediately accepted the offer. However, I soon realised that the trip wasn't going to be a pleasure cruise, it was necessary to maintain a traditional way of life. In the long winter months, my host operated two dog sled teams. The dog teams were the fastest way to commute up and down the frozen coastline in order to visit hunting grounds and smaller outlying settlements, and unlike snowmobiles, they didn't need to drink extremely expensive petrol or require any spare parts or servicing. However, during the short summer season whilst there was no sled pulling to be done, the dogs still needed to be regularly fed. And with no handy supermarket stocked up with tins of dog food in these parts, there was therefore an essential need to go hunting.

Now, I am not generally keen on going out to hunt and shoot things, especially if it is only for sport, but this was vastly different. This was for survival and the maintenance of the indigenous Innuit culture; everything that would be hunted and killed was needed for a valid purpose.

My host walked me down to the small pier, where his friend and regular hunting partner was already preparing the open-decked 20ft boat. Aluminium hulled, it had a small fore cabin and an open wheelhouse. I glanced aft and saw a surprisingly hefty outboard engine, though I was soon to learn why it needed so much horsepower.

Trying to be useful, I stood on the aft deck to cast off the stern line and soon the three of us were speeding out of the small ice-free harbour. Turning out into the bay, I quickly realised the protected harbour was actually the *only* place that was ice-free. The rest of the entire bay was a motorway pile-up of huge icebergs, interspersed with great slabs of thick pack ice and slushy semi-submerged growlers. To my untrained eye, there appeared to be no way through this jumbled up icy maze. Incredibly however, my host then opened up to full throttle, speeding at full pelt towards a narrow gap between two hulking lumps of ice, weighing easily a couple of tonnes each.

"Surely that gap's not wide enough!" I thought.

Amazingly, with only a couple of glancing scrapes off the aluminium hull, we threaded and ricocheted our way through the gap and out into another little patch of open water beyond. Chopping off the throttle, we then came to an abrupt halt. My host, clearly a highly skilled boat-handler then scanned ahead looking for the next gap. Meanwhile, the two-tonne blocks we had just squeezed past, now closed together, shutting off the gap between them.

"Help! We're trapped!" my mind raced.

Yet I needn't have worried. All the ice around us was constantly on the move, pushed around by the strong swirling tidal currents at work below the surface. Dodging through this icy traffic in rush hour, time and again we would dash through a gap, pause, see another gap open up and then dash through again to reach yet more safe open water beyond. At any moment, I worried that we may have become stuck, mid-gap so to speak, in which case our aluminium craft would have formed the squishy filling in an ice block sandwich. Only my host's expertise in reading the mood of the ice, along with his nifty boat-handling skills, averted any of these potential crushing disasters.

By using this fits-and-starts method, we soon reached out into the middle of the ice-strewn bay. The engine was then cut and silence descended. Or nearly so, as the restless ice still constantly groaned and creaked around us.

All was quiet, and it was time for phase two. The three of us scanned the surrounding low-lying ice and pockets of open flat water. We remained silent, watching intently for a distant tell-tale black triangle that would occasionally pop up and break the surface. The first mate spotted one and urgently tapped my host on the shoulder, leading us all to follow his eagle-eyed stare at the water. A seal had poked its nose above the surface to catch its breath while it was busy hunting for fish below the ice. The hunter now became the hunted, as our expert helmsman suddenly now became an expert rifleman instead. He steadied his well-worn .22 rifle on the roof of the wheelhouse, aimed and took his shot.

Crack! A direct hit, first time. Swiftly the sharpshooter stowed his rifle and fired up the engine, racing as fast as possible to the spot where the seal had been. The first mate made himself ready, with a sharply pointed gaff boat hook in hand, to reach down and retrieve the seal carcass.

The need for such speed surprised me as I had kept well out of the way during the whole proceedings. It was later explained that as soon as a seal was shot, its body would immediately start to sink. Failing to quickly hook it with the gaff, the catch would be lost, and we would have ended up "Giving one back to the fish" as they put it.

We carried on in this manner, dodging the ice around the bay, for the rest of the evening, making full use of the long hours of daylight. Three seals were shot, with one of them then being lost on retrieval. At one point, I was rapidly tapped on the shoulder and urged to look up ahead of the boat. A small Minke whale had just surfaced and was heading our way. It slowly came closer, linking a number of small open water 'puddles' together to take a breath in each one. It was truly marvellous to witness such a wild, yet gentle, giant creature so close to our boat. For now thankfully the whale was safe, and I was immediately glad that there was still so much protective ice trapped in the bay. Later in the season there would be much more open water than ice and by tradition, the local Innuit would then organise a fleet of their small boats to take on the hunting of such large prey together.

Heading back to the pier, I suddenly realised how tired I was. I had flown six hours from Narsarsuaq that morning and then embarked on another three-hour boat trip. Sleep came especially easily that night. I would need plenty. The next day was the North Atlantic.

31 July 2015: Kulusuk, Greenland – Reykjavik, Iceland

I hitched a ride back to the airport on the back of a quadbike. The weather looked settled once more, which always helped with my overall morale.

I was about to leave Greenland and therefore had to clear international flight formalities. While waiting for flight plan approval to come through, I had an interesting chat with the Danish ATC in the tower. Whilst I was flying eastbound, he told me of some of the dangers that long-distance westbound flyers had experienced. A surprising number of pilots transiting westward would consider arriving at Kulusuk as having conquered the Atlantic. They would think they had flown the hardest part, across the open ocean and were now safely over land again. This assumption according to the ATC, was a big mistake.

Having thought they were over the worst, from Kulusuk they would then relax their guard and merrily set off, up over the ice sheet, heading directly for Nuuk. The ice sheet, as previously explained, is a huge silent and deadly monster waiting to bite any naively optimistic aviator who would dare cross its path. Numerous such ill-prepared pilots had ended up on the ice and in need of rescue over the years. It was a sobering thought, and I later made my own pre-flight preparations with double extra care.

Right then, this was it! Taking a few deep breaths, I steeled myself for my Atlantic challenge. Take-off from the gravel airstrip was smooth and steady, much as I hoped the whole flight would be. On climb-out I overflew the village, knowing it was the last civilisation I would see until Iceland. This flight would be 99% over water, and a cold, grey, uninhabited North Atlantic water at that.

Heading offshore, I observed that the messy confusion of icebergs and ice blocks from the bay continued stretching far out to sea. Knowing it was not robust enough to allow a safe landing, I was keen to see the ice pack disperse as soon as possible and for the ocean surface to revert to open water. But in the end, I had to apprehensively wait for a full *100 nautical miles* for this to happen, making this by far the single most treacherous stretch of water that I crossed during the entire world flight (and why this crux moment made it onto the front cover of the book...). Eventually to my great relief, the icy menace below finally broke up and melted away, and once safely out of the ice zone, I picked up a strong tailwind and started to make good progress towards Reykjavik.

I began to settle into the long flight and reduced all my actions in the cockpit to the minimum. In such a long cruise over an ocean, with very stable non-turbulent airflow around me, I adopted my familiar routine. I was able to hunker down in my seat and semi-meditate; maximum energy conservation combined with a calm state of mind. My brain nonetheless didn't switch off completely, as I was flying an aircraft after all, so I continued to maintain a background sense of alertness. Had I detected anything unusual, either inside or outside the cockpit, instantly I would have been fully alert again to investigate.

In such a steady Zen-like state of mind, time and distance tended to pass by quickly.

The miles ticked by on the GPS as I cruised along at around 1500ft, and I had little really to focus on ahead apart from some distant cloud formations on the horizon. Far removed from any trading routes, there was no shipping traffic to be seen below. I was completely alone with the ocean.

Suddenly there was movement. Something on the surface caught my eye, a flash of something white. There it was again! Could it be? Yes, it was. It *definitely* was! My first-ever whale sighting from the air.

"Thar she blows! Whale ahoy, me hearties!" I shouted.

I had spotted the distinctive water-spout plume of a large and solitary whale. I was around the midpoint of my crossing, nearly 200 nautical miles from the nearest land in any direction. Acutely aware of how remote and isolated I was out here in mid-ocean, I knew this was definitely no place for any fancy acrobatics. But I simply had to get a closer look at such a magnificent creature. I throttled back the engine and altered course.

The whale, steadily ploughing its way northwards, was huge. Given I was cutting across its path, west to east, the chances of us meeting like this were exceedingly slim. Had I been flying even just a mile either side of my current track, we would never have met.

Circling around overhead, I studied its movement. A sizable Atlantic Ocean swell was running, north to south, and so the whale was clearly having to swim hard against the oncoming waves to make good progress. As I looked on in amazement, I could see that it was so big that the waves were breaking up and over its head, quite similar to how water breaks over the bow of a submarine when it is running along on the surface. Indeed, the whale's whole body was a similar shape to a submarine, though of course without the conning tower!

They both shared a similar streamlined hydrodynamic design, except for one noticeable difference; this particular submarine was *flexing* in the middle. The powerful kicking action of its tail flukes was causing a rise and fall motion, which travelled the entire length of its backbone. I was filled with both compassion and respect for this unassuming gentle giant of the sea, especially as it was having to work so very hard against the challenging swell.

It was such an honour to see it in its own natural environment. I had only ever seen large whales before on TV wildlife documentaries, and they were generally filmed basking in a sheltered bay somewhere, surrounded by whale watchers. In such places they often seemed to surface and take a relaxed, leisurely breath only once every few minutes. Here, out in the restless mid-Atlantic, my whale appeared to be anything but relaxed, it was breathing hard, with a huge exhalation waterspout blowing up every 10 seconds. Ever conscious that time was ticking on and that I still had another 200 miles of ocean to cross, I bade my fellow Atlantic voyager farewell and wished it good luck for the rest of its solitary journey.

As I banked around to get back on track for Reykjavik, I reflected on why the whale's breathing rate had been quite so rapid. It then quickly dawned on me that, of course, it was a mammal. Just like us humans, it was breathing hard because it was exercising hard. I had fortuitously witnessed the normally unseen, unglamorous part of a whale's job. All that fooling around in some shallow Alaskan bay for the TV cameras, didn't quite reflect the lonely graft needed to cross thousands of ocean miles during regular migrations. Little wonder then that they do a lot of singing to themselves on the way.

***

Back on course, things soon settled down again, though I was now increasingly aware that cloud cover, in various layers and levels up ahead, was gradually becoming more joined up and organised. Initially it was well broken, and a patchy layer hung consistently around 800ft to 1000ft above the ocean. This posed little issue as I flew along above it at around 1500ft and I easily maintained constant sight of the surface through the many holes in the cloud below me. However, as the miles ticked by, a more solid layer of cloud began to slowly form above me at around 3000ft. I gradually found myself flying between the layers, still in clear visibility and, with constant sight of the surface, but now also with a growing sense of unease. Gradually the cloud ceiling above me was becoming thicker, its base dropping from 3000ft to 2000ft with occasional wisps of low cloud coming down to 1500ft.

I was forced to fly a bit lower to remain in clear air between the cloud sandwich. Minutes passed and I apprehensively flew on. The broken cloud base below me slowly began to infill and thicken, which was worrying as the visible gaps through to the ocean were gradually getting smaller and less frequent. Legally, flying VFR (Visual Flight Rules), I needed to maintain clear sight of the surface at all times and I certainly didn't want to end up flying blind and suffering total whiteout conditions within the clouds, with no visual reference as to which way was up and which way was down.

Soon, it was command decision time. My two options were to either stay within the sandwich and hope that the two cloud layers, above and below, would helpfully maintain their separation, or to throttle back, lose altitude and then dip down to continue my flight wholly under the lower layer. As the second option appeared to be the safest overall, I carefully considered the remaining holes in the cloud below me, and fortunately the base of the lower level looked to be consistently around 800ft from the ocean. This was at least some good news, even while the rest of the cloud column above it had fluctuated.

Then suddenly, while checking over my shoulder to size up a potentially useable gap, I was caught unaware...

WHAM! I was immediately plunged into some big, big trouble!

I couldn't see a thing. I was surrounded by cloud. I realised that while looking below, a finger of low hanging cloud from the upper layer had now suddenly engulfed me. I momentarily froze. It was one of the worst disorientating situations I had ever experienced.

If I had been in a fixed-wing aircraft, flying VFR, this could have quickly developed into a grave and deadly situation. Without knowledge of the horizon's orientation, a pilot could easily fly their plane into a bad attitude (angle), perhaps by flying on its side or even upside down, or perhaps by entering an unrecoverable stall or spin. I immediately attempted a 180-degree turn to see if I could fly back out the way I came in. But it was no good. Either I was not fully at 180 degrees, or more likely, the cloud had further swirled in and had cut off any rear escape route.

"Help!"

In a matter of seconds, I had gone from normal flight to a toe-clenching, blind panic.

"Don't Panic. Stay calm. You've got this under control," I reassured myself. I had one trump card left to play…

These were terrifyingly dire circumstances for a conventional light aircraft, but I *wasn't in* a conventional aircraft – I was in a gyroplane. And if there is one aspect of a gyro that trumps all other types of fixed, rotary or flex-winged flying machines, it is that it cannot stall. My plan for surviving this potentially life-threatening situation, was to actually *do very little.* I simply pulled back the throttle to idle, held my nerve, and waited. With lack of forward thrust from the engine, the airspeed indicator quickly fell back to zero. Momentarily, I was stopped mid-air, still engulfed within the cloud, but holding stationary. I closely watched my altimeter as it gradually started to show that I was losing height. I knew I was still in autorotation, but effectively I was now also slowly falling out of the sky. I felt reassured that as I was over the empty ocean, at least I didn't have to worry about blindly hitting any other local aircraft, tall radio mast or hidden mountain top in the same vicinity.

All I had to do was wait… 1200ft… 1100ft… 1000ft… 900ft… 800ft…

Where was the cloud base? Had the clouds merged with low mist or a surface fog bank? Would the next thing I spot be the water surface at only a few feet below me? Should I prepare for immediate ditching into the North Atlantic?

I had to calm my mind… I *knew* there was a good air gap below the clouds to the surface, but was that definite? Just wait…

Huzzah!

At 750ft I suddenly popped out into clear air again beneath the clouds, with the ocean gloriously and triumphantly stretching out for miles in every direction. Such a relief washed over me. A moment of distraction had resulted in several anxious minutes of controlled panic. I throttled up and got back on course for Iceland.

With over 100 nautical miles still to go, I now resigned myself to completing the rest of the flight skimming low over the waves. The thickening cloud base remained stubbornly low and gradually dropped further, to only 400ft at times. Worried that I might at any point still encounter low mist or fog ahead, it felt an awfully long run in towards Reykjavik. As I finally sighted landfall up ahead, to my pleasant surprise, the cloud base lifted and the clouds began to break up. I touched down with welcome relief that my first leg of the Atlantic crossing was over, fortunately without too many minutes of extreme drama, though the fickle weather en route had really tested my resolve.

I was whacked. The nervous tension of the flight– firstly crossing the daunting pack ice field, then suddenly being enveloped in cloud and finally having to scud run at about 300ft for the best part of 100 nautical miles – had taken its toll. There would certainly be no flying tomorrow.

1–2 August 2015: Reykjavik, Iceland (non-flying days)

During two non-flying days, due to weather, I was fortunate to be assisted in Reykjavik by a surprise local contact, a fellow Northern Irish pilot John McClean. Many years previously he had met and married a local girl and set up home in Iceland, but still made regular trips back to the Emerald Isle to see family and friends. John acted as my local guide around many of the classic sights, including the spectacular Gullfoss waterfall, the Silfra Fissure (marking the constantly widening boundary between the Eurasian and North American tectonic plates) and the powerful Strokkur Geyser. Rather appropriately, Strokkur is active nearby the site of Geysir, the original geyser that gave the generic name to all such natural phenomenon around the world. Having narrowly missed Old Faithful blowing its top back in Yellowstone, it now felt conciliatory to witness a similar magnificent display in Iceland instead!

3 August 2015: Reykjavik, Iceland – Egilsstaðir, Iceland

Well rested, I returned once more to the business of flying. Psychologically, I told myself this day would be easier. It was to be a low altitude flight around the southern coast of Iceland, which unlike Greenland, had the added luxury of a major coastal ring road to follow. With blue skies on departure, all looked set for a comparatively undemanding day, however unfortunately yet again, this would later prove to be false optimism.

In a way, I had been spoiled by Greenland. The outstandingly impressive scenery of Iceland now just felt a bit tame in comparison. Spectacular? Undoubtably, yes. The Icelandic landscape was dotted with plenty to marvel at: magnificent waterfalls; evidence of recent lava flows, which had poured out over the countryside; resident mini-ice caps and glaciers; and black sandy beaches. But did it scare me? No, not really when compared to Greenland. Similarly, I made the mistake to wrongly assume that the weather, like the 'less scary' landscape, would also remain relatively benign.

As I flew along hugging the southern coastline, I ran into my first problem. A sinister-looking fog bank had been lurking just offshore for the previous 20 miles or so, and then it unfortunately chose to team up with a thick layer of low cloud that was descending out of the nearby coastal hills. Once again, I found myself in a sandwich between a fog bank and a low cloud base. Only now, unlike being far out at sea, I had the added complication of navigating around abrupt craggy headlands and wide coastal valleys. The headlands especially, rising sharply from the sea and disappearing into the low cloud, now became my main concern.

I battled on for a while, each headland eventually providing an escape route through to the next bay beyond. But soon enough I then came to a real showstopper. There seemed to be no way around this particular cloud-blanketed headland. To make matters worse, a stiff headwind had also picked up making progress slow and bumpy close to the turbulent cliffs. I throttled back and semi-hovered, making full use of the stiff breeze. I studied the swirling mist and clouds before me. Momentarily sections of rockface would disappear, while other parts of the cliffs reappeared. It was an extraordinarily confusing, fluid situation.

At one point, I saw brightness beyond the cloud out to sea and manoeuvred out that way, only to have that potential doorway firmly shut again a few moments later. I doubled back inshore again, now fully cursing the fickleness of the weather in these parts. Why couldn't it just behave normally? I was frustrated; the idea that sea fog could even *exist* while the wind was blowing at 30 knots seemed quite alien. I was used to summertime fog appearing back home only in very calm conditions. There, as soon as any light breeze picked up, the fog would rapidly disperse, or the sun would eventually burn it off. Here, the fog was already blowing at 30 knots and the air temperature was exceptionally chilly. There was absolutely no chance of the sun's warmth helping me out at all.

I cautiously checked out a more inland route, and as luck would have it the troublesome headland did not continuously join up with the higher inland hills. There was a small gap in a steep-sided valley, which had been formed by a gushing stream. I dipped down closer to have a look, and yes, a chink of clear daylight existed through the mist ahead. I made a dash for it and emerged on the other side into a completely different scene! The sky opened wide and I was back in clear air. Looking back, I could see what was happening; the stiff breeze was piling the cloud up against the back of the headland and then it was also spilling over the top. Once again, I suddenly felt so small and insignificant, battling as I was, against the huge natural forces at work. Still, my plucky little gyro and I had paused mid-air, and then at the right moment jinked through a narrow valley and hole in the clouds, something that few other aircraft types could have even attempted. Our reward was the welcome return of blue skies ahead.

Soon I passed the seaward edge of the Vatnajökull glacier. Unlike the high glaciers I had passed by in northern Canada and Greenland, this one was much more low lying. Being summertime, the melt water was streaming off its edge, and I was surprised to see how chaotic and *messy* the whole scene was. Big boulders and chunks of melting ice were strewn across the dark black sand. The ice surface itself had a dirty greyish black appearance; it all looked like some massive unorganised scrapheap of natural materials. I was however pleased to see that the whole area, although unkempt and scruffy, was devoid of any sign of human contamination.

I then approached the famous Jökulsárlón Glacier Lagoon, an almost landlocked lake that allowed its adjoining glacier to calf icebergs. The bergs, not quite so large as Greenland's finest, then floated around in the lake. Looking down as I passed by, I could see that the coastal main road used a bridge to cross the lake's narrow outlet estuary as it flowed into the open sea. The newly formed icebergs were trapped inside the lagoon as the bridge was blocking their seaward exit route. It looked like an *iceberg zoo,* with about a dozen or so prize specimens kept under close surveillance from the constant stream of camera-wielding roadside tourists. The only way that a captive berg could ever hope to escape, both the tourist hoards and its own captivity, was to melt away sufficiently within the lagoon and then limbo dance its way under the road bridge – flushed out to freedom at last!

I flew on, pleased that the visibility had now picked up significantly. The downside was that the stiff headwind had also freshened. Over miles and miles of flat estuary sands and shallow inlets, I flew as low as I could to try to minimise the headwind. Skimming along at only 10ft off the exposed windswept beaches and flying at 90 mph airspeed, at times I was barely making 40 mph over the ground. Despite it being a bitterly cold wind, and that it would now take me much longer to reach my destination, hunkered down in my seat I still was happy. I was steadily progressing eastward, albeit painfully slowly; but every mile flown was another mile closer to finally conquering the Atlantic.

4–6 August 2015: Egilsstaðir, Iceland (non-flying days)

The fickleness of the weather skirting around southern Iceland had definitely caught me out. I had naturally assumed when planning the Atlantic crossing, that the hardest sections would be out over the remote ocean. I had thought that flying through Iceland, with the reassurance of civilisation close by and having the coastal road to follow, would be by comparison, a relatively easy flight.

I had of course been proved wrong. So I resolved that for the next leg, from Iceland across to the Faroe Islands, I needed to have as much certainty as possible regarding the weather. Of greatest concern was the wind direction. On the previous flight I had battled for several hours with a strong headwind, but I had emergency options, whether alternate airfields, or even the ability to set down on the coastal ring road if necessary. Once committed to reaching the Faroes, beyond any possible point of no return to Iceland, there would unfortunately be no plan B.

I would have to reach the Faroes and successfully land there or face getting my feet wet.

A healthy tailwind was therefore essential, and I had no option but to patiently sit, study the weather charts and wait in Egilsstaðir for the correct wind conditions to materialise. It took three days.

7 **August 2015: Egilsstaðir, Iceland – Vágar, Faroe Islands**

With the promise of a good stiff breeze behind me, north-west backing to south-west, and with clear skies forecast right across to the Faroes, I was all set. The downside of the wind direction and strength was that my point of no return to Iceland would arrive relatively soon after coasting out over the open ocean, though on the upside at least if all went well, I would reach the Faroes as fast as possible.

The crossing was, as hoped for, quite uneventful. The main highlight was spotting more whales. These were in two groups and judging on the separation of their waterspouts, I estimated four to six whales in each pod. They were noticeably smaller than the large solitary whale that I had seen crossing the Denmark Strait between Greenland and Iceland.

I later read up on the migratory habits of various whale species in the North Atlantic and the large solitary one I saw earlier may well have been a blue whale, as they often migrated solo in this area in the summer months. How fantastic I reflected, to have perhaps just witnessed the largest creature on Earth, right from the comfort of my very own gyroplane armchair!

Some 20 miles out from making landfall with Vágar, the island where the airport sits in the Faroe Islands archipelago, I began to prepare for my upcoming landing. Squeezed into a steep-sided valley that runs down into a deep fjord, the airport runway was surrounded by high sheer cliffs and mountains. With relatively few options to fit a flat airfield into the mountainous landscape, the alignment of the runway was compromised as it had to comply with the topography of the area. It therefore ran along the length of the valley bottom. Confined within such a restrictive landscape, there was little flexibility regarding the actual prevailing wind direction, and this meant that all inbound traffic had to approach either from the north-west along the line of the fjord, or from the south-east through the steep valley and surrounding mountains.

If the prevailing wind was blowing hard from the south-west, as can often be the case in an Atlantic low-pressure system, then a vicious turbulent crosswind was created within the proximity of the airport. Such conditions, as any pilot would agree, are not for the faint-hearted and making a landing approach into Vágar, even for larger regular commercial airliner traffic, was notorious for sudden gusty crosswinds. Indeed, the landing and take-off conditions are so prohibitive that only one local commercial passenger service, Atlantic Airways, has maintained the regular airlink between the islands and the outside world. And even their pilots, who have extensive local knowledge, often have had to abort landings. At such times it's not been uncommon for passengers to be delayed for days while waiting for stormy conditions to ease.

So, with 20 miles remaining before landfall, I scanned the horizon. There was still no sign of any landmass, and I started to doubt myself.

Had I miscalculated? After nearly four hours of featureless, open ocean flying, had I somehow mis-navigated off course and was now missing the islands completely? Surely the GPS was not giving faulty data. I double-checked that both units agreed with each other. Reassuringly they did and I scanned the horizon ever more keenly. I knew that the highest mountain on the Faroes was nearly 3000ft, so I should have been able to see *something* by now.

Slowly a thin black line appeared on the horizon through the grey cloud-leaden skies ahead. At first, I was confused. "That's not a 3000ft mountain," I thought. But drawing closer it dawned on me that what I was seeing was the base of the sea cliffs on the southern coast of Vágar. Now I was able to make sense of the whole picture.

Unlike the weather on the rest of the flight, the Faroes were cloaked and hidden in a thick blanket of cloud, right down to about 300ft above the waves. It was not a welcome sight, damp grey mists swirled above, while an angry Atlantic swell crashed on the sheer cliffs below – wild and forbidding, it was definitely not somewhere to ditch into the water.

A shiver of realisation suddenly washed over me: I had to now find somewhere to land safely in all of that. There was no alternative – I was in the middle of the Atlantic Ocean and there was nowhere else to land. To make matters worse (could it be any worse?), the wind was now also blowing at 35 knots from the south-west. What had been a helpful tailwind on the crossing from Iceland was now a hinderance due to its turbulent effect over the runway. Not only that, but when the damp Atlantic airflow off the ocean hit the steep sea cliffs of Vágar, the rapidly rising air formed a bank of perpetual clouds at only 300ft above sea level. As I watched, I could see the clouds rapidly forming and then being swept up and over the hills, much like a standing wave. I immediately knew that in these conditions, the clouds were not going to magically be blown clear of the hilltops any time soon. This weather was going to continue all day.

Only I didn't have all day to hang about. I had to find a way to land, somehow.

I made my first call with Vágar ATC, stating that I was now visual with the island and making my continued approach from the west. The controller quickly came back to me to establish our comms, but I also could detect some heightened concern in his voice. He strongly advised me *not* to make an approach to the runway from the west, along the line of the fjord. He informed me that due to the severe gusting crosswind conditions, the fjord was currently beset with violent downdraught squalls rolling in over the hills, which could easily knock a light aircraft out of the sky.

Suddenly I felt very vulnerable – I was airborne but facing a very uncertain landing. The non-instrument, VFR approach to the airport, in such low-lying blanket cloud conditions, had to be made very close to sea level, but now the fjord was deemed too dangerous to fly in.

Thankfully the ATC recognised my dilemma. Calming his voice, he came back to me again.

"So, you are flying in a gyroplane, which I guess is very similar to a helicopter for speed and manoeuvrability, correct?

"Correct," I replied, uncertain where the conversation was leading.

"In that case, don't worry," he said, "We have a *back door* approach for you to use."

"OK...," I tentatively confirmed, but my voice was still a little unsure.

"You will need to trust me on this," he said sensing my hesitancy, "but there is another VFR approach that our own search and rescue and medivac helicopters use in these conditions. I think you should be able to use the same route."

"OK. What do you need me to do?" I replied.

"Continue towards the cliffs on the south side of the island, then fly south-east along the coast for about two miles until you see a waterfall dropping straight down into the sea. You won't be able to miss it. And then let me know when you're there."

"OK. I'll look for the waterfall," I said cautiously.

Slightly concerned but also intrigued at what I was being asked to do, I closed in on the cliffs and then changed course to fly along them. I was at around 300ft, maintaining as much height as possible just below the cloud base. The angry Atlantic swell was crashing on the jagged rocks below. It was not a comfortable place to be.

I flew slowly along the cliff edge, to be sure of not missing the waterfall. I needn't have worried, for as I rounded a prominent headland, there it was! A torrent of water, from a small lake perched on the very edge of the cliffs, was gushing over the rockface and cascading straight down into the sea. Quite a stunning sight. I estimated the vertical drop was around 120ft.

"Tower, Golf Oscar X-ray, OK I have found the waterfall. What do I do next?" I radioed.

"That's great. Now, fly in over the waterfall and along the length of the lake. Don't worry that you can't see anything ahead," came his reply.

I'm thinking... "Help!"

"The lake has a dogleg," he continued, "After you fly about 30 seconds, the valley will turn a corner to your left and you should then see the runway straight ahead of you. The runway here has good visibility."

"OK. I will call when I have the runway in sight, Oscar X-ray," I responded hopefully.

Well, this was going to the most unusual approach to any airport I had ever flown into.

I closed in on the waterfall, dropping down to around 250ft for a less obscured view. I then turned out to seaward slightly so I could get a better look in at the 'entrance'. The waterfall and lake behind it were in a narrow valley, forming the lowest point of the cliffs along this part of the coast. The low cloud base formed an impenetrable lid over the top of the shallow valley floor and gave the impression that I was looking into an enclosed letterbox.

And I was supposed to fly *in there*?! How did I suddenly find myself in this bizarre predicament? I took a deep breath, summoned up what bravado I had left in me and pressed on. It was my only way to safely get down out of this place.

Sure enough, as I looked along the length of the lake, it just appeared to be a blind alley, with no way out at the other end. I just had to trust the controller's last words. I banked *Roxy* over and dropped in to shoot through the opening.

As with all restricted valley flying, I stayed slightly off the centre line, so I could have more room to turn back if I needed an escape route. As always, I was grateful that gyros can turn 180 degrees very tightly. The low ceiling gave me about 200ft of height to fly in between the clouds and the lake.

Thirty seconds felt a long time coming!

Just as I felt that I was running out of lake, thankfully right on cue, a side valley opened to my left and to my great relief there were the leading runway lights straight ahead.

My sense of relief however, was extremely short lived. I still had to land safely while dealing with the strong gusting crosswind. Sharp downdraughts caught me on the final approach, throwing me all over the sky. With rapid reactions on the stick and pedals, I was soon fighting to hold a line towards the runway threshold. My wildly crabbing attitude to compensate for the crosswind was worrying. If I landed at this awkward angle or a gust caught me just at the wrong moment, perhaps thumping me into the tarmac, I could easily have barrel-rolled the aircraft over on touchdown. It just didn't feel right at all.

I called the tower.

"Tower, can you confirm that I am the only traffic on approach," I asked.

"Affirm, there is absolutely no one else up flying here at the moment," came the reply I was hoping for.

"OK, because of the wind direction I am going to have to land this as I see fit. Don't worry on my manoeuvres," I volleyed back.

Now it was my turn to reassure ATC not to worry!

I pulled up from the final approach and overshot the runway, maintaining as best I could about 100ft ground clearance, which was difficult to do in the swirling mist that was now being drawn down from the hills overhead. I banked hard right, hemmed in within the tight confines of the valley surrounding the airport, until I was clear downwind of all the airfield buildings. Banking hard right again brought me low over the main terminal building roof, but crucially, it also lined me up nicely with the taxiway that led out onto the runway beyond. I skimmed the terminal rooftop and then making full use of the strong (but still gusting) headwind, I dropped in as steeply as I could. In a manoeuvre that was similar to the one that I made in Le Touquet, I managed to drop in and land short on the taxiway, directly into wind and just before encroaching out onto the runway. It wasn't pretty or conventional by any means, but considering the conditions I had just flown through, it was the best feeling ever to be safely down on terra firma again.

A very relieved voice came on the radio.

"Golf Yankee Romeo Oscar X-ray. Welcome to Vágar!"

The controller's voice was very calm and matter of fact, but in reality his warm, sunny welcome was very tongue in cheek, as both he and I knew that it had all been quite an edgy ordeal. Given the horrendous conditions, we were both just extremely glad that I had made it down safely.

8–10 August 2015: Vágar, Faroe Islands (non-flying days)

It would now be three days until the weather allowed me to continue the flight. After much needed sleep, I was able to better reflect on just how difficult my landing into Vágar had been. I never expected that in all the 23 countries I had flown through so far, ranging from the Equator right up to the Arctic Circle, that right at the end, on the very last landing in the last port of call before finally regaining UK airspace, I would have to endure the worst landing conditions of the entire expedition. Vágar Airport in the Faroe Islands now held that dubious honour. Just when I thought I could begin to relax, the historic first crossing of the Atlantic by gyroplane almost conquered, Vágar proved to be the *sting in the tail* and I very nearly got badly stung. It proved once again that on a pioneering first flight you simply could not assume any degree of real certainty. At every turn, on every flight, it was always a journey into the unknown. I was on a voyage of self-discovery. My own untried instincts and immediate reactions to such new adversity were all I could rely on. My only certainty was that of my belief in my own abilities to cope with whatever was thrown at me.

Sometimes it worked out fine. Sometimes, as with the lake ditching in Thailand, sadly it didn't.

As with Greenland, the Faroe Islands has strong sovereign links with Denmark. In Greenland, I had been given tremendous local ground support by Dan Rasmussen and now he had also arranged a local contact for me in the Faroes, his *equally tremendous* father, Paetur Rasmussen.

It was wonderful to have local support once again and Paetur gave me a fabulous insight into the make-up of the Faroes. Although not the easiest place to reach, of all the destinations that I had visited so far it was certainly one of the most interesting. Paetur gave me a grand tour of the islands, many of which are linked by bridges and tunnels. As we drove around, the summertime weather remained fairly typical, with grey overcast skies, driving rain and squally high winds. With repeated flashbacks to my recent landing, I was so glad to be on the ground.

The islands gave the impression of clinging on to the ends of the world. Worryingly steep, grass-covered hillsides sloped away from the roadsides down towards the sheer edge of the sea cliffs. Grazing sheep, seemingly not so worried as I was, were dotted about on these slopes. If a gust of wind was to unfoot one, I thought its sure fate would be to just roll and roll downhill until finally plunging over the edge and into the angry crashing surf below. I wondered if all the human residents might equally have been hunkered down, clinging to these remote Atlantic rocks for fear of being blown off into the sea. A gentle stroll along the clifftops here would certainly have had its own unique challenges for sure. Many of the traditional houses that we passed by still had grass roofs, and interestingly even in the capital Tórshavn, some more modern buildings had also adopted a similar style.

We stopped for coffee in a quayside café right by the harbour. It was the first taste of European café culture that I had enjoyed for quite some time, and it was great to soak up the lively chat and buzz all around. Looking out from the window, I noted that the whole of Tórshavn's harbour was packed full of huge oceangoing fishing trawlers, transatlantic yachts and other smaller craft, including an ocean-crossing four-man rowing boat. The latter had just rowed in from the UK a few days before. All shapes and sizes of vessels, and now all confined to port, seeking refuge from the angry seas lying just beyond the breakwater.

Fuelled up with caffeine, we continued our tour and Paetur drove us to visit a small and isolated settlement in a remote valley. It was literally at the end of the road and was reached via a road tunnel through a mountain. Before the tunnel had been constructed the only way to reach the settlement had been by boat (when calm) followed by scaling the sheer cliffs, or by foot up and over the steeply sloping mountain. A sobering thought was that if a death occurred in the village, the coffin bearers had the awkward and difficult task of carrying the coffin up and over the mountain to reach the interior of the island, where there was sufficient depth of soil for burial. Imagining the constant struggle just to live in such isolation was hard enough, never mind also having to face such a struggle in death; and all the while being battered from all sides by the wild extremes of weather.

After two days of carefully monitoring the weather charts, the onward conditions were once more clearing sufficiently for what would be my final lengthy offshore crossing back to the UK. My immediate issue however was more local, as the weather around the airport was proving much less cooperative.

I returned to the airfield to check on *Roxy* and to organise the refuelling. There was a good length of daylight and with only an estimated four-hour flight to reach Scotland, I was hopeful that I might have got a weather window to leave Vágar before mid-afternoon. Alas it was not to be, as around lunchtime I was introduced to a medivac helicopter pilot. He had just returned from an emergency call out to one of the outlying islands but had encountered very poor visibility even using the airport's back door route. Unimaginably, it was described as being *even worse* than the day that I had arrived. The pilot, still clad in his full immersion suit, fresh from the battlefield, so to speak, calmly advised me not to go. Such was their extreme weather challenges, I respected the skills and knowledge of the search and rescue helicopter pilots here, more than anywhere else I had visited (though perhaps Kulusuk in Greenland was on a par).

It was therefore an easy decision on my part; I would have to wait yet another day at least.

11 August 2015: Vágar, Faroe Islands – Stornoway, Isle of Lewis, Scotland – Oban, Scotland – Larne, Northern Ireland

The final day of my global odyssey! Or so I thought at the time...

It was however, destined to become quite a long day. Originally, I had planned to complete this phase of the flight over two or three days. Overnighting in Stornoway, I would hopefully have spent some time with the local RNLI lifeboat crew there, before moving on to Oban, where another lifeboat station was located. From there, I had planned to time my final arrival back in Larne quite conveniently, in the early afternoon.

Unfortunately, the vagaries of the weather, had now thrown a spanner in the works. I had already used up my three-day arrival window, with enforced weather-watching in the Faroes. The result of this meant I would now have to concertina three flights together and attempt to fly from the Faroes to Larne all in one day, which was a total of 7hrs 50mins of planned flight time.

It meant an exceedingly early start, but thankfully Paetur was on hand to give me a lift to the airport. Bidding him a fond farewell, I saddled up my flying pony for the final time across the Atlantic and flew off into the sunrise.

The early morning views around the islands were spectacular. The visibility had now improved significantly, and I flew out over the dog-leg lake, in the same way I had arrived four days previously. I could now see all of my approach route clearly, without any swirling mist and low cloud. It all looked much more friendly, though not any less brutal and rugged. The Atlantic rollers had eased off a little, but still enjoyed throwing themselves, crashing and bashing, onto the sheer jagged cliffs. As I re-crossed the waterfall, I set my course direct for Scotland.

It was quite an emotional moment, my final international departure. Next stop, *home turf.*

I had last flown in UK airspace when leaving Stoke airfield to cross the English Channel bound for Le Touquet, on 26 March 2010. Although I had travelled back and forth over the intervening five years, *Roxy* had in all this time remained firmly, defiantly and resolutely *en route.* She had endured five long years of camping out away from home, in far flung hangars, fire stations, a desert petrol station, maintenance workshops, snow plough sheds, an aviation museum, a USAF base and all manner of small grass strips, flying clubs, lean-to sheds and major international airport hubs...

With messages of good luck and a safe flight, I signed off with Vágar Tower and the VHF radio went quiet. It was by now quite familiar; I was well used to solo flying over the ocean with only my own thoughts for company and as usual I quickly adopted my semi-meditative mid-ocean mindset.

At one point, while routinely monitoring my instruments, I was surprised to see a wholly unfamiliar coastline begin to scroll down my GPS screen towards me. For a few moments I was uncertain as to what I was seeing. I definitely wasn't expecting to see any islands out here. I zoomed out on the GPS to get a wider view. The mysterious coastline was still there, only now in more detail, but I still couldn't recognise it. But wait, hang on a minute... Then it hit me. The strange unrecognisable island I had been looking at, was actually the top of Scotland, only viewed upside down! The 'upright' shape of the British Isles is so familiar, to anyone who lives here at least, that to now view and approach it upside down just didn't compute. I had to laugh at my own stupidity, but also took immense satisfaction in the fact that I was arriving back into the UK from such an unusual direction. I had only been able to make this final approach by first flying myself *right around the world.*

The radio soon began to crackle into life again and as usual, I was able to hear shore-based traffic long before being able to speak to them directly. As I listened intently to the strengthening signal, it was fantastic to hear the first clear, Scottish accent from air traffic control after so long flying abroad.

Because of my tight time schedule, my stopover in Stornoway in the Western Isles of Scotland was all too brief. I had barely enough time to complete UK immigration formalities, grab a sandwich and meet the gathered press who were keen to hear my account of the first-ever crossing of the Atlantic Ocean by gyroplane.

Since departing Qikiqtarjuaq, northern Canada on 24 July, it had taken 19 days to reach Stornoway, Scotland. The weather as expected had been very changeable, and together with some Danish bureaucracy in Greenland, had caused most of the delays along the way. The full Atlantic crossing was actually completed in only seven flying days, with a cumulative flight time of 34hrs 20mins. A slow and steady pace, but such was the price to pay for safely pioneering an historic first trans-atlantic gyroplane flight.

Throughout all the efforts, uncertainty and dangers that I had faced, I hoped that perhaps other gyro pilots might now be encouraged to follow on in years to come and directly benefit both from the diplomatic and pathfinding experiences of this maiden crossing.

***

Soon enough I was back in the air and the flight through the Western Isles of Scotland was just sublime. Rare in these parts, the visibility was excellent and free from cloud cover. I could view the intricate layout of the islands before me like a giant 3D model, one that I could now cruise through at will. I passed by the Isle of Skye and the new bridge linking it to the mainland. I could see the entire Cullin Ridge, where 30 years ago while working as an Outward Bound instructor, I had led groups of students on rock climbing expeditions. At Glenbrittle, we had experienced Scotland at its best with wild camping, carnivorous midges and swirling mists.

Passing by Mallaig, I spotted their bright orange RNLI all-weather lifeboat at its berth. A familiar sight and a reminder that I was definitely back flying over home waters. A few minutes of whisky distillery spotting on the Isle of Mull followed and then I made a straight in approach to land at Oban.

This was the last stop before home, only a quick jaunt of 115 miles down the Mull of Kintyre peninsula and then a short hop across the Irish Sea remained. When I had left the UK back in 2010, a cohort of my fellow gyronauts had flown with me in loose formation as an escort, flying over Kent and out over the White Cliffs of Dover. In my sign off radio call with John Butler, I had proclaimed that I hoped to see them fly up to Scotland to greet me coming in at the other end of Britain. At the time, it was fully expected that that homecoming would have been only about four months away. Little did we know that it would turn out to be five years!

But true to their word, a gaggle of gyro pilots did now arrive to meet me in Oban, in order to accompany me on my final leg over to Larne. It was a very special moment meeting up again with John Butler, Adrian Richards and Jon Noble, all of whom had made lengthy cross-country flights up from the North of England to welcome me back.

After a quick catch up and a last cup of Scottish tea we were off. The weather continued to be glorious as we chatted over the radio and dodged about in loose formation down the length of the Mull of Kintyre peninsula. I recalled with great fondness that it was the same friendly banter between friends that had escorted me off the 'UK' premises in 2010. As gyro pilots, we shared a common understanding and love of our unique type of flying machine and enjoyed the camaraderie of flying together. It was a lovely concluding flight and soon enough we were making our final approach into Sandy Bay playing fields.

Last to land, I received a rapturous welcome from family and friends, and from many of the same local townsfolk who had been present on my original departure. The fire brigade was on hand (just in case), as were fellow Larne lifeboat crew members, complete in hi-vis RNLI yellow gear. The latter held up hand flares to give us a good indication of wind drift for landing. The council had done a great job in closing off the field so we could land clear of the gathered crowds, but as soon as I had landed, taxied and shut down my engine, the waiting press pack descended into a media scrum. It didn't matter – I was just so mightily relieved to be safely home and with *Roxy* still intact after such a wildly unpredictable odyssey. The euphoria was slightly tinged with the regret of how the Russians had upset the continuity of the whole circumnavigation. But I quickly reconciled myself with the thought that at least I had tried my best.

After pushing the gyros to overnight in the back garden of our house, the champagne corks popped, and a great party of extended family and friends got underway. A special guest joined us – Barry Jones, who had motorbiked over from England specially to see me arrive home. It was a poignant moment for me as Barry had pioneered the whole idea of trying to fly a gyro around the world. His was the first-ever attempt, and although he was abruptly halted by severe monsoon floods in India, his brave foray of flying a lightweight open cockpit gyro over incredibly long distances and into the unknown opened many eyes. It certainly gave everyone in the gyro community the sense that such a world-circling feat could soon become a reality. It also proved to me, looking on as a novice trainee pilot at the time, that such things were not impossible and in more recent years gave me the encouragement to develop my own circumnavigation campaign.

Along with the American, Matt Hayduk (who had cut short his attempt in Cambodia), Barry and I now made up a very small club of only three would-be gyro circumnavigators.

17

Home: mixed feelings

I was safely home and with *Roxy* wholly intact.

By hook or by crook, I had managed to fly entirely around the world, well the 'free' part at least; Russia being the *only* country out of 24 that had flatly avoided permitting my flight. In the process I had managed to establish 19 new FAI speed and distance world records, including the 'blue ribbon' transatlantic record, the first gyroplane ever to attempt and successfully cross the Atlantic Ocean (both solo and unsupported by any other aircraft). I was able to achieve so many records simply because up to this point in aviation history, gyroplanes had not completed many long-distance international flights.

With the ongoing indifference of the Russian authorities, I now had to resign myself to the fact that they might never allow access for a foreign registered gyroplane to cross through the Russian Federation. This seemed grossly unfair. Whilst I had been consistently prevented from gaining flight access across Russia for *years,* Russian pilots such as the unfortunate Sergey Ananov had seemingly been able to fly freely across Russia and throughout North America unhindered. Sergey had been almost home, and no doubt, barring his ditching, he would have likewise been permitted to breeze on through northern Europe to successfully complete his full circumnavigation back in Russia. It is a quirk of geography that crossing through the Russian Far East and the Bering Sea to reach Alaska remains the *only* viable routing for any light aircraft with limited fuel range capabilities to cross the vast expanse of the Pacific Ocean. It simply cannot be done any other way, and believe me, I investigated numerous alternative options whilst grounded in Japan. The fact that Russia acts as the de facto gate-keeper of all flight access to the Bering Strait, I would have expected that they should have been willing, or even morally obliged, to act in the best interests of all international aviators that needed to pass that way.

But I had tried my best and so now I just had to accept that the reality of the situation was not likely to change much any time soon. So, I concentrated on other aspects of life and had to park the missing part of my Circumnavigation for the foreseeable future.

18

A surprise alliance

In the spring of 2017, quite out of the blue, I was contacted by serial adventurer James Ketchell from Basingstoke in England. Over the preceding years, James had become aware of my global flight and was very keen to come to visit me and find out about my achievement in more detail. At that time he was not a pilot, but he wanted to investigate the practicalities of how soon he could become one, so he could then seek sponsorship towards making his own attempt at a gyro circumnavigation.

Whilst I admired his initial enthusiasm, I had already been contacted over the years by several would-be gyro circumnavigators. Some were much more serious than others, but a few suffered from a sense of over-optimism versus practical realism. I understood the condition well, and indeed I myself had similar thoughts in the early days of planning my flight. It all seemed so easy to imagine that it must be possible to fly around the world in a gyroplane, but of course in reality, getting from that point of initial enthusiasm, even just to the starting line, proved to be much more difficult than I first thought.

Over the next few months, James met with me several times, as I gave both insight and explanation of the key areas and tasks that he would have to consider and plan for. His ongoing drive and eagerness for the task was encouraging. He had previously achieved some notable expeditions: rowing across the Atlantic, climbing Everest and cycling around the world. Becoming aware of how he had achieved these feats however, I could see that they bore little direct comparison to the aviation challenge he was now contemplating.

A key difference was the level of external support he had received, both from people and the environment around him. Rowing the Atlantic was undoubtedly an arduous physical and mental challenge for James, but it took place within the confines of an organised Atlantic rally. He was one of many rowers crossing the ocean en masse, with each rowing a broadly similar course between the fixed start and finish points. The logistics of boats, supplies and safety equipment on such rallies could all be specified, provisioned and scrutineered by the organisers in advance. Although the boats gradually spread out over the ocean en route, his knowledge that there was at least some form of help relatively nearby, which could come to assist in any emergency, must have been a great help psychologically. It was why such rallies were formed, to provide ongoing expertise, built up over many years, and a sense of 'safety in numbers' while crossing the vast ocean. Psychologically, it gives a feeling that you are *not on your own.*

Likewise, climbing Everest was again a very tough physical and mental challenge, but benefits these days by being professionally organised into commercial expeditions. Experienced team-leaders and highly skilled Sherpa-guides are always on hand to help make crucial on the spot decisions and to set up ready-to-use camps on the mountain. Once again, you are not on your own.

Cycling around the world was slightly different. There was a minimum mileage to cover and notional nominated points to reach on the Earth's surface, but the great advantage was that James could pick and choose his planned route and needed only to travel through preferred countries. Selecting perhaps only those countries that were already bike and tourist friendly, he could conveniently avoid and leap-frog over any parts of the world thought to be too dangerous, expensive, bureaucratically difficult, or simply have too extreme a climate or terrain to cope with. With such worldwide flexibility in route planning, it was possible to ensure that friendly assistance was, once again, never that far away should it ever be required.

James now considered flying a gyro around the world as the next big adventure on his list, but it was going to be a vastly different challenge when compared to any of his previous achievements.

Flying solo, unescorted, and out of radio range, James would most definitely be out on his own both physically and psychologically. Once out over the ocean, he would be far removed from any hope of immediate rescue or assistance. An international flight planner could help from afar with flight permissions and ground logistics in foreign countries, but if James suddenly had to land at a remote, desolate outpost in an unfamiliar country, where he had no shared language, again he would feel very much out on his own. Psychologically he would need to strengthen his own self-reliance, his own sense of self-confidence; that, come what may, he would still be OK within himself especially in those extremely isolated situations, where there was just no one else to turn to – which when flying solo on this sort of expedition, occurred much more frequently than not.

Reflecting on these points, I worried that James might be underestimating the level of the task that he was so enthusiastically proposing to undertake. Commercialised adventure, by definition, has had a lot of the previously unforeseen and overly precarious risks ironed out of it. Over time, iconic challenges such as climbing Everest have now become organised, streamlined and packaged. If such ventures were seen to be too recklessly dangerous or unpredictable, the organising companies would quickly go out of business. A participant could certainly still pick up some notable personal achievements, but often only under a protective pre-defined set of rules and well within tried and tested safety measures. Tackling the gyro circumnavigation would be different. It would call on James to build up his experience to be able to robustly construct his *own* cocoon of safety, especially when flying solo, as no one else would be there to either create or manage it for him.

It would also require James to be mentally safe and secure within himself, confident of his own abilities, even while kept busy with a lot of potentially hazardous 'seat of the pants' type flying. Back to basics with no autopilot, no instrument flying and often no air traffic control support over large tracts of remote hostile terrain and ocean. A similar feeling perhaps to the type of flying that was carried out back in the pioneering 1920s and 1930s, where those early brave souls were very much *out there*, on their own physically and mentally, in their lonely open cockpits.

To succeed in flying completely around the globe you are obliged to take on whatever conditions that are thrown at you, coping equally with the rough and the smooth. Cherry-picking the easier countries and perhaps just by-passing the stubborn or awkward ones, is unfortunately not an option. I was therefore concerned early on that James might have been lulled into a false sense of security by his earlier notable achievements. But as he progressed in his training, I was glad to see that he quickly adopted a healthy and respectful cautiousness for what was now going to be a wholly new type of adventure experience.

He still however had a long path to travel before any potential take-off day. Whilst I could perhaps assist and advise where I could, he needed to enable himself to get to the start line, by both raising considerable sponsorship and learning to fly. It would take him a further two years to reach that point...

***

By the early spring of 2019, things had moved on considerably. James now had his brand-new Gyroplane Private Pilot's Licence (PPL(G)) courtesy of gyro instructor Steve Boxhall at Popham Airfield near the south coast of England. I already knew Steve quite well as we had trained together up in Cumbria, under the watchful eye of our flight Instructor Chris Jones, so I knew James would have been trained thoroughly. James had also now secured enough sponsorship to cover his travel expenses and aircraft purchase (a Magni M16C gyroplane registered G-KTCH), and also had a well-advanced route plan worked out with the expert guidance of Eddie Gould of General Aviation Support Egypt. The plan was to broadly follow the same original routing that I had flown. Knowing the route first-hand, I suspected that it was going to be a considerable challenge for such a newly qualified pilot, though at least he would gain some much-needed early experience flying through the string of friendly European countries before being let loose on the much more bureaucratically and physically taxing countries through the Middle East, Pakistan and India.

Preparations were building nicely for a spring departure from the UK, but then suddenly a large spanner was thrown into the works. Quite abruptly, the authorities in Pakistan announced the closure of its entire airspace to all General Aviation traffic. This was immediately a major blow to James's route planning. Without permission to overfly and land a light aircraft in Pakistan, it would be nigh on impossible to reach as far as India directly from Muscat in Oman. It was looking like a potential showstopper for the whole circumnavigation attempt, before it had even got going.

Urgent phone calls and flurries of emails followed, and slowly an alternative plan was formed. Behind the scenes, Eddie had been coordinating with a newly established Russian flight planner, Evgeny Kabarov and his Moscow based MAK Aviation company. Evgeny it seemed, was very confident that Russia was now finally beginning to relax its tight control on its expansive airspace. With routing via Pakistan shut, Evgeny believed that he could now orchestrate a flight through *all* of Russia, not just the short hop across the Far East corner between Japan and Alaska, which had previously been denied to me for so many years. Now, quite incredibly, a proposed trans-Russia flight route across the entire country, west to east was deemed possible. This news was going to be a game changer.

Since landing back in Larne in August 2015, I had always known that *in theory* at least, I could still continue with establishing a full world-circling flight, if only I could somehow be permitted to carry on flying eastwards, across to the Bering Sea and to eventually reach Oregon again. However, I also knew that this remained a theoretical exercise, given Russia's ongoing stand-off regarding permissions. But now that impasse situation was all rapidly changing.

Important phone calls and family discussions followed. It was soon agreed that if I was able to quickly mobilise both *Roxy* and myself, including expediting a one-month Russian tourist visa, then I could combine forces with James so that both our gyros could take on the wilds of Russia together. This would finally allow me to complete the elusive first gyroplane circumnavigation, while at the same time help James get through the first (and most potentially hazardous) half of his own circumnavigation. This would also help to springboard him across the globe as far as the USA and see him well on the way to setting the first FAI world speed record for the fastest eastbound gyroplane over a set distance around the world.

Thus we could each establish our own unique goals for a gyroplane circumnavigation: G-YROX being the absolute first to pioneer and achieve a complete, unbroken, physical circumnavigation, (albeit via a very slow and convoluted journey); and G-KTCH claiming the fastest circumnavigation, a few months later. Given my own disjointed flight could no longer realistically qualify for setting a timed circumnavigation record, I was nonetheless pleased for our whole global gyroplane community, that the first FAI speed record around the world could still be achieved; just as long as James was able to successfully make it back home...

With pre-arranged sponsorship commitments already set up in Europe, James couldn't hang around waiting for me to get ready. He had to set off in early April, whereas I needed at least a few more weeks to literally drop everything else I was doing and prepare once again for a major expedition. Fortunately, a lot of my kit was already to hand, albeit now showing a bit more wear and tear around the edges. It would become a recurring theme over the coming months, with James in a shiny new aircraft with the latest avionics, comms and kit, and me with my aging technology and world-weary, battle-hardened airframe. I took a conciliatory view on this though, with the all-important fact being that I already *knew* what my aircraft and kit was capable of. Tried and tested for thousands of miles, it was robust, reliable and dependable in many situations; but crucially, above all else, I also already knew of its limitations.

It also wasn't the time to teach an old dog new tricks; there was no point starting to learn any new methods or procedures when I already had my own time-served and proven modus operandi under by belt. In this flight, as with all the previous ones, I would just continue on doing what I had always done.

Several day trips by car followed to the Russian consulate in Dublin. Hailing from Northern Ireland, I am allowed dual nationality, so I hold both an Irish and a British passport. Fortunately, the Russian tourist visa was routinely approved without any hitches. Given our chequered past history, I had wondered nervously if my name might have had a big 'undesirable nuisance – do not allow entry' comment placed next to it in their filing system.

With the visa approved, I was good to go. The plan was to fly to England for aircraft servicing and then high tail it across northern Europe as fast as possible to catch up with James in Estonia. From there, we would both enter Russia together on 1 May.

But as usual dear reader, as you might have guessed by now, it didn't all go completely to plan...

19

Northern Europe: UK to Russia

22 April 2019: Larne, Northern Ireland – Kirkbride, Cumbia, England – Shrewsbury, Shropshire, England

For the unbroken continuity of my ongoing circumnavigation, it was arranged with the local council that I could once again use Sandy Bay playing field at Larne Harbour as my onward point of departure. Once again, a supportive crowd of local well-wishers and family turned up to see me set off. And once more the media were on hand to document the welcomed resurrection of the flight. Taking off twice from the same point felt like déjà vu, but little did I know the first time around, that some nine years later I would be now continuing on a *second lap* of the globe!

The fact that I was now aiming to fly right across Russia, certainly caught the media's attention. I was taking on my old nemesis, the very country that had stymied my access across to the Bering Sea for so many years. I was pleased that I was now getting the chance to complete the full circumnavigation, yet still frustrated for every one of my loyal GyroxGoesGlobal followers that it had taken so long to materialise.

After fond farewells, I saddled up the old pony once again, and headed out over the Irish Sea.

My first port of call was Kirkbride Airfield in Cumbia, where I had learnt to fly a gyroplane back in 2005. I enjoyed a quick cup of tea and a chat with my Instructor Chris Jones. I was pleased to be able to include Kirkbride on the circumnavigation route this time, as on the *first lap* back in 2010, I had cut the corner and flown directly to the west of the Lake District on my way for maintenance at Long Mynd in Shropshire. After a good luck handshake with Chris, a second flight quickly got me down to the Midlands and Sleape Airfield, where *Roxy* needed some hastily arranged annual servicing.

23–25 April 2019: Shrewsbury, Shropshire, England (non-flying days)

With the calendar counting down to 1 May, I was keen to get going as soon as possible. But unfortunately, the old saying 'more haste, less speed' now came into play. Because of the tight deadline for entry into Russia, the maintenance had been quickly arranged and many of the necessary servicing consumables and replacement parts had to be sourced and collected with very short notice. It was not the typical, meticulous, cautious and unhurried preparation that you would normally expect before embarking on a major global expedition. The maintenance team at Sleape pulled out all the stops to get me going as fast as possible, but time was now of the essence.

26 April 2019: Shrewsbury, Shropshire, England – Turweston, Buckinghamshire, England – Norwich, Norfolk, England

After three days in the hangar, I was off and running again but continually playing catch up. I called in briefly at Turweston, home to the Light Aviation Association, to have a new radio fitted and re-permit my aircraft over the counter in the LAA office. Next stop was Norwich, which should have been a quick turnaround but wasn't, as refuelling and submitting my flight plan to the Netherlands unfortunately took too long to allow me to arrive at Groningen before they shut for the day. Instead, I had to rest up in a local motel, slowly acclimatising to life on the road once more.

27 April 2019: Norwich, Norfolk, England – Groningen, Netherlands

My first new country en route since 2015 was the Netherlands, which involved a significant 110 nautical mile, over-water crossing of the cold and grey North Sea. If I needed a shake down flight to get me back into expedition mode, this was it. The weather was gloomy and overcast, with low cloud keeping me confined to around 800-1000ft above the occasional white-capped waves. Unlike many of my far-flung, over-water flights, this one was not so lonely. I was flying over the northern approaches to the constantly busy English Channel and could indulge in plenty of boat-spotting. All manner of passenger and cargo carriers, fishing vessels and rig support ships passed by below me. Yet there was surprisingly little traffic around me in the air. Skirting across the north of Europe, I assumed I wasn't on a particularly busy route for GA aircraft, but this lack of congestion suited me just fine. Ghostly forests of wind turbines appeared out of the gloom on approach to the Dutch coast, a flying hazard I would need to watch out for right across the Netherlands and Germany.

Groningen proved very welcoming. The neatly maintained airport even had easily dispensed self-service fuel that could be paid for by credit card. And the resident aircraft handling agent was able to drop me off at a local hotel around 20 minutes drive away. All was going well until I checked in at reception and suffered a sudden sinking realisation – I had left all my credit and debit cards back on the aircraft. A rookie circumnavigator's error for sure! I sprinted outside but the handler had already gone. I was left penniless.

Fortunately, the receptionists were very understanding. After I showed them a picture of *Roxy*, explaining that I had just flown across the North Sea from England, they then appeared to be even more understanding. Though I'm not sure if they were perhaps also showing concern for my sanity. Several phone calls then re-established contact with the handler, who was fortunately passing the hotel later in the evening and he popped in to reunite me with my cards.

28 April 2019: Groningen, Netherlands – Rechlin, Germany

As a broad-brush route plan, I was now aiming for Estonia and needed to chart a direct course to get me there in the minimum number of flying days. Picking a route was easy – I basically scoped out how many daily hops I needed and then scouted around for convenient or interesting landing places at the appropriate distance for each leg. I didn't need the hassle (or expense) of any big airports, though I did need places for fuel and accommodation nearby. In Germany I opted for Mueritz Airpark, 55 miles north-west of Berlin, which was centred around a huge, but now lightly used, Cold War era runway, complete with a myriad of semi-buried blast proof bunker aircraft hangars. Adorned with modern urban graffiti art, the drab concrete bunkers were in stark contrast to the nearby quaint, little flower-festooned town of Mirow, where I was later to find accommodation.

After landing and pushing *Roxy* into one of the dispersed hangars, I hitched a ride into town with the airport manager. He dropped me off at a delightful, family-run hotel on the lakeshore of the Mirower See. Several steins of excellent Benediktiner Weissbier and a fantastic home-cooked meal followed as I briefed my new hosts with my up-coming route plan to cross all of Russia. As always, as soon as I showed them a photo of how small *Roxy* actually was, it immediately gave them a true appreciation of the scale of the challenge ahead.

29 April – 2 May 2019: Rechlin, Germany (non-flying days)

With an onward flight planned towards Poland, I returned to the airpark nice and early to prepare for the day ahead. As I made my customary pre-flight inspection, I ran my hand over one of the three carbon fibre propeller blades to check for any potential stone chips or other damage. However, while doing so, I felt something that wasn't quite right.

Hidden from view, but *definitely* there, was a small notch cut out of the back of the blade. I checked the other two blades and was startled to find a similar notch on each, though these two were slightly less pronounced. What was wrong? I quickly traced the cause of the damage. The auxiliary alternator that was bolted to the rear of my engine, had been replaced back in England during the annual maintenance, but the new unit had not had its fitting to the support bracket correctly adapted to my engine arrangement. The result was that its drive belt was set out of alignment, which meant it was 5mm too close to the back of the prop. The damage must have happened shortly after first start up, post servicing; which meant that I had unknowingly just flown over 110 nautical miles of open water with a compromised set of propeller blades!

I was grounded.

With only three days until I was due to meet up with James in Estonia, I quickly advised both Eddie back in the UK and Evgeny in Russia of my further delay. I also contacted James to break the bad news; there was simply no way that I could now make our 1 May rendezvous in Estonia. The overall plan was quickly revised, with James continuing on into Russia alone on the 1st, arriving in Moscow that evening. A welcoming committee of local helicopters, arranged by Evgeny, was then going to meet him in the air on the approach to Moscow, in order to guide him through the busy city airspace. After rendezvous, the loose formation would then follow the ring road around the outskirts of the city to reach a small regional airfield that was allowed to accept our gyroplanes. Safely delivered, James would then have to wait in Moscow for me to arrive before we could then set off on our trans-Russia adventure together.

Fortunately, at least I was grounded in Germany, the home of the Autogyro factory that originally manufactured *Roxy*. In the next few days, a new set of blades was flown into my location and the auxiliary generator was correctly realigned. That allowed me to then make a ferry flight across to Hildesheim to also replace some leaking oil hoses.

3 May 2019: Rechlin, Germany – Hildesheim, Germany – Rechlin, Germany

My daughter Petra's 18th birthday was spent hopping across to Hildesheim and the Autogyro headquarters. I called her from the car park while *Roxy* was in a maintenance bay. This was yet another example where long-distance family connections were negatively impacted by my dogged and persistent pursuit of this nine-year circumnavigation saga. Petra had been nine and in primary school along with her older brother Felix when I first set off in March 2010. Now she was sitting A-level exams and Felix was already in his first year of university. And yet here I was, *still* making my round the world attempt.

And to think, without diplomatic holdups, bureaucracy and a ditching, the whole flight should have only taken around four months to complete...

With repairs made good, I spent a pleasant final evening with my adopted family at the Hotel Seepromenade. They had been quite surprised when I returned to them after initially being grounded, but their continued friendly company and delicious homemade food helped to keep my spirits up for the rest of the week. There was also plenty of playing cards and telling stories in the evenings. After the rushed start and the unnerving episode of flying a considerable distance with a flawed aircraft, I was now much more settled and ready to take on the Russian adventure head on.

4 May 2019: Rechlin, Germany – Torun, Poland – Kaunas, Lithuania

With *Roxy* deemed fit and healthy again, I was once more good to go. I was also keenly aware that James was waiting in Moscow.

Departing from Mueritz Airfield, I made a low pass over the hotel. It was easy to spot being situated so close to the shore of Mirower See. Suddenly I saw movement below and a flash of white, as bed sheets were being waved at me from the balcony. It was a great send-off. I circled a few times for photos and then with a final big wave of my arm, I levelled out and headed off over the treetops and set course towards the Polish border. It reminded me very much of my flypast of Old Orchard Beach on the coast of Maine. A fleeting final connection with well-wishers on the ground, before heading off into the wide blue yonder.

The flying was easy in this part of Europe. The terrain was very flat and apart from avoiding the ubiquitous forests of wind turbines, navigation was hassle-free. I made a short refuelling pit stop in Torun, Poland, where once again Eddie had arranged some friendly local contacts on the ground to help me. My Turtle Pac was again very usefully deployed to pick up fuel from a local petrol station, where I was also able to grab some food to go. There were few formalities, no hassle on bringing fuel to the aircraft, and payments could be made by credit card… why couldn't all stops around the world be so convenient?

Before long, I was back in the air and heading for an overnight stop in Lithuania, though my arrival in Kaunas soon proved to have its own difficulties. Landing late afternoon, after flying all day, I couldn't find anyone at the airfield. All the hangars were shut, and anyone who had been there during the day had presumably gone home. Reminiscent of Glenns Ferry, Idaho, I decided to hang around a while, hoping that someone, anyone, might turn up and I could get chatting in order to find secure overnight shelter for *Roxy*. After 30 minutes or so, I was finally in luck. A late returning light aircraft appeared and I casually (read desperately) made my introductions and my sales pitch.

"I'm just wondering… if I might find an overnight hangar?"

A few phone calls were made and soon enough I was sorted. I then spent a very agreeable evening in a traditional restaurant with my impromptu local host and guide. The city centre at night looked lovely and I regretted that I couldn't stay a while longer to see the sights properly. But the Russian rendezvous clock was ticking and I was already running too short of time.

5 May 2019: Kaunas, Lithuania – Tartu, Estonia

A taxi dropped me back at the airfield and I let myself out of the hangar. Again, the airfield seemed deserted, but without further distractions, at least it meant I could make a quick getaway. The routing to Estonia saw me overfly Latvian airspace, though avoiding all major traffic areas, it was again a non-eventful flight. Finally, almost a week behind schedule, I arrived in Tartu, Estonia, and I parked G-YROX in exactly the same hanger spot that had been occupied by G-KTCH the week before. It felt good to think that at least I was getting closer, there was now only one more day of flying needed before the two gyros would finally get to meet up.

6 May 2019: Tartu, Estonia (non-flying day)

Gaining entry into Russia was not an easily arranged procedure, as I knew full well having battled with the process for so many years. Now that I was on the doorstep, it took a further day to prepare the final details for my international border crossing flight to Pskov. I was both excited and relieved at the prospect. However, apprehension persisted in the back of my mind as I retained a nagging doubt that for some obscure reason or other, I might still have been denied access, right at the last moment. Thankfully this didn't happen, permission was granted, and everything was set for an early departure the next morning, 7 May, exactly a week behind James.

7 May 2019: Tartu, Estonia – Pskov, Russia – Seredka, Russia – Moscow, Russia

An early start was called for, as I needed to make three flights before the day was done: a one-hour hop to Pskov to clear Russian entry customs and immigration; a 25-minute flight north to Seredka, a small GA-friendly airfield for fuel; and finally, a five-hour flight directly to the outskirts of Moscow. The Russian entry permission, although granted, was not very flexible. It was for entry on this one day only and unfortunately the lack of flexibility did little to accommodate the vagaries of the weather. Forecasted conditions en route were heavily overcast with a significant weather system and rain front directly in my path. I resigned myself to the inevitability that the day's flying was going to be wet, murky and challenging; somewhat in stark contrast to James's flight the previous week, which had been made under gloriously settled conditions and blue skies.

Crossing the Russian border after all my previous permit difficulties was a highly significant moment. Initially at least there was little discernible change in the landscape below me but that all dramatically changed on arrival at Pskov. Landing in persistent drizzle, I taxied off the runway and across a very cracked and broken taxiway toward the terminal building; the airport infrastructure had clearly not been updated for many years.

I was immediately met by a gaggle of uniformed officials who spilled out of a small grey minibus; it was a vehicle that would become very familiar to me in the following weeks, as they were commonly used right across the Russian Federation. Similar in shape to an old VW microbus, only more utilitarian (think Soviet military police rather than Californian surf wagon), it was affectionately referred to as a *Bukhanka* (*Буханка*), which translated to a "loaf of bread".

However, the contrast between this light-hearted mode of transport and the seriously official passengers contained inside was immediately clear. One first glance at these officials and I knew that I had to be on my best behaviour. After hastily gathering up all my aircraft documents, I was squeezed into the back of the bread van and escorted into the terminal for formal proceedings. Thankfully, because James had already passed through the week before, the officials already knew the full procedures for accepting a foreign gyroplane pilot and so the entry process all ran smoothly with minimum fuss. With no fuel to load, I was on the ground for barely an hour before taxiing back out to the runway for a short 25-minute hop northwards.

I was greeted at the small airfield of Seredka with a much more relaxed welcome. My pre-arranged fuel was already waiting, and it was pumped directly into *Roxy's* tanks from a steel barrel. I needed to be fully loaded, both for the long flight to Moscow, and to guard against the murky weather predicted along the way. I therefore needed to have plenty of contingency fuel, for any potential emergency diversion or backtracking en route.

With more than five hours of flying ahead of me, a last-minute visit to the bathroom was also essential. I was directed to a delightful clubhouse that was a log cabin construction – it clearly illustrated that grass roots flying in Russia was just as passionate, as enthusiastic and as friendly as in all the other countries I had visited. It was a far cry from the hard, cold and uncaring image that the Russian security authorities had projected in my direction over the past decade.

* * *

The weather heading to Moscow lived up to its forecast. Initially a manageable soft drizzle, it soon turned into a battle as conditions steadily deteriorated. Gradually the cloud base dropped from 1000ft to around 300ft, forcing me to fly lower than I was wholly comfortable with. Often there were also large unbroken swathes of forest below me, with no roads, logging tracks or even firebreaks of any kind. It was just a solid blanket of densely packed trees. This was becoming an increasingly anxious flight. Indeed, if I hadn't been required to be in Moscow so urgently, I wouldn't have been flying at all.

With more than 200 miles still to fly, I had to console myself that hopefully things would improve once I broke through to the other side of the weather front. I constantly searched for diversion options, as was my usual self-preservation tactic, but the surrounding landscape all seemed identically bleak and desolate. I was flying along in a murky bubble of poor visibility where my view in all directions was barely a quarter of a mile. I was not happy, not happy at all. I studied the too-close-for-comfort treetops, and clutching for mental crumbs of support I tried to convince myself that they looked quite soft, like young saplings that would perhaps bend and flex to absorb any impact with them. In reality though, I knew they were not made of cotton wool. I searched for other positives. At least the terrain remained flat, surely that was a plus?

For a time, I had to weave back and forth around the lowest clumps of cloud base, desperately trying all the while to keep as much gap between me and the treetops as possible. To make matters much worse, I then realised the rain-sodden trees themselves were also generating vapour clouds. Wisps of humid forest mist were rising out of the canopy and at times conspired to join up with the heavy low clouds above. It was like running through a confused, ever-changing maze. With limited visibility, I flew at a cautiously slow 55 mph, making rapid and crucial course-altering decisions constantly, as I kept my aircraft handling responsive and nimble throughout. Several times, I had to put in a hard-banked, full 360-degree go around to try to spot any lighter patches of cloud that indicated the next *bubble of visibility* that I could occupy. It was like aerial steppingstones. In each bubble I would convince myself to feel safe (albeit still trapped over hostile terrain with no visible escape route), before eventually hopping to the next. At least in each one, I could circle and wait for the constantly changing walls of cloud to evolve and shapeshift, until they allowed me a new route onwards. My direct flight path was *approximate* to say the least. It was all I could do to just keep vaguely (within an arc of 90 degrees) on track towards Moscow.

With such a meandering path, progress through the worst of the rain front was slow. I was not enjoying any of this. This was survival flying. I was just about maintaining visual contact in a patch of sky big enough to manoeuvre in, but constantly feeling anxious that I could easily, at some point, run out of safety bubbles. By the time I was a good 30 miles into the worst of it, the thought of maybe having to turn tail and battle my way back out again, became just as daunting an option as pressing on. It was an increasingly desperate situation.

Constantly battling to stay in the air, I tried my best to remain optimistic as I attempted to become more conditioned to my 'new normal'. But the dreadful minutes were slowly ticking by. As bum-clenchingly difficult as it all was, at least I was keeping in the air and I had plenty of fuel, well... for the time being at least. It was unconventional, but it seemed to be working. Out of pure necessity I was being forced to adapt to the immediate situation around me.

But just as I thought it couldn't get much worse, the already dismal conditions ramped up yet another gear. The flat, desolate forest landscape slowly began to *rise*. The undulating terrain began to shape itself into foothills, ridges and valleys. Whereas before I could assume a flat, two-dimensional surface all around me, now I also had height to contend with. Previously, I could hope to escape off to the next bubble in any direction, but now I had blind valleys rising up into the clouds and cloud-covered ridges to deal with.

I could see from the GPS that the bulk of the rising ground was off to my right and so I consciously veered more towards my left, reasoning that the foothills would hopefully be less problematic on that side. Happily my hunch proved to be correct. I ran through wispy light cloud while crossing some minor ridgelines until I was eventually rewarded with a deeper and more promising main valley pointing roughly in the right direction. I gratefully banked down into it and hoped that I was now through the most difficult section. Crucially I was now flying down a valley – not up – and heading towards wider, flatter ground, where the cloud base was lifting.

With the worst of the flying behind me, a small settlement, complete with a deserted, rain-soaked airstrip, suddenly came into view.

"Now you appear!" I muttered to myself. "Where were you when I most desperately needed to land 20 minutes ago?"

Thankfully, the skies ahead continued to brighten. The weather front, as I reached its leading edge, formed a very clearly defined dark line of heavy cloud and it was such a relief to shoot out from under it, with much cheering and punching of the air as I did so; something akin to a bat escaping out of the gates of hell.

The rain had stopped, the air temperature rose dramatically and I now had sunshine; it was a completely different day. I promptly took stock: my red immersion suit was thoroughly drenched, but thankfully I remained perfectly dry on the inside; and although the instrument panel had also taken a soaking, it remained fully functioning. I felt battle-weary and exhausted after so many hours fuelled on adrenaline but was also grateful to have survived such a very lucky escape from the weather. I again thought of how very different James's innocuous flight had been the previous week.

***

After weathering the storms, my eventual arrival into Moscow was sublime. Evgeny had a lot of helicopter buddies based at Heliport Moscow, and similar to James's arrival reception, I too was now going to be met by an escort helicopter on the outskirts of the city. Then the plan was to chaperone me through and around the busy Muscovite skies to an outlying airfield, Myachovo Airport, on the far side of the city.

At the pre-arranged rendezvous spot, I made visual contact and then formed up to act as a following wingman to my local guide helicopter. On drawing alongside, I could see James's beaming face looking out at me from the rear seats. After such an arduous and uncertain mid-section, the rest of the flight now became a breeze. With all the busy ATC radio and flightpath procedures being taken care of, all I had to do was follow the helo ahead of me. We then flew clockwise around the multi-lane ring road that encircles the city, and as with most capital cities, it was heaving in both directions with late afternoon commuter traffic. The whole of Moscow, stretching off into the distance to our right was laid out in all its glory. I was so pleased to finally be here.

I followed the guide helo into land at Myachovo and I was then met properly on the ground by James and a group of local flyers. They had been waiting a week for my late arrival and it was very pleasing to see the two gyros, G-YROX and G-KTCH, finally sharing the same hangar space together. Quickly unpacking my luggage, there was one more surprise to enjoy: a commuter-style flight to beat the surface traffic and bring us right into the heart of the city. We all hopped back into the escort helicopter, and as guest of honour I was given the front left seat.

This was going to be an arrival in style. Taking off once more, we were treated to a magical sunset before landing at the city centre heliport.

The heliport building looked very futuristic, like a large inflatable moon base. Several long hangars were dotted around the multiple helipads, and as I glanced in, I saw more private helicopters parked up in one spot than anywhere else I'd ever been.

For now, these excess luxuries and world-class amenities needed to be savoured, as in a few short days we would be leaving them all behind.

8 May 2019: Moscow, Russia (non-flying day)

After such a long and harrowing recent flight, I was now most grateful to have a non-flying day. It allowed me time to relax, plan ahead with James and take in a whistle-stop bus tour of Moscow. It was also a chance for us to pick up any last-minute items that we might need later in the journey.

The city was full of history, with iconic sights such as the Kremlin, Red Square and the Bolshoi Ballet making it onto the sightseeing itinerary. More unusually, so did a certain large, dominating ornate pink building. This was the home of the FSB, the country's Federal Security Service that, through its deafening silence, had obstructed me from flying across Russia for so many years. It was ironic that now, after all this time, I would catch my first sight of it from the top of a tourist bus. I reflected on how many flight permission applications, embassy letters, diplomatic notes and emails of mine were probably *safely filed* away somewhere in that building, buried under tonnes of other paperwork and likely never to be seen again.

Numerous internal requests for a response on my behalf from the Russian MFA (Ministry of Foreign Affairs) were probably stored in there too as even internally, to another Russian government department, the FSB had consistently over many months and years, declined to make any comment at all. When repeatedly asked for its opinion on the flight (as the FSB acted as a statutory consultee for permission to be finally granted), it completely ignored the request. It didn't say yes but it didn't say no either. It just said nothing, safe in the knowledge that the flight could not actually proceed without its approval. Its officials presumably just sat on their hands, stonewalled everything and hoped the problematic permission-seeker would eventually give up and go away.

9 May 2019: Moscow, Russia – Cheboksary, Russia

After so much solo expedition flying over the years, it felt quite odd to now be preparing to fly with another aircraft. My pre-flight checks had always been conducted as a solitary affair. In my head I have always had a private conversation with *Roxy*, checking and ensuring that she and I were both ready and able to take to the skies. That said, pre-flighting alongside James changed little in my overall thought process. I checked my aircraft in my own usual way and likewise, separately, he checked his. Once we were both happy with our aircraft, we were ready to go.

Heading out east from Moscow the landscape came as quite a surprise. Admittedly, before setting out, I hadn't really known what to expect but this first section reminded me very much of the American Midwest, with vast, gently undulating, cultivated fields stretching out for hundreds of acres in every direction. It was an immediately comforting sight, as any sort of emergency landing would not now be a problem (and happily it would remain this way until we reached the Ural Mountains). Clearly this was a significant grain belt for all of Russia and we took great delight in flying low-level over many of the recently harvested fields. Weaving back and forth, we skirted around isolated woodlands and shot through narrow gaps in the treelines, before briskly pulling up to hop over hedge boundaries and the occasional power lines. This was fun flying in a (mostly) safe, kindergarten landscape and a great first introduction to the whole country. If only the next 5000 miles could all be flown like this.

Occasionally tractors could be spotted, or people working in the fields. I usually remained high to keep a good separation, though

James's exuberance sometimes got the better of him as he swooped down low to buzz past the farmers and give out a *shaka* 'hang loose' hand gesture. I didn't care for it much; on some occasions it just felt like showboating in front of some very hard-working people.

Unfortunately, prolonged low flying over such extensive crop fields caused *Roxy's* windshield, propeller and rotor blades to be covered in the splattered remains of hundreds of bright green bugs. Baked on during the long flight almost to the point of obscuring visibility through the perspex, these proved very stubborn to remove later.

After the sophistication of Moscow, landing at Cheboksary was soon to give us an introduction into what the interior of Russia was really going to be like.

On arrival, we were greeted and hosted warmly. There was lots of local interest in our aircraft and several families dropped by for photographs while we refuelled from 200-litre barrels housed in a tin shed. They even shared ice cream with us as a lovely gesture of friendship. A less lovely experience however was the appearance of a couple of guys who were almost paralytically drunk. They were overly friendly as very drunk people often are, but also were fast becoming a bit of a pest. They insisted on giving us congratulatory vice-like handshakes and manly bear hugs, while their heavy alcohol-laced breath blended subtly with the refuelling petrol fumes. Thankfully we managed to give them the slip before gratefully squeezing both gyros into an already fully occupied light aircraft hangar for the night.

We were then taken to share in a feast of fast food that had been laid out by the members of the local flying club, complete with some equally fast drinking of cognac and beer. The hospitality, as with all of our stops in local airfields throughout Russia, was warm and genuine. This was in stark contrast to the cold impersonal treatment we received from some of the officials at the larger commercial airports.

* * *

Our accommodation proved to be a delightful small hotel, the Hotel Comfort-Place in the suburbs of Cheboksary. Ludmilla, our excellent landlady, was a lovely host and we ended up staying for two nights after some heated words on the phone with our Russian flight coordinator. Evgeny was a helicopter pilot and on examining his proposed forward routing for us, it was immediately clear to me that at some points, he had overestimated the endurance capabilities of our open-cockpit gyros. Our requirements were simply not comparable to flying a helicopter.

He had been insistent that we should fly directly to Yekaterinburg in an effort to maintain his overall schedule. Yet I was equally insistent that we should not. His proposed routing had us flying extremely close to our maximum fuel range and would have completely compromised any safety margins we had regarding weather or other diversions. If a significant headwind picked up over such a long distance, it could easily have added an extra hour onto our flight time, which would then require an extra hour of fuel that we didn't have. We could easily have ended up in the trees, maybe 50 miles short of the destination airfield. I was adamant that Evgeny simply *had* to find us an interim refuelling stop en route. Initially in reply, he flatly maintained there were *no other options,* and that we most definitely had to keep to his schedule by flying direct.This view defied logic, as if *commanding* us to comply with his routing, somehow then would magically enable us to fly farther than it was safely possible to do.

However, after considerable further shouting back and forth on the phone, with James looking on at me somewhat nervously and shocked at my sudden change of demeanour, Evgeny eventually came back with an acceptable interim stop for us near Ufa. It would mean introducing a pronounced dogleg to the direct flight path, but it also meant each individual leg was much safer in overall distance. My stubborn insistence on flying as I saw fit, which allowed for the *actual* prevailing conditions rather than Evgeny trying to railroad us into whatever convenient schedule he had *assumed* we would fly, lost us a whole day. Arrangements had to be altered to allow for our interim stop, but I didn't care. Having already flown 80% around the world, through 28 countries, I certainly wasn't going to be told what to do in such safety-critical circumstances. Evgeny wasn't a gyro pilot and couldn't imagine how very different our safety priorities were, compared to those of a helicopter. Setting down on some remote river sandbank for lunch or to wait for bad weather to clear, just wasn't an option for us. He could suggest all he liked in order for us to maintain his schedule; but at the end of the day, he wasn't the one sitting in the open cockpit.

With the extra day now needed for re-scheduling, it meant we could also relax a little. By chance it was Victory Day, a national holiday commemorating the end of the Second World War, and so James and I were invited to take in the view from a huge dramatic war memorial built on a prominent hill overlooking the town. Earlier in the day, we had each been presented with a commemorative orange and black stripy ribbon, the ribbon of Saint George, and in the evening, we were further treated to a fabulous fireworks festival by the river. It was great to witness regular local people having such fun (and probably explained why the two guys at the airfield had been so drunk earlier in the day).

10 May 2019: Cheboksary, Russia (non-flying day)

After a late night at the festival, we had a welcome catch up rest day for admin and getting washing done.

11 May 2019: Cheboksary, Russia – Ufa, Russia – Yekaterinburg, Russia

With the newly introduced interim stop at Ufa, we now had a busy day ahead with two back-to-back flights, one of five hours and the other, three.

But first, in order to continue east through the Russian Federation and across the Ural Mountains into Siberia, we were required to be checked out by a doctor at the airport. Forms were filled in and questions asked about our physical fitness and our ability to pilot a private aircraft into the more remote interior of the country. All the necessary bureaucratic hoops were jumped through and we were declared fit to fly.

A five-hour-plus stint in the saddle followed, and once again we took delight in swooping low through sprawling, newly harvested crop fields. Gradually, the wide-open stubble fields, now occupied by flocks of grazing birds rather than any people, started to diminish and we encountered the beginnings of the impenetrable flat blanket of trees that would become our familiar landscape for the bulk of the next *4600 miles.* Mentally, I needed to rapidly develop both a love of trees and a sense of resigned acceptance, similar to that felt when out over the ocean waves. Even if I did manage to successfully set down amongst the trees, I had to accept that there would be virtually no chance of any subsequent take-off. The flight would automatically become a search, rescue and extraction mission from then onwards.

The grass strip near the town of Ufa turned out to be a delightful place. It was home to an enthusiastic and lively flying club, one that even had some resident gyros. Unfortunately, almost as I had prophesised on the phone to Evgeny, we had already experienced a significant headwind during our first leg, which meant that we couldn't stay long on the ground. Fuel was thankfully uploaded promptly, so we still had a short time to be hosted in the lovely clubhouse. A lot of club members had turned up at short notice to see us and they were keen to give us some local gifts for our onward journey. I was offered a huge, but alas heavy, jar of locally produced honey. With some considerable persuasion, I managed to swap it for a smaller jar, and I was soon very glad I had done so.

Our departure was now in the full heat of the day, which complicated things, as did the draggy grass strip. Heavy with fuel (and honey), I led out and lined up for take-off with James following on behind. The take-off roll through the grass was indeed sluggish, and as I bumped over the undulating ground it felt that I had little significant lift. With full power, I eventually hauled up into the air, but soon enough settled back down onto the grass.

The hot air and heavy payload were conspiring against me. I throttled down and backtracked to my starting point. James continued to wait for me at the threshold; his brand-new aircraft had barely been run in and his fresh engine and airframe had so far given him very little cause for concern (and it had certainly never spent a few months of its short life disassembled and sprawled out on a Thai table tennis table). I passed him by and lined up to have another go. Thankfully, I had a slightly better performance this time from my 13-year-old steed and I was airborne again. Keeping low and with the nose held level, I attempted to build up groundspeed. I was airborne and very sluggishly climbing out of the airfield, but only just. It was a sickening feeling. My rotor blades were only just holding their own against gravity and I didn't want to upset what meagre lift there was by making any abrupt movements. *Fly straight and level and slowly gain height* was my priority mantra. Unnervingly, directly ahead there was a lake looming and I definitely did not want a repeat performance of my Thailand ditching. I waited until I had as much height as I could before very tentatively putting in a shallow right-hand turn. It was a tense moment. Would I continue to hold my own against gravity, or slowly start to sink, as I had done in Thailand? Thankfully I stayed level, and as I then slowly gained height, the air became cooler. I could feel the rotors had more bite into the denser air and with an ever-lightening fuel load, soon the worst was over and I could relax once more. I made a mental note to try to offload some excess luggage in the next few days. It had been a worrying time and to think, *Roxy* could have been even heavier had I hung on to that original big jar of honey!

The afternoon flight took a further 3hrs 10mins, resulting in over eight hours flying throughout the day. As we closed in on Yekaterinburg, our last obstacle was to cross the Ural Mountains. This mountain range, running north–south across the whole country, forms a formidable physical barrier separating the European Russia of the west from the wilds of Siberia to the east. Needless to say, we approached it with considerable caution. As it turned out however, it proved to be a most benign crossing, with only a series of gently undulating low mountains of about 2500ft to negotiate. The visibility was kind to us also, so it was with great celebration that we dropped down the eastern flanks back to the flat lowland terrain of Western Siberia.

Wow, flying in Siberia! Our Russian adventure had really started now...

The vast landscape stretched out to the horizon in all directions. The ground had poor natural drainage and was extensively flooded and swampy in parts; the blanket-covering of billions of trees was regularly pockmarked with circular lagoons of dark, peaty water. Occasionally we passed by lazy, meandering rivers and I keenly eyed up any long sandbanks that had formed on the inside of the bends. With the complete absence of roads or open fields, these now were the only relatively safe emergency landing spots that remained.

Koltsovo International Airport in Yekaterinburg was an impressive size, yet it was often the larger and more commercial airports like this that were the least accommodating to small aircraft. Whilst being parked up overnight on a remote windswept area of the apron was fine for large commercial aircraft, it was definitely not ideal for us. My first objective therefore on landing was to find some hangarage.

Fortunately, the sudden arrival of two small, UK registered gyros soon attracted an inquisitive crowd of airport workers gathering to take selfies, so I chose them as my target audience for my well-practised 'any chance of a hangar?' routine. James looked on bemused as I managed to convince the managers of a nearby corporate jet maintenance building that we would take up hardly any space in the back of their voluminous hangar. After a few encouraging phone calls seeking permission, we were given the nod to taxi over towards the huge doors and push ourselves inside.

The floor of the hangar was gleaming. A busy GA light aircraft hangar would typically have all its aircraft squeezed in with their wings and fuselages interlocking, but this VIP corporate jet hangar had only two aircraft inside. Happily, they had oodles of space between their tails in which to park our small itinerant gyros and even with their overnight covers on, G-YROX and G-KTCH were hard to spot parked up near the rear wall. It was a great feeling, after such a long day of flying, to head off for the nearby hotel leaving the aircraft in such a warm and secure spot.

12 May 2019: Yekaterinburg, Russia (non-flying day)

As luck would have it, the airport had its own hotel on site. We had wearily checked in with the hope of making a quick turnaround, which would have seen us off again early the next morning. However, events as they happened, played out differently.

Evgeny had assumed that we would be needing avgas at this stop and contacted us in the morning to say that he had a problem getting it to us. His explanation was the avgas was having to be trucked in from 100 miles away and his refueller was having difficulty in getting permission to transport the fuel over such a long distance. This fuel delay was costing us time and as the hours ticked by, the day was steadily slipping away. On the phone, with growing frustration, I emphasised to Evgeny that we didn't actually *need* to run on the hard-to-source avgas at all. In reality, both of our Rotax 914 turbo engines preferred to run on regular unleaded petrol. And what's more, I had noticed while looking out from a hotel corridor, that the airport even had its very own private petrol station to supply its airside fleet of cars and service trucks. The required fuel was all of 100m away, rather than 100 miles.

With airport permission, we could have easily taxied along to the pumps and conveniently filled up with all the fuel we needed. It would also be much cheaper than using the avgas. This option was not allowed however, as aircraft were forbidden to taxi or be pushed into the fuel station. But, it did flag up a workable alternative, that we could simply be supplied with jerrycans of local unleaded petrol instead. As the ongoing avgas fuel delay had now caused the onward flight to be scrubbed for the day, we organised locally to do just that for the following morning.

20

Trans-Asia and the Bering Strait: Russia to Alaska, USA

13 May 2019: Yekaterinburg, Russia – Tyumen, Russia

A daily flying routine between James and me was quickly becoming familiar. As lead out aircraft, I would talk to the tower as I taxied to the runway, with James following on closely behind. Shortly after take-off and upon establishing our initial heading, we would then confirm our chat frequency on the radio. Because I was leading out, I couldn't see James's take-off behind me, so I was always reassured to finally hear his voice and know that he had me clearly in his view ahead. I would then continue on at a slow pace until he caught up close behind and we could settle into our loose flying formation, with G-KTCH typically positioned slightly behind and just off to the side of G-YROX, for the rest of the flight.

After clearing the immediate, busiest area around the airfield, the tower normally handed us over to the regional control frequency, who we then reported to throughout the mid-section of the flight. At this stage, while I focussed on navigating our route ahead, James usually took on the lead comms role for our 'two ship' formation and we would then be periodically deafened by a deep-voiced Russian controller booming out:

"**Golllllllf Kilo Tango Charlie Hotel**. What is your position?"

Sometimes we could give him an immediate reply. Sometimes we were out of range to respond directly. And on occasions we had to consult with each other on the chat frequency to work out what the booming voice had *actually said* in his heavy Russian accent. As the radio coverage became evermore patchy farther east, we also had to rely on giving our position reports via a satellite phone or by relaying our messages via a passing commercial airliner, flying high above us.

On arrival at Tyumen, we were presented with another large airport. There were masses of crisscrossing taxiways, access roads and other infrastructure, and its two vast runways (3000m and 2700m in length) were set in an impressive L-shape configuration. They were wide as well as long, and we could easily have landed widthways on either one.

I had initially felt confident we might again find some help to organise an overnight hangar. Alas, it was a bad case of 'too-big-an-airport-itis'. Considering two world-circling gyroplanes were an unusual curiosity, most small and medium airports usually gave us quite a lot of attention, but a large self-important airport was *far too busy* for any of that sort of nonsense. I suspected we might be in trouble even while taxiing in from the runway. We were directed to park at the very farthest reaches of the apron, alongside a graveyard of scrapped planes that were slowly being butchered for parts, an ominous sign that we were perhaps regarded merely as a nuisance to be tolerated.

Despite the initial cold shoulder, I still put on my best performance to see if we could find any shelter for the night. Initially at least things appeared promising, and we waited patiently for a couple of hours in the hope that we might soon get moved to somewhere better, but eventually the word came back that we just had to stay put where we were.

At least we were able to use the waiting time for some ongoing maintenance, including the fixing of an annoying oil seep that had developed in a banjo pipe fitting under the rear of *Roxy*'s engine.

Basic accommodation was within a walkable distance but because we had hung on at the airport for so long, finding food became our next problem. Our only option was back in the airport terminal where a small café kiosk was able to at least supply us with beer and snacks. It was meagre rations but could easily have been much worse (they could have been out of beer).

14 May 2019: Tyumen, Russia – Omsk, Russia

Breakfast was once again back in the terminal café, (though this time without the beer...). Looking up on the departures board, we were quite amazed to see that **G-YROX** was now displayed as a scheduled flight departure to Omsk. It looked quite odd to see *Roxy* up there in lights alongside destinations such as Beijing, Sochi, Novosibirsk and Moscow. The same display was up on all the departure boards around the terminal. Being a joint flight of two aircraft, they had abbreviated our flight information to the first aircraft that I had listed earlier on their departure form. As we saw G-YROX plastered prominently over all the screens, I think James was a bit miffed that poor G-KTCH didn't even get a mention.

Getting under way, we suffered a lengthy 3km taxi to reach the holding point for the active runway, and then had to endure an additional overly long hold while waiting for the jet turbulence wake from previous traffic to clear. Burning fuel all the while, as if sitting in a traffic jam, I cursed the need for us to visit such large, impersonal, busy airports. But at least our next destination in Kalachevo, on the outskirts of Omsk was going to be at the other end of the scale – as it was a small welcoming grass strip.

The flight was speedy, with a strong tailwind helping to push us along. The downside of this however was that on arrival at Kalachevo, that same strong and gusty tailwind was now blowing directly across the runway. I immediately sensed that this might prove to be a very tricky landing. Rapidly weighing up our limited options, I briefed James on how we would make our final approach.

As with my previous landings at Le Touquet and Vagar, in strong, gusty crosswinds, the safest way to land our gyros in these conditions, was to ignore the convention of a 'normal' fixed-wing final approach and just land directly into wind, across the runway. However here at Kalachevo, several buildings and fences now obscured most of the clear crosswind approaches, but I soon spotted an area where the perimeter fence was set back from the active runway. It gave us a wider box of grass to aim for, so I briefed James to just follow my line of flight in, so that we could then both land directly into the wind.

Banking hard left, I dropped down steeply towards the airstrip and felt a tremendous sense of the ground rushing up towards me. While this was all completely normal for a gyro, to the onlookers waiting for us on the ground it must have seemed like I was willingly setting up for a controlled crash landing. Why else would I be plummeting headlong at 60 knots towards the grass?

Building plenty of momentum in the rotor, I aimed to skim the perimeter fence and then settle further towards the ground as I crossed the runway. The grass box was approaching rapidly, but I pulled hard back on the stick at the last moment to flare *Roxy* steeply, raising the nosewheel high and almost setting the tail onto the ground. As the main rotor caught the air, much like a drag parachute, it snuffed out the last of my forward momentum. My main wheels momentarily skimmed along the top of the long outfield grass, before finally settling in for a gentle touchdown. With a pinpoint, zero-rollout landing, I still had plenty of room to spare as the boundary fence remained a good 20m ahead of me.

I then had a slightly anxious wait for James. I knew he was following in close behind me and would aim to land very close by. However, as I was still facing the fence, I was unable to watch his approach to landing. I was blind and couldn't yet move. If I had started to taxi and turn either left or right of my stationary position, I could have unwittingly put myself right into his flight path. So like a sitting duck, I just had to wait and hope for two things: he wouldn't hit me in the gusty conditions; and he would land short enough to avoid smashing into the boundary fence ahead.

Having just landed, I knew that a short-field, on-the-spot landing in such challenging and turbulent conditions would need James's undivided attention. I therefore maintained radio silence to allow his brain to cope fully with the instantaneous stick and pedal movements required to coax his gyro in for a soft landing.

With a sudden woosh, James swept into my peripheral vision on my left side. Still moving, he was getting close to the fence, but had already pulled on a good flare with the stick. It was amazing how a rapidly approaching fence sharpens the reactive senses, and finally pulling up short, he dropped vertically down the last couple of feet into the long grass. We had arrived!

In the cold gusty conditions, it had been a hard flight of 4hrs 20mins. We looked pretty weather-beaten as we gratefully pushed the gyros into an open-fronted dirt floor hangar. The small aeroclub at Kalachevo, as with the stop at Ufa, again had a lovely enthusiastic, informal and friendly atmosphere as we gathered together for some group photos. With the gyros soon put to bed, we were gathered up into the care of a couple of local entrepreneurs in order to share a ride into the city. Later in the evening, we were treated to some exclusive fine dining in downtown Omsk, and the following morning we were taken to a very modern European-style coffee shop, where the owner invited us to sample some of the best tasting coffee that I had anywhere in Russia.

Friendly hosts and great coffee... We were now settling well into our Russian adventure.

15 May 2019: Omsk, Russia – Novosibirsk, Russia

Still a bit achy from the previous day's demanding flight, I wasn't enjoying the gusty breeze during my pre-flight checks – it was particularly cold and biting. The wind conditions had definitely not eased much in either strength or direction since our dramatic arrival. Fortunately, I soon found a more sheltered sunny spot, tucked in beside the hangar building to finish my pre-flight checks and to repack my luggage. After much friendly banter with the local club members (and making friends with their small aeroclub dog), it was time to go.

In a continuation of our unusual manoeuvres of the previous day, I led us out and lined up at an angle on the far-right edge of the grass runway. Aiming for the far-left edge of the runway (and its nearby fence line) about 100m away, I hoped that even though we were now again heavy with fuel, the strong crosswind would assist us in achieving a relatively short take-off. My early apprehension soon disappeared as we comfortably cleared the fence and climbed into wind to gain height before looping around to give everyone a send-off wave.

Our destination was now Severny Airport, in the city of Novosibirsk (New Siberia). It had once been the main airport for the city, but it closed for commercial operations in 2010 and was repurposed for light aviation and as a heliport for the local police. On making our final approach, the old extensive runway was still visible, though we only required its very short, but relatively clean section of active runway to land.

A few minutes after our arrival, a sleek black R44 Raven helicopter dramatically swooped in to land close by. Its two occupants shut down the helo and then hopped out and came directly over to greet us. One of the figures looked quite familiar, in his own distinctive style… long flowing hair, a tan leather flying jacket, an open shirt (complete with a cravat), and a beard that either Guy Fawkes or Shakespeare would have been proud of. Amazingly it turned out to be Quentin Smith, a world-renowned UK helicopter pilot and better known to many in the aviation world simply as 'Q'. He had been busy giving advanced helicopter training locally with his co-pilot and had decided to pop over and say hello.

It was all quite a surreal experience. I had previously known of Q's global helicopter exploits from afar. For many years he had played significant and key roles in the success of many long-distance flying expeditions. We had never actually met, but now all of a sudden, he had popped up seemingly out of nowhere, to share a cup of tea in the middle of Siberia. We spent an enjoyable hour drinking tea and telling yarns with around 15 or so people, both flyers and locals, all squeezed into a small wooden trailer that doubled up as the pilots' clubhouse.

There was an immediate and familiar meeting of minds; long-distance adventure pilots are something of a breed apart. As they say, it takes one to know one. A significant flight or some particular dodgy situation can perhaps easily be described to anyone, but its true significance, of how it *really feels* to experience it first-hand, is always much more difficult to convey. This aspect is only really understood by those who have already been there, experienced the same sorts of situation, faced the same sort of mental and physical isolation and adversity.

Crossing cold oceans, hot deserts or even the vast emptiness of Siberia in a small, vulnerable single-engine aircraft was not for the faint-hearted, and so no wonder a special sort of kinship develops between those who have *been there, done that.* It transpired that Q and I had actually used many similar routes and stopover points between the UK, Middle East, SE Asia and Japan, albeit a decade apart. Back in 2000, Q had completed an around-the-world flight with Jennifer Murray (first solo female helicopter circumnavigation pilot) and Colin Bodill (first solo microlight circumnavigation pilot), whereas I covered much of the same ground in 2010-11. Even though they had also been accompanied by a fixed-wing support aircraft (handy for transporting extra fuel, excess luggage and an accompanying film crew), the very real challenges of solo piloting their individual aircraft through all sorts of adversities such as brutal weather, niggling mechanical issues and the overall bureaucratic minefield of global flights, remained the same.

Soon enough it was time for them to depart. Twenty-first century photos and selfies were taken to mark the occasion, but considering the enormity of where we were and what we were doing, it felt more like we were posing for pioneering aviation photos from the 1920s instead. Externally, our smiling happy faces were on show for the camera, yet internally, as with those courageous early pioneers, we shared a constant unsettled apprehension of what unknowable challenges awaited us on venturing into the skies. Wishing us a heartfelt best of luck, Q and his co-pilot then climbed back aboard their R44 and as a parting finale, proceeded to perform the most incredible aerial exit manoeuvre that I have ever seen.

Q picked up into a three-metre hover directly in front of us and then slowly reversed away up into the air, tail first. Next, he flew the helicopter backwards at speed and also pushed the tail boom steeply up into the air. The fuselage was now pointing down at the ground at about a 60-degree angle. The machine hung in the air momentarily at this crazy angle before Q encouraged it to fall into a nose-down forward dive, plunging steeply towards the ground. Banking hard and pulling out of the dive enabled him to level out and with a final arcing curve, he slowly circled away from our position, as both pilots madly waved their adrenaline-fuelled goodbyes, and they were *offski*. The whole manoeuvre was one flowing fluid motion, and Q had made the extremely difficult action appear so easy and natural... human and machine working in perfect harmony with the laws of physics. I suppose with a lifetime of flying all sorts of helicopters, he had had a long time to perfect such amazing techniques.

A highlight later in the evening was a visit to a very ornate supermarket. Before the flight, I had wondered just how well provisioned the towns and cities would be once we travelled into the more remote areas of Siberia. In Novosibirsk city at least, I was pleasantly surprised to see a huge and varied array of food and drink on display. Though perhaps unsurprisingly, about 70% of the alcohol shelf space appeared to be devoted to a myriad of Vodkas. A large four-tiered cascading fountain stood at the entrance to the shop, where the tills were somewhat bizarrely adorned with wooden fretwork trestles and floor-to-ceiling blue lace curtains. But apart from this local 'Arabian Nights' décor, the actual produce for sale was all *top notch* and reasonably priced. We were able to stock up on a few emergency and essential items, just like a couple of cowboys filling our saddlebags with precious *vittles* before heading out into the wild west. Only in our case it would be the wild east, in just a few days' time.

16 May 2019: Novosibirsk, Russia – Krasnoyarsk, Russia

As each day wore on, the overwhelmingly vast Siberian landscape became that little bit more familiar. I was gradually becoming accustomed to the endless carpet of trees, and the lack of roads, people and landing places. Between the 'islands' of populated cities, I felt it was very similar to crossing the oceans. Exposed to such an intimidating and dangerous landscape for any length of time, I seemed to grow ever more accepting and comfortable with the constant challenge and the inherent risks. It was perhaps a human coping mechanism that all pioneering explorers must use. That said, I never became more complacent, as of course all the risks remained very real.

With this newfound familiarity, I also thought back to how I had felt encountering the edge of a large expanse of desert for the first time. Initially I had found myself edging along its flanks for as long as possible, staying within a few miles of the relatively safe farmlands and road network. But before long, I rationalised the risks, reasoned with my fears and persuaded myself that it would be OK to venture out into this unknown type of wilderness. Such apprehension subsequently cropped up with every new type of hostile terrain I flew over, and these forests of Siberia were no exception.

Luckily for us, on our arrival at Krasnoyarsk, the main international airport had a smaller outlying neighbour situated barely a mile away. Krasnoyarsk Cheremshanka Airport proved to be much less busy and was a perfect size for us to use. In advance of our arrival, James's DHL sponsors had put him in contact with their regional representative and he had agreed to meet us. This immediately gave us a *friend in camp* and made our overnight logistics that much easier to arrange.

We were pushed into a hangar with a fabulous highly polished floor, one that you could have happily eaten your dinner off. It made such a contrast from the moss-covered earthen floor we had experienced in Omsk a few days before.

17 May 2019: Krasnoyarsk, Russia (non-flying day)

Since leaving Moscow, flying across the Russian interior had been tricky in terms of potential headwinds associated with the flat exposed terrain, but the added complications of rising ground and mountain weather had not yet been a worry. This was soon to change however in the next few days, notably on a two-day foray through higher ground to reach the small town of Taksimo. Both there, and farther east when reaching the town of Tomtor (following the ominously named Road of Bones), we needed a window of several successive days of settled mountain weather in which to quickly bounce in, stay overnight and then bounce out again. These were not places that we wanted to end up being stuck in for several days. Good timing and an accurate forecast were therefore essential. We had been fortunate so far in avoiding weather delays, but we were now stalled for a day whilst the logistics of upcoming airfields and weather patterns were assessed and reconfigured. As ever, it gave us extra time to catch up with some admin, rest up, take stock and work on any minor mechanical issues.

In the late afternoon back at the hotel, James and I chatted and sipped well-earned beers beside a wall-to-wall, floor-to-ceiling window overlooking the street below. The late sun was streaming in and we were glad of a little oasis of calm normality. We were now thousands of miles from home turf, but slowly Russia was beginning to feel ever more comfortable and familiar. James had spotted a Russian McDonald's just around the corner from our hotel, and he was keen for us to go-grab ourselves a Russian *Big Mac.* Perhaps unsurprisingly, we soon discovered that the food, the service, the décor and the layout were all practically identical to the McDonald's outlets in every other country around the world. Siberia may have been geographically very remote from Western culture, but it was certainly not isolated from the West's pervasive, far-reaching influence when it came to selling burgers.

18 May 2019: Krasnoyarsk, Russia – Bratsk, Russia

Relaxed and recharged from our day off, we made quick progress towards Bratsk. The swathes of blanket tree cover were now periodically broken once again by hundreds of acres of sprawling farmland, interspersed and dotted with smaller copses of trees and hedgerows. Temporarily freed from the constant danger of having to make a forced landing into the thick forest canopy, we found this intermittent open terrain to be a most welcome and relatively safe playground. Flying at a low level, we could once again skim across the empty fields and weave through the stands of individual trees.

Like in Krasnoyarsk, we avoided using the main airport in Bratsk as we had a much better alternative. We headed for a gravel strip on the outskirts of town, near Morgudon. Our approach path brought us close to a huge industrial plant, twinned with a belching smoke plume which we had seen for many miles before our arrival. We were met upon landing by a fantastic local pilot who was a real flying enthusiast. Amongst a wide selection of aircraft that he had hangared was – of all things – a Aérospatiale Gazelle helicopter.

The hangar had large glass windows, which allowed the late afternoon sun to stream in. It was lovely to be unpacking our gyros in such a warm and welcoming, dry space. We were also met by yet another local DHL agent, Ivan, who had travelled quite a way to meet up with us. He quickly became our local guide for the evening, and being an international freight handler, he was also able to lighten our luggage, by organising the shipping of some unneeded kit back to the UK.

19 May 2019: Bratsk, Russia – Kazachinskoye, Russia

The gravel strip was fortunately well maintained, and a few minutes after a dusty take-off, I throttled back to let James catch up with me. We then headed on together towards a large lake that lay directly in our flight path. To our surprise and much like I had experienced previously in northern Canada, large panels of thin ice covered the entire lake. They were much too thin to land on without breaking through to the icy water below. Fortunately, I was suited and booted as normal, wearing my trusty immersion suit, lifejacket, GPS tracker and personal locator beacon (PLB). My life raft was also permanently stowed directly under my left knee for good measure.

As a general rule, I preferred to always be prepared for any eventuality, regardless of the terrain below. Unfortunately, James had not yet decided to kit up in his immersion suit and lifejacket. Who could blame him? We were currently in the middle of a predominantly landlocked and heavily forested landscape after all. The sudden appearance of an expansive frozen lake had taken us unawares, and whereas I remained completely unfazed and charged on out over it, James was understandably much more reticent. He tried to minimise his time over water by tiptoeing around the edges, but in the end, the lake had to be crossed and James was forced to endure a nervous ten minutes doing so. Even the remotest chance of an over-water or wide river crossing en route after that, saw James immediately donning his lifejacket before take-off. Long-distance flying lesson learned: always expect the unexpected.

Landing at the small town of Kazachinskoye was supposed to be for a quick fuel stop only. We had made good time from Bratsk, only three hours in the air, so we expected a fast turnaround to allow us to make a further four-hour flight to Taksimo in the afternoon. Alas it was not to be.

Soon after our arrival we sensed there was a problem; the airport was deserted, there was no refuelling handler waiting with supplies, or even anywhere to grab a quick bite to eat. There was nothing except a desolate windswept apron that was dusty, deeply cracked and full of weeds. We kicked about and explored around some long-abandoned Soviet-era buildings close by. At one point, a ramshackle car appeared.

"Ah great, at last the fuel?" I hoped.

Ah again, maybe not... A local family – mum, dad, teenage daughter and a small boy aged about four – spilled out of the car, keen to have a look at these strange flying machines. They were very welcoming and friendly, and as the small boy sat in *Roxy* for family photos, I offered them all some chocolate. Even though we shared no common language we still happily enjoyed each other's company. After a short conversation between the parents, the father then hurried off to bring us something from the car; it was a half-bottle of a brown coloured vodka-type drink. I couldn't tell whether it was shop bought or a home-brewed hooch, but I knew that it was a kind gift nevertheless (even though we couldn't possibly drink it while flying). There was also another gift – a large frozen fish – wrapped up in a plastic bag. Quite what the hell we were supposed to do with a frozen fish at that precise moment was not important. What *was* important was they had clearly offered us whatever it was they had readily available, whether suitable or not. And I felt it was a very touching and generous gesture.

On the fuel front, it was still not looking hopeful. We waited and waited with the precious afternoon slowly slipping away. Several increasingly frustrated phone calls with Evgeny back in Moscow followed, with him repeatedly reassuring us that the refuelling guys would be there soon. They eventually did turn up, but it was infuriatingly late in afternoon.

Evgeny was full of expectation that we would now be soon on our way, but I wasn't having any of it. The day was now completely lost. There was no way we were going to set off on a four-hour flight in the evening. It would have been madness, as anything could have gone wrong in the failing light. I had to resort to yet more shouting on the phone. Once again, there was an attempt to cajole us into following his 'convenient' schedule, but this was at the risk of compromising our own self-imposed margins of safety. There was no doubt in my mind that we would be now staying put overnight.

It was not ideal. As the curious local family had proven, this part of the airfield was not at all secure and anyone could have easily wandered in overnight. As we wrapped up the gyros as securely as we could, there was talk of a local night watchman being put on guard overnight, but we saw little evidence of him during our stay.

Whilst unlucky with the fuel debacle, we had much better luck with the accommodation – a plush, two-apartment log cabin no less. James took the upstairs flat, while I dropped my bags in the ground-floor one. I very much enjoyed the contrast of this simple accommodation, out in the wilds of rural Siberia, compared with the big urban places we usually stayed in. This relaxed, idyllic existence made for a peaceful evening. But my new-found tranquillity was soon rudely shattered early the next day…

20 May 2019: Kazachinskoye, Russia – Taksimo, Russia

BANG! BANG! BANG!

I awoke with a jolt at 6am. Someone was urgently hammering on the cabin door, and I jumped out of bed to open it. It was our local handler, who was aggressively demanding that we get up immediately and be ready in a few minutes to be taken back to the airport. This was not what we had arranged the night before; we had planned to be picked up at 8am after at least having had breakfast and got ourselves repacked. There was no way we could be rushed and bullied into taking on another long and uncertain day of flying before we were fully ready. The handler continued shouting for us to "Go [to the] airport, now!".

There was no real emergency going on, the sense of urgency was only being created to fit in with the handler's own agenda, not ours, so I shouted back in anger. I stated that we were just not ready to "Go airport, now" and that we wouldn't be "Going airport" until 8am, as previously arranged. I added that I refused to take any orders from someone who had already messed up our whole previous day with refuelling issues. As he heard 'fuel' being mentioned his whole aggressive demeanour dropped, as he knew full well that he had already caused us a lengthy delay and was no longer in any position to make any *urgent* demands of our time. I had won the argument.

Over many years, in many countries, I had experienced similar pushy handlers who expected me to fit in with *their* own scheduling and agenda. This was despite it being *me* who was ultimately footing their bill, and *me* who was taking all the consequent risks in the air if the aircraft was badly or dangerously packed after I had been rushed or hassled to quickly "go now" whilst still preparing for flight on the ground.

Standing in the cabin's doorway, I couldn't give a monkey's hoot about the handler's schedule. Somewhat crestfallen, he slumped off to make some phone calls in his car. I closed the door and went back to bed, still fuming.

As instructed, he returned at 8am to find us fully packed up and ready to go.

Back at the airport, Evgeny came on the phone to try to placate everyone and smooth over the cracks. He had been badly let down by the local refuelling fiasco and as a pilot himself, he empathised with our position. He was beginning to finally realise (after two weeks) just how arduous flying an open cockpit gyro over such challenging terrain actually was. With some much-needed mutual respect restored on both sides, he went on to offer me some sage advice for our next leg to Taksimo. It was a wise and welcome instruction that we could both easily agree on.

"After Lake Baikal," he said, "you will fly for two days west of the Stanovoy [Mountain] Range. There are no main road crossings on this route, only the railway line. Stay close always to the railway. *The railway equals life.*"

Thankfully, unlike James and I, the gyroplanes had remained completely undisturbed overnight and given that the fuelling had been carried out the evening before, we were able to quickly re-pack and get on our way.

* * *

Soon enough, as we began to climb and traverse our way up and through the first significant mountains since crossing the Urals, we were quite suddenly met with a spectacular sight. Visibility at this point was around 100 miles, and away off in the distance towards the south-west, stretching as far as we could see, was the mighty Lake Baikal. It was still partly frozen on its surface, and we only skirted around its northern flank, but its description as one of the world's most spectacular natural lakes was well founded. Incredibly, the lake extends to about 350 miles in length and in parts is around 50 miles wide.

Our onward route, continuing through the mountains towards Taksimo, was equally stunning. The main peaks were now towering way above us, but the valley floor thankfully remained wide and flat, with the reassuring presence of the railway line meandering its way along its length. As we continued to shadow it for hundreds of miles, I was constantly reminded of Evgeny's cautionary words, "the railway equals life". After so many recent days of flying over the predominantly flat Siberian plains, it was a gentle introduction into the much more remote and potentially hazardous high mountain flying that was yet to come, beyond Yakutsk, on the final quarter of the trans-Russia flight.

Taksimo marked the halfway point on our current two-day foray through the mountains. A small-scale regional airport, it had several regular scheduled flights to larger destinations and all the trappings of a busy commercial terminal, albeit all squeezed into a quaint compact wooden building. Once again, the gyros had to endure another night outdoors, whereas James and I managed to do slightly better, sharing a clean-but-threadbare twin room at a local hostel for workers.

I always looked on our various ad-hoc accommodations as *character-building* and enjoyed being in the midst of local Russian people. Evgeny had initially been worried that we might not have the standard of accommodation that he assumed we would need, but I just liked it even more for its honest authenticity. For food we were taken to a local bar/restaurant, which, with its extensively black painted interior, also appeared to double up as a night club. As it was still early evening, the only other guests were two drunk guys, who were kept busy propping up the bar.

21 May 2019: Taksimo, Russia – Olekminskiy, Russia – Yakutsk, Russia

During the daily pre-flight inspection and re-packing on the apron in Taksimo, a small group of local people came to visit. They were keen for photos and to see the 'flying motorbikes' that were blazing their way across Russia. One of the ladies, Natalya, presented me with a traditional good luck talisman that she had made. It was a small round disc about 10cm across and represented the sun, and hence good weather. Made with beads and what looked like reindeer fur set in a ring around the outside, it was intended to be worn around the neck like an Olympic medal. But as I put it on, I was worried that it would flap around in the wind when I was airborne. I thought for a minute about what to do with such a personally meaningful fluffy gift.

Then I had a brainwave... fluffy dice! As with the ubiquitous dice that can be seen hanging in countless boy-racer cars, I was able to *pimp my ride* and have *Roxy* wearing the talisman instead of me. With no rear-view mirror to hang it on, I swiftly lashed the disc securely onto the top of the instrument panel instead, where it would be most protected from the elements.

As an aside, the talisman has stayed attached there ever since. And many times afterwards, I was encouraged by glancing down at it, especially while in the midst of adverse or uncertain flying conditions. It was a constant reminder of that simple act of kindness and concern for my safe travel from a thoughtful Russian lady, who I had only met for a few brief minutes back in Taksimo. Quite often, flying eastwards late in the day, the western setting sun would cast its light over my shoulder directly onto the instrument panel. On such occasions the shiny beads of the talisman really sparkled with friendliness.

After 4hrs 30mins of flying from Taksimo, we arrived at a small airfield in Olekminskiy for refuelling. The surface was unusual because it was made of heavy red clay. Typically baked hard in the summer sunshine and then presumably frozen solid in the winter, it was currently neither. Soaked by recent heavy rains, the taxiways in places were now thick with sticky mud. I managed to pick my way around the worst parts, but James unfortunately fell foul of one innocent-looking patch, which soon resulted in his wheels and undercarriage being completely caked in red clay gloop.

Unlike our last refuelling fiasco, happily the fuel here was already waiting for us in 40-gallon drums. G-YROX and G-KTCH were both refilled up to the brim to see us safely all the way to the city of Yakutsk, another four hours or so away.

The second flight of the day went smoothly, but an awkward headwind picked up as we cleared the last of the Stanovoy Range foothills and began to follow the banks of the mighty Lena. The river was a tremendous work of nature, carving a continuous gorge for itself about 40m deep out of the surrounding flat lands. We flew at a low level to stay out of the headwind as best we could and followed the river for over 300 miles while it guided us all the way to Yakutsk.

Occasionally, we spotted small clusters of wooden shacks beside the riverbanks. Appearing long-since abandoned, we later found out that they would sometimes still be used by hunters or travellers during various parts of the year. Flying the river route was comforting as there were numerous sand bars and islands along its length that could have been landed on in an emergency. And, like flying the railway line before it, if anything had gone wrong in such an otherwise flat and featureless forested landscape, this time it was the *river* that equalled life.

The day's headwinds had really slowed our progress, and we landed at Magan Airport on the outskirts of Yakutsk a good hour later than we anticipated. We had been flying a total of nine hours over the two flights and were glad to be landing before sunset. On final approach, however, Magan's runway had one last surprise for us.

The whole area, we would soon find out, had been significantly affected by melting permafrost. The result was that the elderly concrete runway had become undulated like a huge, corrugated washboard. I was very thankful that a gyro can land at a walking pace, and so I was able to pick the smoothest part I could find on the cracked and upheaved concrete. Just a last dash of added adrenaline after a long and tiring flying day.

Alas as we taxied in, it appeared that our day still wasn't quite done yet, as a film crew and local newspaper reporter had been waiting for hours to meet us. So in the dwindling twilight, we yet again had to put on our best cheery and happy faces for the cameras. It had been an exceedingly long day and we now needed a solid rest.

22–27 May 2019: Yakutsk, Russia (non-flying days)

Traversing the terrain ahead for the rest of the Russian leg was now going to become ever more technically challenging. Siberia had been remote enough, but the Russian Far East region that we were fast approaching was going to be even more isolated, rugged and cold. It was also increasingly lacking in emergency support should we ever need it. Our next two flights were going to be once again into the mountains, this time the Verkhoyansk Range, which formed a dauntingly impressive wall of peaks up to 8000ft high, some 230 miles east of Yakutsk.

While planning for the next flight to Tomtor, I found a reasonable route that would at least give us the comfort of some sort of a road nearby. The ominously named Road of Bones would ultimately lead us all the way through the mountains to Magadan, some two days flight away.

The difficulty was that we didn't want to become stuck for any length of time in Tomtor. It was a small village with very few local amenities. If the weather closed in badly in the middle of the mountains, we might have been forced to stay there for perhaps a week or more, until flying conditions improved again. Our best option now was to sit and wait in the much larger city of Yakutsk until an ideal weather window appeared, one that would give us at least two consecutive clear days. This would allow us to fly through the mountains into Tomtor and then quickly fly out again the next day to reach the low-lying coastal city of Magadan.

The risks however of flying to Tomtor were difficult for me to both predict and mitigate. From Yakutsk, there was firstly 230 miles of heavily forested, flat plateau flying to cross, before even reaching the mountains, with practically no alternate landing options close by. Then there was a real possibility that we might reach the mountains, only to then find them impenetrable, due to the unpredictability of mist and cloud blocking our onward path at any time. Perhaps forced to turn back, we would then face a daunting slog, possibly against a stiff headwind, all the way back to the relative safety of Yakutsk. Worse still would be if we managed to enter the mountains and go beyond the point of no return for fuel range, only to be then engulfed on all sides by the weather. There was therefore no doubt in my mind (and it was easy to convince James the same way), that we simply had to wait until the weather was right.

Little did we know then, but it would be nearly a week before the next suitable weather window materialised.

One positive aspect of our enforced delay was that, with Evgeny's assistance, we were able to get an extension to our one-month visitor visas that were only valid for May. The problem had been magnified by my delayed initial entry into Russia, our various further delays along the way and now the added delay of waiting for weather in Yakutsk. We were clearly not going to make it out of Russia by the end of May, so after some discussions between Evgeny and the authorities back in Moscow, we spent several days visiting different local government offices in Yakutsk before our passport visas were duly amended. There was much relief all round.

During the process, we were guided with great efficiency around a plethora of non-descript government buildings dotted about the city. It was fascinating to visit the *inner sanctum* of these local government offices and I'm sure that few people, foreigners or Russians alike, were ever normally permitted to venture beyond the formidable front desk officials. It felt that we were given VIP status, a far cry from me having to wait in long queues within the Russian consulate buildings of Dublin, Manila and Tokyo, while trying to negotiate my onward flight from Japan.

* * *

With a few days to wait until the extended visas would be issued, there was a chance to relax a little and take in the sights of Yakutsk, reputed to be the world's coldest city, enduring an average winter temperature of -40°C. Happily though for us, in late May, it was a relatively balmy 20°C, which made for a very pleasant stroll in the bright sunshine. The whole city was within the permafrost zone, and as a result all the buildings were constructed a few feet above ground level and supported on concrete stilts. But unfortunately, the slow thawing of the permafrost in recent decades due to climate change has now become a serious concern for the region.

A visit to the world-leading Mammoth Museum, which is attached to Yakutsk's North-Eastern Federal University, showed us how the thawing tundra was slowly revealing its secrets. Inside their research labs, but kept deeply frozen, were some incredibly well-preserved woolly mammoths from the far north of Yakutia. When later invited to handle a mammoth's tooth, I was surprised at just how heavy it was.

Another trip was to the Museum of Permafrost, which was carved into a hillside. After passing through several sets of insulated airlock doors, we entered into a labyrinth of tunnels that remained at a constant temperature of -18°C, but without a refrigeration unit in sight. Fragile ice crystals hung off every surface, sparkling in the coloured floodlights and forming a surreal, other worldly backdrop to the intricate ice carvings that were scattered about on display. Bathed in the frigid atmosphere, it was such an extreme contrast to the sweltering deserts of Saudi Arabia and oppressive heat of central India.

Once back in the city and wandering around the busy streets, the urban ambiance felt surprisingly modern and cosmopolitan. Trendy coffee shops had a bohemian western vibe, while fast food burger joints and more traditional restaurants alike, all had a wide and varied menu.

One of the most intriguing local dishes I tried was frozen raw fish. It resembled curled strips of shaved ice, which I then dipped into a dry mix of salt and pepper before eating. It was thin enough to melt as you ate it and had the curious texture of a fishy ice lolly. Nonetheless, the taste was very pleasant, just like cold Japanese sashimi (though without the soy sauce and wasabi).

As the days rolled on, we began to make ourselves at home, even appearing as studio guests at the local TV station. We went on to give several interviews to local journalists and also visited a nearby school.

Another highlight of the week was a visit to Mr. Dapper's barber shop. To me, a defining trait of any long-distance journey is getting a haircut. It's something that sets a traveller apart from a tourist, as it is not an essential activity for people on a short holiday. As my circumnavigation journey took so long to complete, I ended up in barber shops in some tremendously far-flung places: Thailand, Borneo, Philippines, Japan and the USA. I was now able to add Yakutia to the growing list.

Normally for speed and simplicity, I always opt for a 'Number 3' with clippers, which results in all my hair being sheared to a length of 3/8 inch. It's something akin to mowing the lawn, with a bit of neat edging done around the ears and neck and can usually be all done in 10 minutes flat. Mr. Dapper however (for it was the very man himself that went to work on me, while James was assigned his talented assistant) managed to turn it into a full 45-minute session of creative *coiffuring.* Clipping, washing, combing and buffing was followed up with copious slicking of hair, using various mystery bottles of hair product, and yet more combing and buffing until eventually... *et voilà!* My hair was so neat and tidy that it rivalled the 18th green at St Andrews or Augusta. As fantastic as it looked, we were now also extremely late for a pre-arranged newspaper interview back at the hotel. Full of apologies for being so delayed, at least when we eventually arrived, we were both looking uber-presentable for the photos.

A little later in the day, I had hoped that we might meet up with Sergey Ananov, who was the Russian R22 helicopter pilot I had been waiting for in Nuuk, Greenland, when he was forced to ditch in the Davis Straight. He was due to be in Yakutsk, but alas Evgeny got late notice that he wouldn't be able to make it. Such a pity, as I was looking forward to meeting him face to face and sharing our global adventure stories. Hopefully someday our paths will finally cross.

* * *

Our urban distractions continued all week, but always in the back of my mind was the technicalities of the upcoming mountain flights. Several times, a two-day weather window began to look promising, only for the forecast picture to then deteriorate a few hours later returning us back to square one. There was no point in trying to convince ourselves that perhaps a poor forecast might not be *too* bad. Such casual optimism might have been OK when avoiding a light rain shower on a stroll around the local park, but in our case, unfavourable weather had much more serious consequences.

I had already heard of the notorious Road of Bones. The film actor Ewan McGregor and his buddy Charley Boorman had rode along it during their globe-trotting motorbike journey, the *Long Way Round*. They travelled eastbound from London to New York overland, shipping the bikes over the Bering Strait along the way. Their arduous account, filled with hardship and uncertainty, left little doubt of the road's hazardous remoteness. With rickety bridges across raging torrents, and endless miles of rough dusty tracks winding precariously through high mountain passes, it was a road of legend. For our flight, following the road through the mountains would at least provide some sense of security, as we could use it for an emergency landing. Yet I was also keenly aware that such a self-rescue option might only allow us to jump out of the frying-pan and straight into the fire.

Most worrying was the prospect of being closed in within a steep-sided mountain valley, with the path ahead over a mountain pass blocked by low cloud and mist. But to mitigate that risk, I devised a creative plan that would hopefully allow us to escape such a dire situation, a plan that only perhaps a gyroplane pilot could ever hope to use.

The night before our departure into the mountains, I shared the plan with Eddie back at his home office in the UK. As usual, he would be constantly monitoring our flight remotely in real time by following our updated GPS tracker signals online. I explained that if the trackers indicated that we had suddenly stopped in the mountains, he should hold off immediately alerting search and rescue. Instead, he should watch closely to see if the signals then begin to move slowly along the road. My plan was that if we were indeed cut off and unable to cross over a mountain pass, we had the novel option to land on the road, align the rotor blades fore and aft and then simply ground taxi both aircraft up and over the mist-shrouded pass and down into the next valley.

Once safely down and clear of the cloud base, I proposed that we could hopefully then take off again from the road and continue merrily on our way. It was a comforting thought to have such a practical (albeit highly unorthodox) solution for this very real risk. Though I doubt such a radical technique would ever be featured in any *Beginners Guide to Mountain Flying* textbook!

28 May 2019: Yakutsk, Russia – Tomtor, Russia

At last, with a promising forecast it was time to get going again. The journey back out to Magan Airport was a rather wild ride as the road surface was broken and undulated crazily, all thanks to the slowly thawing permafrost. At one point I closed my eyes, thinking back to carefree summer holiday journeys bouncing over similar bumpy roads on Achill Island on the west coast of Ireland. Those roads weren't deformed from thawing ground however, but rather from the underlying peat bogs. Alas my happy childhood memories proved fleeting and all too soon the familiar, constant apprehension of dealing with the uncertainty of crossing the Siberian wilderness crept back into my thoughts. The Russian transit, previously felt to be quite manageable, was now gradually becoming ever more intimidating by the day.

The flight *towards* the mountains was, as predicted, uneventful. The view up ahead though, was much less benign. Like a massive granite wall, the mountains just started abruptly, rising dramatically from the forested flat lands and with no gentle rolling foothills in which to acclimatise. Leading our route in, I had to make sure I found the correct valley. With such a long and technical flight ahead, I knew we had very little room for any navigational errors. Finding ourselves flying up the wrong valley could have been a very costly mistake.

Almost immediately, the valley sides became quite steep, and within a few short meandering bends the flat plains behind us were obscured from view and all but forgotten. We were at once thrown into the technicalities of mountain flying, but at least the road snaked reassuringly along the valley floor below. Having already flown through some seriously rugged mountain landscapes – navigating the jagged ridges of Oman, crossing the Thai border from Myanmar, traversing the high Rockies, negotiating northern Canada and crossing the ice sheet of southern Greenland – I was fairly familiar with what to expect and most importantly how my aircraft could perform. James on the other hand, being a relatively novice pilot, to date had virtually no such gyroplane experience in these extreme environments. This gave me some added concern, as this wholly unforgiving terrain could yet prove to be an extremely dangerous training ground for attempting to 'learn on the job'.

The strong cross-tailwind that had previously helped push us along over the forests was now an extra hazard. We had to be cautious of where to position ourselves within the steep valley walls to avoid the vicious downdraughts spilling down from the higher peaks. I had to directly eyeball the terrain ahead on each winding bend and determine our best route through the valley. I flew a few hundred metres ahead of James to allow me space to suddenly change course, if needed. I was then able to report back to him on each bend, advising where the best position was to stay in the updraughts and how to avoid the worst of any downdraughts. The confused rough terrain made it tricky to get it right every time however, and occasionally a sudden sharp downdraught still seemed to arrive out of nowhere. This often caused *Roxy* to drop like a stone towards the jagged rocks below, both rapidly focussing my mind and sharpening my adrenaline-fuelled reactions. Fortunately, the situation was usually short lived, as I instinctively battled the invisible enemy with rapid and fluid use of stick, throttle and pedals, until I could wrestle and cajole my way back out into more stable air once more. Danger averted, there would then be a quick call back to James to warn him to avoid following my *exact* path in that area.

We tiptoed onwards, picking our way from one zone of relative safety to the next. In order to traverse the highest mountain pass, we had to climb to a very chilly 6500ft and well above the surrounding snowline. So it was with much relief when this barrier was finally crossed, as it marked the end of the highest ground (for now at least). It was then all downhill and a relatively flat valley run for the rest of the way to Tomtor.

Passing through these high mountains marked another significant milestone for me. I was once more passing through 140 degrees east of Greenwich, the same longitude as Shonai Airport in Japan (some 1700 miles to the south). From this point onwards, until my arrival once more on the Pacific coastline of Oregon, USA, I would be flying over the last remaining lines of longitude in my journey to fully circumnavigate the world. This would also include crossing the International Date Line in the Bering Strait, something I was looking forward to very much.

Tomtor proved to be a particularly interesting stopover. We were not exactly sure what accommodation to expect, but it turned out to be a delightful, self-catered guest house. Surprisingly, the owners were actually quite used to hosting foreigners, as travelling film crews and the like often visited to document daily life in what is the coldest inhabited settlement on Earth. The record-setting temperature of -71.2°C was recorded just a few miles up the road.

Self-catering meant that we now needed to go shopping and our hosts advised us to visit a small nondescript house just off one of the main streets in town. Unfortunately, large puddles of melted permafrost had partly blocked off many of the rough roads and tracks around the place, though helpfully between the buildings, numerous rickety wooden duckboards had been laid out across the soggy ground to aid our progress. At one point we also had to clamber over a large, heavily lagged overground pipe that was running between buildings, which was presumably part of a district heating system. Eventually, after much teetering, scrambling and vaulting, we were finally directed around the back of a house and into a small one-room shop. Although the stock on display was extremely limited, there was at least enough to make a basic picnic: apple juice, a sort of fritter in breadcrumbs, pasta, coleslaw, yoghurt and tinned fish.

As it turned out, it all tasted great. We were at that point, where we could have eaten anything and been incredibly thankful for it.

29 May 2019: Tomtor, Russia – Magadan, Russia

Road of Bones, day two… and the morning weather was mercifully remaining stable.

The mountainous terrain now became a little more user-friendly as the valleys gradually became much flatter and wider, and happily this easier flying continued until the last 80 miles or so around Magadan. Then the mountains once again became steeply jagged, with the valleys more winding and closed in. The Road of Bones also took a circuitous route at this point, skirting around to the north-west of these higher peaks. On previously studying the charts, I could see that continuing to follow the road and its main valley, would add considerable mileage to our journey. I could also see however that with some careful navigation, we could take a short cut through a side valley that would hopefully then deliver us safely out of the mountains quite close to Magadan's Sokol Airport.

As soon as we arrived at the entrance to the intended side valley, I looked nervously along it to gauge its suitability. It looked promising, with clear visibility. And it also opened up nicely as it dropped away in altitude. Advising James to follow me in, we left the relative safety of the road behind and I soon made friends with a wide and winding river instead. As it flattened out into the coastal lowlands, it displayed numerous long sandbanks that were ideal for emergency landing spots. However, the weather on this coastal side of the mountains had now changed dramatically. Heavy, grey rain-bearing clouds began rolling in off the Sea of Okhotsk, and so our final approach into Magadan was a wet, murky and dismal affair. I didn't mind too much though, as we had just conquered two of our most unpredictable mountain days and could now look forward to the next few days of lowland coastal flying.

Sokol was a main regional airport, and it had an expansive apron with plenty of parking. As always, I tried as hard as I could to get some overnight shelter for the aircraft in one of the many inviting hangars and storage sheds. It would have been so nice to get out of the persistent drizzly rain, but my efforts were to no avail. So once again, we had to wrap up G-YROX and G-KTCH and leave them parked up out in the open overnight, just a few yards from warm and dry shelter.

Magadan was the principal city in this part of the Far East region, and while driving in from the airport we were asked where we might like to stay. After two days in the mountains and our recent frugal accommodation in Tomtor, James was keen to return to a bit more luxury. Rather hastily, he asked the driver to take us to the best hotel the city had to offer, thinking that in such a remote outpost the best hotel might translate to be a mediocre one by European standards. This proved to be a costly mistake. We were duly dropped off at a suburban hotel where the rooms were more luxuriously appointed than any we'd previously stayed in, and where the reception staff proceeded to put us into two of their best penthouse suites. Arriving late and leaving early the next day, it was frustrating that we had precious little time to appreciate any of the luxury that was on offer. Unfortunately (though unsurprisingly), even though we had hardly used the place overnight, the next morning we were still each presented with a hefty *luxury bill* to match the rooms.

While *Roxy* had been stuck in Japan, I had many times planned and re-planned all the possible routings from northern Hokkaido up through the Russian Far East region. Flying north from Japan, I had ideally planned to route around the western shoreline of the Sea of Okhotsk to reach Magadan. But now, by a twist of fate, I had finally actually made it to Magadan by flying in from the west instead. Broadly speaking, these two approaches were the only feasible gyroplane circumnavigation routes (eastbound) around the world: a southern route (such as my original routing to Japan) and a northern route (crossing Russia), separated by the impenetrable Himalayas in the middle. Approaching the Bering Sea, both routes coincided in Magadan before following an identical route north towards the Bering Strait and Alaska, the only route available to get across the Pacific Ocean.

It was therefore an incredibly special moment to finally reunite with what would have been my original southern routing up through

Russia, having planned for it so carefully ten years earlier. The next few stopovers, from Magadan up to Provedinia Bay, already felt like familiar old friends to me, even though I had never actually been there. I had spent many hours peering down at them all from Google Earth. Small random settlements, hidden away in a vast country, and yet all just happening to be the correct distances apart to allow an adventurous gyroplane pilot to hop, skip and jump between them.

I had long searched and researched for answers to basic questions online: would they have an adequate runway? communications? fuel? food? accommodation? Well dear reader, we would now find out *first-hand* in the next few days.

30 May 2019: Magadan, Russia – Evensk, Russia

As the reassuring Road of Bones had finished in Magadan, there were now no further long-distance highways to follow until Anchorage, and I once again had to constantly keep my eyes open for any safe landing spots en route. I was happy however to be once more returning to the coast, having had my last sniff of salty air while crossing the North Sea to the Netherlands over a month previously. After crossing a 115-mile peninsula to the east of Magadan, we finally joined the coastline and began a 200-mile seaside jaunt north-east to Evensk. These miles of terrific coastal flying turned out to be some of the most memorable of the whole Russian transit.

When looking at this section of coast on Google Earth, the entire shoreline appeared to have a white line drawn along it. Yes, all *200 miles* of it. In reality, I discovered this whiteness to be a wave-cut pebbly beach, which was backed by a steep escarpment of ragged cliffs, topped off by a uniform blanket of trees. An emergency landing would have been possible on the beach but, because of the many large boulders, randomly strewn about, a touch down would have been similar to Neil Armstrong's landing of the LEM *Eagle* on the moon. Though I was not sure I would have been as successful or as graceful as him at last minute boulder avoidance whilst landing, using the *mark one eyeball* technique.

Potential emergency landings aside, this was now beach flying *on steroids.* James took up position, some 100m astern of me, and off we blasted, skimming and weaving above the pebble shoreline and boulders, across the bays and around the headlands for almost 200 straight miles. Incredible.

We were also extremely lucky with the weather; the visibility was gin-clear, the sky was blue, and there was only the slightest breath of wind.

Along the way, something up ahead didn't look quite right. Away off in the distance, one of the big, scattered boulders seemed to be moving. I double-checked, but sure enough I was not seeing things. As the object grew ever larger, it suddenly dawned on me what it was. I hastily triggered the radio.

"BEAR!" I excitedly shouted.

"What?" James was seemingly incredulous.

"A BEAR! I shouted again, "Right in front of me. He is now running up the beach towards the cliffs. Look, exactly where I am now. I'm just crossing over him."

"Oh yes, I can see it now!" James gleefully replied, "I'll get a camera ready."

And that was that, our first sighting of an East Siberian brown bear. It looked to be a large juvenile who had wandered down onto the rocks in search of food. With no immediate tree cover it was very visible and something of a sitting duck for James's camera. Little did we know then, but we would end up seeing another 14 bears during the day's flight. Most were single foragers, but at one point, we also saw a family group of a mother and two cubs. Sometimes we would circle around to take another look, but at a distance, so to not frighten them. As with the camels in the Saudi desert, the bears became quite a common sight after a while. But they remained captivating, perhaps because an angry wild bear could have potentially caused us much more harm on the ground than a wild camel.

A more sobering sight came into view shortly afterwards – it was the tattered skeleton of an old airliner. Similar to a DC-3 Dakota, it was half hidden by undergrowth on top of a flat headland. Amazingly, parts of its bright silver metalwork still glinted a little in the weak afternoon sun. I pondered on how on earth it had got there. Had it simply crashed in bad visibility, or had it tried to make a bush out-landing of some sort and then failed to take off again? It was a stark reminder (though none was needed) of how brutal and uncaring such a place was if you were unlucky enough to get into any sort of trouble.

Yet as the afternoon wore on, it wasn't the risks that were at the forefront of my thoughts, but rather the feeling of rare privilege to be witnessing first-hand something quite so marvellous. And how lucky to be here and to experience it all in such rare calm and clear conditions. Technically, to be in such a place felt raw, edgy and brutally isolated. Emotionally however, its very isolation also gave it a peaceful, calm and unspoilt serenity.

Later, I again spotted something unusual up ahead. In the water this time, tight to the shoreline, was a submerged white blob moving towards me. As I approached, I was astounded to see the blob was not one, but seven white shapes in the clear, shallow water. They were beluga whales!

This pod had arranged themselves in a very clever formation as they hunted along the shoreline. By swimming in unison, in a tightly slanted line formation, with the one closest to the shore positioned at the rear of the slant, any unlucky fish that happened to be in the shallows were then corralled between the whales and the beach. There was nowhere to escape to, except into the waiting jaws of the inner-most whale who was directly benefitting from the coordinated efforts of the other six. I watched as the whales slowly rotated their positions in the line, rather like a peloton of *underwater cyclists*. This meant each whale could in turn benefit from being in the tail end feeding position. It was so wonderful to observe such evolutionary innovation at work in nature.

* * *

Evensk, when it finally appeared in the distance, was like a little oasis of human survival surrounded by a vast and inhospitable wilderness. The runway, rough and ravaged by the harsh winter conditions, sat almost at right angles to, and directly adjoining, the pebble beach shoreline.

This was definitely not, however, an idyllic beach holiday destination. The foreshore was strewn with the rusting hulks of small cargo vessels, hauled up from the water onto the gravel. Some were obviously shipwrecks, battered by countless storms and destructive waves laden with pack ice. However, it soon became apparent on closer inspection, that some of the other rusty old heaps were still in fact fully functioning and operational. Much like resupplying an isolated island community, the ships simply ran their bows up onto the shingle beach in order to unload their essential cargo.

The compact town was a fascinating mix of aging and decrepit soviet-era concrete accommodation blocks and smaller wooden prefab houses. Similar to the Innuit settlements that I passed through in the north of Canada, the open spaces around the weather-beaten buildings appeared messy; dusty dirt tracks, scrubby vegetation and long-abandoned, scrapped and rusting equipment contributed to the overall ramshackle scene. Though of course, it was easy to forget in these extremely short summer months that for the majority of the year, all this mess could rather conveniently remain hidden under a thick blanket of snow and ice.

Accommodation was somewhat *spartan* but adequate, a small apartment in one of the slightly better-clad concrete block buildings. It reminded me of a vacant student flat. My room had a basic bed, chair, desk, net curtains, two very utilitarian teacups and lino flooring. Relative luxury when considering our geographical location. The view from the first-floor window overlooked the dirty gravel road and another decrepit soviet-era building opposite. Studying it closely, it reminded me of the type of old abandoned house that would perhaps feature well on the set of a disaster movie. Beneath the building's aged, corrugated asbestos roof were peeling window frames and a patchwork of shabby grey render that had been plastered over repeatedly through the decades. The crumbling render was now flaking off in huge chunks, like serious sunburned skin. I counted four different layers, no doubt documenting the building's history throughout its ravaged life. In the rear 'garden', unkempt and heavily overgrown, the skeleton of a large glasshouse still stood; now an abandoned relic, it was another reminder of the former soviet optimism to prevail and thrive throughout all parts of its territory, even in such a harshly remote corner as this.

The whole place felt noticeably quiet, with minimal traffic as there were no roads beyond the edge of town. Quiet that is, apart from a strange and constant, dull thumping sound.

On an evening stroll to look around, I discovered the source. An aging and very decrepit power station, blackened by many years of constant toil and looking well beyond its sell-by date, was providing the town with its electricity. The thumping engine and belching chimney could have been a scene straight out of the darkest days of the early industrial revolution. Gazing down from Google Earth you can plainly see it has created a dark smudge and blackened roads, right in the middle of town. Definitely not pretty, but nonetheless it provided a vital heartbeat, keeping the town alive.

It was a subtle reminder that we were venturing into seriously inhospitable territory. Self-reliance and self-resilience were going to be watchwords from now on. The end of the Road of Bones in Magadan had marked the end of all overland transport links and we would now have to 'island' hop every day, from one totally cut off settlement to the next; right through the Russian Far East, across the Bering Strait and for most of the route down through Alaska. Fully linked-up civilisation would only return once we reached Anchorage and the relative comfort of following the mighty Alaskan Highway onwards south into Canada.

However safe arrival in Anchorage, as it turned out, was still over two weeks away.

31 May 2019: Evensk, Russia – Markovo, Russia

The recent shoreline flying had been exhilarating, both in scenery and wildlife. From Evensk however, we now had to head inland, cutting across the top of the Kamchatka Peninsula and through the Chukotka Autonomous Okrug to eventually reach the northern port city of Anadyr. Lying at almost 600 miles to the north-east, Anadyr was marginally too far to reach in one hop, but fortunately the small settlement of Markovo was positioned in between, at 390 miles along the route.

The terrain was now slowly changing, from flat swampy valleys to low rocky mountain ridges of around 2000ft. We could comfortably pick and choose the crossing points of ridgelines without the risk of being closed in by steep, high-sided valleys and mist. Fortunately, the weather conditions were also kind to us, at least while in the air, though that all dramatically changed as soon as we arrived in Markovo.

Perched on the ever-shifting floodplain of a crazily meandering river, the gravel runway at Markovo was only a few feet above normal water level. The whole area was quite used to having regular floods, and as we skidded and bumped our way along the loose gravel taxiway we were met with some concerned local faces. We soon learned that the heavy rain we had experienced while in Magadan had moved north ahead of us, soaking the mountain ranges we had just crossed. Crucially, that water had to run off somewhere and it was now predicted that the runway at Markovo would be under water within the next 24 hours!

To make matters worse, we were also being told that our next flight from Markovo to Ulgony Airport near Anadyr, was not permitted if it involved flying during the weekend. The clutching hands of bureaucracy at work once again.

Oh, and by the way of impeccable timing it was now, of course, late Friday afternoon.

We had very few options. If we held off the next flight until Monday morning, the whole airfield was surely going to be flooded by then. There was no suitable high ground to escape to on the broad low-lying flood plain, and even if we did somehow lift the gyros clear, it would be many more days before the waters subsided enough for the gravel runway to become usable again. Our priority was clear; there was absolutely no way we could stay here beyond a single overnight stop.

Our only tactic was to plead with the local authorities to make us a special case. Could we possibly be allowed to fly on the Saturday because of the exceptional circumstances? Several phone calls were made on our behalf, and we waited apprehensively for a reply.

We were not left to idle however, as fuel soon turned out to be our next big issue. In such a remote area, fuel was understandably a precious commodity, and there was a lively debate as to what was available to suit our needs. With no avgas to be had, I persuaded them that regular unleaded petrol, the same that was in the rickety cars, outboard motors and other machinery dotted around the place, would also be fine for us. I could see that our hosts were still a little unconvinced, but miraculously they became much happier after I was made to sign a declaration that we had taken on fuel entirely at our own risk.

Whilst our hosts were all smiles again, they weren't the ones who were going to have to use this fuel of a totally unknown *vintage*... and it took several tense minutes in the air on the next flight, monitoring the engines closely for any coughing and spluttering, before James and I could also start to smile again.

Soon enough news came through that we had been given special clearance to allow us a Saturday 'ferry-flight' to reposition the aircraft at Ulgony due to the expected floods. While we had been discussing the fuel situation, we were also being plagued by huge (and thirsty) mosquitoes. Being down so close to the river, with many oxbow lakes dotted about full of stagnating water, it was of course their perfect habitat. So the news that we were indeed getting out of here first thing in the morning came as an extra welcome relief.

1 June 2019: Markovo, Russia – Anadyr, Russia

We were making steady progress, with only two more Russian stopovers before the Bering Strait. The landscape continued to change, dense forest slowly giving way to swampy tundra and exposed rock. Approaching the coast from the west, the air temperature dramatically dropped, with a biting wind being drawn in off the still frozen seas around Anadyr. The last hour of the flight was particularly chilly, causing a gradual sapping of heat from our bodies' extremities. I wiggled my toes and fingers to keep some circulation going and hunkered down in my seat, trying to keep out of the icy airflow as much as possible, hoping all the while for a reviving hot shower later.

On reaching the port of Anadyr, the sight of the frozen bay stretching out as far as the eye could see was captivating. I was well used to ice-covered water by now, as I had experienced plenty in northern Canada, Greenland and more recently on Lake Baikal, but my fascination and fear remained. I could see the ice-locked harbour, with its ships tied up waiting to be released by the mid-summer thaw. It was such an alien sight for someone who hails from Larne in County Antrim, where our coastal waters are warmed (slightly) by the Atlantic gulf stream. The ships in our harbour would have to occasionally remain tied up because of a few days of stormy weather, but never because they were trapped in port by ice!

Our approach to Ulgony Airport, on the opposite side of the bay, allowed us to fly in directly over Anadyr, the regional capital and hometown of some 16,000 people. Neatly laid out, it was clearly a larger, more prosperous, modern settlement as befitting its status. Yet it still was dominated by the ubiquitous coal-fired power station positioned slap-bang in the centre of town. Its twin cooling towers were huge scaffold edifices of rusty brown steelwork, that sat rather jarringly in stark contrast to the surrounding brightly painted soviet-era apartment buildings.

We flew on, dashing across the two-mile wide frozen estuary to reach the airport. Although a regional hub, traffic was quiet and we were cleared to land on runway 19 into a biting crosswind. Being a strategic airport, the closest main hub to Alaska, it was not surprising to find that the runway length was immense, almost two miles long. With James following on behind, I made the final approach to the 19 threshold as instructed and then elected to fly a few feet above the runway along its entire length to land, directly into wind, at the far end. The tower, as with other bigger regional Russian airports, instructed me to park on the farthest stand away from the buildings. Shortly afterwards, James pulled up alongside and we were hurriedly approached by a no-nonsense official.

"Passport! Passport now!" he barked.

Not one pleasantry, nor even a muted "Hello" or "Welcome to Anadyr."

It was clear that we had once more reached *border territory*, with all its associated strict formalities of checks, customs and immigration. We had been blissfully free of such bureaucracy while flying throughout the domestic interior. Not since Pskov had we had to appear happy in order to appease any overly officious customs officials. If nothing else it demonstrated that their approach towards customer relations was at least *consistent*, being equally hard-line-authoritarian in both the far west and the far east of the country.

* * *

We were now only two flights away from reaching Alaska, but we had the Bering Strait to tackle first, and as always, it was clear that the weather was going to play a crucial part in making a successful crossing. Waiting for the right weather, perhaps for many days, was therefore also going to be critically important. Once again, I was very keen to try to negotiate some shelter for the gyros and not have them stuck out on the apron in all weathers, as had happened in Magadan. As if to emphasise the harsh conditions, the late afternoon wind coming off the frozen sea was bitterly cold.

At first the answer to my well-practised, "Any chance of a hangar?" enquiry was, the by-now-familiar, flat "Nyet." I argued the point, pleaded the point, looked hangdog and dejected, pulling out all the stops. Yet, nothing… James looked on with resignation, but by now I was in never-say-never mode.

With no progress, I decided to change tack and employ a softly, softly, more circuitous approach.

"Well, if we have to stay out on a stand," I reasoned, "can we at least be given permission to move to that much more sheltered area, in close to those buildings and out of this freezing wind?"

I pointed over to some very tempting maintenance hangars a few hundred yards away. A few phone calls and yes, we were OK to relocate.

Phase one complete!

We quickly taxied across to our more sheltered stand and made busy unloading our luggage. If we were going to be held up here a few days, it was yet another good chance to get some admin and washing done.

As we were now much closer to the buildings, we were also much more visible (and accessible) to various airport maintenance staff. Several appeared from their offices to check out the gyros and take photos. Once again, I got hustling on the issue of hangarage, only now with a much wider audience and eventually I struck lucky. In conversation, I *casually* pronounced that back in Yakutsk we hadn't needed formal hangar space at all; we had just made do with a big shed, used to store the snow-clearing trucks. I continued to steer the conversation in that direction as there just happened to be a very similar type of shed sitting right behind us. Before long the penny dropped. A few more phone calls were made and… *Voilà!*

Phase two was complete!

The gyros were soon safely (and warmly) tucked up indoors next to the slumbering snow-blowing machines in their summer hibernation, and with this minor victory won, we were in a buoyant mood as we were given a lift in a minivan down to the shore. Our spirits were then raised even more with what happened next.

The two-mile stretch of water separating Ulgony Airport and Anadyr now became our next barrier to cross. In the long winter months, it was simply a case of creating an ice road between the two shorelines.

And in the short summertime this was replaced by a seasonal ferry service. However, there was also a brief period of a few weeks each spring, when the ice road was too slushy and unstable to use, *and* the ferry couldn't yet break through the thick layer of ice. And these were precisely the conditions that we now faced. We didn't need to worry though because a novel solution was at hand. We were dropped off on the shingle beach with our luggage and asked to wait. Soon enough a small but very noisy little boat came racing across the ice towards us. Only as it came closer, I realised that it wasn't a boat – it was a *hovercraft*! Weaving this way and that to navigate through the larger chunks of thawing sea ice, it was a perfect solution to a very real problem. A fleet of about five craft were being used as a taxi service, taking about five minutes to cross from one side to the other.

Like a couple of excited schoolkids on a day trip, we clambered into the small cabin while still on the beach. Moments later we were up and away, dropping sideways down the beach and out across the icy melt water. Our pilot was a young boy-racer, who was obviously well practised in hovercraft handling. I think he treated us to a bit of an extra joy ride, seeing we were foreigners; he even managed to coolly monitor the text messages on his phone as we careered along. It was so weird to be blasting across the cracked ice at around 40 mph. Several times we were heading straight for a large chunk of ice, only for the hovercraft to glide straight over it, with hardly a bump. What a fantastic way to travel. The ever-shifting sea ice conditions meant we took a lengthy dogleg across the estuary. The only other vessels on the water were the other hovercraft zipping here and there.

We rapidly closed-in on our approach to the Anadyr shoreline at the same breakneck speed, which was slightly disconcerting. But with skilful precision, our boy-racer hit the upslope of the beach at just the right point and with just the right momentum, so that the craft drifted into a beautiful sideways arcing turn. At the top of the beach, the noisy engine was cut, and we quickly squatted down onto the rapidly deflating skirts.

What a most spectacular way to *arrive*. Though I'd humbly say, it still has to take second place to landing a gyroplane on a windy day.

2–5 June 2019: Anadyr, Russia (non-flying days)

Making the briefest of stops in Markovo to avoid the impending floods, had felt like trying to step quickly and as lightly as possible onto a shaky rock whilst crossing a stream. In Anadyr we now felt much more secure again, back on a more stable footing as it were, and paused to assess the upcoming weather picture around the Bering Strait for the days ahead. While waiting for the next favourable flying window, we spent a few pleasant days mooching around town.

It was surprisingly well presented, with brightly painted residential blocks, clean streets (complete with flower beds) and a well-stocked supermarket within its own small shopping mall. On most days, we dined in a café bar located upstairs in the mall, or alternatively in our hotel's own small restaurant, where one evening we got chatting with another circumnavigating pilot. Like us, he was also taking advantage of Russia's gradually opening skies, though he was flying his fixed-wing plane in the opposite (westbound) direction. He had just arrived in from Nome, Alaska and I quizzed him about the flight conditions he had faced en route. Alas, whereas his aircraft had the fuel range to fly directly from Nome in one hop, we still required two days of flying to complete the same journey in reverse.

On an exploratory walk around town, we were given a guided tour of a fantastic wooden church. The interior was brightly lit and stunningly decorated with lots of shiny gold and vividly coloured religious paintings. It felt that the brilliance of the interior was designed to provide a very welcoming haven for people, especially during the long dark days of an icy winter. Another welcoming sight was Anadyr's huge marine and workwear shop, which we later happened upon at the edge of town. I was pleased to find that they stocked a comprehensive, no-nonsense range of 'polar bear strength' arctic puffa jackets, designed to keep out the bitingly cold wind. I gladly bought one and proceeded to wear it as an extra protective layer under my immersion suit; it proved so effective that I then made use of it permanently, all the way down to sunny California.

6 June 2019: Anadyr, Russia – Provedinia Bay, Russia

I had watched the forecast weather charts for days as we now had a similar logistic situation to the two-day mountain flight to Tomtor and Magadan. Provedinia Bay, the last stop in Russia, was similar to Tomtor, a basic outpost surrounded by remote and hostile terrain. We needed the weather, visibility and particularly the wind directions to be favourable and consistent, to allow a two-day transit to reach *both* Provedinia and then quickly on across to Nome in Alaska. Safe arrival in Nome would mark the achievement of a major logistical and technical hurdle, crossing the Bering Strait, where Asia and North America are almost within touching distance of each other. However, as the crossing point was situated at the confluence of ocean currents between the Arctic Ocean and the northern Pacific, the weather conditions, despite any favourable forecasts, were still going to be notoriously changeable. We would need a hefty dose of good fortune to make a drama-free crossing.

After five days of patiently watching and waiting, we were getting as good a forecast as we could expect and decided to go.

With trepidation and nervous excitement held in equal measure, we progressed once more north-east along the shoreline. Around an hour into the flight, some 80 miles east of Anadyr, we passed a significant milestone. Watching the GPS, I saw the nav coordinates suddenly switch from measuring longitude as 180 degrees east to reading 180 degrees west of the Greenwich prime meridian. We had just literally flown across the back of the world! Although now technically in the Western Hemisphere, global geopolitics dictated that we still had to wait until the Bering Strait to cross the next navigational milestone, the International Date Line.

Visibility remained good as we followed the coast, at least for the first 100 miles or so. Yet as we cut the corner to cross a wide inlet, the first wisps of cloud began to build at around 800-1000 ft. For the next

50 miles, staying above it, I watched it carefully. Thankfully it remained a thin layer as I could still easily see the whitecaps of the breaking waves below. With 50 miles still to run to reach Provedinia, however, the clouds began to thicken considerably, and the sea surface below became increasingly obscured. To add to the complexity, the coastline now consisted of steeply sloping rock faces and mountains. One option might have been to stay low, hugging sea level under the increasingly blanketing cloud. I considered it but was worried that there might also be pockets of sea mist under there. With practically zero visibility, trapped a few feet above the sea and with an invisibly hostile rocky shoreline close by, it was an option I didn't like at all.

I advised James to keep me glued in his sights as I maintained our course above the low cloud and picked our way along the coast. The nearby mountain peaks helpfully poked their heads above the clouds and by matching these to my GPS screens, I was still able to retain an overall picture of the obscured topography below. I navigated carefully, as even on a clear day, Provedinia Bay might have been a bit tricky to find. It is kept protected from the worst of the arctic climate by being located within a complicated series of sea inlets and gorges, and I definitely didn't want us to overshoot and perhaps descend into the wrong valley.

This was fine for now as we could keep in clear visibility, but inevitably at some point, we were still going to have to descend through the clouds to land. I thought through the strategy. Our best plan was to arrive (as close as possible) overhead of the airport and then make a cautious slow vertical descent through the clouds, much as I had done previously on my flight over the Atlantic. We could then hopefully emerge through the cloud base above the airport and have a clear view of the runway for a normal landing.

The key word in that last sentence however was *hopefully,* as a constant nagging doubt remained in my thoughts – what if instead of finding a clear view, we emerged from the cloud base and then immediately ran straight into a thick surface mist or coastal fog?

So late into the flight, finding an alternative landing option was now highly unlikely and we had little choice but to push on, closely monitoring the troublesome cloud formations below. As we approached the last headland and inlet that would guide us slightly inland to the airfield, I began to realise that the clouds, streaming slowly ashore from the open sea, were now gradually piling up *in slow motion*, against the near vertical sea cliffs. The heaped clouds, with nowhere to go, were spreading upwards against the mountains. However, much more worryingly, it appeared that they were also spilling *downwards*, into the clear air gap close to sea level that I had been so desperately relying on. This was a serious issue, some light wispy sea mist might not have caused a problem, but this was heavy, moisture-laden oceanic cloud.

I immediately scanned the way ahead for better options until suddenly something caught my eye. A glimpse of land, a flat green valley bottom. How could this be possible in the blanketed whiteout that had been tormenting me for hours? I quickly worked it out.

The clouds had been piling up on the open-water side of the mountains and had been halted in their tracks. Consequently, on the sheltered inland side of the mountains, a hole or rip had developed in the cloud cover. A huge wave of relief washed over me, and I quickly relayed the good news back to James.

"There's a hole! I shouted gleefully, "I've spotted a hole in the clouds and can clearly see the valley below. We can just drop through there vertically and then we'll find the airfield no problem."

Wow! I could hardly believe how rapidly our luck had changed for the better. We had certainly used up a fair chunk of our allotted good fortune already; and we hadn't even reached the Bering Strait as yet.

Making a very relieved landing on Provedinia's rough gravel strip a short time later, I took a moment to collect my thoughts and gazed skywards and then at the surrounding mountains. The thick clouds were sweeping past all around us, but a big, beautiful circle of blue sky remained permanently above our heads, a natural phenomenon caused by a timeless battle between the winds aloft and the mountains below.

I pondered that it was perhaps why the airfield had been built in this precise spot in the first place. I for one and James for two, were mightily glad it had.

Soon enough we were safely parked on the small gravel apron. Once again there was no sheltered hangar, or even the slightest chance of a maintenance shed to be had. The gyros would just have to spend their last night on Russian soil out in the open. Again, we were immediately approached by customs officials, a whole troop of them this time. Dressed in smart uniforms with wide-brimmed caps, they seemed a much friendlier bunch than we had previously encountered. Perhaps being stationed out in Provedinia Bay was such a quiet posting that any passing foreign aircraft was regarded as a big event. Larger aircraft easily had the range to fly directly between Anadyr and Nome, and so I got the impression that we were definitely something of a rarity. They were soon busy taking selfies and group shots of us all standing in front of the aircraft, though rather unfairly, for *security reasons* we weren't permitted to take any photos of them. They were good-natured however, and we were even given a ride into town in the back of their large truck.

One younger officer spoke quite good English and so volunteered to help us while we were being allocated rooms in yet another Soviet-era concrete block of apartments. It was interesting to note that accommodation in these buildings became gradually more dilapidated and rundown the further east we travelled. This was not surprising as the basic living conditions got steadily worse too. The state-supported population of Provedinia Bay back in Soviet times was planned to be around 8000 to 12,000. More recently, with the mass exodus of people looking for easier living conditions and better job prospects, the population had dropped to less than 2000 people. As a result, the majority of the drab, grey concrete buildings were left derelict and crumbling, giving a strange eery feeling of being in a forgotten war zone or a post-apocalyptic zombie movie.

The local people by contrast were full of life. In the evening, our customs officer guide took us to eat in the town's only café bar. We were suddenly very hungry and were given homemade burgers, which went down a treat. We also called into the shop to buy some provisions for breakfast. It contained a fascinating Aladdin's cave of produce, mostly frozen, tinned or dried goods, and all with a long shelf life. Though often not long enough, as it appeared many of the items were now well past their sell-by date. We were unlucky to have missed the summer-season arrival of the re-supply ship, which was expected within the next week. Faced with such a drastically restricted choice, we just had to make do with a couple of large cans of tinned fruit in syrup.

7 June 2019: Provedinia Bay, Russia – Nome, Alaska, USA (landed on the 6 June)

A big day had arrived. It was to be the first-ever attempt to make a crossing of the Bering Strait by gyroplane. As always, the weather en route was uppermost in my thoughts. The flight to Nome, Alaska would not be such a great distance, around 260 nautical miles and 3hrs 30mins or so in the air. But the technical challenge was considerable.

The first hurdle was to get out of Provedinia. After being dropped off by car at the airport, we were soon subject to a rigorous customs exit procedure. The fact that both aircraft were so small helped; there was very little room available for smuggling anything out of the country. Yet the paperwork and customs declarations were still under the same scrutiny as if we were a large foreign passenger or business jet.

Thankfully the large hole in the clouds above us, which had so recently saved the day, was still in situ. However, so were the thick murky clouds all around us. On the way in, before dropping through the hole, I had spotted that the bulk of the troublesome blanket cloud had been piled up out to sea to the south-west of us. By contrast, the conditions in the opposite direction, to the north-east, had looked much more promising as the sky in the distance was again becoming much clearer; and fortunately this was in the direction of our onward route. But that had been yesterday's weather... As I now sat on the ground warming up the engine, I looked up through the hole and sincerely hoped that those same clear skies to the north-east would still be there.

The engine warm up took a long time as the air temperature overnight had been close to freezing. The air was also saturated, with almost 100% humidity and felt damp and heavy. This was also combined with a biting wind chill. It was difficult to comprehend that this was early June.

I initially thought that with the engine thoroughly warmed up, as with cold winter flying back home, there would be no major problems in performance. Take-off and climb-out, into the cold and thick sea level air, would provide more air density for the rotors to bite into while making a tight spiralling ascent, to climb ourselves out of the hole. The plan after that was to simply fly above the coastal cloud blanket until we reached the clearing skies beyond.

Alas, as events unfolded, it did not turn out to be all that simple.

As per usual, I led out onto the runway with James following close behind. Take-off from the loose gravel was bumpy but quite routine and I flew straight ahead at a constant rate of climb to clear the runway. James radioed to confirm he was also now airborne and following my track. Banking to the left, I made a tight spiralling ascent, using as wide a radius as the hole in the clouds would allow.

After a good four minutes of hard full-throttle climbing, I was able to break out on the top of the clouds and into a gloriously sunny day. I immediately scanned the horizon up towards the north-east. I was relieved to confirm that we still had the same cloud-free conditions as I had seen the day before. Yet my relief was very short lived.

On the climb-out, I had detected that something didn't quite feel right with the pitch function of my control stick. The stick felt heavy in my right hand. Once I had throttled back and levelled out above the clouds the condition worsened dramatically. It felt as if the stick was constantly wanting to pull forward out of my hand. Had it done so, the aircraft would have instantly pitched nose downwards into a steep dive or even into a catastrophic forward somersault. I was acutely aware of a highly dangerous condition called a 'powered pushover', where a sudden downward nose pitch causes the thrust of the engine to push the Gyro over the top of itself. This in turn, reverses the airflow through the main rotors and unloads the rotors with immediate disastrous and unrecoverable results.

I gripped the stick hard, counteracting the constant strong pull forward that the aircraft was exerting on it. It was a worrying situation. If I had relaxed my arm or lost my grip, even for a split-second, the stick would have flung forward and violently pitched the aircraft into a deadly pushover.

Thankfully, I didn't panic. Indeed, feeling somewhat calmly detached for a few seconds, I looked down at my right hand and very slightly relaxed it to try to gauge the severity of the pull. It was immediate and forceful.

"OK, I don't need to do *that* again," I thought.

Realising the acute life-threatening seriousness of the situation, I sought desperately to work out what was wrong. The pitch of the main rotor is directly controlled by the control stick via a series of push-pull rods that run up both sides of the rotor mast. In normal operation, there is a small pneumatic piston that helps trim the pitch mechanism whilst in flight and this neutrally balances the stick pressure and movement, fore and aft, for the pilot. However, as I repeatedly tried to apply more trim via the trim switch, it seemed that the whole system would not hold pressure. With all pitch trim on the stick now lost, it was clear that something was drastically wrong within the pneumatic system itself.

One thing was certain, there was no way I could fix it while up in the air. I was still able to fly but only by resisting the constant (and deadly) pull forward of the stick in my hand. I briefly wondered if we could carry on, that perhaps the fault, which may have been temporary, might fix itself over time. However, with more than three hours flight time remaining, over such hazardous terrain, I immediately knew that that would have been a very foolish option. My arm was already starting to ache from the constant (and considerable) effort required.

There was no option, I had to return to Provedinia.

I then suddenly remembered I had James following behind me.

With all my own problems within the cockpit I had forgotten to keep James up to speed. I triggered the radio.

"Sorry matey, I've got a real problem here with my control stick. We'll have to turn back."

It was a serious undertaking. We had already cleared customs and immigration and were now considered to be an outbound international flight. I hoped our sudden unexpected return wouldn't cause any issues.

Banking around, I once more led us down through the cloud hole. Thank goodness it was still open. My main concern was just to get safely back on the ground as quickly as possible, before both the grip of my hand and the strength in my forearm faded. With so much going on, my landing was understandably a little ragged. We then taxied back to the stand amidst surprised airport officials, who had quickly come back out to meet us.

I now had to be very guarded and a bit vague when explaining our sudden return. I wanted to avoid appearing to have a major technical problem, as this might have resulted in them grounding me instantly until a suitably qualified engineer could sign off the aircraft as being once again airworthy. As you can imagine, the practical logistics of getting someone 'suitably qualified' to Provedinia would have been mind-boggling.

In any case, I wasn't even sure what the problem was. I began a thorough check of the pitch trim linkages and pneumatic system. Now back on the ground, everything appeared to function normally, making the tracking down of an intermittent, transient fault much more elusive. Though on the plus side, at least I could establish nothing was physically broken, as getting a replacement part delivered would have been a similar logistical nightmare.

Slowly as the precious minutes ticked by, I reasoned out a possible cause and effect of what the issue could be, or now (hopefully) *had been.* The air, since our arrival at Provedinia, had been laden with a lot of moisture and we had also been continuously skirting close to high-humidity cloud on the previous flight. In addition, the runway and apron had been very dusty on our arrival and it had also been a very cold night for the gyros sitting out in near-freezing conditions. In such an environment, I wondered could some transient dust or ice particles have perhaps adversely affected the pneumatics? Something that had subsequently been blown (or melted) out of the system while I was applying repeated pressure cycles during my diagnostic tests? It would certainly explain why everything suddenly went back to normal. One big question remained however – would the fault *return* once I got back in the air? There was only one way to find out…

Much relieved that at least the system seemed to be again working fine, I was able to play down the whole issue with the concerned officials who looked on.

"No problem guys," I reassured, "just a small adjustment was needed while I was on the ground. Nothing to worry about."

With the clock constantly ticking and still faced with an arduous flight into the unknown, we once more saddled up and headed for the runway. I glanced anxiously upwards and thankfully the beautiful blue-sky hole was still with us. The stick felt normal on take-off. Five minutes into the climb-out, *good,* the stick still felt normal. Ten minutes, *better,* all still OK… I began daring to hope that the issue had already now resolved itself. Time would tell, and happily to my great relief, the issue never did return. Clear of the cloud at last, we continued our Russian coastal track north-east, to reach the Bering Strait.

***

I had wondered for over a decade what it would be like to cross this narrow strip of water. Whilst flight planning, I was surprised to realise how close the Alaskan and Russian coastlines actually were to each other. Approaching from the Russian side, I kept a watchful eye on both our course and on the weather ahead. Then, while scanning the horizon to the north-east, I spotted something.

"I can see Alaska!" I proclaimed.

"Whereabouts?" James replied.

"Away off on the horizon. Look at about 2 o'clock," I answered.

All that was visible were the peaks of some far-off mountains, but they definitely weren't in Russia. It was a moment of great excitement for us, equivalent perhaps to the shout of "Land ahoy!" to the pioneering navigators of sailing ships exploring the world's great oceans.

Our Russian adventure was almost over and within the next hour or so we would cross the International Date Line, literally flying ourselves 24 hours backwards into yesterday. But Russia was not quite done with us yet, as she had one more spectacular sight to offer.

Once again out of the corner of my eye I spotted movement. We were still tracking the Russian coastline, but also slightly offshore.

"Whale! I've seen a big whale!" I proclaimed (again...).

"Where?!" James replied.

"I'm flying just over it now. Look below where I am."

I had first spotted the whale's distinctive waterspout, a sight I would never forget while making my crossing of the Atlantic in 2015. The experience now, however, was quite different as the state of the sea was much calmer. Soon enough we spotted numerous whales, easily recognised by their waterspouts and sometimes by a curious trail of discoloured surface water following in their wake (I later learned that that was actually *whale poo...*).

Once again, I felt so honoured to be able to witness such majestic, gentle creatures in their natural habitat. James was able to make a few low-level flypasts and managed to get some great photos while he dashed about here and there, like a kid in a toy shop. I was still very much concerned about my earlier technical issue with the pitch trim and decided my best action was to remain flying high and steady, so as not to stress poor *Roxy* more than absolutely necessary.

As we closed in on the Bering Strait, yet again a thick low-level cloud layer began to build up out to sea. Inland on the Russian side, things still remained completely clear, so I maintained our route to follow along the edge of the cloud bank. The Alaskan mountain tops were getting much closer now and we were treated to the unforgettable sight of both Russia and the USA occupying the same horizon. The advancing blanket of cloud appeared to be halted right in the narrowest section of the strait, seemingly stuck in the bottleneck between the two continents. Farther north, beyond the strait and towards the Chukchi Sea and the Arctic Ocean, the sky was a clear and brilliant blue. Onward routing was therefore simple, we would continue to skirt the northern edge of the Bering Strait cloud blanket.

Our next waypoint was to pass the Diomede Islands. Like two huge, steep-sided boulders plonked in a narrow river, they sit right in the middle of the Bering Strait. Big Diomede is Russian and Little Diomede is American, and quite amazingly they are only two miles apart.

As in Provedinia Bay, the clouds spilling in northwards from the Bering Sea, were piling up on the two islands' southern flanks, shrouding the sea cliffs completely. Originally, I had thought it would be fun to make a figure-of-eight flight around both islands while we had a good look at them, but the cloud proximity put a stop to that idea. Instead, I led us through in an elongated S shape between the two islands, which still gave us a spectacular view of each island on both sides. I was particularly impressed by the feat of engineering that had been needed to install a small outpost of buildings on Little Diomede. With no flat land around the shoreline, it was perched like a small seabird colony clinging to the side of the steep rugged cliffs.

We pressed on. After our challenging arrival at Provedinia, I was constantly concerned about what the large blanket cloud would be doing on the Alaskan side. We had flown as far north as we needed to go to cross the strait, but now we had to fly southwards to reach Nome. Glancing seawards to the south, the cloud rather worryingly did look to be massing again. Yet more trouble ahead, I wondered.

We quickly closed on the Alaskan shoreline and were greeted by a very reassuring sight. Just on the northern edge of the thick cloud layer and right next to the beach, was the small town of Wales, Alaska. A welcome sight indeed as they also had a lovely runway. We called the airport tower and heard our first American ATC voice welcoming us to Alaska. I immediately felt very relieved. If we now suffered any further weather difficulties between here and Nome, we at least knew that the runway at Wales had clear visibility for us to return to.

More good news came when Wales ATC reported that Nome was also currently cloud-free, even though to us that seemed highly unlikely, given our present cloud-filled horizon. Thanking them for their warm welcome, we pushed on again, comfortable in the notion that the conditions should become clear again as we closed in on Nome.

That comfort, however, was a long time arriving, as the blanket cloud conditions worryingly persisted with us for the next *80 miles.* But sure enough as we finally closed in on Nome, the cloud cover dramatically dispersed, as if held back by a protective ring of mountains, at a radius of some 20 miles from the town.

We were elated, landing finally on US soil in the late evening. As with Provedinia, the night-time air temperature was dropping fast, but thankfully I was able to quickly organise hangarage for us with Bering Air, whose main maintenance hangar was based in Nome. I was heartened to find that all the folks working at this family-run business had a great team spirit. Maintaining their aircraft and helicopter fleet far removed from the usual ancillary support services provided around larger airport hubs, reminded me very much of the mindset of Air Inuit in north-east Canada. Both of these companies provided a vital local service, and in such remote locations their aircraft mechanics and engineers had to be multi-disciplined, highly skilled and very self-reliant. In a way, they were a modern version of the highly resilient frontiersmen of old.

And talking of frontiersmen, soon after bedding down the gyros, we were taken into town to check-in at the aptly named Nome Nugget Inn (after all, we were now in gold prospecting country).

After crossing the International Date Line, we had landed in Nome on 6 June, having gained a whole day en route. But by the time we finally checked in, it was nearly midnight. We were dog tired after the tensions of the day, but we were still able to find late-night burgers and chips in a bar and ceremonially paid for them using the *mighty greenback*. We had definitely arrived in the USA!

21

North America: Alaska, USA to Canada to USA

7 June 2019 (again): Nome, Alaska, USA (non-flying day)

Although staying in Nome was uber-expensive, we really needed a non-flying day to rest up and mentally decompress from both the excitement and trepidation of completing our last few days in Russia. Crossing the Bering Strait had also been a pioneering historic achievement and marked a highly significant personal moment. I immediately felt that a great weight was lifting from my shoulders, as I had now crossed the last serious expanse of open water that was necessary to complete my circumnavigation (having already previously crossed the Atlantic). All that remained now was to continue flying down the west coast of North America until I arrived, once again, back at my original 2015 're-start' point in McMinnville, Oregon; thus allowing me to finally *close the loop* on my complete and unbroken lap around the planet.

Undoubtably, every long-distance, light-aircraft pilot retains a 'what if' worry when faced with serious over-water crossings. What if the engine faulters mid ocean, or an electrical or a mechanical failure occurs? What if the weather turns nasty? What if there are navigation issues? What if I have a fuel problem or even an acute medical problem?

On reaching Alaska, I was finally able to banish those worries entirely. All of my circumnavigation flying from now on, no matter how hazardous, would at least be over (or very close to) land. Nice, safe, *dry land.* After any emergency landing, I retained a reasonable chance of taking off again after repairs, an option that was simply impossible out at sea. Sitting and chatting in a Nome coffee house, James was acutely aware that, whereas I had now completed my oceanic flying, he had only started his. He still had his biggest challenge of all looming large ahead of him; the North Atlantic crossing. His background anxiousness felt vividly familiar, as I too had needed to mentally cope with exactly the same feelings, over a very extended period of years. But his own worries were probably not now helped by the fact that I had finally overcome that major mental hurdle, whereas in his own mind, James still *had it all to do.* Whilst I empathised with him as best I could over coffee, the unavoidable, most brutal fact remained; he couldn't complete his own circumnavigation without first conquering the Atlantic.

My own big ocean-crossing worries may have been removed, but the transient trim switch fault over Provedinia Bay still niggled away in my mind. It was a given that James had much more flying still to do, but he also had youth on his side and was in an aircraft not long out of the factory. *Roxy*, by comparison, was now 13 years old and had already physically flown almost one and half times around the world. Likewise, I was almost 10 years older than when I had started this project. Both man and machine were now feeling their age...

Physically, I was beginning to feel slightly underpowered. Periodically, I had a sort of tiredness or weariness, which even a good night's sleep could not fix. I simply put it down to the general stress and gruelling length of the whole journey, exacerbated by a touch of sunstroke or even mild dehydration. But the feeling stayed with me, off and on, for the remainder of the trip. I would not find out the true cause of this creeping malaise, until returning to Northern Ireland some two months later.

Health issues aside, the immediate upside was that, in Alaska, life once again began to feel very familiar. There were no language difficulties, flight planning was hassle-free and once down into the lower 48 states, fuel, accommodation, food and stopover airfields were going to be (by and large) both cheap and plentiful.

By contrast, Nome was a fascinating *outpost* of American resilience. Its close historical connection with prospecting for gold meant it strongly retained a frontier town feel. There was still an assumption that people could make their fortune here, dredging the nearshore sandbanks and sifting for gold in the sediments washed down from the mountains. But the logistics of living and re-supplying in such a place also ensured that everything was charged at a premium price.

With such relative normality, it was easy to forget for a moment that we were still seriously far north, just below the Arctic Circle. We had a lot of extreme terrain still to cross before we could finally consider ourselves completely out of the wilderness. Our short respite was over, we needed to get going again.

8 June 2019: Nome, Alaska, USA – McGrath, Alaska, USA

There were two options open to us to reach Anchorage: we could opt for a longer route and continue to hug the coastline; or we could take a more direct routing cross-country, which would mean flying over the imposing Alaska Range mountains situated north of Anchorage.

In the end, it was not our decision – the weather made it for us. Taking advice from local aviators, it was clear that the coastal route at this time of year could be fraught with bad visibility and coastal fog banks. We had already experienced more than enough of these difficult conditions on the Russian side of the Bering Strait and so we plumped instead for the inland routing and I set to work finding us a flyable route through the mountains.

The Alaska Range is the highest in the world outside of Asia and the Andes, and it is home to Denali (20,310ft), the tallest mountain in North America. Crikey, safely navigating through 20,000ft peaks felt a little daunting to say the least, but thankfully our local advisors told me of a possible workaround option. The plan would be to use Rainy Pass, a relatively low-level valley route through the mountains, but it was only flyable when the conditions were favourable. As with the mountain flying in Russia, it would rely on waiting for the right weather window, which we hoped to do in the small riverside town of McGrath.

Initially at least, flying south-east from Nome was quite similar to Siberia; there were no roads, yet plenty of trees, rivers and lakes. And the bears were just swapped from the East Siberian brown bear to the Alaskan Peninsula brown bear (aka peninsular grizzly). But at least there were no longer any Siberian tigers to worry about…

Occasionally, we overflew rough gravel or dirt airstrips used by bush pilot prospectors to commute to their remote gold mines. There would often be a cluster of ramshackle buildings nearby and a fast-flowing river course. The river was frequently dammed in terraces to provide the catchment of gold-bearing sediments and silts. The old wild west image of panning for gold by hand had now become highly mechanised, with washing, sifting and grading equipment used to efficiently process tonnes of gravel, rather than shovelfuls.

I wondered why certain mountain streams we flew over were being worked heavily, while others still looked pristine and untouched. It could have simply been ease of access. Everything had to be flown in and out and finding suitable terrain that was both flat and long enough to land on was scarce. As we later crossed the flat plains of the mighty Yukon River, I allowed myself to daydream that a gyroplane-flying bush pilot, able to make use of a much shorter runway, would have a significant advantage over the pilot of a fixed wing aircraft when prospecting for a new claim. On flying in, the shovel and panning dish would just have to be strapped to the outside of the gyro as there would be no room on the back seat; it would already be occupied by camping equipment, vittles and the 'Klondike' pot belly wood burning stove.

"Hot diggity! There's *still* plenty of hidden gold in them thar hills!"

9–11 June 2019: McGrath, Alaska, USA (non-flying days)

Arriving at McGrath, we had little knowledge of what to expect. It had been picked as a suitable stopover point purely for logistical reasons, as it was roughly halfway between Nome and Anchorage and would provide an ideal base for monitoring the upcoming Alaska Range weather. As luck would have it however, we were treated to one of the best stopovers that we could have hoped for.

We were generously hosted by the owners and staff of Hotel McGrath, who immediately recognised the pioneering challenges we were facing in flying our tiny open cockpit aircraft over such vast distances and in such an unforgiving landscape. They were well used to welcoming intrepid travellers, albeit mainly in the winter season, given that the town is one of the official checkpoint stopovers for the annual 1049-mile Iditarod Trail Sled Dog Race. Rather incredibly, the record race time is a little over eight days to complete the gruelling course, from Anchorage to Nome, which often involves battling whiteout blizzards, gale force winds and biting sub-zero temperatures.

The Purpose of our wait in McGrath was twofold: crucially, we had to ensure that the weather in the Rainy Pass through the Alaska Range was flyable; and we also needed to organise some additional forward planning.

After our extended flights through Russia, both G-YROX and G-KTCH were needing their regular airframe maintenance and engine services. As we approached the Bering Strait, I had been keeping in email contact with John Hereward back in the UK. He had previously flown out to Thailand to extensively rebuild *Roxy* after my ditching episode, and since he was already fully qualified, with many years of experience of working on both my Autogyro MT-03 and James's Magni M16C aircraft types, he was now our ideal choice to perform the required aircraft services jointly on both machines.

Whilst still in Russia however, it had been very difficult to predict exactly when we might arrive in Anchorage, which logistically was the easiest place to arrange for John to meet us. As it turned out, we ended up being a few days ahead of John's Anchorage arrival, which then gave us an extra reason to rest up in McGrath for a few days longer.

McGrath's two resident aircraft mechanics kindly offered us use of their maintenance shop hangar for the gyros and the McGrath Hotel management very generously gave us free board and lodgings for the duration of our stay. We were billeted in one of their rental houses, which was mainly used throughout the popular hunting season. We also borrowed two bikes that allowed us to cycle around the entire road network of the town. It was only a few miles, but it was fun to explore on ground level. Mentally, it was like being on a small holiday island for a few days, amid the constant background nervous tension of flying across the wilderness.

* * *

McGrath was a relaxing oasis where we could browse the General Store and pay a visit to *both* bars. In McGuire's Tavern we spent time signing banknotes to leave as mementos on the wall, and from Joe's Bar we were invited for a 'beer and guns' river trip with two local hunters.

Growing up in Northern Ireland, I had developed a natural aversion to guns. In our troubled society back in the 1970s, they were not so much associated with sport or recreation, but rather something much more sinister; so the guns aspect of the river trip didn't really hold much attraction for me. That said, I was still very keen to see the construction of the small hunting cabin that we were going to visit.

We took a fast riverboat up one of the smaller tributaries to the main river that snakes its way past McGrath. Being on a flat plain, this smaller creek, like the main river, meandered, twisted and turned back on itself in dramatic loops. It was great fun blasting around the bends at high speed, constantly watching the banks for any sightings of big wildlife, such as moose or bears. Soon enough we pulled up at a small ramp next to a great little cabin, only accessible from the river. Hand crafted from all manner of repurposed wood, the backwoods cabin reminded me of childhood adventure stories about Davey Crocket, the 'King of the wild frontier'.

The beers were duly unloaded, and some makeshift shooting targets were set up in the woods. We all needed ear protectors as the guns were ear-piercingly loud. Like a full set of golf clubs, there were different rifles and handguns for different purposes. While James had instruction on how to fire them all, I stuck to just looking on, slightly bemused, with a beer in hand. I had no real curiosity in firing any of them, but I must say the spectacle of the firepower was certainly dramatic. One of the rifles, on a semi-automatic setting, was like something straight out of a war movie. A machine gun that could spray out a hail of bullets in seconds. I wondered however, aside from target practice, what civilian purpose owning such a thing could possibly serve. Unlike skilfully using a regular, single-shot hunting rifle with great care and precision, where was the skill in mowing down a fleeing animal in a hail of bullets?

Back in town, we toured about for a few days on our bikes, seeing the sights and appreciating the exercise. I enjoyed examining the forest floor in close detail, the small plants, mosses, lichens and shrubs. I had obviously seen a lot of trees from above in the past month, but rarely (thankfully) ever got to see them close up on the ground. It was fascinating to compare the different species types with those of our own more familiar UK woodlands back home.

On one exploration we happened down a small track near the river. At the end was a small wooden cabin that was occupied. Thinking we had gone the wrong way, we were just turning to backtrack when a friendly voice called out.

"Hello there!"

We looked behind us to find an elderly native Alaskan lady waving us back. We then had a lovely hour or so chatting with her, learning about how her life was mapped out by the seasons and traditional migrations. Much activity was influenced by the river and the fish it contained. I was amazed to hear that one of her winter specialities, popular with her extended family, was a sort of ice cream made of fish. Alas it was not the right season to make it. I would have loved to have tried her fishy ice cream recipe, particularly after having tasted jellyfish ice cream in Japan and frozen raw fish curls in Russia.

On returning to town, we saw a crowd of firefighters who had assembled by the runway. Specialist equipment was strewn all around them, being checked over with great care and we wondered what they were up to. Soon they were called for a briefing, and we later learned that they were a bunch of *fire-jumpers* preparing to parachute into a nearby wilderness area to combat wildfires. I was most impressed, such an amazing, though dangerous and difficult job to perform, yet here they were, calmly and quietly going about their heroic deeds with such little fuss. True heroes, one and all.

Later in the day, a light aircraft returned to McGrath from its regular monthly shopping trip to Anchorage, and as it disgorged its contents of newly bought spares and equipment into several waiting pickup trucks, I was able to confirm that the Rainy Pass was currently flyable, with settled weather conditions all the way to Anchorage.

It was time for us to move on.

12 June 2019: McGrath, Alaska, USA – Willow, Alaska, USA

Recorded for posterity, like some old black and white pioneering photo shoot, we pushed our gyroplanes off the apron and lined them up directly outside Hotel McGrath's front door. They were like a couple of old stagecoaches or charabancs that were about to head out on some wild west adventure. Our visit felt to be such a rare event that I wondered whether McGrath might *ever* see another gyro passing by in the future.

After a warm send-off from all our new friends, I led us out and briskly climbed up and away from the airfield, whilst James looped around to make a lower-level farewell flypast along the river. I was still cautious having suffered my trim switch issue in Provedinia Bay and felt the need to gain plenty of height as quickly as possible. I didn't want to have any technical issues whilst only scraping the treetops.

Settling into the flight, my full attention was focussed ahead as the mighty barrier of the Alaskan Range loomed into view. Visibility was good and glancing away far off over to the east it was easy to spot the highest peak in the range. Even from *140 miles* away, Denali dominated the skyline.

Careful navigation was now needed. As with the previous mountain transits in Russia, I needed to make sure we flew through the correct sequence of valleys to transit the Rainy Pass. The valleys were steep and cut deep through the towering peaks all around. It was easy to see why the Rainy Pass had such a fearsome reputation in poor weather conditions. If the cloud base settled down into the valleys, becoming trapped underneath would be like flying along in an oversized drain-pipe. In the tightest section, going by the ominous name of Hell's Gate, a light fixed-wing aircraft would struggle to have enough room to make a 180-degree turn, without either climbing blindly into the cloud, or scraping its wingtips on the steep sidewalls. They would be flying up a blind alley without being able to escape back out of it. Reassuringly, at least we were slightly better off in gyroplanes, as we could turn tail on a sixpence should the need have ever arisen.

It must be said – despite the complex terrain, the view was spectacular. The valleys twisted and turned dramatically, and as I banked steeply around each tight bend, the next section ahead would suddenly reveal itself. Constantly, I mentally ticked off the sweeping bends and side valleys en route to prevent becoming lost or disorientated. Our relatively 'low-level' route was still up at roughly 4900ft and had we strayed into the wrong side valley we might have had to climb considerably higher in order to escape out of it. Getting lost while in this maze of mountains didn't bear thinking about.

With the highest pass crossed in the middle of the range, my technical workload of pathfinding reduced considerably, and mentally at least it felt all downhill from here. Slowly the valleys began to widen and flatten out and I took comfort that we had finally crossed our last true wilderness before Oregon. Once we reached the Anchorage area, we would then again have the reassuring comfort of roads to follow.

Now clear of the complex barrier of the Alaskan Range, I was able to predict with better certainty when we could rendezvous with John Hereward in Anchorage. We still had a few days in hand and so opted to overnight at a seaplane base in Willow. Once again, our local hosts were fantastic. They had a large (and full) hangar, but we still managed to squeeze both gyros into it. To add to the adventure, we also slept in there too! Under the wing as it were, in amongst all the aircraft.

Tucked up in my sleeping bag, I felt a similar warm glow as I did after crossing the Bering Strait. In Nome, I had realised that I would no longer have to face ditching into open water, and now I had the same realisation about landing out in forested wilderness. In any emergency situation from here onwards, I could head towards a plethora of small airstrips, or if more urgent, opt for a wide road, a cultivated field, a golf course or even a large Walmart parking lot.

I spared James too much celebration. Even though I was elated at being so nearly home and dry, he still had a very long way to go in his circumnavigation journey.

13 June 2019: Willow, Alaska, USA – Anchorage, Alaska, USA

Different challenges now presented themselves. After so much airspace freedom adventuring around in the wilderness on our own, it came as a real shock to the system to be now suddenly plunged back into the tightly controlled, congested skies surrounding Anchorage. The place appeared packed, with all kinds of light aircraft whizzing in and out of the various local airfields scattered around the city. Outlying bush pilots were commuting back and forth on shopping trips, floatplanes were linking up with their lake and river bases and likewise all manner of sightseeing helicopters and small commercial planes were also plying their trade. For somewhere so removed and isolated from the rest of the country, it certainly was a busy place.

The formalities of arrival and radio procedure into Merrill Field Airport were straight forward enough, but it all just felt very rushed. Leading us into land, I was aware of departing traffic below us queuing up and waiting for their take-off slots, as well as an increasing line of air traffic approaching on long finals behind us. Everything had to be expedited; we needed to land quickly and then get out of the way fast. Unfortunately, in haste on landing, we were directed to taxi off onto the opposite side of the runway to where we wanted to be. It then took another 20 minutes of patiently waiting on a taxiway before a gap in the runway traffic finally allowed us to cross and reach our parking area.

I was almost missing empty Siberia.

We were hosted by the fantastic aviation charter business Lake and Peninsula Airlines, *Lake and Pen* for short. They kindly allowed us full use of their aircraft maintenance shop, which was essential as John would need to perform full services on both aircraft in the coming days. Being able to readily borrow a few hand tools when needed was also a big help.

With G-YROX and G-KTCH sorted, we still needed to find accommodation. We wanted to be close to Lake and Pen's office during the upcoming servicing and to find somewhere reasonably cheap, as we were likely to be now grounded here for a week or so. At US$50 a night, the Mush Inn, just across the street, seemed to fit the brief. It was a bit rough and ready, but as with all our other previous dodgy lodgings, I convinced James it would at least be *character-building.*

The thin laminate wood-effect walls in my room still had various impact holes punctured into them from previous disgruntled guests, and the thinnest of carpet was of that certain appearance and sticky texture that discouraged me from taking off my shoes, ever. At least the bed was safe, being the relatively cleanest place in the room. Unfortunately, James's first room reeked of cannabis smoke, so he was quickly moved, and I also got an upgrade on the second day, to a room with a better (ie. working) shower.

14–20 June 2019: Anchorage, Alaska, USA (non-flying days)

As in McGrath, bikes seemed to be the best option for getting around town. Being a popular cruise ship stopover, the downtown area was much more touristy than we were used to. Gaudy souvenir emporiums and T-shirt vendors seemed to occupy every other shopfront. These were interspersed with the impressive front lobbies of international hotel chains, though in stark contrast, there were also a lot of homeless people and drug addicts dotted about on the streets outside. Perhaps they were drifters, who had migrated into the big smoke to seek their fortune, but instead had now somehow ended up jobless and living rough.

The Mush Inn for all its downsides, actually started to feel quite homely after a few days. I could ride my hire bike right up to my motel room door, wheel it inside and store it securely. I certainly couldn't have done that very easily in some fancy 10th floor suite of the nearby Sheraton Anchorage Hotel and Spa. The bikes would have caused mayhem in their crowded lifts for a start, chain oil and cocktail dresses don't mix too well...

As the week went on, necessity proved the mother of invention. As we were assured of being in one place for a few days, I took the opportunity to get some much-needed washing done. With so few spare clothes, it was always a bonus to have at least semi-clean clothes to change into.

In my sumptuously appointed Mush Inn *suite*, I took stock of what I had to hand: some left-over Russian handwashing powder that I had last used in Anadyr; a working shower with hot water; and a 2ft-high plastic wastepaper bin. With a thorough pre-clean, the bin soon became a makeshift washing tub. I took a stroll outside and found a branch of a small tree to fashion as a large stirring stick. I was all set. After the washing and several rinses in the shower tray, I was ready for the next (and most tricky) stage, the drying.

Having a very sparsely furnished room now proved to be decidedly useful. All I had was the bed, a freestanding table and a bedside cabinet. Oh, and a parked bicycle... In my bags, I found some lengths of thin rope and straps used for luggage lashing, but alas with the wafer-thin walls, there were no wall lights, picture frames or built-in furnishings to tie a washing line to. I then had an idea. I took the table and turned it upside down. I now had four sturdy table legs to string the straps around. Next, wedging the table so that it wouldn't slide, I stretched the ropes right across the room and lashed them to the equally wedged bike. Job done! A bespoke multiple indoor clothesline that only needed me to perform a limbo dance twice each time I needed to get to the doorway.

21 June 2019: Anchorage, Alaska, USA – Tok Junction, Alaska, USA

John had made a sterling effort to complete his full maintenance programme on both aircraft in the short few days we had available, despite feeling a little under the weather from a combination of jet lag and a bug he had picked up en route to Alaska. It had been nice to catch up with him again and to hear the latest news of the gyroplane community back home.

As for James and I, with renewed confidence in our freshly serviced aircraft, it felt good to get back in the saddle again. Routing onwards from Anchorage once more presented us with a choice. We could elect to stay close to the Pacific Ocean all the way down to Oregon, which would mean facing the ever-present risk of fog banks, desolate fiords and an inhospitable coastline; or we could move inland, but then have to negotiate the high peaks of the Pacific Coast Ranges later in the journey. The latter option offered one significant advantage: we could opt to follow the world-famous Alaskan Highway. The choice therefore was a no-brainer, being possibly the longest emergency runway ever built, the highway won.

Quickly picking up the route of the highway, navigating south-east out of Anchorage was a breeze. Like a true pair of aerial motorbikes, we meandered alongside the road, banking steeply around the bends and keeping the road surface within a short landing range. The dense, hazardous forest, sprawling out to either side, suddenly didn't matter anymore. We now had an asphalt safety net below us for the whole of our journey through western Canada and ultimately down into the lower US states. If anything went wrong in the air, we now had the option of landing and even taxiing along the road for miles in order to reach help.

We were in high spirits, and the mood was so relaxed that at one point we even had the luxury of choosing to stop for a *comfort break* when we passed over a remote gravel runway. As if pulling into a roadside layby, I quickly looped us around and we landed, took a few photos, had some snacks, had a pee and climbed back into the air, all in about 15 minutes flat.

Accommodation stopovers were now planned out according to how far along the road we could fly before reaching a suitable airstrip. Tok Junction was our first selection and it fitted the brief nicely, with both a choice of handy roadside motels and a diner called *Fast Eddie's.* I took a selfie with James next to the restaurant sign to send to our very own fast Eddie sitting at home in the UK. Although the motel rooms initially appeared in a better condition than those in Anchorage, alas it was not the case. Both James and I awoke to find our bodies covered in tiny red marks; overnight the bed bugs had been a-biting.

While accommodation was proving to be decidedly hit or miss, at least finding fuel in the land of plentiful gasoline was not a problem. Every town we passed by had at least one roadside gas station, with brimming tanks of 95 octane gasoline. It was a long-distance gyro pilot's dream come true.

22 June 2019: Tok Junction, Alaska, USA – Alaska Highway, Yukon, Canada

Walking (and itching) our way back to the airstrip in the morning, I noted that we passed a gas station run by the Three Bears Alaska Outpost. It was about a quarter of a mile along the highway and rather helpfully, on the same side of the road as the airstrip. I also noted that, again rather conveniently, that side of the road also had a narrow bike lane pathway, about 8ft wide, which ran along parallel to the main highway. With a plan hatching in my mind, it seemed that fortune was now going to favour the bold.

After re-packing the gyros and getting ready to refuel, I asked James to follow me. Initially puzzled, the penny soon dropped when he saw me start up my engine and taxi off the apron to reach a dirt gravel access road. We then scooted along our newfound cycle lane/taxiway towards the gas station. Pulling up close to the pumps we cut the engines early and coasted into the garage forecourt to line up for the pumps like a couple of touring motorbikes. After smiling for many selfies and answering numerous questions from curious locals and tourists alike, we were soon re-scooting back to the airstrip and were ready for departure in record time. Once more the versatility of flying a gyroplane shone through.

Our road-hugging flight continued, progressing along the Alaskan Highway through southern Alaska and then flying into Canadian airspace. It was a first for James, and my second arrival in the country since leaving Houlton, Maine back in 2015. Then, as now, the distinctive red maple leaf Canadian flag fluttered on a white flagpole below. Eddie, from his home office in the UK, had arranged for us to clear customs formalities with the Canadian authorities on arrival in Whitehorse, so we nonchalantly overflew both the US and Canadian border checkpoints in turn.

All was good. For the moment at least everything around us seemed to be running along smoothly and to plan. Until suddenly, with a tremendous flash in the sky, it wasn't!

With only 35 miles or so left to run before reaching Whitehorse, I rounded a bend in the road to be met by a vicious-looking thunderous sky ahead. It dominated the skyline and fully occupied the wide valley basin. Initially, I spotted a chink of brighter sky above the right-hand side of the valley, so I radioed back to James to explain that we could possibly squeeze through it. He replied that he would follow my lead, but as we closed in along the valley, the conditions grew darker and more menacing by the second. The clear gap was still there, but heavy rain was now also falling up ahead, further reducing our visibility. My gut feeling was telling me to be extremely cautious. The idea of pressing on was becoming ever more marginalised and I also had James to consider, following on behind. At such tricky moments, my greater flying experience automatically made me our 'crucial decision maker', and I didn't want to now lead him into a potentially hazardous situation. To check on his whereabouts, I radioed again to confirm that he had me well in his sights. The last thing we wanted in marginal visibility was for us to lose sight of each other.

And then it happened. An almighty flash of lightning and crack of thunder, almost on top of us.

Decision made. With a fast-changing thunderstorm now bubbling up over the hills all around us, we needed to get out of the sky as soon as possible. I quickly scanned our options and spotted some open fields on a nearby ranch close to the highway. But as I dropped down closer, I noticed that they were being used for grazing horses and were criss-crossed with electric fencing.

"James, the fields are no good," I radioed. "We're going to have to land on the road, and as fast as possible. It'll be fine, just follow me in and keep an eye out for any road traffic."

I had made several such out-landings on roads previously, most memorably in Saudi Arabia (twice) and India. As long as the road was clear of both traffic and powerlines it was relatively straightforward. And here we had the added advantage that, for safety reasons, it was generally accepted that light aircraft could land on the Alaskan Highway, in the event of being caught out by any sort of emergency or bad weather. Moreover, all powerlines that follow the road had been set well back from the roadside on purpose, so to give adequately wide wing clearance for any fixed-wing aircraft making a precautionary landing.

The winds suddenly picked up from the emerging thunderstorm – they were confused, squally and violently buffeting, but still no match for a couple of gyros who were now on a mission.

Dropping out of the sky and banking hard left brought me in line with the road below. Helpfully James then flagged up that through the murky conditions he had just caught sight of a layby farther ahead, which gave us a perfect place to set down and get off the road as quickly as possible. I extended my final approach a little and landed, rolling off onto the truck stop area with the rotor still turning. James popped into view behind me a minute later and we were safe, at least for the meantime. We climbed out and congratulated each other on what had just been a wild five minutes. James got his camera out and was busy filming our situation when another almighty crack of lightning struck a prominent rocky outcrop, only about 100m away. The bolt kicked up a plume of smoke and vaporised rock. Safely on the ground, it was an amazing thing to witness first-hand.

We hurried to get the gyros under their covers as by now the rain was pelting down. There were a couple of big wooden toilet cabins in the rest area, so we sheltered in the doorway while we took stock of our situation. We had landed around 35 miles from our intended overnight stop in Whitehorse, barely half an hour's flight away. However, we also had plenty of daylight remaining, and so I presumed that we could still hopefully get going again once the storm has passed. This plan however didn't sit so well with Canadian customs and immigration...

We had no mobile signal, but we could still communicate by text using the Garmin satellite trackers. The ever-vigilant Eddie back in the UK was straight onto our case, and acting as middle-man, was able to liaise directly with the police and customs officers in Whitehorse to advise them we were at least safe on the ground, albeit 35 miles away. A message then came back, via Eddie, that we were to stay put, *exactly* where we were, until the officers came out to meet us. Technically, as we had now already landed in Canada, without clearing customs after leaving Alaska, I presumed they wanted to check our aircraft paperwork on our first point of landing.

So, we obediently waited...

The storm cleared after an hour as predicted and the ground dried fast from the heavy rain.

We still waited, standing around in the truck rest area, kicking our heels and wondering why customs were taking so long to reach us.

And so we waited some more...

The light now was starting to fade, soon we would no longer be able to make it to Whitehorse before dark.

No one came.

It was now too late in the day to fly on.

What to do?

Neither of us fancied hanging out in a toilet block all night, and we already had perfectly good accommodation booked in Whitehorse.

But just then, the cavalry arrived. Not in the form of a police truck as expected, but in the form of a holiday camper van, complete with a fabulous family inside, who were returning to Pennsylvania from a long-distance road trip vacation in Alaska. They were also heading for Whitehorse but had pulled over into the layby to take a good look at our strangest of road-going vehicles. We got chatting about our predicament and soon the kettle was on and very welcome hot chocolate was being passed around. What a fantastic stroke of luck on such a desolate stretch of road! Consequently, when the officers failed to show, we wrapped up the gyros as securely as possible and gratefully accepted a lift in the camper all the way into Whitehorse.

The next morning, word came through that customs would visit us at our hotel. It was only then we found out the whole story as to why they hadn't turned up the previous evening. Apparently, they had set off to come and find us but only drove 25 miles and then gave up and returned to town. Although we had to remain calm, apologetic and conciliatory in front of these officers, inside I was fuming. Having initially instructed us that *under no circumstances* were we to move from our landing spot, *why* hadn't they tried harder to find us? And *why* didn't they tell us they'd called off their search? Had we known, we could have easily flown to Whitehorse before nightfall to meet them there instead.

To add further insult to injury, when I then asked if they could take us back to retrieve the aircraft they had caused us to abandon in an unsecure truck stop 35 miles away, they said it was not possible. Their alternative suggestion? To take a taxi, a ride that subsequently cost us C$100! Welcome to Canada... Grrrr!

23 June 2019: Alaska Highway, Yukon, Canada – Carcross, Yukon, Canada – Dease Lake, British Columbia, Canada

On the bright side, even though the taxi back to the truck stop was expensive, the friendly driver later acted as an excellent impromptu road traffic controller, stopping all passing vehicles momentarily as I led us out of the layby to speedily take off from the highway.

Having already completed the customs entry paperwork, we now no longer needed to fly into Whitehorse. The downside of that however meant we also missed out on getting refuelled at the airport. But I already had an alternative plan up my sleeve.

The previous night I had found a small local town called Carcross on Google Earth. Peering down from orbit, I could see they had a gravel airstrip close to the town centre, and with the additional help of Google Street View, I was then able to see that they also had a gas station, only a couple of hundred yards up the road. Bingo! My overnight plan was all set...

Once more James followed my lead as we banked in hard and steep to land on the rough gravel of Carcross airstrip. Pausing only to stop the main rotors, we taxied to the highway, looked left and right and then nipped across the road to reach the gas pumps. As with Tok Junction, our sudden arrival caused a plethora of camera phones to be hurriedly fished out of pockets. It turned out to be a perfect little stop, as after re-fuelling, we pushed over to the small on-site diner and had ourselves a lovely lunch.

This was definitely *the* way to travel.

Arriving at Dease Lake, the airport appeared deserted. After waiting for the usual 10 minutes, in case someone had seen us fly over the town and had driven out to the airport to get a closer look, we fired up the engines and taxied along to the Pacific Western Helicopters service hangar at the far end of the runway.

Thankfully, inside we soon found some friendly local aviators, who offered us overnight hangarage as well as a welcome ride to a small hotel in town, the Northway Motor Inn. Close to Highway 37, it was surprisingly busy with tourist traffic for such a small settlement, and we were fortunate to get both accommodation and a set menu meal in the restaurant, just before they closed.

24 June 2019: Dease Lake, British Columbia, Canada – Smithers, British Columbia, Canada

The IFR (I follow roads) navigation continued south from Dease Lake to Smithers, over endless pristine pine forests, sparkling rivers and shimmering lakes. It was relaxing to think that we could now expect this sort of *safety-net flying,* cruising along at 500ft above the road, all the way down to the Washington State border.

The airport at Smithers was also very quiet but I soon got chatting to a pilot at a helicopter charter company based on the airfield. He was kept busy ferrying research scientists back and forth to various remote drop-off and pick-up points. It must have been an interesting job, with lots of multiple short flights every day and getting to regularly fly into some very wild and unusual places. We were kindly given overnight space in his hangar and spent a relaxed evening in a nearby, pleasantly landscaped, two-story motel, the Aspen Inn. The early evening was warm enough to eat outside and we shared some beer and stories with our new pilot friend until the sun went down. Alfresco dining was a comforting sign that warmer flying days were soon hopefully on their way.

25 June 2019: Smithers, British Columbia, Canada – 108 Mile Ranch, British Columbia, Canada

Our flying road trip continued south as we followed the highway for most of the day. I was constantly amazed by how stark the contrast was between the small settlements huddled along the roadside compared to the vast wilderness that existed only a few hundred yards back into the surrounding forests.

At one point, I was taken aback by a sobering sight. As I led us along, following the thin black ribbon of tarmac meandering through the trees, I was in *energy-saving-mode,* both physically and mentally. Hunkered down in my seat, I was monitoring everything, but at the same time seeing very little. All was quiet and calm. James meanwhile, was following along in our usual loose formation about 100m behind me. We then passed by yet another small village on the roadside and I glanced down to admire some immaculately tended back gardens behind a prestigious row of large, well-to-do houses. The neatly cropped lawns, the hot tubs and barbeque decks hinted of a luxurious outdoor lifestyle. A crowd had gathered on one of the decks, perhaps for a family gathering or a birthday party and all appeared engrossed in their various conversations. A sudden movement however, in the scrubland about 100m behind the house, then caught my eye. Shifting my focus, I was then amazed to see that it was a huge grizzly bear slowly ambling along!

It was incredible to see these two worlds juxtaposed so closely together like this, one completely wild and the other completely urbanised. Thankfully neither appeared to be aware of the other, though I did briefly think of trying to loop back to shout some sort of a warning to the people. But on reflection, I saw they had a good boundary fence in place and that the grizzly, now sniffing at the ground, didn't appear to be overly interested in gate-crashing his neighbour's party. In any event, had he been invited, nibbling on light canapés and quaffing numerous glasses of prosecco would have been a tad socially tricky considering he was only equipped with big furry bear paws.

I quickly flicked myself back into *energy-saving-mode* and flew on.

Our choice of small, less busy airfields that just happened to be about the right distance along the road each day, was working out well. We always eventually found someone locally to chat to, and South Cariboo's 108 Mile Ranch was no exception.

It was another lovely stopover and G-YROX and G-KTCH were hosted in a huge, scrupulously clean hangar along with some local helicopters. As an added bonus, for accommodation we were able to stroll across from the entrance gate and check in to a well-appointed holiday lodge across the road. Later in the evening we were given a lift in a pickup truck to the nearest gas station to fill up on gasoline. I used my trusty Turtle Pac as usual and James made do with a borrowed 200-litre barrel.

Suitably fuelled, we were ready now for our last flying day in

Canada. All being well, our next stop would see us cross the border and back into *the good old US of A.*

26 June 2019: 108 Mile Ranch, British Columbia, Canada – Port Townsend, Washington, USA

Pushing south from 108 Mile Ranch we encountered our last significant physical barrier before reaching the freewheeling, easy-rider, US West Coast; we had to navigate through the steep, rugged mountains of the Pacific Coast Ranges. Fortunately for us, our keep-safe-close-to-civilisation main highway continued to lead us along the lowest and most navigable path. Though it did take us through some spectacularly tight and twisting river gorges that were cut deep into the barren rock-face. Snaking along the riverbank, the road closely followed the raging river in the centre of the gorge, and it was also soon accompanied (on the opposite bank) by an equally snaking railway line. Both road and rail links were remarkably busy with traffic, in what was probably the mother of all transport bottlenecks as it was the only viable commercial traffic route through the mountains for many miles around. And on this particular day, it also happened to include a couple of opportunistic globe-trotting gyroplanes, looking for their easiest route south.

The frequent trains proved to be the main spectacle, each with several engines coupled together to both haul and push their hundreds of payload wagons in long metal snakes up and down what seemed, on occasions, to be quite steep inclines. Some trains even had engines placed halfway along them, to add extra muscle to the task. It reminded me of the similarly long iron-ore trains that I had seen over on the east coast of Canada, on the 2015 flight from Sept-Îles up to Schefferville.

Flying along in such a confined vertical-sided gorge, I had to remain constantly vigilant to locate and avoid hard-to-spot powerlines, masts and lattice pylons, especially if they suddenly appeared after flying around a blind bend. It took an hour or so of intensely focused flying to pass through the most technical part of the mountains and then, quite suddenly on rounding yet another bend, we broke out onto the wide flat plains of the western seaboard.

Once again, I felt elated at reaching yet another milestone, as navigating us safely from Alaska down through the Pacific Coast Ranges, had been the last major mountain challenge of my entire circumnavigation flight. It was all hopefully flat open landscapes and plain sailing from now on, to reach my finishing point in Oregon, a few short days away.

Soon enough, with all eyes on the GPS screen, we crossed the 49th parallel of latitude that denoted the border between the USA and Canada. It was an interesting sight as the actual line of the border in these parts was mapped out on the ground by a line of regular field posts and wire fence, stretching off as far as the eye could see in both directions. At any point along it you could easily have hopped over the 4ft wire, from one country to the other and back again, as many times as you liked. It was such a contrast to how the border now appears across the southernmost reaches of the USA.

Shortly afterwards, now flying in US airspace once more, we landed in Port Townsend, a quiet (yet still international) airport situated north of Seattle, at the mouth of Puget Sound. As expected, the local customs formalities arriving in from Canada were exactly that, a formality. Especially as we had also been in Alaska only a few days previously.

I was pleased to discover that the airfield also had its own excellent aviation museum, and even more pleased when they opened the big exhibition hall doors and allowed us to push the gyros inside for the night. As always on such occasions, I like to think that *Roxy* had a great night, sharing adventurous flying stories with all the other exhibits in the hall.

27 June 2019: Port Townsend, Washington, USA – Scappoose, Oregon, USA

This was a significant day for me, as it marked my return to Oregon. Back in 2015 I could never have predicted that I would now be returning, some *four years later,* to finally complete my circumnavigation of the globe. After all, at the time, I had just shipped *Roxy* over from Japan and so had been forced to accept that my goal of an unbroken circumnavigation was probably no longer ever going to be achieved. But the satisfaction now, after eventually finding a workable solution that *did* allow me to complete my unbroken loop of the planet, felt all the more special.

It certainly seemed that *good things truly do come to those who wait...*

Setting out from Port Townsend, I briefly considered taking us on a south-westerly route to pick up and follow the coastline. We could then have overflown Tillamook, the most westerly starting point for my coast-to-coast flight back in 2015, but it would have made for a lengthy looping diversion, and I was keen to avoid any repeat of the poor weather delays I had experienced in the coastal hills the first time around. We therefore made a more direct beeline towards my original restart point at the Evergreen Aviation and Space Museum in McMinnville, and by fortunate coincidence, Scappoose also happened to be on the same direct path; so I looked forward to calling in en route to catch up again with Jim Vanek and his Sport Copter team.

As we closed in on the approach to Scappoose, with about 12 miles to run, we tracked along the eastern bank of the Columbia River. I was amazed at the volume of shipping that was plying up and down the channel and chatted to James who was following along behind in our loose formation. Then, as we turned a bend in the river, I suddenly had a flash of recognition.

I felt a warm glow of familiarity; ***I had been here before***. I recognised the features of the landscape from my various local familiarisation flights back in 2015. I shared the moment with James on the radio.

"I've been here before!" I called, "I recognise everything about this place. That's it! It's done! *Roxy* is the first gyroplane to have flown completely around the world!"

With much shared celebration over the radio, we closed in on Scappoose and continued the celebrations on the ground, when greeted by the Sport Copter crew. Technically speaking, landing at Scappoose did physically close the loop for my circumnavigation, having taken off from the same spot on 4 June 2015, but in my own mind, I regarded returning to McMinnville as the ultimate start and finish point of my unbroken global journey. It was where I had re-commenced flying on 1 June 2015 after *Roxy* had been shipped directly there from Japan.

Pushing G-YROX (and accompanied this time by G-KTCH) back into Jim Vanek's maintenance hangar was a special feeling. Jim quickly noticed that my rudder trim tab was missing (a small tab of metal that helps the aircraft to fly straight without slight rudder pedal correction). It had been a victim of *hangar rash* at some point, suffering damage on the ground, rather than in the air. He immediately set about shaping me a replacement one, which was much more robust than the original. As an added touch, for posterity, he also etched his name onto the alloy tab with a small hand-drill; there was no way that signature was going to rub off anytime soon!

A short time later, I had the great pleasure of returning and introducing James to the same Scappoose Creek B&B Guest house that I had used on my previous visit. I was pleased to see that it still had its small herd of llamas grazing in the adjoining field. In the evening, Jim picked us up and we had a very pleasant evening in a local floating restaurant.

28 June 2019: Scappoose, Oregon, USA – McMinnville, Oregon, USA

This was it, this was *the day* I had worked towards for so long. All being well, I would succeed in completing the first physical flight of a gyroplane around the world, a feat that has eluded aviators since the birth of gyroplane/autogyro aircraft back in 1923. A pioneering effort that was 96 years in the making. The last remaining fundamental type of aircraft would now be able to achieve its historic maiden global flight.

Walking back to the airport from the B&B, it all felt quite surreal. It was only a short flight of 40 minutes, and I was scheduled to land at the museum at midday, but all morning I was buzzing with a heightened awareness, everything seemed extra meaningful and significant.

This included James's reaction to the upcoming flight. Rather than wanting to accompany me on my final landmark flight to McMinnville, he preferred to let me arrive there on my own. By way of explanation, he described this to be "my big day", as the media spotlight would no doubt be focussed on G-YROX, as the first gyroplane to finally encircle the world. Instead of flying with me, he elected to stay back in Scappoose and follow along to the museum much later in the day, after all the expected media interest had died down. Initially I thought his reaction had been a bit odd and I wasn't sure of why, after all our constant close flying together over so many weeks, he didn't now want to witness, first-hand, this final milestone being reached. I reasoned that perhaps he preferred to be absent in order to stay focussed on his own ongoing circumnavigation journey. I had successfully finished my challenge, but he potentially still had a lot of extremely uncertain, difficult and challenging flying ahead, not least the psychological mind games that would be necessary in attempting his own crossing of the North Atlantic. I also wondered if perhaps he wanted to avoid any confusion in the eyes of his various sponsors; if he had arrived with me and then got roped into giving any press interviews, it may have given out a mixed message to them. As events unfolded later in the day however, I was still being interviewed by a local Oregon TV crew when he flew in, so he didn't manage to entirely avoid the media attention after all.

At the appointed hour of midday, I put in a few circling orbits over the top of the museum buildings to announce my arrival. As prearranged, I spotted good friend and museum docent Tom Halvorsen waving from the ground. He had positioned himself to momentarily halt any traffic on the museum's access roads. This then gave me a clear run at landing wherever I needed to, depending on the wind direction. As it happened, I elected to land on a quiet gravel section of the road system, right in front of the space exhibition building.

What a feeling! Overwhelming relief that I was down safely and that *Roxy* and I had finally, successfully, and *Gloriously* finished our nine-year quest to achieve the first circumnavigation of the world in a gyroplane aircraft.

Engine still running but main rotor stopped, I followed Tom in his familiar blue jeep around the perimeter roads to end up where it all started, outside the huge hangar doors to the rear of the exhibition halls. Rather appropriately, this was also exactly the same spot where we had first unloaded *Roxy* from the Japanese shipping container in the autumn of 2014. And even more appropriately, as I shut down the engine, the next people that came over to welcome me were Terry Naig and Larry Wood who, along with Tom Halvorsen, had been a tremendous help during my first visit.

We all chatted for ages before I finally climbed out of my seat. It was still incredible to think that I had literally flown myself around the world since I last saw them. Many of the docents on duty also gathered around, for photos and congratulations. There was much catching up to do with them all.

22

North America: completing the circumnavigation

29 June 2019: McMinnville, Oregon, USA (non-flying day)

After a good night of rest at Tom's place, who again was acting as my impeccable host, James and I spent a very welcome non-flying day relaxing and looking around the museum exhibits, including of course the world-famous main attraction *The Spruce Goose.*

I had time also to reflect a little on the completion of the circumnavigation. After the intense flying of the past two months, across Europe, Russia, the Bering Strait and Alaska, I was finally able to ease off on the single-purpose focus that I had placed on myself. Despite all the considerable setbacks and challenges, I had successfully achieved the historic, first physical flight of a gyroplane around the planet and had now become the first gyro circumnavigator. I had also helped to guide James across the wilder parts of Russia and Alaska and safely down into the lower 48 states of America, putting him well on his way towards establishing the first gyroplane speed record around the world. We had crossed some extraordinarily vast and hostile terrain together, but at last I could now feel my overall burden of responsibility towards our joint flight gradually lifting.

The four-year enforced delay in returning to Oregon had scuppered any hope of me continuing to set a realistic speed record. In the same timescale, a person could have run on foot around the planet – *twice over.*

For historical completeness however, I had continued to diligently collect the take-off and landing certificates as per the FAI rules at every stop from Larne to McMinnville. These were to provide physical proof, if ever it was needed, that I did actually fly the entire route as described in this book. It seems hard to believe that by the time of final reckoning, I had eventually flown over 27,000 nautical miles, through 32 countries (instead of the original 24) and had ended up looping one and a half times around the world in order to finally achieve the unbroken circumnavigation.

Between 2010 and 2015, I had already set 19 FAI world records for gyroplane flight, including what I still regard as the most technically significant achievement of them all – the first gyroplane crossing of the Atlantic Ocean. And although the FAI *speed* record around the world ultimately became technically unattainable for me, I was more than happy to have still achieved my core pioneering and historically significant objective; to complete the first *physical* gyro circumnavigation around the globe, regardless of any arbitrary man-made timescale.

I reflected on why it took so long to complete the task. From the outset, I was attempting a type of circumnavigation that had never been achieved before. Every aspect of it, aside from Barry Jones' inspirational initial attempt, was pioneering, untested and unknown, and surrounding the entire journey was a backdrop of constant uncertainty of it actually being achievable at all. The major diplomatic impasse of being denied access to cross Russia had been the single biggest contributor in causing the long delays, but these diplomatic barriers were completely out of my own control. Try as I might, over many consecutive years, it was simply *not my fault* that the Russian Security Services continually decided to hold off on allowing the permission. Had that permission not been withheld initially during 2011, I could have continued to fly the course of my original routing attempt, transiting the Russian Far East immediately after Japan; followed by crossing the Bering Strait, continental USA and the North Atlantic, to have completed the full unbroken circumnavigation by the late summer of that year. But that scenario had not been allowed to happen. Instead, I found out first-hand the hard way, that a maiden pathfinding journey was always much more difficult and uncertain to achieve than any subsequent journey made by those aiming to repeat the feat at a later date. Once something is achieved for the first time it loses much of its worrying uncertainty, as now it had been proven to be physically possible. Embarking on an untried and untested maiden flight and finding myself constantly at the mercy of its unpredictability, I soon realised that it was always much harder to lead than to follow.

I was not alone however, in being painfully slow to achieve a historic first circumnavigation; the first sailing ship took three years to complete its journey, as part of the Spanish Magellan expedition, between September 1519 and September 1522. They too were dogged by all sorts of diplomatic difficulties, mishaps en route and navigational uncertainties. Of the five ships that originally set out, only one eventually managed to make it successfully back to Spain. Likewise, of the four US Army Air Service biplane aircraft that took off together from Seattle, USA in April 1924, aiming to complete the historic first aeroplane flight around the world, only two successfully made it back again to their start/finish point some six months later.

When attempting to pioneer and path-find something that has never been done before, it's a given that constant uncertainty and the hazards of the unknown go with the territory. What *is* certain however, is that a successful outcome can never be guaranteed. Set in this historical context, I now regarded my own disjointed and long-delayed journey as perhaps being not so unusual after all.

James on the other hand, still had a lot of serious flying to do before he could finish his own circumnavigation back in the UK. He needed now to significantly build up his overall mileage by performing numerous zigzag flights all over the USA in order to make up the minimum qualifying distance for his FAI speed record attempt. Setting such a speed record would be meaningless unless it was measured against a set minimum distance flown and the FAI uses the circumference of the Tropic of Cancer (19,863 nautical miles; 22,858 miles; 36,787 kilometres) as its benchmark for this purpose. By zigzagging around in the States, G-KTCH's overall global mileage could be quickly built up whilst remaining wholly within a singular, light aircraft friendly country. This was technically still within the rules, but perhaps akin to running a marathon and completing half the distance running safely around a running track rather than out doing battle with the less predictable hazards of the open road. All I could hope for was that after our many long hours of expedition flying together, James had now picked up enough *on the job training* to allow him to capably continue on his onward journey solo around the States, and to then also take on his ultimate challenge of crossing the North Atlantic.

Having safely arrived on the US West Coast, I felt my ad-hoc role of being at times both an aerial chaperone and mentor, had now run its course. James would soon have to increase his pace, in order to build up his required mileage count, whereas I was now looking forward to slowing down on my own flight schedule. I had a good three weeks available before my next fixed objective, which was to arrive in Wisconsin for the huge annual EAA AirVenture Oshkosh convention at the end of July.

For now though, from McMinnville our immediate intentions were to fly on together for a few more days, down the entire US West Coast to reach San Diego. From there, we would both head east for a couple of hours, up and over a last obstacle of high ground, before bidding each other an airborne farewell over the radio and splitting off in different directions. James to head back up north on his first 'zig', and me continuing east for a time to follow the Mexican border.

Even though I had had a good night's sleep at Tom's house, I woke up feeling drained of energy and general vitality. As with a few previous mornings, I put it down to the general fatigue of the punishing flight schedule we had taken on over the past hectic weeks. I hoped that a few rest days and some gentle, fair-weather, beach-flying down the Oregon and Californian coastlines, would soon result in a speedy recovery.

But still, during the next few days, a nagging self-doubt continued. Perhaps I was just getting far too old for this sort of high-level mental and physical self-punishment. I just didn't seem to be bouncing back each day with the same vigour as I remembered previously.

It was as if a creeping malaise was slowly taking me over from within, though for the time being at least, I thankfully remained completely oblivious to the extremely serious nature of what would slowly and gradually develop inside my body over the next two months.

23

North America: West Coast, USA

30 June 2019: McMinnville, Oregon, USA – Crescent City, California, USA

Our flight plan now was to head out to the coast and then follow it as closely as possible, all the way south through Oregon and California, almost to the Mexican border. It was going to be a fantastic road trip on our '*le formidable*' flying motorbikes, making the American dream of cruising down the Big Sur in an open-topped sports car just look like *small beer.*

I had flown many training sorties back in 2015 out to the coastline from McMinnville, so I knew what to expect when we reached the beach. Turning south, we encountered hundreds of miles of pristine sand and foaming waves crashing straight off the Pacific Ocean, interspersed with harsh rocky headlands and sea cliffs. Pockets of human settlements were scattered here and there, squeezed tightly into coves or perched remotely on clifftops. The Oregon coast appeared to be much less developed, still more natural, than its more brash and bawdy southern neighbour, California.

We blasted along the beaches in perfect visibility. Frequently popping up below us were clusters of cars and trucks with beach barbeques on the go and occasionally these were accompanied by racing quad bikes ripping around in tight circles while carving their doughnuts into the sand.

Boy-racers on shiny quad bikes, charging along the beach at full throttle and thinking they were impressively cool (but probably were just annoying to all the other regular beach goers), were one of my favourite targets. I would cruise up alongside them unannounced, then slow down to match their speed and give them a little wave. In that moment, in a quick exchanged glance of defeated acknowledgment, *I knew* that *they knew* that their noisy, bumpy, ground-hugging vehicles could no longer be seen as the *kings of the beach.* There was now a new kid on the block, one who *really* knew how to fly! Point proven and with all the boy-racer *pumped up egos* suitably punctured, I then smoothly throttled up the pace and showed them *Roxy's* tail rudder as I zoomed off down the beach at 100mph towards the horizon.

On other occasions we came across a different sort of vehicle zipping about, but unlike the quad bikes, these had to be avoided at all costs. Flashes of coloured fabric in the sky initially announced their presence: kite surfers. From the air, kite surfer control lines were virtually invisible to us, and these posed a great threat to our fast-spinning rotor blades. With the promise of a deadly entanglement, they were by far our most dangerous hazard on the beach. Fortunately though, the relative closing speeds between a gyro cruising along at 75 knots (86 mph) and a kite surfer at say 20 knots (23 mph) led to an easy avoidance manoeuvre on our part. All we had to do was simultaneously pull up and steeply bank over in a sweeping curve out towards the open sea, thereby leaving a wide safety margin of clear airspace around them.

Arriving in Crescent City, we were once again winging it with small friendly airfields. It turned out to be a pleasantly relaxed local stopover with self-service fuel and no onerous airspace restrictions or overly bureaucratic fuss. Lovely!

1 July 2019: Crescent City, California, USA – Little River, California, USA – Half Moon Bay, California, USA

Another day of coastal flying saw a near-repeat of the previous day, only now we had reached northern California. I knew that this region was famous for having the tallest Sequoia (giant redwood) trees in the world and I was now keen to spot them. The coastal forests were certainly impressive as seen from our elevated viewpoint, but alas with so many trees to look at, I was unable to spot the tallest one of them all, a coastal redwood named Hyperion that stands at an incredible 115.85m (380ft). Rather appropriately, I later learned that its exact location is a closely kept secret to protect it from any unwanted human interference.

Assisted by a brisk tailwind, our beach-flying adventure continued southwards. And as was the case on the Alaskan Highway, two hours into the flight we spontaneously decided to call in at the next suitable airfield for a rest stop. This happened to be Little River, a small airstrip set back about a mile inland and tucked in amongst a dense, blanketing pine forest. After ten minutes or so on the ground, we saddled up again, taking off in a northerly direction into the wind. I led us out and climbed high into wind to gain a healthy separation from the trees below. Only then did I allow myself to bank left by 180 degrees to re-join the beach and pick up once more on our lovely tailwind.

James took off a minute or so behind me, but then decided to 'cut the corner' and began to bank around left at a much lower level than I had, just above the treetops. I had by now completed my turn and so glancing down and across to spot where he was, I immediately recognised his somewhat precarious position, skimming just above the treeline. I grimaced to myself; it did not look a comfortable place to be. During my own climb-out, I had felt that the wind just above the treetops was strong, gusty and very turbulent. He was now trying to climb out through this confused turbulence whilst flying low-level and downwind. I watched on fearfully. At any second, a violent downdraught could have easily forced him down into the trees. Painfully slowly, he began to claw his way up into the sky and to regain a similar altitude to me. I felt it had been a tense moment, but James casually remarked later that it had just *been a bit bumpy* for a while there over the trees. Mulling it over, I don't think he quite realised the extent of the potential danger he'd put himself in by turning downwind so soon.

Near the end of the flight, we closed in on San Francisco Bay. We turned a final headland and *there it was*... The Golden Gate Bridge! For a moment it seemed so strange to look at, almost unreal, like someone had built a huge, highly accurate and detailed model of the bridge and had then placed it as a feature in a giant model village.

We were flying seaward of the bridge, which meant the famous streets of San Francisco formed a dramatic backdrop and the entire inland bay area stretched out before us. The former prison island of Alcatraz stood out stoically in the middle of the bay, while hundreds of white sails, jet skis and speedboats dashed and splashed busily about near the shoreline.

Reducing speed, I was able to turn into wind and hold position in a slow hover for a while to take it all in. Next, I overflew around the southern end of the bridge to have a better view of Alcatraz and checked via the radio to see where James was. He had been orbiting around close to the bridge, to get some close-up selfies. A few minutes later, the next radio call had him whooping and hollering with excitement as he had just flown *under* the bridge. I was unsure if that was actually allowed (while touring France in 2009 there had been a strict 1km exclusion zone for aircraft around the Millau viaduct) and we were both then worried about being met by some blue flashing lights as we landed at nearby Half Moon Bay. As it happened, fortunately for James and much to his relief, no police turned up to arrest him for 'reckless flying'.

Once again, as with previous smaller airfields, we were hosted by some terrifically kind local flyers and even managed to squeeze both gyros into a single T-shaped hangar that was only meant to hold one fixed wing aircraft.

2 July 2019: Half Moon Bay, California, USA – North Los Angeles, California, USA

Flying the Big Sur was a real blast. All day long I marvelled at the architecture of the many grand private mansions, tucked away from the main road, that had been creatively constructed to maximise their ocean views. I hadn't realised just how populated this coastline had become, but from the air we had the best views of it all. Sprawling estates, private golf courses and sumptuous villas clinging onto clifftops were all on display as we buzzed along. I was concerned however for some of the more precarious cliff-edge residences, having flown over evidence of past landslides and rockfalls and I wondered what would become of all this opulent living should the San Andreas Fault ever decide to shake itself into the history books yet again.

Our Californian road trip continued as we cruised past Santa Cruz; its rocky headland was setting up endless, perfectly formed waves for the surfers, who were all floating in small sociable groups below us, no doubt waiting for the best sets of waves to roll in.

North of Santa Barbara, we headed inland to avoid some busy restricted airspace and made an aerial rendezvous with American Peter Kalev, a fellow gyro pilot. He had kindly volunteered to guide us in through the highly congested airspace around the greater Los Angeles area so we could land at Whiteman Airport. As with our escorted flights around Moscow, it was so much easier to follow a local guide at such times, one who knew all the local radio procedures and airspace restrictions. With less navigation and comms to worry about, both James and I had more time to look out and enjoy the spectacular view.

Los Angeles as seen from the air, really was the epitome of modern urban sprawl. Peter led us in onto long finals for runway 12 at Whiteman and on approach, I was surprised to see that the alignment of the single runway conformed with the grid system of urban roads that surrounded it and not necessarily with the prevailing wind direction. Either that, or the road system had been designed *after* the runway orientation had originally been set (perhaps an aviation version of *chicken and egg!*).

After taxiing to the hangars, Peter warmly welcomed us more properly on the ground, and I was able to thank him for all his expert local help and guidance. A short time later, a broadly grinning *family emissary* also turned up to greet us, my nephew David, who happened to be now living in LA. He had come to pick James and me up from the airport and we spent two very relaxing nights at his place along with his wife Chloe. We enjoyed all the beer and comforts of regular home living, while catching up with their news.

3–4 July 2019: North Los Angeles, California, USA (non-flying days)

Sightseeing was the first order of the day and David took us on a grand tour of the sights of downtown LA and the surrounding hills. I found that a day spent doing such regular touristy things was always a great mental break from flying.

On the 4th of July, amid all the Independence Day celebrations, we intended to move on south toward San Diego. However, on returning to the airport I had hoped to address a propeller pitch/vibration adjustment on *Roxy* that had crept in over the past few days. Alas, despite much fine tuning, tweaking and tinkering, time ticked on through the day and without fully solving the issue, another plan was needed. It was decided that James would continue on solo to San Diego in the late afternoon, while I would stay and hop over to Hawthorne Airport on the south side of LA in the morning. There, I hoped to be able to get some additional help with the propeller from resident gyroplane chief instructor, Henry Boger, and his maintenance team at Adventure Air.

To get an early start in the morning, I stayed at a local motel across the street from the airport. On check-in, I was met with thick bulletproof glass at the reception window and paid upfront in cash for a somewhat dark and dingy room. Clearly of *character-building* grade, the accommodation helped set the scene nicely for the restless night ahead.

The immediate surrounding neighbourhood was known to become quite rowdy later in the evening, and for personal safety, I was advised that under no circumstances should I leave my room after dark. That was fine by me as I was feeling dog tired again as usual. The local 4th of July celebrations however, only helped to further magnify the mayhem, as huge window-rattling explosions, occasionally mixed in with some light-hearted *recreational gunfire* for good measure, went off for most of the night, in all directions around me. The big bangs were far louder than regular fireworks, and when combined with vibration-activated car alarms and police sirens, it was like trying to sleep in a war zone.

5 July 2019: North Los Angeles, California, USA – South Los Angeles, California, USA – San Diego, California, USA

Heading for Hawthorne, Peter once again was on hand to escort me south of LA. In loose formation, we flew close to the world-famous Hollywood sign, swept past the downtown area and picked our way through the congested skies around LAX International Airport. On landing, I was soon able to get the propeller issue resolved, with the enthusiastic help of both skilled mechanics and local volunteers alike. Their positive can-do attitude towards getting problems fixed was uplifting, and in keeping with the tremendous spirit of cooperation and camaraderie that can be found in gyro communities all around the world.

Piloting gyros, in all their forms and keeping them flying, was definitely a collective team sport.

Interestingly, while on the ground, I was reminded of another 'team sport' outfit that was situated just around the corner from Hawthorne Airport. It was the Californian HQ for Elon Musk's phenomenally successful SpaceX company, and apparently, according to local gyro folklore at least, Elon had even been spotted taking more than a passing interest in gyroplanes.

With the technical issues all sorted, I was ready to continue on south to San Diego and catch up again with James. A pleasant late afternoon flight of 1hr 40mins saw me buzz past the stunning extensive port facilities of Long Beach and arrive at Montgomery Field, San Diego.

I was met by James and the esteemed Australian gyroplane pilot, Andy Keetch. Andy was one of the true pioneers of early long-distance gyroplane flight, having set numerous cross-country speed records all over North America in his famous Little Wing LW-5 Autogyro named *Woodstock*. I had seen his aircraft (now retired from active flying) on display in the EAA museum, Oshkosh when I had passed through there in 2015. And now, here I was, honoured to meet up with the very man in person.

6–7 July 2019: San Diego, California, USA (non-flying days)

As luck would have it, San Diego was also home to another record-setting global pilot, Robert DeLaurentis (aka the *Zen Pilot*). There was a common link with Robert, as over the years we had both worked closely with our friendly mutual flight planner, the ubiquitous Eddie Gould. Robert kindly hosted James and me in his fantastic apartment, which had magnificent views overlooking both the world-renowned San Diego Zoo and – away off in the distance – Naval Base San Diego, the home port of the US Navy Pacific Fleet. Robert was mid-way through planning his next huge aviation challenge, a fixed-wing circumnavigation flight that would require him to fly solo across both poles. I thought I had flown in some pretty remote spots within the Arctic Circle, until he showed me his charts of Antarctica.

The next day James decided to spend his time catching up with computer admin back at the apartment, so I took a long walk out with Robert around the extensive park near the zoo. We chatted easily, having much in common regarding our long-distance flights, both past and future. He had a very calm, confident and relaxed manner, hence earning him his moniker – the Zen Pilot. His cool calm demeanour greatly reminded me of the search and rescue pilots that I had met in Greenland and the Faroe Islands; no heroics or attention-seeking egos there, just highly skilled pilots quietly and diligently going about their regular business, yet all the while achieving *great things* in the process.

In these few short days, I had met some very inspirational people and I was yet to meet one more before leaving, a university professor and gyroplane historian, Dr. Bruce Charnov. As soon as I heard that he lived in San Diego, I knew I wanted to meet up with him if possible. His authoritative book, *From Autogiro to Gyroplane* published in 2003, had a memorable influence on my decision to become a gyro pilot. As a rookie trainee, I had read it avidly from cover to cover. It laid out the complete history of our unique aircraft type, with its notable milestone achievements over the decades, so that in a historical context it could be directly compared with all other types of flying machine. I remember feeling at the time that the glorious history of the gyroplane, although much varied and extensive over the years, was crucially not yet complete. As not one of these machines had ever flown around the world.

To me this felt like a burning injustice; the poor gyro had thus far been left out of the *circumnavigation club*, stuck away in the dusty back corner of the hangar and forgotten about. It later became a significant part of my motivation to correct this injustice, to put things straight and help complete the gyroplane's historic story, by eventually flying one completely around the globe.

And incredibly, I had now gone and done precisely that. And even better, I was also able to relate this story directly to Dr. Charnov in person, no less. What a fantastic day.

24

North America: Oshkosh bound, USA

8 July 2019: San Diego, California, USA – Gila Bend, Arizona, USA

The flight out from San Diego was the last one that James and I took together – it was a day short of two months after we had set out on our first, which was from Moscow on 9 May. Turning eastwards and inland from the coast, we slowly climbed our way up and over the Laguna Mountains, the lowest route available north of the Mexican border, to cross into the interior states of the USA. After 3hrs 30mins of flying, we closed in on the small settlement of Gila Bend, which was where we parted company. Over the radio we wished each other good luck and to stay safe for the rest of our respective journeys. James then turned north, to fly farther into Arizona, whereas I continued eastward, following the Mexican border towards western Texas.

Shortly afterwards, I landed at Gila Bend airport. I was relieved. With James now safely launched merrily on his way, I was able to slow down the pace of my own flying by significantly shortening my flight distances. Over the following days I remained puzzled as to why I felt increasingly washed out and lacked my usual endurance and stamina. Once again, I just put it down to the general rigors of the flight and additionally the extreme heat that was now building as I moved away from the West Coast. The sweltering desert conditions across southern Arizona and New Mexico certainly didn't help my energy levels, but it was still an amazing and fascinating landscape to fly through. I stayed overnight at a local roadside motel chain, America's Choice Inn, which had towering giant cactus plants outside the front lobby, complete with iconic side branches sprouting out like arms. It was a desert scene straight out of a classic wild west movie. At the neighbouring truck stop and fuel station, they even had a road sign that read: "CAUTION: Watch for rattlesnakes". I made a mental note to add this extra check to my pre-flight routine the following morning. Finding a stowaway snake in the cockpit whilst airborne was to be avoided at all costs!

9 July 2019: Gila Bend, Arizona, USA – Douglas, Arizona, USA

Throughout the day, I skirted just north of the Mexican border. It was incredible to witness the stark contrast between the two sides of this international boundary. There were huge tracts of scrubland between border settlements, where the border was represented merely by a thin line of wire fence planted in the sand. But as I passed more populated areas (in either country), the fence often became much more visible and fortified, and in parts it resembled 'The Wall' that US President Trump had so famously championed during his term in office. It was interesting to see however, from my unique elevated viewpoint, that the fortified fencing only lasted maybe a few miles out into the desert on either side of the border towns, before reverting to scrubby desert and minimal fencing once more. Perhaps beyond these points, would-be border migrants were simply put off by the brutally harsh desert landscape. Given it was teeming with rattlesnakes and spikey cacti, it was certainly not somewhere I wanted to land in an emergency anytime soon.

The desolate and parched desert scenery stretched for countless miles in all directions. At one point, I noticed a familiar sounding town appear on my GPS and detoured slightly to go check it out. It was a small settlement but with an internationally recognisable name,

Tombstone, Arizona. Flying over this arid landscape, I could really imagine the hardships that anyone trying to travel overland by horseback or dusty stagecoach must have experienced back in the wild west days. Given the oppressive heat, on riding into town who could blame them for diving fully clothed into the nearest horse trough and then bursting through the saloon swing doors to order a shot of Red Eye Whiskey at the bar. From the air, I looked out for the nearby OK Corral (famous for its gunfight) and the Boot Hill cemetery. Though unfortunately, without a town tourist map plotted on my GPS screen, I wasn't quite sure if I had actually seen them or not!

Approaching the US border town of Douglas, I was surprised to find that their local airport runway was placed very close to the border fence line. So close in fact, that in order to line up on finals to land, I had to actually extend my glide path out over the boundary of the border. So, for a short time, I could technically claim that I was flying in Mexican airspace! However, it was probably an even shorter jaunt than my foray into Iranian airspace over the Gulf of Oman, and I was soon making my touchdown back in the USA.

Now, what about that shot of *ol' Red Eye...* Set 'em up, Bartender!

10 July 2019: Douglas, Arizona, USA – Fabens, Texas, USA – Van Horn, Texas, USA

My tour of the old wild west continued along the border and across the famous Rio Grande north of El Paso. Avoiding the city limits, I then skirted south-east to pick up the river once more and followed its course into Texas. The heat and relatively high-altitude flying across New Mexico had taken its toll, so I sought refuge at Fabens Airport, a small, quiet airfield close to the highway I-10. Besides picking up fuel, I slept for about half an hour on a sofa in the air-conditioned pilots' lounge area of the FBO flight office. I decided that I was just not cut out for these flying conditions; besides soaring temperatures, I was also flying consistently about 4000ft higher than I was used to when following coastlines. My increasing lack of energy didn't help either.

Dragging myself back into the air in the early evening, I was relieved to find the worst heat of the day had subsided, making for a more relaxed flight into Van Horn.

11 July 2019: Van Horn, Texas, USA – Ozona, Texas, USA

Initially, I had planned to route directly eastward, towards the Gulf of Mexico. I was aiming to follow its coastline north-east as far as the Mississippi Delta and then accompany the mighty river northwards. However, Hurricane Barry had recently taken up a brooding residence in the Gulf, which instantly scuppered my coastal beachcombing idea. Instead, I had to make an early turn northwards, up through western Texas, which by way of consolation, rewarded me with its own tremendous landscape. It gradually became far greener than I had previously imagined, with lakes and trees returning and huge sprawling ranches appearing (often with their own airstrip). I could easily see why distances, like everything else, appeared to be so much bigger in Texas... It came as no surprise to learn that geographically the *Lone Star State* was almost the same size as Europe!

I was very impressed with Ozona Municipal Airport when I landed. It immediately reminded me of the well-tended grounds of some exclusive country club, with trees, manicured lawns and neatly painted fences. But fortunately for me, this picturesque parkland just also happened to have a fully functioning runway running through it. On arrival, I spent an hour or so chatting with the friendly FBO staff. I no longer had any sense of an urgent, onwards agenda to contend with and so I relished the feeling of once more becoming an unhurried, solo aerial adventurer.

12 July 2019: Ozona, Texas, USA – Taylor, Texas, USA

Feeling like a baton in a relay race, I now happily fell into a run of stopovers where I was passed from one kindly gyro community host to another, all the way up through the American Midwest towards the Great Lakes. First up, was a fantastic two-night stopover with a fellow gyroplane long-distance record holder, John Craparo. The most interesting of his various jaunts had been a two-man, multi-record setting, transcontinental flight in October 2015, which took him (and gyro chief flying instructor Dayton Dabbs) on a three-leg journey from Dallas to Los Angeles and on to New York, before returning to Dallas. This was followed up by a diplomatically significant, two-ship gyro flight in May 2017, from Texas to Cuba and back; again, John was flying with Dayton, with Mike Baker and Jonathan Prickett in the second gyro. Through pioneering these notably adventurous flights and many more besides, both John and Dayton have continually contributed greatly in stretching the envelope and expectations of what modern cross-country gyro flying is capable of in the USA.

13 July 2019: Taylor, Texas, USA (non-flying day)

A most enjoyable day was spent sightseeing locally with John and catching up with Dayton at the airfield, where I also had a first try of a gyro equipped with a Rotax 915 engine (an advance on my 914 model). The day included a tasty trip to the renowned Louie Mueller Barbecue shack for lunch and a trip to Gumbo's restaurant in Georgetown in the evening along with fellow pilot John Nagle and his partner.

14 July 2019: Taylor, Texas, USA – Justin, Texas, USA

Passing on the gyro host baton, I was next invited to the delightfully named Propwash Airport nearby to Justin, Texas, in order to spend some time with avid gyroplane enthusiasts Mark Airey, Mark Rhoads and Christine Toevs. The latter of whom had brought her TAG (Titanium AutoGyro) aircraft over to get serviced with visiting TAG manufacturer, Neil Sheather, from Australia. Mark Airey's set up was fantastic, as his house and hangar were built immediately adjacent to the end of the runway.

15 July 2019: Justin, Texas, USA (non-flying day)

I had a relaxing day chatting and hanging out with everyone, including giving an extended kitchen table interview with Ira McComic, a Vietnam veteran Cobra helicopter pilot, passionate gyroplane enthusiast and highly regarded aviation author. With an unassuming yet very knowledgeable style of questioning, he made being interviewed a real pleasure. I was sad to learn recently that he has since passed away (January 2021). I remain honoured and privileged to have had that brief opportunity to share in some of his fascinating aviation stories.

16 July 2019: Justin, Texas, USA – Ponca City, Oklahoma, USA – Junction City, Kansas, USA

It was time to move on and to also say farewell to Texas. I headed into the rolling farmlands of Oklahoma and slap bang into the middle of *Tornado Ally*, which I hoped was now past its annual peak season. For a time, I skirted along the flank of a large heavy rolling cloud that continued to darken and become ever more menacing as the minutes ticked by. I didn't like what I was seeing, so I decided to land at the nearby Ponca City Regional Airport and sit out the worst of the afternoon storms on the ground. Fortunately, the terminal building had a very inviting on-site restaurant, so I treated myself to a brief lunch stop until the skies brightened once more. A short hop in the late afternoon then saw me cross into Kansas and arrive with fellow gyro pilot Mark Sodamann at Freeman Field Airport, near Junction City. Taking up the gyro host baton, Mark and his wife Fran put me up in their fabulous house for the night. After giving an impromptu interview to one of their neighbours for a local news article, I relaxed around the big dining table with them all until late in the evening; we chatted of all things gyro and of past travel adventures in Ireland. But little did I know, that the next morning would start in a much less relaxed manner!

17 July 2019: Junction City, Kansas, USA – Kirksville, Missouri, USA – Biggsville, Illinois, USA

The layout of Mark and Fran's house on a sloped elevation, was such that the guest room was on the same level as the rear garden and below the main living space. My bathroom was the next door along the hallway from my room, and in the early morning as I opened the bathroom door, a movement in the hallway caught my eye. Not quite believing what I *thought* I saw, I ran upstairs to find Mark and we both went down to investigate. There was nothing amiss in the hallway, just a sumptuous grey carpet and a couple of white store cupboards. We opened one and looked in cautiously... nothing, except for a few small cardboard boxes. Still convinced that I had definitely seen *something* earlier, we approached the second cupboard door... a slight indentation in the carpet below the door was our first clue, and as Mark stepped forward, I took a step back in response. He opened the door and then immediately shut it again. Yes, he confirmed, I had indeed seen something.

It was a snake, about three feet long!

Thankfully it turned out to be a non-venomous gopher snake. But hailing from Ireland where we famously have no snakes (thanks to the legend of St. Patrick), I hadn't known that at the time! Mark fetched a long stick and managed to expertly pin the snake down on the carpet before releasing it unharmed back into the garden undergrowth. He was equally as surprised as me, as he had never had one come into the house before (or since!)

Such nerve-jangling *Indiana Jones* adventures... and all before breakfast time!

* * *

The day's flying was once again hampered by unsettled thundery weather, forcing me to land at Kirksville, Missouri for a time, to wait for the darkest clouds to disperse. At every interim stop, I took some time to sit down and rest, yet only to get going again without feeling properly rested at all.

I was now well within the Corn Belt of America, and my next stop off point was a delightful 'farm strip' called Beulah Land Farm Airport. On arriving overhead, I found the airstrip initially tricky to locate. It was camouflaged and hidden within vast cornfields that were growing hundreds of acres of six-foot high maize plants. As I landed it was like descending into a narrow corridor, as the horizon on both sides disappeared behind the solid green walls of cornstalks. I taxied over the hard-packed bumpy earth towards the only building I could recognise as possibly being a hangar. The whole place appeared deserted, and it was only after hanging around on the ground for half an hour or so, that a bright yellow crop-sprayer aircraft suddenly swooped down out of nowhere to land. As it taxied over to a large road tanker truck nearby (presumably full of agri-spray chemicals), I was amazed at how big the spray plane was. The pilot, Matt Defenbaugh, was also a single-seat gyro enthusiast and kindly offered me a place to stay for the night on the farm.

It was a very special evening with Matt and his family gathered in the farmhouse kitchen. I had landed in many remote places during my global journey and had been hosted by numerous friendly people, but to land in the middle of a sprawling US cornfield and then to stay on a working farm was yet another wholly unique and fascinating experience.

Once again, the flexibility and adaptability of the gyroplane made it possible to be equally at home either in complying with a tightly controlled international airport, mixing it with the military jets and personnel on an airbase or just kicking back and spending some quality time with a 'flying farmer' on a hard-to-spot rural farm strip. I felt so privileged and fortunate to be flying one of the best 'all-rounder' types of aircraft there is.

18 July 2019: Biggsville, Illinois, USA – Lansing, Illinois, USA

Taking off from the cornfield proved to be just as exciting as landing had been. I aimed to minimise my take-off roll as much as possible as the rough dirt and rock-hard surface gave my relatively small wheels a lot of unwanted extra vibration. I quickly hopped off the ground and then flew at a couple of feet above it to build up my airspeed. For a short time, I was flying at eye-level with the top of the corn, and this gave me an odd feeling of flying at speed *through* the crop, rather than above it. Soon enough though, I climbed away, curved around over the farmstead to wave my goodbyes, and set course for a previous 2015 stomping ground, Lansing, Illinois.

I enjoyed a brisk tailwind from the south-west which helped push me along over the green sea of maizefields, which stretched from horizon to horizon. And as with the 'real' sea, the stiff breeze made constant patterns of gusts and lulls over the surface of the crops. It reminded me greatly of flying through the fields of France on my first flight abroad, over a decade before; *Roxy* and I had certainly flown many more miles together since then...

19 July 2019: Lansing, Illinois, USA (non-flying day)

After a four-year gap (and a full circumnavigation of the globe), it was fun to be hosted once again by members of the gyro club at Lansing Municipal Airport. This time around, I was kindly hosted by George Smundin, another great stalwart of the local gyro community. As luck would have it, George lived next to a hairdresser who had a home salon, and so I was able to receive my final *expedition haircut* before heading out for the evening to a local restaurant with many of the club members.

20 July 2019: Lansing, Illinois, USA – Oshkosh, Wisconsin, USA

This was the day that I had both hoped for and anticipated, ever since I had last called into Oshkosh in 2015. I was about to join around 10,000 other aircraft and arrive at the world's largest fly-in event: EAA AirVenture 2019.

On first glance, the arrival procedure (published online) had appeared a little daunting, but once studied carefully it all made much more sense. Gyros fell into the ultralight/microlight category of aircraft and as such, had their own dedicated flight corridor to make their approach. This narrow corridor was strictly controlled both in width and in height, so that it avoided all other types of aircraft, which had their own entry procedures into the airfield. I would fly in the corridor and enter a small orbiting circuit that passed overhead of a grass strip, adjacent to the main runways, and then be allowed to land. The plan had been well-practised during previous years, only unfortunately *this year* the weather had obviously not read the briefing notes…

The flight from Lansing had started well, with a spectacular shoreline flyby of the downtown Chicago waterfront. George had arranged that he and a few other club gyros would fly with me for this first section, and in loose formation we were treated to a fantastic view of the cityscape. Skirting along the shore of Lake Michigan, we were well below the height of the famed skyscrapers, especially the iconic Willis Tower, while other familiar landmarks swept past too, such as Soldier Field NFL stadium, Grant Park and Millennium Park. I even spotted the huge 'shiny bean' art installation *Cloud Gate* as I flew by.

As we approached overhead Navy Pier, George and my impromptu flight escort took their leave and doubled back home to Lansing, leaving me once again flying solo. Only I wasn't entirely alone. I soon began to see many small black dots scattered around in the sky, and they were all slowly converging on my route. I quickly realised that with so many light aircraft making long cross-country flights (and of course all inbound for Oshkosh), the local patch of sky was rapidly going to be filled with traffic of all shapes and sizes. Many of them were flying much faster than *Roxy* and me and soon I was being overtaken on all sides. Some were in loose formations, others flying solo like me, but all had one goal: to arrive and safely land at Oshkosh. For a while everything felt OK as the different types of aircraft were heading for different rendezvous and entry points around the airport perimeter. All I had to worry about was spotting any other microlight/ultralight traffic that were also headed for my small entry corridor in the sky.

Everything remained fine until the weather decided to throw in a curve ball...

A huge rainstorm was brewing directly in my path, and as I assessed its possible potency, I considered my options. Looking around, all the other aircraft seemed to have now completely scattered, presumably each adopting their own diversionary tactics. The thick dark clouds looked menacing, but the storm was slowly moving and starting to track off slightly to my right. In response, I veered off to my left, hoping to skirt around the edge and escape the worst of the rain front. However, I didn't veer quite wide enough, and soon enough I was caught under a tremendous sudden cloudburst. For a long ten minutes, I was buffeted about in severe turbulence and squally heavy rainfall, and the air temperature dropped sharply for a time. To maintain visual contact with the ground in such increasingly dreadful conditions, I needed to skim over the fields at barely 200ft. The rural roads that crisscrossed my path were dotted with powerlines, grain silos and tall radio masts, all lurking semi-hidden in the driving rain. I was not in a happy place. I had to escape.

I knew the closest edge of the rapidly developing storm was still farther out to my left, so I made a sharp bank in that direction and pushed on. More long minutes passed until miraculously I punched out through the edge, under a wall of cloud towering above me and back into bright normal flying conditions. I kicked myself that I hadn't taken a wider course earlier on and had mistakenly assessed the storm to be more localised than it turned out to be. Another hard lesson learnt; I was never going to do that again in a hurry!

After so much aerial drama, finding the entry corridor for the AirVenture ultralight circuit proved quite straightforward. Only the troublesome Wisconsin weather had one last parting gift to bestow. I arrived overhead the grass landing strip only to find it had been severely waterlogged (from the same storm that had affected me) and the runway was now temporarily closed in order to keep its soft grass surface in good condition for the rest of the event.

Damn!

I began orbiting in a holding pattern around the small overhead circuit, pondering what to do. Luckily the ground marshals quickly realised my dilemma and contacted me on the radio; they had a small, traffic-free window on the main runway, and they allowed me to briefly veer out of my circuit to land on the very end of it. With dozens of arriving aircraft expected imminently behind me, I briskly landed and taxied off the runway at the first available turnoff, before being warmly welcomed in by the army of bright orange clad volunteer marshals. I was mightily glad to have got down safely; it had been one last eventful moment of a very eventful day.

Roxy was duly pushed over to the ultralight airstrip where I was met by Geoff Downey, the EAA's volunteer Chairman of Rotorcraft. The recent rainstorm that had shut down all ultralight operations also had a heavy knock-on effect on many other aspects of the AirVenture site. Many of the camping areas had been heavily waterlogged, both flooding out tents and making many RV camping areas inaccessible to vehicle traffic. Not ideal when many thousands of campers were still expected to arrive from all over North America in the following days. I tagged along with Geoff in his pick-up truck as he made a damage inspection tour of some of the more badly affected parts of the camping grounds. Surveying the muddy scene, I needed little reminder that Mother Nature could be both a swift and awesome disruptor to any best laid plans of mere humans.

Later in the day, like some cold war undercover spy exchange, I was taken to a little-used junction of the perimeter road where I was delivered from Geoff's truck into the hands of my soon-to-be-new-handler and impeccable host, Steve Owen. A seasoned 28-year volunteer of the EAA flight line operations team, Steve was now a permanent resident of Oshkosh. Back in the day, he had originally arrived from the UK to volunteer and then subsequently met his future-wife-to-be, Pat... and the rest as they say, is history.

21–29 July 2019: Oshkosh, Wisconsin, USA (non-flying days)

I commuted into the show every day with either Steve or Pat and was delighted when I was given the opportunity to help out with the North 40 flight line ops team who were kept extremely busy, receiving incoming aircraft and directing them into their allotted parking spaces. With upwards of 10,000 aircraft to park in just a few short arrival days (and to subsequently release again back into the air at the end of the show) this operation needed military precision and an army of bright orange clad, baton-waving volunteers. The pilots of some popular fixed-wing aircraft types organised themselves into arriving *en masse* and it was not uncommon to have perhaps 90 identical aircraft, such as Bonanzas or Cessnas, land simultaneously; touching down, three at a time, on a main runway. They would then form a long conga line of taxiing planes heading directly into a designated area of empty grass outfield.

It was not to stay empty for very long. In a constant stream, the planes were directed in by a line of energetic marshallers to be parked neatly, head to toe, in an oversized, real-life version of *Tetris.* The 'North 40' referred to an area of grass outfield that encompassed *forty acres...* and when filled, that was a full forty acres of tightly parked aircraft! Quite an incredible sight to behold.

As a complete rookie at aircraft parking, I thankfully was mainly assigned the easier roles of first getting a pilot's attention (by holding my marshalling baton wands vertically upwards above my head) and then either: waving them on to the next marshaller in the line or turning them down into the next parking row in the sequence. It was great fun, adrenaline-filled and definitely the closest I'll ever get to being an aircraft handler on a busy aircraft carrier deck. Expertly coordinated and managed by Carol Garceau and Sandy Strebel, the large team of flight line volunteers worked tirelessly and so precisely in such difficult and potentially dangerous situations. After all, propeller blades and people don't mix well when manoeuvring together in close quarters.

I especially admired the marshalling team's *can-do* philosophy, its fabulous sense of camaraderie, and the peculiar hierarchy of status that successive years of volunteering could bestow on the more senior marshallers. The numerous mission patches festooning their bright orange hats or waistcoats, each earned annually for volunteering at the show, were real *badges of honour*, and these most seasoned volunteers were duly given the respect that their many past years of experience deserved.

As unsure and (a little) awestruck as I was on my first arrival, being immediately greeted by friendly and skilled volunteer marshals made all the difference to me in making the complicated seem so easy. On behalf of visiting pilots from all over the globe, (orange) hats off to all the AirVenture volunteer aircraft handling teams, both on the ground and up in the ATC control tower.

***

The days at the show passed quickly, and aside from helping to park planes, I took *Roxy* out for a little exercise most days, putting in some orbiting laps around the ultralight circuit for the benefit of the crowds that had gathered to watch the assortment of rotorcraft types take to the air. I was also interviewed on Oshkosh's very own TV output, being beamed to the big screens all around the grounds. Such was the eclectic mix of aviation guests on the live broadcast, that immediately before me on the line-up was a space shuttle astronaut and after me was Charles Lindbergh's grandson. When not busy flying, *Roxy* spent most days proudly on display in front of the Autogyro USA trade stand, where people could have a closer inspection of the first gyroplane in history to conquer the world.

During the show, some more familiar faces arrived. James, who was still midway through his zigzagging speed record attempt, had been escorted into the show by a flight of Magni gyros that had come up from Texas. He was however only able to stay for a couple of days, as the clock was still ticking and he needed to make haste for his appointment with the North Atlantic. As he prepared to set off again, I was once more able to wish him good luck for the rest of his flight back to the UK. It turned out to be the last such meeting that we had together during the whole expedition.

As the show was drawing to a close, there was one more person that I simply *had* to find. Amid the plethora of packed exhibition halls and flashy aviation trade stalls, I tracked down a modest display stand tucked in alongside the mind-boggling array of latest avionics, aircraft accessories and *must have* gadgets. I made my approach through the busy crowds and *yes*, there was someone there, manning the stand. It was the trade stall for Turtle Pac and the man before me was none other than Laszlo Torok. I had first made contact with Laszlo 10 years earlier, and he had discussed, designed and produced *Roxy's* bespoke fuel bags by way of sponsoring my circumnavigation efforts. He had given me a decade of support, but in all that time, we had never actually met face to face. I think he was as surprised to meet me at the show as I was to finally get to meet him. We spent a great afternoon and early evening, first at his stand and later at a nearby food and beer tent, chatting and catching up on my flight. I was so grateful to be able to thank him in person for the fantastic Turtle Pacs that he had supplied over the years, particularly the bespoke designed *Saki Barrel.* My entire journey, especially with its long ocean transits and countless off-airport trips to find fuel, would have been made a lot harder (if not impossible) without having my trusty *flexible friend* sitting in the back seat.

30 July 2019: Oshkosh, Wisconsin, USA – Mentone, Indiana, USA

With AirVenture 2019 coming to an end, most of the visiting aircraft had now gone and *Roxy* and I enjoyed a much quieter departure compared with our rather soggy arrival. My final remaining mission was to head to Mentone, Indiana to attend the Popular Rotorcraft Association (PRA) annual convention and fly-in. By flying south to Chicago and then turning east, directly to Mentone, it was an easy afternoon flight, both for navigation and weather. On landing, I was happily reunited with some recent gyro friends, who were now fast becoming old gyro friends. Mark Airey, who had hosted me down in Texas, continued his fantastic hospitality by allowing me a berth in his motorhome, which was parked up next door to an ingeniously designed rig owned by Christine Toevs, consisting of a fabulous all-in-one gyro transporter and live-aboard trailer.

31 July – 3 August 2019: Mentone, Indiana, USA (non-flying days)

The PRA gathering was a much more laid-back and homely affair compared with the extremely busy Oshkosh show. It was the perfect afterparty, where I relaxed and spent time chatting with the wide variety of gyro enthusiasts, who had gathered from all over the US.

On one of the days, to my great surprise and delight, I met Paul Salmon. Like Andy Keetch in San Diego, Paul was another prolific FAI record setter for rotorcraft. At the latest count, Paul holds 23 FAI current world records (15 set by gyroplane and 8 set by helicopter), while by comparison I have 19, Andy has 18 and James has 8 (all set by gyroplane). We ended up having a great chat and even took a short flight out together around the local area.

Aside from aircraft demonstrations, trial flights and competition flying at the airfield, many interesting radical designs and concepts (both old and new) were discussed and showcased over the four days of the convention, including a very impressive single seater with jump take-off capability. I even found time to sew up a pair of my ripped shorts while gathered around sharing gyro stories in the open-sided dining area.

Winding down after the hectic pace of the summer's flying was exactly what I needed, particularly with my ongoing lack of general vitality, energy and stamina, which was still giving me much cause for concern. One last push, back to the EAA Museum at Oshkosh and I would be done with flying for the foreseeable future.

4 August 2019: Mentone, Indiana, USA – Harvard, Illinois, USA – Oshkosh, Wisconsin, USA

After a fantastic last evening of fireworks and farewells, at the annual PRA Convention banquet and prize giving dinner, it was an emotional moment having to saddle up my pony knowing that it was for the very last time. I retraced my route back west, escorted for a while by Christine in her TAG gyro accompanied by Mark in the back seat. When they finally waved goodbye and banked away to return to Mentone, I was left alone with my thoughts of soon finally finishing this world circling adventure. I recalled back to my first day, in a shiny red suit and shiny yellow aircraft, nervously striking out over the Irish Sea. That was almost a decade ago and I hadn't been at all sure of whether I could succeed. Yet now, here I was; I had finally done it and at long last I was relieved to be rapidly closing in on the home straight.

Once more I gave the built-up downtown Chicago area a wide berth, before heading north directly towards Oshkosh. En route, I stopped at the least busy end of the grass strip at Dacy Airport in order to rest up, stretch my legs and have a snack; I was in no particular hurry, as long as I arrived at the rear of the EAA Museum buildings before they closed for the day. Fortunately, Pioneer Airport's grass strip was immediately adjacent to the museum and so it gave me a perfect final landing spot to aim for.

Soon enough, I arrived overhead and was cleared to land at my own discretion. I overflew the field to check all was clear and then swooped around in a long lazy descending arc to line up for a short final run in to land. It was a pin-point landing, witnessed only by a handful of late visitors scattered about and Ben Page, the curator of the museum. I was soon to entrust the safe keeping of *Roxy* into his capable hands, while she was put on prominent display in the main exhibition hall. Taxiing over to Ben and shutting down the engine for the last time, I suddenly felt a real sense of closure.

Wow!

It was complete.

My epic, nine-year global challenge had just finished.

I would never again feel compelled to do something so extreme and so uncertain, over such a long period of time.

My relief was absolute, I never needed to do this... *ever again.*

Over the following two days, *Roxy* was prepared for display. The first task was to run the engine briefly one last time while a chemical aerosol solution was sprayed directly into the air intake system. This allowed the interior surfaces of the engine to be coated with preservation spray in order to ward off long-term internal corrosion. The process was aptly named *pickling the engine.* All the electronics were then disabled with the removal of both batteries, and as with all the permanent exhibits, any remaining fuel in the tanks was completely drained to minimise any potential fire risk whilst on display.

But one more task remained before setting *Roxy* amongst the other exhibits... Ben had arranged for a mannequin to wear my specially designed Ursuit drysuit, helmet and lifejacket. We wrestled the now decidedly weather-beaten and sun-bleached red suit onto the dummy and it all worked very well, apart from making 'Captain Norman' about four inches taller than yours truly!

My lasting impression was of leaving G-YROX surrounded by iconic and historic aircraft on all sides, including the much-admired 1930s' adventuring autogyro *Miss Champion* and Andy Keetch's multi-record setting gyro, *Woodstock.* Gleaming proudly under the bright museum lights, *Roxy* immediately fitted in with her new surroundings. No doubt she now had many a tale of globetrotting adventures to share with her fellow pioneering exhibits.

25

Heading home

My last evening was spent very pleasantly with Steve and Pat before commencing the long trek home, crossing the North Atlantic back to the UK on a commercial flight. I was in seat 45D, tucked in right at the back of the economy seating, but while cruising effortlessly across the Atlantic, it felt like the best seat in the sky. I could stand up and walk around, use the restroom and even visit the galley for a snack... actions that are taken for granted by packaged air travellers the world over, yet now they all felt so fantastically *luxurious* to me. The crossing merely took hours rather than weeks and I was soon back on terra firma, although this time, without the empty Turtle Pac tucked under my arm and the lingering whiff of my favourite *Eau de Gasoline* cologne.

I was amazed to find many of my extended family and local friends had gathered for a celebratory welcome home party, which came as a lovely surprise, and a great evening was had by all. The garden, where we had stored the gyros overnight back in August 2015, had been especially spruced up for the occasion by Felix, Glen, Andrea, Petra and Jakob. It was lovely to think that I could now spend a lot of time in that garden without needing to worry any more about the flight. Repeated waves of relief and a warm glow came over me to know I didn't have to worry about completing it ever again.

One surprise, however, that none of us had expected, turned out to be not so welcoming... Over the following two days, what everyone initially thought was suntanned skin became ever more yellow. I had developed jaundice.

Given jaundice has around 28 different causes, I was immediately taken to hospital for what turned out to be 10 days of extensive tests. I was later confirmed to be suffering from a relatively rare form of bile duct cancer (cholangiocarcinoma). Without any warning, this news hit like an express train. Aside from my previous weeks of growing malaise and tiredness while crossing America, there had been little sign that anything so sinister was lurking just around the corner. That was of course until my bile duct system got completely blocked up and then abruptly turned me a nice shade of Homer Simpson yellow.

Within a few short weeks I had gone from making pioneering history by circling the world in a gyroplane, to facing the prospect of a long, yet for me an all too familiar path, of gruelling chemotherapy treatment, with a highly uncertain and grim prognosis for long-term survival.

It looked like I wasn't going to be given a choice as to what my next project in life might be... My next adventure into the unknown had already been chosen for me.

Postscript

Two years on from the completion of my flight, I am pleased to report that my health condition has gradually improved and has now remained 'stable' for some time. This has so far been achieved both through medical interventions and life choices on my part. The combined regime included enduring an initial six months of chemotherapy, and adopting an ongoing ketogenic (low carbohydrate/high fat) diet, which is supplemented with occasional shiatsu sessions and weekly hyperbaric oxygen therapy. (All actions that are thought to give cancer cells a really hard time). Although not entirely out of the woods as yet, I remain positive and pragmatic about the future (much like I was when I had bowel cancer treatment previously).

Dealing with and adapting to the unknown challenges that the global flight frequently presented, has given me a solid set of coping mechanisms for living with my current condition. If an upcoming situation looks challenging, I can always reassure and remind myself that I have probably already been in a far more onerous previous predicament. Bizarrely, it is a logic that has actually now come full circle. To reassure myself in tricky situations during the flight, I often reminded myself that I had probably been in a far worse situation during my first cancer episode. But now, in the midst of my second cancer episode, I frequently remind myself that I was perhaps in a far worse tricky situation during the flight...

It's strangely ironic to think that my gyroplane circumnavigation was so neatly bookended by cancer. Still, on a more positive note, there has also been plenty of 'living life to the full' in between!

Some of the reasons I had for starting the whole flight project underwent an evolution as time progressed in my journey, so much so that by the end, they were not necessarily the same dogged and battle-weary reasons that I had for getting it finished.

Part of that evolution means I can never again look upon any adventure with the same mindset… When I am now often asked what my "next big adventure" is, I can honestly say that I now no longer need one. My sense of adventure has been fully satisfied.

Through completing this global flight, I've finally arrived in a rarefied place, beyond the need to seek out any more self-fulfilment or self-discovery. And thankfully I have also been fortunate enough to have lived to share that story with everyone.

Unlike perhaps modern *serial adventurers,* who ultimately seem trapped in a sort of perpetual unfulfillment, despite all they achieve, I can now rest easy in the knowledge that I have gone well beyond any lingering sense of unfulfillment. I made a journey that contained such extreme unknowable and extraordinary experiences that I will never feel compelled to push myself out into such intense levels of adventurous uncertainty, ever again.

This quote from celebrated global adventurer Sir Francis Chichester in his 1964 autobiography *The Lonely Sea and the Sky,* perhaps gives some sage advice for all present and future adventurers:

"I would feel an intense depression every time I achieved a great ambition; I had not then discovered that the joy of living comes from action, from making the attempt, from the effort, not from success."

As one of my most inspiring role models, Chichester attempted to fly around the world in an open cockpit Gipsy Moth biplane, often flying at about the same airspeed, range and altitude as I did in *Roxy.* Coincidently, his global flying effort was also abruptly halted upon reaching Japan and had to be abandoned there. Not to be thwarted in his circumnavigation goals however, he swapped from flying to sailing. And subsequently in 1966, he became the first sailor to achieve a singlehanded circumnavigation of the world (west to east) using the open ocean clipper ship trading routes via the great capes. Some weeks later, on his safe return to the UK, he was knighted by Queen Elizabeth II. Fittingly, Her Majesty used the same ceremonial sword that the royal court of Queen Elizabeth I had used to knight one of the earliest globe-trotting circumnavigators of them all, Sir Francis Drake, in 1581.

Unfortunately, fast forwarding back into the 21st Century, there have thus far been very few opportunities for my post-circumnavigation celebrations, primarily due of course to the ongoing Covid 19 pandemic. Whilst in the USA, I was honoured both at Oshkosh with a Gyroplane Champion 'Lindy' award (an Oscar-like statue of Charles Lindbergh) and at the PRA convention with the Marion Springer Community Award for the promotion of gyroplane flight across the USA and beyond. Shortly after completing my flight, I was further honoured to be commissioned as a Kentucky Colonel by the Commonwealth of Kentucky and inducted as a fellow of the American Civil Wings Society. Perhaps the most fitting of awards though was again by the PRA, when they also presented me with the plaque for the Farthest Flown Aircraft Award. After flying right across Europe, Asia and America in the previous few months, even by the most conservative estimate, I had probably beaten the next farthest-flown candidate by a good 10,000 miles! The most unusual accolade was to be accepted as a life-time member of the Goldfish Club. Often referred to as the most exclusive and difficult club to join in the world, it is entirely made up of aviators who have, at some point in their flying career, survived an aircraft ditching into water. Fortunately for me, the club committee were quite accepting that my ditching into the lake in Thailand easily qualified the awarding of my membership.

I have been rather disappointed that, as of yet in the UK (aside from becoming a Goldfish!), there has been little formal recognition that on the 28 June 2019, I completed the first, physically unbroken circumnavigation of the world in a gyroplane. This in turn earned *Roxy,* my trusty steed, the accolade of becoming the *First Gyro* to have flown completely around the globe. The disappointment wasn't so much for me personally but more for the global gyroplane community. If this maiden circumnavigation had been made by the first helicopter, first airship or first rocket, there would surely have been much more of an official fanfare to mark the occasion. Once again, the humble gyroplane appears to have been consigned to the very back corner of the airport hangar; a poor relation perhaps in the minds of mainstream aviation officialdom. And yet the incredible fact remains that the gyroplane was the *very last* type of aircraft to fly around the world. At least one example of all the other six fundamental aircraft types (fixed-wing aeroplane, flex-wing aeroplane, airship, free balloon, rocket and helicopter) had already completed a circumnavigation and had been duly recognised for doing so. Until humanity comes up with a brand-new way to fly, there are now no more maiden circumnavigations of fundamental aircraft types left to achieve. This written account of the *First Gyro*, represents both the *first* gyroplane and the *last* aircraft type to conquer the world.

Whilst the first physical circumnavigation has had little formal recognition to date, the same cannot be said of the first speed-record flight around the world. After waving James farewell in Oshkosh, he went on to complete his own uninterrupted circumnavigation, which in total took him 175 days to fly through 13 countries. He was subsequently (and correctly) awarded an FAI record for setting the 'fastest speed around the world (eastbound) by gyroplane'. However, after this award was ratified, an additional certificate was created for James by the Guinness World Records (GWR) organisation proclaiming the world record was for 'the first circumnavigation of Earth by autogyro'. This of course was not historically correct, as it should have more accurately read either: 'the first *continuous* circumnavigation of Earth by autogyro' or 'the *fastest* circumnavigation of Earth by autogyro' and should not have implied, by lack of clarity, to be the first [absolute] circumnavigation. I was extremely disappointed with James that, even though he would have known that the citation was minimally worded (no doubt even before its first publication), he still allowed it to be used without further clarification or immediate correction. It was incredible to think that he could read, display and stand by such wording and still portray the certificate as being completely 100% accurate, whilst knowing full well the background facts and the whole truth that it clearly was not. His glib acceptance that such a *part truth* could conveniently be inferred to be the *whole truth* has no doubt had the effect, in some impressionable circles, of side-lining and 'airbrushing' my own circumnavigation flight right out of history... as if somehow, my flight never actually happened at all. This has been extremely frustrating especially after the considerable effort that I had put in to help him in both preparing and safely achieving his own circumnavigation, all done in a spirit of friendship and camaraderie, to help a fellow gyro pilot to achieve his goals on behalf of our worldwide gyro community. Subsequently, and presumably on the strength of his all-encompassing GWR 'endorsement' (which no doubt added considerable leverage), James swiftly went on to be awarded both the Royal Aero Club's Britannia Trophy and the Royal Automobile Club's Seagrave Trophy. It's quite amazing what a little *selective wording* can help to achieve... though I can't help also thinking that such notable and illustrious achievements might forever feel to be a little *hollow*, especially after considering the full story of how *exactly* they came to be awarded.

* * *

But, for the very last time *dear reader*, I digress! By writing this account of my journey, I have been allowed to relive it in a way that I have always wanted to do. Sharing such a solo-pioneering, personal experience with you all has been an extremely rewarding one. I could never have imagined how the flight would eventually turn out; events were so unexpected, situations so unpredictable and chance happenings so extraordinary. It was an incredibly enlightening, yet humbling experience.

Since my return I have often been asked what my most enduring impression was after undertaking such a global challenge. My answer is always the same – the overwhelming kindness and generosity of people. Time and time again throughout the 32 countries that I visited, whether I felt vulnerable, exposed, insecure or apprehensive, they were always willing to help me, often at a moment's notice, to get back up into the air and over the horizon towards my next port of call. My faith in the goodness of humanity was renewed constantly; I soon found that there are not just *some* good people in the world, goodness and kindness exists *everywhere*, in every culture and society, if only people were permitted to show it, and perhaps in some countries, trusted with the opportunity to express themselves more freely.

During the flight, I was on the receiving end of much camaraderie, positive encouragement and good humour, often in situations where there was no common language to share. Though in the end, this simply didn't matter as we humans are an adaptable species and there was *always* a way to find friendly communication and a meeting of minds, even without the need for any words to be spoken.

But for now, I think I have spoken quite enough words!

So on behalf of *Roxy*, myself and everyone around the globe that has played even the smallest part in the *GyroxGoesGlobal* and *First Gyro* story, I thank you all for giving us such a wonderful worldwide welcome.

Norman Surplus
February 2022

Afterword:

A few months prior to publishing, my old medical nemesis from 2003 returned.

Detected on regular CT scans, a resurgence of my bowel cancer led to ileostomy surgery in late January 2022. The operation was led by my consultant surgeon Miss McBride and the tremendous team of nurses and staff of ward 7 South at Belfast City Hospital. I now face the prospect of yet a further course of chemotherapy in the near future. As a final ironic twist of fate, as if taking me back to the beginning of my whole journey through cancer treatment, my lead consultant oncologist this time around will once more be Mr Harte, who had initially treated me in 2004.

My unknowable adventure through life continues...